The Romani Movement

Studies in Ethnopolitics

General Editors: **Timothy D. Sisk**, University of Denver, and **Stefan Wolff**, University of Bath

This new series focuses on the growing importance of international and external influences on ethnopolitical issues, such as diplomatic or military intervention, and the increasing effects of the forces of globalisation on ethnic identities and their political expressions.

Disputed Territories: The Transnational Dynamics of Ethnic Conflict Settlement
Stefan Wolff

Peace at Last? The Impact of the Good Friday Agreement on Northern Ireland
Edited by **Jörg Neuheiser** and **Stefan Wolff**

Radical Ethnic Movements in Contemporary Europe
Edited by **Farimah Daftary** and **Stefan Troebst**

The Romani Movement: Minority Politics and Ethnic Mobilization in Contemporary Central Europe
Peter Vermeersch

Modernity and Secession: The Social Sciences and the Political Discourse of the Lega Nord in Italy
Michel Huysseune

The Romani Movement

Minority Politics and Ethnic Mobilization in
Contemporary Central Europe

Peter Vermeersch

Berghahn Books
New York • Oxford

First published in 2006 by
Berghahn Books
www.berghahnbooks.com

©2006 Peter Vermeersch

All rights reserved. Except for the quotation of short passages for the purposes of criticism and review, no part of this book may be reproduced in any form or by any means, electronic or mechanical, including photocopying, recording, or any information storage and retrieval system now known or to be invented, without written permission of the publisher.

Library of Congress Cataloging-in-Publication Data

Vermeersch, Peter, 1972-
  The Romani movement : minority politics and ethnic mobilization in contemporary Central Europe / Peter Vermeersch.
    p. cm.
Includes bibliographical references and index.
ISBN 1-84545-164-3 (alk. paper)
 1. Romanies--Europe, Eastern--Policies and government--20th century. 2. Romanies--Europe, Eastern--Politics and government--21st century. 3. Romanies--Europe, Eastern--Government relations--20th century. 4. Romanies--Europe, Eastern--Government relations--21st century. I. Title.

DX210.V47 2006
323.1191'479047--dc22

2006042833

British Library Cataloguing in Publication Data

A catalogue record for this book is available from the British Library

Printed in the United States on acid-free paper

ISBN 1-84545-164-3 hardback

Contents

Acknowledgements	vi
List of Tables	x
List of Abbreviations	xi
Introduction	1
1 Identities, Interests, and Ethnic Mobilization	12
Romani Identity and Interests: An Overview	13
Theories of Ethnic Mobilization	28
2 The Development of Minority Policies in Central Europe	45
Legacies: Communist Policies and Institutions	48
The Domestic Political Context of Romani Mobilization: Institutions and Policies	63
Allies and Opponents	94
3 Ethnic Politics from Below	102
Romani Identity and Electoral Politics	104
Nonelectoral Romani Mobilization in Hungary: Actors and Issues	123
Nonelectoral Romani Mobilization in the Czech and Slovak Republics: Actors and Issues	133
4 The Power of Framing	150
Problem Definition in the Accounts of the Activists	151
Subject Definition within the Romani Movement	159
Policy Perspectives: Top-Down Problem and Subject Definitions	168
Assessing the Effectiveness of Romani Movement Frames	180
5 International Responses	184
International Governmental Organizations: Institutional and Political Responses	187
Third Parties: The Role of Transnational Advocacy Networks	200
6 The Romani Movement in Theoretical Perspective	213
Culture, Inequality, and Ethnic Mobilization	214
Solving the Puzzle? Strengths and Problems of the Competition and Political Process Approach	220
Notes	231
References	239
Index	257

Acknowledgements

I remember exactly when and where Tcha Limberger told me about his dream. It was a gray and frigid afternoon in midwinter 1995 in Kraków, and we were walking to the railway station. Tcha was a friend visiting from Bruges, my hometown in Belgium, and I was studying abroad in Poland for eighteen months. Tcha, being an unusually talented musician, and blind, carried his violin and a tape recorder everywhere he went through the city; he was on a constant search for new sounds and musical impressions. The street musicians in the heart of Europe, who continued to play their instruments even if the streets were blanketed with snow, had whetted his appetite. His dream was to go to Budapest, live there for a year, and learn to play the *magyar nóta*, an old repertoire of Hungarian popular songs made famous by Gypsy bands like those of the round-faced violin virtuoso Roby Lakatos. I was afraid at the time that Tcha's plan was overly romantic, that Hungary would not be the welcoming fairy-tale world he imagined it to be, that the traffic in Budapest would be implacable to someone who could not see it, and that the traditional Romani family orchestras would not be as open to outsiders as his Manush family in Belgium had been.

Three years later Tcha had learned to speak Hungarian and had persuaded me to come to Budapest. We were in the beautiful but crumbling neighborhood around Klauzál tér, sitting at a table laden with pancakes in the small flat of one of the city's masters of the *magyar nóta*. By then I had become interested in minority politics, so I talked with the *primas* about his dealings with the local Romani activists. But soon the topic of conversation inevitably shifted to music, and he and Tcha became increasingly engrossed in a technical discussion about finger grips and wooden bows. The outside world no longer existed; I rubbed a clear patch on the window and saw nothing but a thick evening mist.

I remember how impressed I was by what I thought was the deeper meaning of this little scene: how mutual passions could inconspicuously remove barriers between people, countries, and cultures. The music in this room had made the geographical distance between Belgium and Hungary meaningless; ethnic differences no longer appeared to play a role in this setting; even language had become close to superfluous. Yet I knew that outside this flat there was a world of barriers. In many places in Central Europe, groups of people were mentally or physically isolated from the rest of society, not only in forgotten industrial wastelands and impoverished villages, such as I had seen in central Romania and in the eastern parts of Hungary and Slovakia, but even in the poorer districts of the capitals. In 1990, the year that I began to study Slavic languages and

Eastern European Studies, many had believed that the psychological and political barriers that divided Eastern and Western Europe would soon disappear. A few years later, however, many people realized that other divisions continued to mark the continent. The division separating those known as "Roma" from other groups in society was a case in point.

I also realized that in Hungary, as in other countries in Central Europe, a growing group of people was trying to organize a movement aimed at finding ways to overcome this barrier. These efforts, and the additional difficulties they often created, were taking place at the margins of politics and society, and they were not a frequent topic in mainstream political science. Yet the more I was thinking about them there in Budapest, in that small apartment, sitting at a kitchen table listening to two violins being tuned to pitch, the more I thought they were important. It was there I decided what I wanted to do: write a book about them.

This task was challenging, and if I was able to accomplish it, it is to a large extent thanks to the support and help of a considerable group of people. First of all, I wish to thank the many people across Central Europe who opened their doors and generously shared their thoughts. They were an invaluable source of information. A lot of material from these meetings and interviews did not make it to the book, but every talk was crucial in advancing my knowledge about the Romani movement. I have listed the names of a number of my interviewees in the text where appropriate. In addition to those, I would like to thank the following people:

In Hungary: János Báthory, András Biró, Ágnes Daróczi, Antónia Hága, Aladár Horváth, Jenő Kaltenbach, Blanka Kozma, József Krasznai, Gábor Miklosi, Attila Mohácsi, Gyula Náday, Éva Orsós, Béla Osztojkán, György Rostás-Farkas, Gabriella Varjú, György Kerényi, Csaba Tabajdi, and Jenő Zsigó.

In Slovakia: Gejza Adam, Marek Baláž, Jozef Červeňak, Vincent Danihel, Ladislav Fízik, Agnes Horváthova, Juraj Hrabko, Václav Kappel, Robert Kašo, Anna Koptová, Miroslav Kusý, Jana Kviečinská, Miroslav Lacko, Tibor Lorán, René Lužica, Ivan Mako, László Nagy, Klara Orgovánová, Amalia Pompová, József Ravasz, Ladislav Richter, Silvia Rigová, Ladislav Šana, and Martina and Nataša Slobodníková.

In the Czech Republic: Eva Bajgerová, Jarmila Balážová, Viktor Dobal, Ondřej Giňa, Karel Holomek, Monika Horáková, Roman Krištof, Barbora Kvočeková, Margita Lakatošová, Marta Miklušáková, Vladimír Mlynář, Robert Olah, Milan Pospíšil, Emil Ščuka, Petr Uhl, Ivan Veselý, and Petra Zhřívalová.

I would also like to thank the people who gave up their precious time to help me organize my research visits and arrange the interviews (and who themselves were often very informative), in particular Ingrid Baumannová, Edith Bartko, Claude Cahn, Sándor Gallai, Attila Halász, Jessica Houghton, Deyan Kiuranov, Helena Kozlová, Nora Kuntz, Angela Kóczé, Natália Makovská, Marta Miklušáková, Viktória Mohácsi, John Murray, Alice Nemcová, Helena Sadilková, Michael Vašečka, and Ferenc Zsifkó. For providing background information on the Romani movement in Belgium I would like to thank Wolf Bruggen and Toon Machiels.

This project took me not only to Central Europe but also to the four corners of the academic world. I have benefited a lot from the advice, the kind support and the encouraging comments provided by a wide range of scholar in universities in Europe and North America. I am particularly indebted to Will Guy, Graham Holliday, Eben Friedman, and Martin Kovats. Many thanks also to Thomas Acton, Judy Batt, Alexandra Bitušiková, Colin Clark, Raymond Detrez, Paloma Gay y Blasco, Nicolae Gheorghe, Sarah Kate Rose, Simon Thompson, David Crowe, Tim Haughton, Krista Harper, Ilona Klímová-Alexander, Laura Laubeová, Elena Marushiakova, Dimitrina Petrova, Vesselin Popov, Eva Sobotka, and Nidhi Trehan. Thanks also to Stefan Wolff and Timothy D. Sisk for their interest in including this work in the Series on Ethnopolitics.

I also owe special thanks to all my colleagues and former colleagues in Leuven for their help and companionship, especially Katlijn Malfliet, Frank Delmartino, Jan Beyers, Marleen Brans, Ana Maria Dobre, Sam Depauw, Edith Drieskens, Dirk Jacobs, Bart Kerremans, Bart Maddens, Riana Prinsloo, Anton Stellamans, Ronald Tinnevelt, Katia Vanhemelryck, Lien Verpoest, Nico Vertongen, and Balázs Vizi. My research visits to Central Europe, as well as other parts of the research process were funded mainly by the Belgian Fund for Scientific Research, Flanders (FWO-V).

In addition, I am particularly happy to be able to list here some of the people whose friendship I enjoyed during the years I was working on this project: David Van Reybrouck, Wilfried Swenden, Gommaar Maes, Jan Desmet, Caitlin Bergin, Steve Sanford, and Pascal and Lode Vermeersch. Thanks so much to you all for the encouragement, the travel stories, the jokes, the music, the poetry, and the late-night conversations about the complexity of ordinary life. My gratitude also goes to my parents, Annie Bisschop and Antoine Vermeersch, who supported me enormously along the way. I reserve my utmost thanks for Véronique Philips, who has been part of it all from the beginning. To her I dedicate this work, with love.

A final word about Tcha. While I was trying to make sense of Romani politics in Central Europe, Tcha learned to play the *magyar nóta*, got married to Dorka whom he met in Budapest, and managed to become somewhat of a local celebrity in the Kalotaszeg region of Transylvania. Now he and Dorka live together with their three-year-old son, Tódor, in a small village near Ghent in Belgium. One of these days I should pay them a visit.

Peter Vermeersch
Brussels, October 2005

List of Tables

1.1 Estimated Romani populations in Europe. The ten countries with the largest Romani populations in percentages.   17

1.2 Official and estimated Romani population figures in the Czech Republic, Hungary, and Slovakia in the 1990s.   18

1.3 Official census results for "Romani nationality" in 1990/1991 and 2001.   19

2.1 Summary of the seven cases.   93

3.1 Overview of elected Romani candidates in the national legislatures of the Czechoslovak Federation, the Czech Republic, and the Slovak Republic (1990–2002).   107

3.2 Overview of elected Romani candidates in the Hungarian parliament (1990–2002).   113

5.1 EU funding through the Phare programs. Grants made available for projects that explicitly support Romani communities.   207

List of Abbreviations

ANO	New Citizen's Alliance (Alliancia Nového Občana)
CIT	International Gypsy Committee (Comité International Tzigane)
CMSP	Hungarian Gypsy Solidarity Party (Cigányok Magyarországi Szolidaritási Pártja)
CPRSI	Contact Point for Roma and Sinti Issues (OSCE)
CSCE	Conference for Security and Cooperation in Europe
CSCE US	Commission on Security and Cooperation in Europe (United States Congress)
CSO	Committee of Senior Officials (OSCE)
ČSSD	Czech Social Democrat Party (Česká strana sociálně demokratická)
DHR	Democratic Movement of Roma, Slovakia (Demokratické hnutie Rómov)
DÚ	Democratic Union, Slovakia (Demokratická únia)
DÚRS	Democratic Union of Roma, Slovakia (Demokratické únie Rómov)
ERRC	European Roma Rights Center
ERTF	European Roma and Travelers Forum
EU	European Union
FCNM	Framework Convention on the Protection of National Minorities
Fidesz	Federation of Young Democrats, Hungary (Fiatal Demokraták Szövetsége)
Fidesz-MPP	Federation of Young Democrats—Hungarian Civic Party (Fiatal Demokraták Szövetsége—Magyar Polgari Párt)
FKGP	Independent Smallholders' Party, Hungary (Független Kisgazdapárt)
HCNM	High Commissioner on National Minorities (OSCE)
HSD/SMS	Self-governing Democracy Movement/Association for Moravia and Silesia (Hnutí za samosprávnou demokracii-Společnost pro Moravu a Slezsko)
HZDS	Movement for a Democratic Slovakia (Hnutie za demokratické Slovensko)
ILO	International Labor Organization
IMF	International Monetary Fund
IRU	International Romani Union

KDU-ČSL	Christian Democratic Union—Czech People's Party (Křest'anská a demokratická unie—České strana lidové)
KPSS	Communist Party of the Soviet Union (Kommunističeskaja Partija Sovetskogo Sojuza)
KSČ	Czechoslovak Communist Party (Komunistická strana Československa)
KSS	Slovak Communist Party (Komunistická strana Slovenska)
MCDP	Democratic Party of the Hungarian Gypsies (Magyar Cigányok Demokrata Pártja)
MCDSz	Democratic Alliance of Hungarian Gypsies (Magyarországi Cigányok Demokratikus Szövetsége)
MCESz	Association of Roma in Hungary for the Safeguarding of Interests (Magyarországi Cigányok Érdekvédelmi Szövetsége)
MCKSz	Hungarian Gypsy Cultural Alliance (Magyar Cigányok Kulturális Szövetsége)
MCSzDP	Hungarian Gypsy Social Democratic Party (Magyar Cigány Szociáldemokrata Párt)
MDF	Hungarian Democratic Forum (Magyar Demokrata Fórum)
MDP	Hungarian Workers' Party (Magyar Dolgozók Pártja)
MG-S-ROM	Specialist Group on Roma/Gypsies/Travelers (Council of Europe)
MIÉP	Hungarian Party of Justice and Life (Magyar Igazság és Élet Pártja)
MSzMP	Hungarian Socialist Workers' Party (Magyar Szocialista Munkáspárt)
MSzP	Hungarian Socialist Party (Magyar Szocialista Párt)
NATO	North Atlantic Treaty Organization
OCKÖ	National Gypsy Minority Self-Government (Országos Cigány Kisebbségi Önkormányzat)
ÖCO	National Gypsy Self-government (Országos Cigány Önkormányzat)
ODA	Civic Democratic Alliance (Občanská Demokratická Alliance)
ODIHR	Office for Democratic Institutions and Human Rights (OSCE)
ODS	Civic Democratic Party, Czech Republic (Občanská demokratická strana)
ODÚ	Civic Democratic Union, Slovakia (Občianská demokratické únia)
OF	Civic Forum, Czech Republic (Občanské fórum)

OH	Civic Movement, Czech Republic (Občanské hnutí)
OSCE	Organization for Security and Cooperation in Europe
OSI	Open Society Institute
PER	Project on Ethnic Relations
POS	Political Opportunity Structure
RIS	Slovak Romani Initiative (Rómska iniciatíva Slovenska)
RIZS	Romani Intelligentsia for Coexistence, Slovakia (Rómska Inteligencia za Spolunaživania)
RNC	Roma National Congress
ROI	Romani Civic Initiative, Czech Republic (Romská občanská iniciativa)
ROI-SR	Romani Civic Initiative, Slovakia (Rómska občianska iniciatíva)
ROMA	Political Movement of the Roma in Slovakia or ROMA (Politické hnutie Rómov na Slovensku—ROMA)
RPS	Roma Press Center
SDK	Slovak Democratic Coalition (Slovenská demokratická koalícia)
SDKÚ	Slovak Democratic and Christian Union (Slovenska demokratická a krest'anská únia)
SDĽ	Party of the Democratic Left, Slovakia (Strana demokratickej ľavice)
SD-LSNS	Free Democrats/National Socialist Liberal Party, Czech Republic (Svobodné demokraté-Liberální strana národne sociální)
SMK	Magyar Coalition Party, Slovakia (Strana maďarskej koalície)
SNS	Slovak National Party (Slovenská národná strana)
SOPR	Party for the Protection of Roma in Slovakia (Strana ochrany práv Rómov na Slovensku)
SPI	Party for Labor and Security, Slovakia (Strana prace a istoty)
SPR-RSČ	Assembly for the Republic-Czechoslovak Republican Party (Sdružení pro republiku-republikánská strana Československa)
SzDSz	Alliance of Free Democrats, Hungary (Szabad Demokraták Szövetsége)
SZETA	Fund Supporting the Poor, Hungary (Szegényeket Támogató Alap)
SŽJ	Party for Social Security, Czech Republic (Strana za životní jistoty)
UN	United Nations
UNDP	United Nations Development Programme

UNHCR	United Nations High Commissioner for Refugees
US	Freedom Union, Czech Republic (Unie svobody)
US-DEU	Freedom Union/Democratic Union, Czech Republic (Unie svobody—Demokratická unie)
VPB	Vote for the Future, Czech Republic (Volba pro budoucnost)
VPN	Public Against Violence, Slovakia (Verejnost' proti násiliu)
WRC	World Romani Congress
ZRS	Workers' Association of Slovakia (Združenie robotníkov Slovenska)

Introduction

The collapse of communism and the process of state building that ensued in the 1990s have highlighted the existence of significant minorities in many European states, particularly in Central and Eastern Europe. In this context, the growing plight of the biggest minority in the region, the Roma (Gypsies), has been particularly salient. Like no other ethnic label in Central and Eastern Europe today, the name "Roma" brings to mind dramatic images of mass unemployment, poverty, ill health, discrimination, and social exclusion. This is true even in parts of the region that are now generally considered to have successfully transformed themselves after the collapse of communism. In countries like Hungary, the Czech Republic, and Slovakia, new opportunities and freedoms have emerged, but large parts of the population have lacked or have been denied the means of participating in the advancement. There have been few signs of hope for the Roma. Transition to democracy and the free market even appears to have heightened their plight, or at least made it more visible.

The question that lies at the heart of this book is: How have the Roma themselves responded to this state of affairs? Have there been attempts by Romani activists to redress the grievances of the Roma and make their presence felt on a political level? Have the Roma raised a political voice? In other words, have there been any attempts to establish a Romani movement? And if so, what has determined its successes and failures?

Rather surprisingly, few social scientists and other external observers have highlighted the role of Romani activists or have concentrated attention specifically on issues that concern the Roma as a political movement, such as the role of ethnopolitical organizations; the development of group interests; or the impact of ideas on political strategies and identity formation.[1] This does not mean that the predicament of the Roma in Central and Eastern Europe has gone unnoticed. Rather to the contrary: since the beginning of the 1990s, it has elicited discussion far beyond the borders of the region. International human rights organizations and journalists, for example, have published a torrent of articles and reports documenting the desperate conditions in which many Roma live. At times the Roma even reached international newspaper headlines, like for example in February 2004, when the bleak outskirts of Trebišov, and other towns in Slovakia, suddenly became the scene of Roma rioting and protesting against government measures aimed at reducing long-term unemployment benefits. Many observers have also been disquieted by the general public attitude toward this population and the way some politicians have used them as an exploitable topic to appeal to resentful, xenophobic sentiments in the electorate. The high levels of discrimination and segregation prompted academic scholars, independent organizations, and international institutions such as the World Bank and the United Nations Development Program (UNDP) to find reliable ways to assess the precarious economic and social situation of this population.

This burgeoning literature is undoubtedly interesting and important, but it largely neglects an equally interesting and important topic: the role of the Roma and their supporters as political actors. This is a topic that for a number of reasons merits increased attention from students of ethnic politics in Central and Eastern Europe.

First of all, the Romani movement represents a remarkable mixture of successes and failures. Since the beginning of the 1990s, a considerable number of Romani activists and organizations have been actively engaged in one or other form of ethnic politics. They have been able to attract the attention of international organizations and have found access to domestic governmental institutions. They also have successfully constructed and disseminated the term "Roma," which now—as the director of one advocacy group described it—"has come to dominate the official political discourse, at least in Europe, and has acquired the legitimacy of political correctness" (Petrova 2003: 111). At the same time, however, they have manifestly failed to mobilize the Roma into a political mass movement. This is an intriguing puzzle. Why has mass mobilization failed? And what explains the fact that, despite this failure, the issue of Romani treatment has found its way to international and domestic policy agendas?

Secondly, the Romani movement in Central and Eastern Europe represents a form of ethnic mobilization that does not seem to fit the patterns of ethnic mobilization that are considered typical for the region. Unlike many other instances of minority activism in Central and Eastern Europe, Romani activism has never been seen as a threat to the stability and the territorial integrity of an existing state. Few, if any, Romani activists ever demanded territorial autonomy, there have been no irredentist claims, and there have been no instances of large-scale violent conflict about a territory between camps of Roma and other groups. This latter fact presumably explains why the Romani movement has largely fallen outside the scope of most scholars in Central and East European affairs. One does not have to be cynical to realize that violence usually attracts increased attention from the media as well as from scholars. The large body of literature on the Balkans is a case in point. Given the devastating impact of violent conflict on entire populations and the moral confusion that besets observers when they see images of what Susan Sontag has called the "pain of others," the eagerness to describe and comprehend bloodshed is quite understandable. However, from an academic perspective, the study of nonviolent ethnic relations is itself as important as the study of violent conflict, because it is only by examining different forms of ethnic politics that we can approach a fuller understanding of the phenomenon. In this way Rogers Brubaker has rightly argued that we should be analytically attuned to "negative" instances of ethnopolitical group formation, because this not only enlarges the domain of relevant cases but "helps to correct for the bias in the literature toward the study of striking instances of high groupness, successful mobilization, or conspicuous violence" (Brubaker 2002: 168). For this reason, there is also much to learn from developments in the study of ethnic relations in Western European countries, where there has been an increasing awareness of the new political assertiveness among immigrant populations and of ethnic relations as a specific field of political contention within the contours of stable, democratic states (Koopmans and Statham 2000).

Another reason for studying the Romani movement is that it allows one to draw attention to the role of political factors in the process of Romani identity formation. This is an important task. Much of the existing literature has cast the Roma exclusively in primordialist terms. The Roma are very often depicted as an immutable, archaic, traditional, arcane, secluded and "unconstructed" ethnic group. They are portrayed as a group that is marked by a set of particular, distinctive, and usually negative characteristics. But defining the Roma in terms of "typical properties" is tantamount to neglecting the contemporary insights of social anthropology and social psychology about the relational nature of ethnicity. And what is worse, it easily perpetuates misleading stereotypical images of them as eternal nomads, criminals, outsiders by choice, or a people with a preference for living in poverty on the margins of society.

My approach starts from the premise that, as any other ethnic identity, Romani identity is the result of a complex process of labeling, categorization, and self-categorization. To study the Romani movement means to study that process of labeling, categorization, and self-categorization in political action. A serious analysis should not simply focus on specific forms of lifestyle, traditions, descent, language usage, and so forth; it should ask why and in what social and political circumstances such phenomena become generally accepted as markers of Romani identity.

Such an approach builds on a tradition in social anthropology that understands ethnicity, not in terms of group characteristics, but as a form of social organization (Barth 1969; Eriksen 2002; Jenkins 1997; Roosens 1998). Like all forms of identity, ethnic identities are not given; they belong to—as Charles Tilly has formulated it—that "potent set of social arrangements in which people construct shared stories about who they are, how they are connected, and what has happened to them" (Tilly 2003: 608). Ethnic groups should not be understood as natural units that have always been there and therefore automatically constitute the basis for political action; on the contrary, conceptually and empirically, it makes more sense to understand them as the result of social and political processes of categorization.

Although this view may seem obvious enough, it is worthwhile highlighting its importance briefly because it is not the usual perspective in many popular narratives of recent events in Central and Eastern Europe. The popular tropes that are used to describe the ethnic heterogeneity of the region often convey the image of a natural world resembling a mosaic of neatly segmented and ethnically bounded population groups. To give just one example, *National Geographic* once described the Caucasus as a volatile area "because it is dauntingly complex, with 50 ethnic groups and nationalities spread like a crazy quilt across a California-size territory" (Edwards 1996: 126). In this oversimplification, ethnic groups appear as static, natural, quantifiable, quasi-territorial entities. They seem independent of political and social factors and removed from inclusion in that other often oversimplified category, "the state." *National Geographic* even suggests that these entities are responsible for bringing about certain political and social developments; the Caucasus is volatile, it is contended, *because* there is ethnic heterogeneity. The mere existence of ethnic differentiation is viewed as a cause of political mobilization along ethnic lines; and as a consequence ethnic groups are easily portrayed as the "protagonists" (Brubaker 2002: 164) of mobilization, not as the "products." Such an approach toward reality is (to say the least) problematic because it precludes large areas of research into the role of political actors—state institutions, ethnic activists, organizations, politicians, and so forth—in articulating particular identities and creating ethnic groups.

In sum, I argue that it is important to look at the *political* dimensions of Romani identity and to examine the political factors that have contributed to the emergence of Romani identity as an ethnic label and a frame of reference for political group formation and policy making in Central and Eastern Europe.

Two additional remarks need to be made about this task at the outset. First, by arguing for the inclusion of political factors in the study of ethnic identities, I do not mean of course that ethnic identity formation is influenced by political factors alone. There are various studies in social anthropology, cognitive sociology, and social psychology, all of which have fruitfully demonstrated the range of circumstances that may produce collective identifications as well as internal images of the ethnic self. What I do argue is that focusing on political factors is of crucial importance if one wants to understand how ethnicity works in current societies. Political factors are likely to be essential in the construction of ethnic groups because such factors are directly related to the power structure of a society (Bulmer and Solomos 1998: 823), which in turn determines access to resources and the representation of interests, all central to those excluded from the mainstream.

Second, by conceptualizing ethnic identity as a "frame" and a "social arrangement," I do not mean to argue that Romani identity is not "real." Neither do I mean to deny the reality of the experiences that people have lived through as a result of their identification as Romani. On the contrary, what makes people understand certain identities as "ethnic" is precisely the general agreement among them that such identities depend on immediate descent, and are thus given, natural, and inescapable. Many of the people who are discussed in this book take the existence of ethnic groups simply for granted. Participants of ethnic politics usually sincerely believe that their ethnic identity is an immutable bundle of innate characteristics, even though that identity is clearly dependent on social and political negotiation. The environment in which they find themselves further solidifies this tendency to think in "ethnic totalities." This is what has been called "participant primordialism" (Smith 1998: 158), a phenomenon that is certainly present in and around the Romani movement. For many people Romani identity is not a matter of much choice.

As David Laitin has noted, people are limited in their senses of self by "the prevalent typologies of identity that surround them" (Laitin 1998: 20). In analyzing an ethnic movement, however, one should not simply take the perspective of the participants; one should try to explain why and how participants have come to experience certain labels as predominant and inescapable sources of identification. It is again Rogers Brubaker who has provided useful vocabulary to deal with this problem. Referring to Pierre Bourdieu's writings on language and symbolic power, he argues that "ethnopolitical entrepreneurs" invoke ethnic groups in order to call these groups into being. Analysts should not replicate such primordialism. They should "try to account for the ways in which—and conditions under which—this practice of reification, this powerful crystallization of group feeling, can work" (Brubaker 2002: 167). In order to accomplish this, Brubaker has suggested a "non-groupist" approach: a research strategy that seeks to "specify how—and when—people identify themselves, perceive others, experience the world and interpret their predicaments in racial, ethnic or national rather than other terms" (Brubaker 2002: 175). This is precisely what I aim to do: offer an analysis that does not presume the existence of ethnic divisions as a natural, cultural, or historical fact, but instead focuses on how ethnic divisions are invoked by contemporary social and political actors in the present circumstances, and investigate whether and how historical, cultural, or other justifications are utilized in this process.

Overview of the Book

This book consists of an introduction and six chapters. After this overview of the various chapters of the book, the remainder of this introduction will provide a brief outline of some of the basic choices that underpin the empirical research presented in the main part of the book.

Chapter 1, then, sets the general empirical and theoretical context. It starts with a discussion of how outsiders, mainly academics, have defined Romani identity and interests. The purpose of this discussion is to provide some background for the debates on identity and interests that have taken place *within* the Romani movement and that will be the focus of the following chapters. The latter part of chapter 1 discusses the theoretical framework. It considers various theoretical models for explaining ethnic mobilization. Is ethnic minority mobilization mostly dependent on the solidarity ties springing from a common culture? Should importance be attached to the calculations group leaders make on the basis of their assessments of economic and political competition? Or, are developments primarily influenced by government policy, state institutions, and the dominant political discourse? These questions roughly coincide with the different theoretical perspectives on ethnic mobilization that can be found in social movement literature.

Chapter 2 provides a synthesis of policies aimed at Gypsies and (later) Roma in the countries covered by this study. It deals with both pre-1989 and post-1989 policies, with the examination of the older policies undertaken in order to provide a context for understanding more recent policies.

Chapter 3 is devoted to exploring and charting the actions of Central European Romani activists, their opinions and their interpretations of events. It will attempt to offer insight into the heart of contemporary Romani activism in Central Europe by describing the positions that some of the important movement leaders or putative leaders have found themselves in and the dilemmas they have been faced with.

In Chapter 4 I focus on the interaction between activists and policy makers. More, in particular, I explore the divergent ways in which Romani movement leaders have understood and framed their cause, and I investigate how government policy documents have interpreted the matter.

This discussion is complemented, in Chapter 5, by research into the international political context. The chapter deals with the impact of international organizations, in particular the European Union (EU), the Council of Europe, and the Organization for Security and Cooperation in Europe (OSCE), on the development of domestic Romani movement action in Central Europe.

Finally, the concluding Chapter 6 brings together the empirics with the theories dissected in earlier chapters. It asks which of the various theoretical models presented in the beginning of the book offers an apt and sufficiently comprehensive theoretical framework for understanding and explaining the developments of the Romani movement in Central Europe.

Some Notes on the Empirical Research

Geographical Limits

With so vast a geographical area encompassing the Roma, certain regions are better represented here than others. I have chosen to conduct a comparative study of three countries in Central Europe: the Czech Republic, Slovakia, and Hungary. From the beginning of the 1990s until 2004—the decade that covers more or less the chronological range of this study—these three countries shared a number of striking similarities. Not only were they closely related to one another because of their communist past and their recent histories (most clearly in the case of the Czech and Slovak Republics, which formed one country before 1993); they also harbored quite comparable expectations for their political future. Visions of a common political fate were embodied in the name "Central Europe." Together with Poland, these three countries encouraged the public acceptance of that name in order to dissociate themselves from terms with a less profitable political overtone such as "Eastern Europe" and the "Balkans" (Ash 1999; Kürti 1997; Zeigler 2002). More importantly, with the introduction of the freedom of association in the late 1980s and early 1990s all three countries saw the rise of organizations and activists seeking to defend the interests of ethnic minority citizens. After 1993, at the time when the international community had become aware of the renewed saliency of ethnic issues in Europe, the policy responses toward these minority claims were closely monitored by Western institutions, not least by the EU, which all three aspired to join. In particular the treatment of the Roma in Central Europe became subject to international scrutiny as waves of refugees began to migrate to wealthier countries.

But there were not only similarities. There was also significant variation with regard to the way in which the three countries responded to ethnic minority demands. For instance, while Hungarian policy makers chose to adopt special policies to protect and promote the cultural autonomy of national minorities, in Slovakia and the Czech Republic policies granting cultural autonomy to minorities did not immediately find political support. In contrast, Slovak and Czech traditions generally emphasized the principle of the equal treatment of all citizens, including those belonging to minorities. There was also a considerable variation in the development of the Romani movement in the three countries under consideration. Whilst there were periods during which Romani activists sought a kind of political unification through the participation of ethnic parties in national elections, there were also times when they reverted to more direct methods of protest. Moreover, the effects of Romani mobilization in the 1990s were very diverse. Virtually all Romani parties failed to attract voters, yet some Romani activists were able to find access to domestic governmental organs. At times when Romani protest against domestic policies was weak, certain Romani activists, usually in coalition with advocacy organizations, were still able to draw international attention from such organizations as the Council of Europe, the OSCE, the EU, and—to a lesser extent—the United Nations.

Sources

The empirical investigations of the Romani movement presented in this book rest in part on data derived from secondary literature, existing surveys, and independent expert reports. The bulk of it, however, is based on interviews and conversations with more than sixty representatives or members of organizations that aim to represent or protect the Roma. Through these interviews, I sought to acquire information about various subjects such as the current perceptions of the movement, the present opinions about Romani identity, the present opinions about the problems facing the Roma, the dominant ideas about what could be done about them, and the motivations of (putative) group leaders to start organizing. Furthermore, I asked about topics that related to the daily practice of ethnic mobilization, the extent of networking between organizations (and the obstacles to it), the perceived divisions within the movement, and the attempts made at influencing the policy-making process.

My analysis of government policies is mainly based on official documents collected through state institutions on the national and international level. On domestic levels, the most relevant organs contacted were the Government Council for Romani Community Affairs (Rady vlády České republiky pro záležitosti romské komunity) in the Czech Republic (formerly the Interdepartmental Commission for Romani Community Affairs), the Government Commissioner for the Solution of the Problems of the Romani Minority in Slovakia (Splnomocnenec na riešnie problémov rómskej menšiny), and the Office for National and Ethnic Minorities in Hungary (Nemzeti és Etnikai Kisebbségi Hivatal). On the international level, documents were collected through the Secretariat of the OSCE in Prague, the Contact Point for Roma and Sinti Issues at the OSCE's Office for Democratic Institutions and Human Rights (ODIHR) in Warsaw, the Council of Europe's Specialist Group on Roma/Gypsies/Travelers (MG-S-ROM), and the Directorate General for Enlargement of the European Commission.

It is important to note that both the information obtained from the activists and the official documents are not to be understood as unproblematic representations of reality. Just as reports published by activists are likely to contain some bias, government reports and policy documents offer little information as to what policies actually look like when they are implemented. One may assume that there exists a certain discrepancy between the content of the policy programs and their practical implementation. It is even one of the frequent complaints made by Romani activists that official plans look acceptable on paper but are not properly executed. Good intentions do not suffice, they contend. Policy makers, on the other hand, have often deflected criticism by arguing that activists unfairly trivialize every attempt made by the government. The discussions illustrate that both policy programs and activist accounts are not fully to be trusted as descriptions of reality. They are, however, more reliable sources when it comes to examining the views, understandings, and positions they represent. In other words, they are political documents. As such they offer an insight into the perceptions of the actors involved in the political game of policy making, ethnic interest representation, and identity formation.

Conceptualizing the Movement

Like many ethnic movements, the Romani movement in Central Europe is complex and diffuse. It consists of both officially recognized and informal groupings, and it encloses organized as well as less organized associations. For this reason, the word "movement" has to be nuanced; it must not be understood as a clearly defined and bounded collection of officially recognized organizations, but as a conceptual term denoting the totality of activities carried out in the context of defending and cultivating a shared Romani identity. Moreover, the Romani movement is not monolithic but rather fragmented, and it is in constant flux. It would be virtually impossible to paint a picture of the Romani movement in its entirety. Informal structures, such as friendship ties, may have had their particular significance for bringing about movement activities, but they are difficult to investigate and trace in a systematic way. For this reason, I decided to focus primarily on those activists who form what can be called the *formal* side of the movement—they are important members of organizations that in one way or another attempt to represent Romani interests or are supportive organizations that aim to assist, protect, or to mobilize the Roma. Information about informal networks will occasionally appear in this book when their importance is particularly clear, but on the whole the following chapters are mainly concerned with organizations that formally exist, in the sense that they are registered, or at least recognized by a considerable number of people, and that their activities are to some extent documented. They include "classical" ethnic movement organizations as well as ethnic political parties and supportive organizations (organizations that share the goals of the movement, but do not identify themselves as Romani).

With Romani activists connected to both formal and informal organizational structures and finding themselves both inside and outside the official public institutions, it comes perhaps as no surprise that mapping out the various key players of the movement turned out to be a time-consuming exercise. Matters were made even more difficult by the fact that in the course of the 1990s and the early 2000s many new organizations arose while others disappeared or changed their names, alliances, and leaders. On the other hand, having to devote much time to observation and multiple fieldwork trips was not a disadvantage. It allowed me to gain a better idea of what sources of Romani activism were the most stable and influential ones. During extended periods of stay in the three countries I could also observe directly how particular conflicts and cleavages within the movement developed over time.

Terminology and Spelling

Finally, before turning to the main part of the book, it is worth adding a few words on the basic decisions I had to take with regard to terminology and spelling. This book discusses the "Roma" and the "Romani" movement; I use these names deliberately because they are closely linked to the process of political mobilization. The word "Roma" (plural) is based on the meaning of the word in the Romani language for "man" or "husband" ("Rom") (Gheorghe 1991). The word "Roma" is a noun and "Romani" is an adjective. Although there is some disagreement whether this is linguistically correct (some authors prefer the word "Roms"), it corresponds to current standard usage in international literature.

In Slovak, Czech, and Hungarian one will often hear or read the words *cigán*, *cikán*, and *cigány* to refer to the same population. When quoting an original text or speech that contains one of these designations, I use the English term "Gypsy" to differentiate from the terms used for self-designation. However, some considerations must be kept in mind with regard to this translation. Although I capitalize the word "Gypsy," in Hungarian the word *cigány* is not as a rule capitalized, just as other nouns referring to members of national or ethnic groups are not capitalized. Although the word sometimes has derogatory overtones, it is also very often applied as a neutral term. In Czech and Slovak, nouns that refer to ethnic and national groups are normally capitalized; nevertheless, there is a tendency not to do this with the words *cigán* and *cikán*. The authoritative Czech language dictionary published in 1952 did not capitalize the word *cikán* and defined it as "a member of a nomadic nation, symbol for mendacity, thievery, vagabondage" (Ulč 1995: 2). This no doubt reflects the popular usage of the word as an insult, as is the case in Slovak. Nevertheless, I also translate these terms as "Gypsy" in English. The reader is, however, asked to bear in mind the possible negative connotations of the word in the original Czech or Slovak text. There is also the fact that Czechs and Slovaks increasingly use the words *Romové* and *Rómovia*, which easily translate as "Roma." While adjectives in Hungarian, Czech, and Slovak are generally not capitalized, I nevertheless consistently capitalize the adjectives "Romani" and "Gypsy" in English.

That terminology and spelling is usually considered very important in the study of Romani affairs reflects the importance that is attached by both Roma and external observers to the nature of Romani identity. In fact, together with the claims that activists make, identity formation is a crucial component of the movement they try to form. That Romani activists, supportive organizations, and governmental actors have framed Romani identity and interests in different ways will become clear in Chapters 2 to 5. Chapter 1 starts from the question of how external observers have viewed Romani identity and interests.

Chapter 1

Identities, Interests, and Ethnic Mobilization

This chapter has two objectives. First of all, it will set the general context of this study by reviewing some of the most important current descriptive literature on the Roma. In order to create an ethnic movement, organizations and individual activists need to specify their ideas on two crucial components of political action: identity and interests. With regard to the Roma, it may therefore be asked: What is Romani identity? And what issues should Romani activists try to place on the public policy agenda? These are questions that have plagued many activists consistently. Later in this book, I will examine how Romani movement organizers in the Czech Republic, Hungary, and Slovakia have responded to them; how they have demarcated the boundaries of Romani identity and defined their interests. Answers to these questions have not only been given by activists, however; they have also been increasingly formulated by academics and other external observers. The writings of the latter are not merely important within the confines of academic study; they have clearly left an imprint on nonspecialist literature, popular thinking, and the views of the activists themselves. Before turning to the central actors of the Romani movement, it is therefore useful to start with an outline of the dominant ways in which academics and specialists have understood Romani identity and Romani interests.

The second purpose of this chapter is to lay out the theoretical framework of the study by asking what general theoretical approaches are applicable to the dynamics of Romani political mobilization. To do so I canvass the current theories concerning ethnic mobilization. There is a specific branch in social movement literature that has focused on the emergence and development of national and ethnic movements. In the latter part of this chapter, I discuss this literature and critically examine the three broad sets of factors that authors increasingly emphasize: political opportunities, mobilizing structures, and the processes of perception and interpretation.

Romani Identity and Interests: An Overview

Romani Identity

There have been many discussions on identity-related topics in Romani studies. One minor approach has been to consider the name "Roma" as a constructed category, and not as an entity in reality. Will Guy (2001b), Judith Okely (1983), Michael Stewart (1997), and Wim Willems (1995) are some of the scholars who have adopted categorization perspectives that are more or less similar to the one I propose. In most of their work, these authors have tried to understand Romani identity not as a matter of biology, lifestyle, descent, or any other group characteristic; but rather as the product of classification struggles involving both classifiers and those classified as Roma. That is also how they have considered a plethora of other group labels: Gypsy, *Zigeuner*, and *Tsigane*; their equivalents in the Central European languages such as *cigán*, *cikán*, *cigány*, and so on; and the appellations that have served to label subidentities such as Kalderash, Manush, Caló, Vlach, Romungro, Beash, Sinto, etc.[1] A characteristic of most of these names, and certainly the more widespread ones, is that they carry with them a myriad of negative and romantic connotations. The introduction of the term "Roma" therefore clearly represents an attempt to break away from social stigmas and to produce a more positive, more neutral, and less romanticized image. In this sense, the usage of the name Roma is closely connected with the process of Romani political mobilization. Consequently, the name cannot be separated from the movement. Nicolae Gheorghe and Thomas Acton, both academics who have been involved in the international Romani movement, were hinting exactly at this aspect when they noted the following:

> Not all those politically defined as Roma call themselves by this name; and some of those who do not, such as the German Sinte [sic], outraged by what they perceive as claims of superior authenticity by Vlach Roma, even repudiate the appellation Roma. The unity of ethnic struggles is always illusory; but to the participants the task of creating, strengthening and maintaining that unity often seems the prime task. (Gheorghe and Acton 2001: 58)

Not all authors, however, have shared this view. On the contrary, there is a strong tendency in the literature to understand Romani identity in terms of real common properties and objective characteristics. Perusing the work of the most influential authors writing within this tradition, one can roughly distinguish three main conceptualizations of Romani identity. These conceptualizations are not universally regarded as mutually exclusive, but they do represent quite distinctive perspectives.

The first defines the Roma as a historical diaspora. Scholars such as David Crowe (1995), Angus Fraser (1995; 2000), Ian Hancock (1992; 1997), and Donald Kenrick (1978) have all—in one way or another—understood the Roma to be a once bounded but now fractured community with common historic roots and common patterns of migration. What they have done is far more than simply search for historical evidence confirming the presence of the Roma; they have instead claimed a past through assuming the existence of the Roma as an enduring historical subject. They have usually viewed the Roma as the descendents of a population that traveled from the Punjab region in northwestern India and arrived in Europe at the end of the thirteenth century. A well-known proponent of this hypothesis is the Romani activist and linguist Ian Hancock. In comparison to those of many others, his theory is surprisingly specific. Hancock believes that the "ancestors of the Roma were members of the Kśiattriya or military caste, who left India with their camp followers during the first quarter century of the second millennium in response to a series of Islamic invasions led by Mahmud of Ghazni" (Hancock 2000: 1). Hancock's idea is based mostly on linguistic investigation and builds on a research tradition that goes back to the latter part of the eighteenth century. At that time a number of people in different places—most notably the German historians Johann Rüdiger and Heinrich Grellman—for the first time forged a link between the Romani language and the Indoaryan languages of India (Fraser 2000: 21) and contributed to the idea of the Roma as a people (*Volk*).[2] The idea of the Romani language as evidence for the existence of a once intact, original Romani culture in India was dominant among scholars studying Roma throughout the nineteenth century. It even served as a basis for the establishment in 1888 of an academic collective in England under the title of the Gypsy Lore Society.

The diaspora perspective has not remained above criticism. The two most prominent critics have been the anthropologist Judith Okely and the social historian Wim Willems. Okely (1983) has suggested that linguistic connections to Indian languages need not necessarily point to the Indian provenance of the group, since the language itself could have traveled along trade routes between East and West without the actual migration of an ethnic group "carrying" that language. According to Okely, the tendency to take the diaspora perspective for granted unnecessarily puts a large number of different people under the same category and sets them apart from European culture—in other words, it "exoticizes" them. She claims that such a perspective also inhibits good scholarly work on this subject since it neglects the group's own criteria for membership (Okely 1983: 13).

Willems (1995), on the other hand, has focused not on the categorized but on the categorizers. His work has dealt in particular with the role of the classic "gypsiologists" (Heinrich Grellman and George Borrow) and the Nazi psychiatrist Robert Ritter in creating "the Gypsies" as a people with common origins in India. Willems has argued that current ideas of the Roma as an ethnic diaspora have their basis in a process of deliberate fabrication that started in the eighteenth century and reached well into the twentieth century, involving "gypsiologists" as well as governmental, judicial, and religious authorities.

The second conceptualization of Romani identity has focused on issues of lifestyle and behavior. Jean-Paul Clébert (1972) is one of a number of authors who have alluded to the idea that Roma are to be recognized by their desire to travel. Similarly, Angus Fraser (1995), Ian Hancock (1992), Jean-Pierre Liégeois (1994), and Andrzej Mirga and Lech Mróz (1994) have referred to other common cultural practices (elements of religion, habits, rules of cleanliness, musical traditions, etc.) and interpretations of the world (sometimes called Gypsiness, řomanipé or romipen) as allegedly objective elements of ethnic group identity. One author even suggests that on the basis of the standards of ancient Romani traditions, a distinction can be made between "orthodox" Roma and those who conform less to common cultural practice (Barany 2002: 13). A radical version of the lifestyle perspective argues that the Roma are related to one another exclusively in terms of their behavior; it concludes that for this reason they should not be seen as an ethnic group. Some of the arguments put forward in Lucassen et al. (1998) could be read in this way, especially when the authors argue that authorities applied the word "Gypsy" to groups that were not related in any ethnic sense but shared an itinerant lifestyle. Most versions of this perspective in Romani studies, however, accept the existence of Romani ethnicity and even agree with the thesis of a common Indian origin. Their emphasis is not on the common origin in itself, but rather on its effects on matters of lifestyle and habits.

The existence of a typical "Romani lifestyle" is sometimes referred to by those advocating the introduction of special rights for the Roma. For example, Colin Clark has argued that the nomadic way of life of those known as Gypsies and Travelers in the United Kingdom is a lifestyle that should not just be retained, but one that "should be respected and even promoted as a valid and legal way of life" (Clark 1999). Unfortunately, however, some of the writings that fall within this perspective have been pivotal in preserving stereotypical thinking about the Roma as inherently nomadic, marginal, "untrustworthy, primitive, childish and sorely in need of firm guidance and control" (Fraser 2000: 21). The notion of an allegedly intrinsic connection between Romani identity and deviant social behavior has frequently appeared in policy documents ever since the first large-scale assimilation campaigns in the Austrian empire under Maria Theresia (1740–80) and Joseph II (1780–90). In current academic literature one sometimes finds allusions to the idea that Romani identity revolves around a preference for marginality. In 1972, for instance, an article in *Urban Life and Culture* called the Roma "an outstanding example of a people ... whose culture allows them to survive and even flourish in relatively impoverished environments" (Kornblum and Lichter 1972: 240). On the subject of nomadism, it is remarkable that the idea of the Roma as a wandering people has proven persistent even in the face of empirical evidence refuting such a view. Today the overwhelming majority of those who are seen as Roma in Central Europe live in settled communities—as their ancestors have done for many years. Still, romantic stereotypes of them as wanderers abound.

The third conceptualization focuses on the issue of biological kinship. Whether all Roma are genetically related is a vexed question. In 1992, Ian Hancock argued that this was indeed the case by stating that the Roma made their journey from India to Europe "intact" (Hancock 1992: 139). According to Hancock, the absorption of non-Roma into their ranks during travel "can account for some of the factors which distinguish one [Romani] group from another, [but] it has not led to the dissolution of the Roma as a genetically related people" (Hancock 1992: 134–35). This view is, of course, closely related to the diaspora perspective, but unlike that approach, the biological perspective emphasizes the supposedly natural bonds within and among small, tribal communities. Romani identity is here primarily defined along lines of alleged genetic or phenotypic characteristics. For Hancock, promoting this view is clearly part of an endeavor to emancipate the Roma. Assimilation policies of the past were often based on the argument that the Roma do *not* constitute a separate "ethnic" group, but are merely vagrants who have isolated themselves from mainstream society. The concept of genetic kinship, in Hancock's view, serves to refute that argument.

But biological theories of ethnicity remain extremely controversial. Not only are they reminiscent of the racist ideologies of the nineteenth century; they also remind us of the type of racial ideology that marked the rise of Nazism in Europe and the eugenic movement in the United States. More specifically, reference to the alleged biological deficiency of the Roma is closely associated with the eugenic work on Roma done by the infamous German youth psychiatrist Robert Ritter and his associates in the latter half of the 1930s (Willems 1995). Inspired by Nazi ideology, Ritter tried to establish a link between heredity and antisocial behavior. He argued that "Romani genes" had affected the German "race" and in this way had led to the creation of people "of mixed blood" (*Zigeunermischlinge*). According to Ritter, most of the Roma in Germany were "of mixed blood" and, in the context of Nazi belief in *Rassenhygiene* (racial hygiene), needed to be completely eradicated (Burleigh 2000: 372–74). This view provided license for a practice of sterilization, deportation, and mass murder (Benz 2002; Nečas 1999). During the war the Roma became a target for total genocide, and survival was often solely dependent on the level of local non-collaboration in the various areas of Europe under Axis control (Lutz and Lutz 1995). Biologists now recognize the fallacy of biological determinism and the invalidity of the concept of "race" as a natural perceptual scheme or a biological category (see, e.g. Allen 1990; Gilroy 1998; Tucker 1996); there is as much genetic variation within what we call racial groups as there is between them, writes Lawrence A. Hirshfeld (1996). Yet the idea of the Roma as a biologically distinct and naturally inferior group remains surprisingly persistent. It is heard frequently in everyday talk, and, what is perhaps even more alarming, it continues to surface in some of the darker corners of the academic literature.[3]

As the above overview illustrates, a classification of the literature according to three ways of circumscribing Romani identity cannot be anything else than a blunt analytic tool for exploring a complex and heterogeneous field of academic discussion. Many authors have looked at the Roma in more than one way, and some of them have, of course, changed and adjusted their views over time.

Given the disagreement among scholars about what constitutes Romani identity, it is not at all surprising that there has also been some degree of polemic concerning the number of people said to possess that identity. To offer an idea of the size of the Romani minority in Europe, it is customary among activists, governments, and academics to present some of the available population statistics. One example of this is the often-cited estimates compiled by the London-based advocacy organization Minority Rights Group. According to these figures, the total Romani population in Europe amounts to at least six million people, with large concentrations in Macedonia, Romania, Bulgaria, Slovakia, Hungary, Albania, and the Czech Republic (Liégeois and Gheorghe 1995). Table 1.1 is based on the Minority Rights Group estimates compiled by Jean-Pierre Liégeois and Nicolae Gheorghe, and presents the percentages and absolute figures for the ten countries with the largest proportion of Romani

Table 1.1 Estimated Romani populations in Europe (percentages and absolute figures). The ten countries with the largest Romani populations in percentages.

	Percentage Romani population %	Romani population in absolute figures
FYR Macedonia	12.0	240,000
Romania	10.0	2,150,000
Slovakia	9.4	500,000
Bulgaria	8.9	750,000
Hungary	5.6	575,000
Yugoslavia	4.0	425,000
Albania	2.9	95,000
Czech Republic	2.7	275,000
Spain	1.8	725,000
Greece	1.7	180,000

Sources: Romani population figures are averages of the estimates in Liégeois and Gheorghe (1995: 7). Total population estimates come from the *World Bank Data Profiles* available at http://www.worldbank.org/data/countrydata/countrydata.html (2002).

citizens. Presented thus, the figures appear to suggest that there is complete clarity about the size and boundaries of the Romani population. This is quite misleading. When one reads further through the literature, one comes across figures that differ substantially from those offered by Liégeois and Gheorghe. Three areas of disagreement are apparent.

First of all, there are huge differences between estimated and official census figures. According to the Bulgarian anthropologists Elena Marushiakova and Vesselin Popov, the minimum number of Roma for the whole of the Central and Eastern European region (thus excluding Western European countries) is, based on censuses, about 1.5 million; while the maximum estimate, if one includes those of Romani activists, is around 6.3 million (Marushiakova and Popov 2001a: 34). Indeed, for the Czech Republic, Hungary, and Slovakia, one sees a large gulf between the official census figures and the available estimates (see Table 1.2).

Secondly, among the estimated figures themselves there is no clear consensus either. In fact, every new source seems to bring forth new figures, with sometimes spectacular differences in both percentages and in absolute figures (again, see Table 1.2).

And thirdly, there is also a striking variation among the available official census figures over the years (see Table 1.3). Despite the fact that estimates indicate a continuing growth of the Romani population over the last decades, official census figures have increased only slightly or have even decreased (again, see Table 1.3). The Czech case has been the most surprising example of this. The figure given in the census held in the beginning of the 1990s was regarded as manifestly too low by virtually all of the observers and activists to whom I spoke in the Czech Republic. However, the long-awaited 2001 census yielded an even lower result of only roughly one-third of the previous official figure. The census figure dropped to 0.1 percent of the population, notwithstanding that census forms had been made available in the Romani language. The most recent census figures in Slovakia and Hungary indicate the modest

Table 1.2 Official and estimated Romani population figures in the Czech Republic, Hungary, and Slovakia in the 1990s.

	App. total population	Official number (1990/1991)		Lowest and highest estimates in secondary literature	
Czech Republic	10,300,000	32,903	(0.3%)	150,000–300,000	(1.5%–2.9%)
Hungary	10,200,000	142,683	(1.4%)	550,000–800,000	(5.4%–7.8%)
Slovakia	5,300,000	83,988	(1.6%)	458,000–520,000	(8.6%–9.8%)

Sources: Total population estimates come from the *World Bank Data Profiles* (2002) available at http://www.worldbank.org/data/countrydata/countrydata.html. Official total Romani population figures come from official censuses taken in 1990 and 1991: Český statistický úřad, *Sčítání lidu, domů a bytů*, http://www.czso.cz (2001); Központi Statisztikai Hivatal, *Népszámlálás 2001*, http://www.nepszamlalas2001.hu (2002). Highest and lowest Romani population estimates are compiled by Druker (1997).

Table 1.3 Official census results for "Romani nationality" in 1990/1991 and 2001.

	1990/1991 Census		2001 Census	
Czech Republic	32,903	(0.3%)	11,716	(0.1%)
Hungary	142,683	(1.4%)	190,046	(1.9%)
Slovakia	83,988	(1.6%)	89,920	(1.7%)

Sources: Český statistický úřad, *Sčítání lidu, domů a bytů*, http://www.czso.cz (2001); Központi Statisztikai Hivatal, *Népszámlálás 2001*, http://www.nepszamlalas2001.hu (2002); Štatistický úrad Slovenskej republiky, *Sčitanie obyvateľov, domov a bytov*, http://www.statistics.sk (2001).

beginning of an opposite trend. However, the increases in the number of Roma were well below the expectations of many Romani activists in both countries.[4]

What do these differences mean? Besides the fact that the numbers represent various methods of collection—some of them evidently more sophisticated than others—the numerical differences are primarily the result of a process described earlier as "categorization." In this way, population numbers are not a simple reflection of some kind of "reality" that exists outside categorization, interpretation, and self-identification. As David Kertzer and Dominique Arel have argued, censuses do not merely reflect reality but play a key role in its construction (Kertzer and Arel 2002). While census figures are based on self-declaration, estimates typically rely on categorization by others. One may conclude from the conspicuously low official figure that many of the people who are usually considered as Roma do not want to use that name to identify themselves in public.

However, not a lot of people would agree with what might appear to be the obvious conclusion, that less than 2 percent of the citizens in the Czech Republic, Hungary, and Slovakia are ready to identify themselves as Roma in daily life. All three governments have in so many words admitted that the census figures are considerably skewed. They rely on the willingness of people to state their ethnic background on an official written form or to declare it before an official administrator. Even if people commonly identify themselves as Roma, they may not always want to do so before an official administrator. A reason for this, some authors have pointed out, may be related to bad memories within Romani families with regard to the abuse of ethnic registration forms by the Nazis during the Second World War (Druker 1997: 22–23). Others have speculated about a general climate of distrust between Roma and officials, and the fear among Roma of some kind of reprisal (Clark 1998).

Figures reflecting self-declaration are thus problematic, but so are estimates based on external categorization. The figures are dependent on those "doing" the categorization. It is not unimaginable that estimations distributed by politicians and activist organizations are sometimes rounded up for political reasons, or at least are not viewed as critically as would be appropriate.[5] In other cases, simply a different "perspective" can lead to very different figures. Independent research in 1993 and 1994 by the Hungarian sociologists Gábor Havas and István Kemény, for example, resulted in a figure of 482,000 (4.7 percent) Roma in Hungary, on the basis of identification by direct observers: schoolteachers, headmasters, social workers, and doctors were asked to identify those they considered to be the Roma of their communities (Havas and Kemény 1999; Kertesi and Kézdi 1998). The expert estimations on which the Minority Rights Group report is based are very different, since identification in this case seems to have relied, not on the judgments provided by direct observers, but on those of the compilers themselves.

The uncertainty and disputes surrounding the demographic data illustrate quite clearly the difficulties that mark all attempts at conceptualizing identity as an objective property. With each new perspective on Romani identity, new figures arise. For this reason, careful consideration of how to define Romani identity is not only important in academic literature; as we will see, population numbers and conceptualizations of identity have notable consequences for activists as well as for policy makers.

Romani Interests

Discussions about statistics lead us to the second important element that lies at the heart of any project of political group formation: interests. Interests are the values and goals that group leaders seek to defend. Not all values and goals are automatically interests. As some analysts have pointed out, they only become interests when they relate to public policy (Baumgartner and Leech 1998: 23–24). With regard to the Roma, one could define interests as those public policy goals of which activists believe they will benefit all Roma. Important in this conception is that, like identities, interests are not given; they are to a large extent formulated by activists and organizers who make their own assessments of the needs of the group. In other words, interest formulation depends on problem analysis. In the case of the Romani movement, analyzing problems clearly involves not only Romani activists and organizers. Outside the domain of direct political activism, there is a large body of expert literature about the needs of the Roma, which is equally important for the formation of interests. Most of that literature focuses on the material conditions of Romani life. In particular, it argues that the principal issues that need to be tackled by the authorities are discrimination, unemployment, and poverty.

The persistence of discrimination against the Roma in Central Europe is pointed out by a range of sociological research projects. There is a wealth of material to demonstrate that Roma systematically lack protection and experience unequal treatment in education and the judicial system. According to a research report published by the OSCE's High Commissioner on National Minorities (HCNM):

> Romani communities are the subject of hostile perceptions across an extraordinary range of countries. In some, politicians and citizens feel few scruples about expressing derogatory stereotypes of Roma. In this climate, Roma have been prime targets of skinhead violence and, at times, what must be properly called pogroms. (HCNM 2000: 3)

Although human rights organizations have been highly active in documenting and publicly disclosing instances of discrimination, it is difficult to find reliable numerical estimates of the impact of this phenomenon. For the most part, organizations as well as independent scholars have focused on providing in-depth descriptions of individual cases. Stories often reveal more than numbers, especially when one wants to say something about the causes of discrimination. And indeed, what worries observers in particular are not merely the instances of discrimination, but the underlying attitudes. Examples can be given for the three countries under consideration. One author notes, "Czech views include a vocal current among the majority population that seeks to discriminate against Roma, to isolate or even eliminate them from the Czech social space" (Fawn 2001: 1196). To substantiate this, the author cites an opinion poll that finds that 45 percent of Czechs favor the departure of Roma from the Czech Republic and 90 percent of Czechs have an "aversion" to Roma and would not have them as neighbors.

Although there exists a myriad of large-scale opinion surveys that demonstrate the prevalence of hostile attitudes toward Roma, the results are quite difficult to use for comparative purposes. The questions asked in these surveys and the applied methods of inquiry usually differ substantially from one opinion poll to the other. It is therefore useful to rely not solely on opinion surveys to substantiate this point, but complement such data with findings resulting from less general and more in-depth research projects. One interesting project in the Czech Republic, for example, was a detailed discourse analysis of four television debates that were broadcast between 1990 and 1995 (Leudar and Nekvapil 2000). In this case, the researchers coded the transcripts of these debates and specifically tried to find out how descriptions of Roma were used and warranted. They concluded that there was very little to learn about the Roma. Most of the qualities ascribed to the Roma were negations of what Czechs find desirable in themselves, and the Roma were often characterized by the absence of positive qualities (Leudar and Nekvapil 2000: 507).

In Hungary, a number of research projects pointed to the prominence of stereotypes concerning "Romani criminality" (Tomka 1991). A survey in 1994 led to the conclusion that approximately 64 percent of the Hungarian population agreed with the statement "the predisposition to crime is in the Gypsies' blood" (Fábián and Sik 1996). The indications of a general negative opinion about the Roma were supported by the data of the 1997 Hungarian Household Panel (Csepeli et al. 1999). A part of the questionnaire in the latter research contained six views on the Roma. The preferences of the respondents, who had to indicate whether they agreed or disagreed with particular statements, revealed their inclination to assume a causal link between the occurrence of criminality and Romani identity, rather than to suppose a causal link between social conditions and criminality. The opinion to which participants had to respond in this survey was, "There are just as many criminals among the Roma as among the non-Romani population living under the same circumstances." A total of 59 percent did not agree with that statement, 33 percent agreed, and 8 percent did not know. In the interpretation of the researchers these findings suggest that only one-third of the Hungarian population agrees that living conditions play a crucial role in the emergence of criminality. For the majority of the respondents ethnic identity is the decisive factor (Csepeli et al. 1999: 461).

Other research confirms this general hypothesis. For instance, Hungarian sociologists György Csepeli, Antal Örkény, and Mária Székelyi found that Hungarian police officers widely believe that there is a direct connection between crime and ethnicity; 54 percent of the officers questioned by these researchers stated that they believed a criminal way of life is a key element of Romani identity (Csepeli 1998). Other scholars focused on the media. Between November 1996 and October 1997, Gábor Bernáth and Vera Messing gathered and analyzed 508 articles from two national and four regional daily Hungarian newspapers that featured news on minorities (Bernáth and Messing 1999). The researchers found that by and large the distribution of topics reflected the social roles typically attributed to Roma by the majority. These ascribed roles pertained to ethnic conflict, exotic culture, and criminality. Moreover, the newspapers studied in this research clearly carried the suggestion that a strong bond exists between criminal behavior and Romani identity. When reporting on crimes committed by members of other minorities or, indeed, by ethnic Hungarians, the media rarely if ever mentioned the ethnic origins of the suspects (Bertnáth and Messing 1999: 36).

Working with a similar research design, researchers in Slovakia gathered 1,990 sources of information on Roma between June 1998 and May 1999 in both the electronic and printed media (Benkovič and Vakulová 2000). On the basis of a content analysis of the articles, they concluded that there was a tendency to report the ethnicity of the suspect when the information was negative. On the basis of a more general overview of press coverage of criminality, the researchers found that such ethnic labeling was not applied to any other minority group. They reported that they did not find a single piece of information in which the ethnicity of a

Slovak citizen other than Roma was mentioned when an individual was suspected of committing a crime (Benkovič and Vakulová 2000: 18).

Stereotyping and discrimination is seen by many organizations and independent scholars as the underlying cause of two other problems: the concentration of poverty and unemployment among the Roma. The HCNM report argued that:

> Roma face profound challenges in virtually every sphere of social life: rates of unemployment, poverty, illiteracy and infant mortality are staggeringly high among Roma. In a classic downward spiral, each of these problems exacerbates the others in a self-perpetuating cycle. (HCNM 2000: 7)

It is quite clear that many current descriptions agree on the fact that in a large number of countries Roma live in dismal economic circumstances. This is true in particular for the countries under study in this book. On the basis of general domestic indicators such as GDP (gross domestic product), life expectancy, education, and adult literacy, one might be tempted to argue that the Czech Republic, Hungary, and Slovakia have been able to secure their advance toward stability and prosperity. In the 2001 *Human Development Index* of the United Nations Development Program (UNDP), they were three of the forty-eight countries ranked under the category "high human development" (in places 33, 36, and 35, respectively) and together with Slovenia, Estonia, Croatia, and Lithuania (29, 44, 46, 47) they were the only postcommunist countries in this category (UNDP 2001: 141). But separate national UNDP reports suggest that there are striking inequalities within the Central European countries as regards unemployment, level of education, housing, and poverty. Absolute poverty rates summarized in a World Bank report suggest that, notwithstanding generally low poverty rates, there are significant groups at the very bottom of the income distribution, especially in Hungary and Slovakia (World Bank 2001: xiii). These pockets of great poverty, the report claims, are usually found in areas that are populated by people who are identified as Roma.

Although the deplorable situation among Romani populations is common knowledge today, it is nevertheless difficult to find any reliable statistical representation of this state of affairs. In the three countries under study, there is no official registration of ethnicity with regard to unemployment and social benefits. However, unofficial figures have sometimes been kept by employment offices, based on the judgments of the administrators about who is and who is not Roma. These data clearly show the concentration of poverty within this group. They suggest—albeit in varying ways—disproportionately high levels of unemployment, the existence of a huge social and spatial distance between Roma and non-Roma, and the prevalence of a very negative image of the Roma in the non-Romani environment.

For Slovakia, current descriptions seem to indicate that the situation is critical, particularly within the estimated 600 "settlements" (*osady*) in the rural periphery—most of them in the eastern parts of Slovakia, notably in the Prešov and Košice regions—but reportedly also in the Banská Bystrica region in Central Slovakia.[6] These communities of Roma living in poor-quality housing outside or on the edge of the main residential areas are characterized by high unemployment and material deprivation (Buček 1999; Vašečka 2001: 192).

On the basis of registries from the National Labor Office in Slovakia, which until 1998 contained a reference to ethnicity, the World Bank published figures for the registered unemployment of those considered as Roma in Slovakia. These figures show an increase in the share of Romani unemployment from 15.5 percent in 1991 to 19.2 percent in 1997 for the total number of unemployed citizens in the whole of Slovakia. The World Bank also showed that the last available figure for the proportion of Roma eligible for unemployment benefits (that of 1995) is as low as 5.3 percent of all citizens eligible for benefits (World Bank 2001: 109). The fact that the portion of the Roma receiving unemployment benefits is so low is considered to be linked to the long duration of their unemployment.

An even more tragic picture of Romani unemployment in Slovakia emerges when regional figures are taken into account. The World Bank cites a 1997 survey by the Slovak Ministry of Labor, Social Affairs and Family, which estimated that in eastern districts with large Romani populations (e.g. Košice, Spisská Nová Ves), Romani employment in 1996 was as high as 40 to 42 percent of the total number of unemployed (World Bank 2001: 109). Moreover, in 1999 the World Bank found that around the Western Slovak town of Malacky official unemployment among Roma ranged from 60 percent in integrated areas to nearly 100 percent in isolated settlements, while the overall unemployment rate for the district was 13.5 percent. Similarly, in the northeastern district around Stará Ľubovňa and around the south-central town of Rimavská Sobota, the unemployment among those seen as Roma was between 80 and 100 percent, while the total unemployment rate for the district was around 35 percent (World Bank 2001: 110).

That the problem of long-term unemployment in Slovakia has reached dramatic proportions in the so-called "Romani settlements" can also be derived from a 1999 government report which states that, of the 124,031 registered inhabitants in those settlements, only 8,664 (slightly less than 7 percent) were officially employed in 1998—a figure which, according to the report, included 5,940 women on maternity leave and 1,066 people attending vocational training (Government of the Slovak Republic 1999a).

For the Czech Republic, a numerical assessment is even harder to make since even fewer official and unofficial statistics are available. Unemployment statistics in the Czech Republic do not indicate ethnic identification. Yet there are some reports that attempt to make generalizations on the basis of other data. One overall numerical assessment comes from a government report published in 1997. On the basis of a crude estimation, it states that while in that year unemployment in the Czech Republic was generally 5 percent, unemployment among the Roma was estimated to be roughly 70 percent, and in some places amounted to 90 percent (Council for Nationalities of the Government of the Czech Republic 1997). Another report builds on unofficial records kept by employment offices in 1997 to estimate that about 47 percent of all Czech Roma were at the time dependent on social welfare (Kaplan 1999). According to the same report, important evidence can be derived from data about the number of people who are actively looking for a job and are registered at employment offices. Results for March 1998 suggest that in that month the unemployment rate among Roma was 3.4 times higher (18.9 percent) than among non-Roma (5.5 percent). Some of the more recent reports conclude that unemployment among Czech Roma fluctuates between 40 and 50 percent (UNDP 2002: 36), while others maintain that the actual rate must be around 60 or even 70 percent (Ministry of Labor and Social Affairs of the Czech Republic 2002). There is a more general consensus among researchers on the underlying reasons. Qualitative research on Romani unemployment in the Czech Republic has suggested that the very high levels of unemployment are largely due to the restructuring and deregulation of the labor market, compounded by deficient education and discriminatory practices (Guy 2001c: 296).

In Hungary, too, changes in the labor market—especially the disappearance of workplaces where unskilled workers were employed—have resulted in unprecedented levels of unemployment among the Roma. Although official statistics are not available for Hungary either, an indication of the extent of Romani unemployment is offered by the figures that have been compiled in a 1993–94 National Roma Survey involving a sample of about 2,000 households. According to that research, merely 30.8 percent of Romani men were employed at that time. Gábor Havas and István Kemény cite figures for 1993 from the International Labor Organization (ILO) which show that registered unemployment among all Roma in Hungary was at the time as high as 49.7 percent (Havas and Kemény 1999: 365). The most severe unemployment was found in the northeast of Hungary, where rates were as high as 59 percent among the Romani population and 17 percent among non-Roma (Kemény 2000: 32). According to the same authors, there was a continuous decline in the number of registered unemployed (both among Roma and in society as a whole) between 1994 and 1999. They presumed this was primarily caused by an increasing number of people giving up registration at employment offices after losing all hope of finding work. According to the 1999 Report of the Republic of Hungary for the Implementation of the Council of Europe Framework Convention for the Protection of National Minorities:

> The unemployment rate in the entire population is 8%–10%, while it is four or five times greater in the case of the Gypsy minority. There are settlements where 90%–100% of the Gypsy population is unemployed. The studies that analyze Gypsy unemployment prove that the Gypsies' inclination to work is basically not lower than that of non-Gypsies living in similar conditions. The unemployed Gypsies, however, have considerably worse chances for making a return to the labor market than non-Gypsies since they have been unemployed for considerably longer. They usually live in small settlements, in regions that are short of jobs, which makes it hard for them to even take part in retraining programs as well as to find employment. (Hungarian Government 1999, Art. 4)

According to Kemény (2000: 34), the catastrophic situation with regard to Romani unemployment in Hungary is to a certain extent mitigated by the fact that an unclear portion of the officially unemployed Roma are engaged in the "gray" and "black" economies (mainly agriculture and small trade) as a means of subsistence. The 2002 UNDP/ILO report relies on a survey among 5,043 individuals in five countries (Bulgaria, the Czech Republic, Hungary, Romania and Slovakia) to conclude that unemployment figures among Roma are lower than what is commonly believed. The report claims that a considerable number of Roma have found income-generating opportunities in the informal economy.

Many human rights groups and Romani organizations have pointed to survival strategies among Romani communities as the result of lack of opportunities on the regular job market. This state of affairs is also perpetuated to some extent by the general situation of Romani children in education. According to a recent report by the UK charity Save the Children:

> In the Czech republic, Roma/Gypsy children are about 15 times more likely than non-Roma/Gypsy children to be placed in special schools for children with learning disabilities. ... In addition, the special school system, in which 75 percent of children are Roma/Gypsies, is effectively a substandard segregated system. (Save the Children 2001: 34)

The same organization also documented a very low intake of Romani students by the Hungarian and Slovak regular education systems. This has led to a segregated system of education, with those children who are perceived as Roma systematically dropping behind in relation to non-Romani pupils, and eventually giving up all ambitions in this field. As a result of very low preschool attendance in Slovakia, Roma tend to withdraw from regular primary and secondary education. In Hungary, most Roma in secondary education are to be found in vocational schools. This sector of education has been "particularly hard hit by economic changes that have severely reduced the value of qualifications from these institutions as a means of gaining subsequent employment" (Save the Children 2001: 121).

Comparable research projects in Central Europe have pointed to phenomena that accompany the occurrence of discrimination, unemployment, and poverty: an alarming health situation and distressing material and environmental conditions. Hungary, in particular, has a growing body of literature and statistics on these issues. To mention just one example, in 2001 and 2004 the School of Public Health of the University of Debrecen published the results of field surveys that were carried out in order to gather information about the living conditions in Romani settlements in the country (Népegészségügyi Iskola 2001; 2004). It found a total of 557 "settlements" (*telepek*) that were characterized by low levels of convenience and quality (lack of brick walls, power supply, sewage system etc.), a high population density and an unfavorable location. Virtually all of these settlements were exclusively the home of Roma. The highest numbers of settlements were found in the counties of Bács-Kiskun, Borsod-Abaúj-Zemplén, and Tolna.

The above overview is, of course, far from exhaustive, but it nevertheless shows that descriptive reporting and analytical studies are remarkably consistent when it comes to defining the concerns of the Roma. There is no complete agreement on the exact numbers, but there is consensus on the topics of concern. Most of the literature on the Roma carries a fairly explicit message. It argues that authorities should be putting much more work into combating discrimination, living conditions, segregated education, poverty, and unemployment. It is significant that only a much smaller portion of the literature is concerned with issues related to the protection of Romani culture and language. One example of the latter is a book published in 2000 by the Gypsy Research Center (*Centre de recherche tsigane*) in Paris in collaboration with the University of Hertfordshire in the UK dealing with the Romani language (Bakker et al. 2000). The main objective of the publication was to debunk some of the popular myths about that language, but it had also a direct political agenda. The seven authors, who come from various European countries, joined in an international effort to advance the idea that the Romani language should be further standardized, preserved and disseminated through education and media. At first sight this could be seen as a striking example of a group of scholars advocating a Romani interest that most other authors have more or less ignored. But even in that publication, there was a strong reference to other aspects of the Romani experience. The authors asserted, for example, that "many Roma have problems much more serious than the preservation of the language" (Bakker et al. 2000: 116).

The same kind of hesitancy can be found in another small portion of the literature: the writings that propose to pressure for demands relating to the protection of specific forms of lifestyle. Authors place such demands promptly into perspective when the discussion shifts to issues of material inequality and discrimination. The Hungarian sociologist János Ladányi summed up this point during a Romani studies conference in 2000, when he argued that the Roma should not be concerned in the first place about their right to be different, but should give priority to demands for equality and equal treatment.[7] The scholarly consensus holds that Romani interests in Central Europe primarily need to be seen in connection to material circumstances, poverty, and discrimination. As one collection of scholarly articles published in 2001 summarized the issue: The Roma "are present in every country yet remain on the margins of society without a nation state to defend them as they suffer the sharp pain of racist assaults and the more grinding pressures of material deprivation and daily humiliation" (Guy 2001d: xiv).

It should not come as a surprise that this academic analysis of the current state of affairs has served—albeit in a variety of ways—as a basis for the political action of Romani activists and the organizations that seek to represent, defend, or speak for the Roma in Central Europe. Indeed, influencing and shaping the general perception of the current plight of the Roma by highlighting external observations by (academic) researchers has been considered to be an essential part of any attempt to attract attention to the situation of the Roma. It has also been regarded as a crucial element in the process of mobilizing people to become actively engaged in an ethnically based Romani movement. Before proceeding with the empirical study of the dynamics of this process of Romani mobilization in Central Europe, however, the remainder of this chapter first lays out a general theoretical framework for studying ethnic mobilization.

Theories of Ethnic Mobilization

In order to review the available theoretical perspectives on ethnic mobilization I draw on two bodies of literature: (a) the literature on political mobilization and social movements; and (b) the literature on ethnic identity and ethnic politics. The combination of these two academic debates is not self-evident. In the past, issues of identitification have not always found their way to debates on political mobilization. As Charles Tilly has observed, many people have regarded identity claims primarily as "a form of self-expression, or even self-indulgence—what others do when they are too comfortable, too confused, or too distressed for serious politics" (Tilly 2003: 609). Tilly's argument is that identity claims and their attendant stories do constitute serious political business. It is a premise I start from, too.

Let me first consider briefly the concept of political mobilization. In a general sense, political mobilization is the process by which political actors organize collective efforts in order to attempt to bring about political change. These efforts include the representation of the interests of a constituency, the construction and formulation of these interests, and the attempts to persuade constituents that the way in which interests are formulated and defended will effectively lead to change. In short, political mobilization is the process of actors finding active adherents to a collective cause and managing to express that cause in public action (Stone 1998: 217).

What should be clear from this definition is that I am adopting a broad understanding of minority mobilization. The focus here will not be restricted—as is sometimes the case with other authors—to the formal political participation of ethnic minorities, referring exclusively to the electoral behavior of the individual members of an ethnic group, their involvement in political parties and their interest representation in parliament. Arguably, such a narrow view of political participation is inspired by the classical division social scientists have made between the political significance of political parties and interest representation in state institutions, on the one hand, and the social and cultural (but supposedly less political) weight of social movements, on the other (Kriesi 1993: 2–3). This is clearly an oversimplified view since it presumes the existence of a homogenous political mass which seeks representation through established channels. Of course, social movements have important cultural and social implications; but they are also inherently political. As it was formulated in one now classic international comparative study on political action, nonelectoral and noninstitutionalized types of public action in liberal democracies—such as protests, for example—should be regarded as important forms of political action because they reflect "newly emerging interest cleavages" (Barnes et al. 1979: 38).

Moreover, it is no doubt true that in the second half of the twentieth century the articulation of collective demands of social movements in Western European democracies was increasingly addressed at political authorities, and that social movements therefore came to play a very direct role in politics. Hanspeter Kriesi even proposed the term "social movement politics" to describe the increasing tendency of Western European citizens in the latter half of the twentieth century "to take recourse to unconventional, extra-parliamentary means of action" (Kriesi 1993: 2). It is appropriate, however, to employ the term "political mobilization" to refer to a broad field of influence that includes aspects of both electoral and nonelectoral forms of political involvement, the reason being that, as in Western Europe, a great deal of ethnic politics in contemporary Central Europe is likely to be located outside the existing formal institutional arrangements. In this respect the abundant literature on the link between civil society development and democratization in Central and Eastern Europe and the significance of the growing presence there of associations that mediate between individuals and the state is particularly pertinent (e.g. Hann and Dunn 1996; Rueschemeyer et al. 1998).

In the light of the current overwhelming interest in the link between ethnic groups and political mobilization, it is perhaps surprising that theorizing on ethnic mobilization in political science literature cannot look back upon a long history. Traditionally, political scientists used to consider the possible ethnic dimensions of political mobilization as of secondary importance. Not that ethnic politics was entirely discounted; but scholars often assumed that ethnic solidarities in politics would be abandoned with the ongoing development of modernization and the spread of liberal-democratic values (Kymlicka 2000: 184). This argument was not necessarily influenced by the analogous Marxist reasoning that class identity would prevail over other types of identities through the struggle against capitalism (Glazer and Moynihan 1974). Before the 1960s, mainstream political science was influenced by the assimilationist view in sociology and regarded ethnicity as a transitional phenomenon or as a factor that did not have any influence on the formal political system (Taylor 1996: 886; Vermeulen and Govers 1994: 2). In some cases they even thought that ethnicity would disappear from the political vocabulary. Prior to the 1990s, many authors in Western Europe and North America had long dismissed the subject, and even predicted the decline of ethnic attachments in politics. The "liberal expectancy" (Glazer and Moynihan 1974: 33) of mainly American theorists was tantamount to the idea that ethnic identities were merely transitory and would vanish into an ethnic melting pot with the advancement of liberal democracy (Moynihan 1993: 27–28).

The resurgence of political mobilization of territorially based linguistic groups in Western Europe in the 1970s contradicted the expectations of classical social theory—as can be witnessed from the mobilizations of the Bretons and Corsicans in France, the Celtic-speaking populations in Great Britain, or the Flemish-Walloon cleavage in Belgium (Ragin 1987: 133). Ethnic differences within one country did not seem to erode, a phenomenon that made the need felt for additional theorizing. However, it was the surge in ethnically based conflict in the last decade of the twentieth century that again changed views on ethnic mobilization, this time quite radically, and refocused attention on the need to think about the relationship between ethnicity and politics.

Indeed, over the last decade or so political scientists have written a considerable amount of literature on the phenomenon of ethnic mobilization. Through perusing this vast literature, roughly four overall explanations can be discerned, or, perhaps more accurately, four different perspectives on ethnic mobilization:

1. a "culturalist" perspective, which emphasizes the significance of strong subjective bonding and values within ethnic groups for shaping the lines of ethnic mobilization.
2. "reactive ethnicity" perspective, which argues that the primary cause of ethnic mobilization lies in the coincidence of ethnic bonding and relative deprivation.

3. "competition" perspective, which focuses on ethnic leaders making rational calculations about their identity and invoking ethnicity in their struggle for resources and power.
4. "political process" perspective, which emphasizes the role of the macro-political context—the institutional environment and the dominant political discursive context—in determining patterns of ethnic mobilization.

Each perspective differs in the sense that each considers a different set of factors to be primarily responsible for causing and shaping ethnic mobilization. That being said, it should be noted that the distinction between them necessarily involves some simplification; certain nuances are not dealt with and differences are emphasized over similarities. Nonetheless, the distinction offers a useful analytical device to structure the literature and gain insight into the pattern of explanatory variables that theorists have considered to be pivotal in driving ethnic mobilization. We will take these perspectives in turn, in the following pages.

The Culturalist Perspective

The culturalist perspective distinguishes itself from other approaches by its view on the role of culture in the process of ethnic mobilization. Culture here refers to the values, symbols, and interpretations of meaning that are shared by the members of a group.[8] The culturalist perspective regards the cultural socialization process as the most fundamental factor explaining ethnic mobilization. In other words, the fact that members of an ethnic group share a common culture determines the group's pattern of ethnic mobilization.

There are different versions of the culturalist argument. Many authors have propounded views that are only implicitly culturalist. George Schöpflin, for example, argues that the persistence of ethnic communities is in large part related to the process of "cultural reproduction." Ethnic groups employ instruments of cultural reproduction such as dress, dietary codes, language, symbols, rituals, monuments, and so forth, to "reaffirm their community" (Schöpflin 2000: 56–57). One could read this as a plea in favor of taking culture as the essential basis of an ethnic community's political continuity. In other words, cultural group solidarities lead to distinctive modes of community affirmation among ethnic groups. However, Schöpflin carefully points out that in political development there are other identity-forming processes at play besides cultural reproduction. Identity politics is not only influenced by culture, but also by the state and by civil society. That cultural reproduction in Central and Eastern Europe has gained prevalence over the other identity-forming processes is, according to Schöpflin, the result of the weakness of the state and civil society in that region. In other words, ethnic identity is the result of a pre-political process of cultural reproduction and people revert to that identity when other identity-forming processes fail. "It is not the case that in the postcommunist world, people are obdurate in their attachment to 'outdated' ethnic identities, but rather that the institutions of the state and civil society are weak and not trusted, whereas ethnicity has authenticity" (Schöpflin 2000: 31). Of course, this argument is not entirely satisfying since "authenticity" implies an external arbiter who sets the standards for authenticity.

A similar nuanced embracement of the role of culture in the political development of ethnic communities can be traced in the work of Anthony D. Smith. In essence, Smith advances the proposition that a nation as a political entity has a cultural basis in the form of an ethnic community (*ethnie*).

> Though not all cultural differences reflect ethnic differentiation ... the persistence over centuries of separate styles attached to particular peoples in certain areas does point to the longevity and widespread incidence of *ethnie* in all periods. Along with polities, religious organizations and class, ethnicity provides one of the central axes of alignment and division in the pre-modern world, and one of the most durable. (Smith 1997: 33)

In the academic literature on the roots of nationalism, there is a host of authors who generally consider nations to be political entities derived from ethnic groups sharing a particular culture. The works of authors such as Walker Connor, Steven Grosby, Donald Horowitz, and James G. Kellas differ in many aspects, but on a deeper level they share the idea of the existence of a cultural basis for political nationalism (Connor 1994; Grosby 1994; Horowitz 1985; Kellas 1991). On Smith's reading, these authors can collectively be called "perennialists." They accept the modernity of nationalism as a political movement, but regard nations as updated versions of immemorial culture-based ethnic communities (Smith 1998).

These scholars have mainly discussed the historical origins of nations and nationalism without directing attention to the impact of culture on contemporary political movements. Other authors, however, have explicitly accepted the idea that ethnic identities are based on cultural givens and natural affinities that have an overpowering emotional and nonrational quality determining current patterns of ethnic mobilization (Allahar 1996; Oberschall 2000: 982). One school of thought in international relations literature argues that culture should be seen as the crucial independent variable explaining economic and political developments. Samuel P. Huntington, for example, notoriously contends that cultural explanations should be central to our understanding of why particular societies achieve or fail to achieve progress in economic development and political democratization (Harrison and Huntington 2000). In this literature, ethnic groups are mainly discussed in the context of violent conflict. In Huntington's view ethnicity is based on cultural attributes such as religion and traditions. Throughout long periods of history, it is argued, such cultural attributes have influenced population groups so profoundly that it becomes easier to engage them in ethnic conflict.

The basic assumption that governs this literature is that ethnic mobilization is the reflection of cultural structure. The obvious conclusion, then, is that people from the same ethnic group will have some sort of a natural connection because of their shared culture and will therefore organize in similar ways. Their social or economic situation may to a certain extent thus facilitate or suppress mobilization, but it is ultimately the cultural content that forms the backbone of the mobilization process. On the basis of the assumption that action is expressive of culture, the argument is made that each ethnic group should exhibit a unique mobilization pattern (Ireland 1994: 8). It is, in this perspective, also expected that the same ethnic group in different societies will adopt roughly similar forms of mobilization.

Culturalist explanations of ethnic relations have been employed in many descriptive accounts of Central and Eastern European politics. The argument underlying these contends that the communist political systems attempted in vain to suppress the original cultural solidarity in society, and that—after the downfall of these systems—the cultural reality of old solidarities and rivalries resurfaced. Culturalist explanations nevertheless have been subjected to a number of criticisms. The first criticism is that the culturalists have too readily taken for granted that an ethnic group is characterized by a shared culture (Barth 1969). Culturalist explanations have created the impression that ethnic groups are naturally occurring entities with a unique and fixed cultural essence, a view that is close to an extreme form of primordialism. There still exists a research tradition in social anthropology that claims that ethnic groups should be retained in anthropological analysis to designate more or less coherent cultural entities (de Heusch 1997). It is, however, a minor tradition, and it has been criticized by most of the major authors in the field (Eriksen 2002: 57). In most cases, critics contend, it is difficult to define the cultural essence of an ethnic group, and therefore culture is too diffuse to be a useful explanatory variable. As Nathan Glazer has responded to theories that follow Huntington's line of thinking, "What does Italy in the large tell us about the typical Italian immigrant, poor, from the south, uneducated? Are we to take him as an example of the culture and civilization of Catholic Europe, of the Mediterranean, of peasant life, all of which and more may be considered to mark him?" (Glazer 2000: 223).

Secondly, some authors contend that culturalist explanations of ethnic mobilization tend to be tautological. The cultural perspective explains ethnic mobilization by reference to cultural solidarity, without, however, making a clear distinction between cultural solidarity and ethnic mobilization (Olzak 1998: 188). Even in cases where proponents of primordialism remain far removed from theories of biological determinism or ideas of ethnicity as a means of categorizing people into frozen hierarchies, they have still tended to attribute uncritically a general explanatory quality to the cultural content of an ethnic group without making clear what the difference between cultural content and ethnic identity actually is. They have defined ethnic groups in terms of incompatible cultures and have then seen this incompatibility as the primary source of ethnic rifts in a society. The culturalist perspective, in other words, considers ethnic identity to be determined by culture, but suggests at the same time that the individuals of a group have a common culture *because* of their common ethnic identity. Obviously, such reasoning leads to circular explanations of ethnic mobilization and, perhaps, to self-fulfilling prophecies.

Another criticism is that culturalist descriptions fail to appreciate the role of agency. By excluding the role of agency, these theories manifestly fail to account for the fact that individuals and groups can change both their culture and their ethnic identity, consciously or unconsciously, or that their ethnic identity can assume a different meaning over time, dependent on the political circumstances. Moreover, it neglects the role of individual leadership and strategy. This criticism often points to the existence of empirical evidence suggesting that leadership and strategy exert a great influence on ethnic bonding. According to one study on immigrant minority mobilization in Western countries, ethnic bonds, "if not wholly invented by political leaders and intellectuals for purposes of social manipulation, are at the least linked to specific social and political projects" (Ireland 2000: 270).

Reactive Ethnicity

In contrast to the culturalist perspective, the "reactive ethnicity" approach does not consider ethnic mobilization as the mere natural and automatic consequence of the existence of separate cultural groups. In this perspective, the rise of ethnic mobilization is prompted by the unequal division of resources along ethnic lines. The term itself is strongly associated with the work of Michael Hechter on ethnic mobilization in the Celtic fringe of the British Isles in the early 1970s (Hechter 1975). In Hechter's formulation reactive ethnicity means that ethnoregional loyalties and conflict within a state may be strengthened as a result of increasing levels of economic inequalities between the core and the ethnically distinct periphery. Although Hechter applied this approach specifically to offer an explanation for territorially based ethnic identities, similar theoretical perspectives were applied to explain instances of ethnic mobilization that are less connected to the core-periphery distinction. A prominent example of this line of reasoning was Bonacich's "split labor market theory" (Bonacich 1972), which holds that ethnic antagonism is generated by the competition arising from a differential price of labor for the same occupation. Ethnic mobilization in this version is dependent on the economic competition between ethnically differentiated segments of the working class.

Theories that could be considered as similar to the "reactive ethnicity" approach have also been applied to explain revolts in American ghettos (Blauner 1969) and more recently to explain ethnic mobilization of immigrant minorities in Western Europe. Beatrice Drury offers an example of the latter. According to her observations, ethnic minorities in the United Kingdom are likely to mobilize when they experience discrimination and problems which arise from poverty and social deprivation; when they perceive that they are being denied equality of opportunity and an equal share of society's resources; and, if they believe that there are very few alternative avenues to social and economic mobility (Drury 1994: 16).

A number of important criticisms have, however, led to a reconsideration of this theoretical approach. First of all, economic disadvantage is clearly not a sufficient condition for the occurrence of ethnic mobilization. It is not so difficult to find examples of economically disadvantaged ethnic groups that do not engage in politics or protest. The level of mobilization does not seem to be dependent on the level of disadvantage. Conversely, if ethnic mobilization occurs, it is not necessarily accompanied by economic disadvantage. Some scholars, for example, have pointed to the resurgence of ethnic solidarities in regions that are economically advantaged relative to other areas (Coughlan and Samarasinghe 1991: 4; Smith 1981).

Furthermore, the "reactive ethnicity" approach as it is set forth in these works is relatively close to the structural-functionalist perspective on social movements, which considers social movements to be side-effects of over-rapid social transformation (della Porta and Diani 1999: 4). Structural-functionalists view social movements as manifestations of feelings of deprivation and aggression resulting from a wide range of frustrated expectations. The approach has been criticized by social movement scholars who have argued that there is little or no relationship between variations of relative deprivation and the pace and timing of collective protest (Fox Piven and Cloward 1995; see also Tilly 1978). The hypothesis that situations of deprivation automatically produce mobilization reduces such mobilization to an agglomeration of individual behavior. Della Porta and Diani (1999: 5) note that such a perspective ignores the importance of the dynamics by which feelings experienced at the level of the individual give rise to phenomena such as social movements. Structural-functionalist theories on social movements have also been criticized for regarding activists as irrational actors. Action thus comes to be "devalued as reactive behaviour, incapable of strategic rationality, isolated from the conflicts it [seeks] to express" (della Porta and Diani 1999: 7).

In response to this criticism a number of social movement scholars have focused on the resources that movement organizations and movement entrepreneurs need in order to be able to engage in political action; their approach has become known as "resource mobilization theory." Resources such as money, expertise, access to networks and people permit social actors to take strategic decisions with the purpose of mobilizing for social and political change. Taking social movement actors as rational actors has provided an important inspiration for theorists on ethnic mobilization focusing on the role of leaders. The latter perspective is what I have called the "ethnic competition" perspective.

Ethnic Competition

According to the competition model—and largely in keeping with the reactive ethnicity approach—society revolves around a struggle for scarce resources, and solidarity occurs in relation to these resources. It differs from the reactive ethnicity approach in three ways.

First, the competition perspective argues that it is not economic deprivation that gets people to mobilize. On the contrary, economic advancement of previously disadvantaged groups can result in an escalation of inter-group conflict. According to this view, the mere fact that groups can compete for the same resources as a result of their economic advancement may contribute to conflict.

Second, while the reactive ethnicity approach usually regards mobilization as an automatic response to situations of deprivation, the competition perspective emphasizes "the entrepreneurial role in ethnic politics: how the mobilization of ethnic groups in collective action is effected by leaders who pursue a political enterprise" (Barth 1994: 12).[9] Within this perspective emphasis is placed on the ability of political entrepreneurs to respond to economic and political circumstances. This perspective does not pay much attention to beliefs in common origin, but instead claims that the idea of an ethnic group refers sociologically to an overlap between patterns of (positive or negative) recognition and of resource allocation (in the broadest sense, of which economic resources are simply one important instance) (Crowley 2001: 102).

Third, in contrast to most culturalist and reactive ethnicity approaches, the competition perspective regards ethnic group identity not as a preexisting fact, but as a phenomenon that arises during the process of ethnic competition. In order to defend material interests, self-proclaimed group leaders invoke an ethnic group identity. In this way their identity and interests are mutually reinforced. According to Daniel Bell, ethnicity in the competition perspective "is best understood not as a primordial phenomenon in which deeply held identities have to reemerge, but as a strategic choice by individuals who, in other circumstances, would choose other group memberships as a means of gaining some power and privilege" (Bell 1975: 171). The assumption underlying this theoretical perspective is that politics is not an automatic reflection of ethnic divisions. On the contrary, ethnic divisions are invoked through a political struggle against situations of marginalization and inequality. For example, certain leaders may find it useful to organize a group around a common ethnic identity when they sense that this group has been placed in a specific position in the workplace, experiences a common form of discrimination, or suffers from income inequality.

The element of economic positioning has attracted a lot of attention in neo-Marxist treatments of ethnic minority mobilization in the West (Miles 1989; Rath 1991; Solomos and Back 1995). With regard to immigrant populations, the argument has been made that the common "class" identity of immigrants determines the nature of their involvement in politics (Ireland 1994: 6). In other words, ethnicity may be the modality in which immigrants experience class relations in Western Europe. Ethnic minority development has, in this view, not been the result of a natural bonding, but a by-product of the concentration and isolation of immigrant workers in a specific workplace. Other authors approaching ethnicity from this perspective have emphasized that it is not only the economic position that contributes to the construction of certain patterns of ethnic minority mobilization, but also the differential distribution of political power (Oberschall 2000: 983).

The competition perspective has been inspired by what has been called an instrumentalist critique on primordialism. Instrumentalists disagree with the assumption held in the primordialist accounts that ethnicity is strongly determined by a common ancestry. In particular, instrumentalism has responded to the "hard" version of primordialism, which holds that mutual ties of blood somehow condition reciprocal feelings of trust and acceptance (Allahar 1996: 6). As a result, instrumentalism has directed attention toward ethnicity as a calculation of social, economic, and political profits carried out by political elites.

Joane Nagel, for example, has argued that the occurrence of ethnic minority mobilization is the result of individuals engaging "in continuous assessment of situation and audience, emphasizing or deemphasizing particular dimensions of ethnicity according to some measure of utility or feasibility" (Nagel 1996: 23). Some theorists have contended that ethnic identity directly evolves out of elite competition (Brass 1991). One of the important points of reference in this literature is the work by social anthropologist Fredrik Barth. Although the element of political competition was only implicit in his most influential work—written in 1969—on ethnic groups and boundaries, by 1994 Barth was contending that political factors deserve more attention. He suggested that the creation of ethnicity should not be seen as taking place only on the interpersonal level but that it is also dependent on collective action (Barth calls this the "median level"). The importance of Barth's view for students of political relations was primarily that it cleared a way for studying the role of elites and their strategic action in the construction of ethnic boundaries. In other words, the interactional element introduced by Barth's 1969 article was taken a step further and brought into the scope of theories of political competition.

The competition model characterized influential writings of a number of authors in political science, such as Paul Brass (1991), Abner Cohen (1996), and Michael Hechter (1996).[10] In different ways they have all adopted a more or less explicit instrumentalist view of ethnic identity formation, offering a great deal of attention to the role of elites who engage in struggle for political power, maximization of preferences, and rational choice. A number of these authors have also devoted attention to the circumstances that constrain the making of strategic decisions. Also Barth himself had become increasingly aware of this; in 1994 he argued that the state should be taken into consideration as an important factor determining mobilization patterns (Barth 1994: 19). Consequently, several other researchers have begun to draw attention specifically to the fact that ethnic identities appear to be dependent on ethnic classifications promoted by political elites and the state.[11]

Political Process: The Dynamics of Opportunity Structures and Framing

This last aspect of the competition approach comes close to what may be called a "political process" perspective. This perspective seeks to fuse attention to competition with attention to a socially structured context. Like the competition perspective, the political process perspective regards as important the activities of those who present themselves as leaders of ethnic minorities, their resources, their ability to make public claims in the name of the minority, and their attempts to garner mass support. But the political process perspective directs attention to two additional elements: "political opportunity structure" and "framing."

The inspiration for this perspective has come from the literature on new social movements, which submits that collective action is more than just the result of strategic and instrumental rationality (Cohen and Arato 1995: 510). It is important to recognize, this literature argues, that social movements evolve around the articulation of identity and the awareness of the influence of power relations on the creation of identity. Divisions in society are not simply reflected in politics, neither are they merely the result of strategic action. Divisions are constructed through politics within the context of dominant perceptions in society. In contrast to the culturalist and the competition perspectives, the political process perspective on ethnic mobilization argues that there is a two-way relationship between political action and interests. Interests are not just "out there," waiting for ethnic leaders to organize around, but are shaped by the institutional environment and the discursive context.

While the competition perspective focuses on resource competition as the most important factor influencing patterns of ethnic mobilization, the political process perspective attaches crucial importance to the institutional environment (the political opportunity structure) and the symbolic and discursive dimensions of mobilization (framing processes) —both fields of influence that have been taken into account in the comparative analysis of social movements (McAdam et al. 1996). This approach sets ethnic identity against the broader picture of social movements utilizing identity as a basis for mobilization in search of access to political power, material resources, and the control of representation.

Political Opportunity Structure (POS)

Recent writing on social movements has drawn attention to the role of the institutional structures of the state in determining patterns of mobilization. This has been conceptualized as the "political opportunity structure" (often abbreviated as POS) of a movement (McAdam et al. 1996; Tarrow 1994). The POS refers to the complex of formal and informal political conditions into which a movement must enter when it becomes active. On the one hand, it refers to what can be regarded as the stable properties of the institutional environment, such as the state's propensity to repression or the openness of the institutionalized system (in this case, for example, the official recognition of ethnic minorities or the existence of special channels for minority representation). On the other hand, it refers to less stable factors such as the presence or absence of elite allies, or the shifts in political alliances (in the case of ethnic movements, for example, the political position of other identity groups). According to the brief definition offered by Sidney Tarrow, the POS comprises "consistent—but not necessarily formal or permanent— dimensions of the political environment that provide incentives for people to undertake collective action by affecting their expectations for success or failure" (Tarrow 1994: 18). A frequently used way of conceptualizing the POS is offered by Hanspeter Kriesi and Marco Guigni (1995: xiii–xvi). These authors have argued that the POS is made up of four components:

- national cleavage structures (the established political conflicts in a country, which arguably impose important constraints on newly emerging movements);
- formal institutional structures (institutional make-up of the stable elements of the political system, such as parliament, public administration, or other more direct democratic procedures);

- prevailing informal strategies in dealing with social movements (strategies members of the political system typically employ to deal with social movements);
- alliance structure (cyclical elements of change in the political system such as the availability of influential allies or the shifts in ruling alignments).

The theoretical influence of POS perspectives in the study of social movements must be seen in the context of crucial developments in social movement theory in the 1970s and 1980s. As I have already outlined, the structural-functionalist approaches (authors such as Neil Smelser and Arthur William Kornhauser), which regarded social movements as uncalculated and irrational by-products of large-scale social transformations, were criticized from a "resource mobilization" angle (Oberschall 1973; Zald and Ash 1966). So were the collective behavior perspectives, which conceived social movements as collective initiatives aimed at enforcing new values and norms in reaction to a changing environment. The resource mobilization approach regarded collective movements as forms of "conventional" political behavior by actors who calculate the costs and benefits of their collective action in relation to the limited material or nonmaterial resources available. Social movements were thus no longer seen as simply reactive or grievance-based collective phenomena, but as conscious actors (professional social movement organizations became a primary focus), making rational choices within a political system (della Porta and Diani 1999: 9).

Resource mobilization approaches in turn were criticized for ignoring the structural context of contentious politics. The political and institutional environment, and particularly the relation between institutional political actors and social protest, was the main concern of those who became known as the "political process" theorists (della Porta and Diani 1999: 9). Key to their line of argumentation was that the characteristics of the external environment, especially the openness or closure of the political system, were relevant to the development of social movements (Eisinger 1973). Their concept of POS, which has been applied and established in social movement research by authors such as Charles Tilly (1978), Doug McAdam (1982), and Sidney Tarrow (1983), referred to both the general receptivity of a given political system to the collective contention by social challengers and the formal access points they have to the institutions of the political system (McAdam 1996). In the "new social movements" tradition researchers applied the POS concept mostly in comparative research designs, trying to account for the cross-national differences in the appearance and organizational form of comparable movements on the basis of the properties of the national political systems in which they are embedded (McAdam et al. 1996: 3).

The POS perspective provides an important point of support for studying the formation of ethnic mobilization (Koopmans and Statham 2000). Scholars writing about ethnic minority mobilization within this perspective have been attentive to the properties of the political context that facilitate or constrain the formation of a certain movement identity. Moreover, the theory is compelling because it responds to an intuitive feeling that social movements will act in accord with the institutional opportunities and constraints with which they are confronted in a given political system. Such an idea is also related to what James March and Johan Olsen have labeled "the logic of appropriateness" (March and Olsen 1989). This approach argues that the strategies and preferences of actors are determined and created by institutions. "Institutions create or socially construct the actors' identities, belongings, definitions of reality and shared meanings" (Rothstein 2000: 147).

Interestingly, the POS perspective has served as a primary source of inspiration for an emerging research tradition among scholars who have attempted to understand the political mobilization of immigrant minorities in long-standing Western democracies (Bousetta 2001; Castles 1995; Favell 1998; Ireland 1994; Jacobs 2005; Martiniello and Statham 1999). The argument held in common by these researchers is that the shape of the institutional political context is a key variable influencing and fostering the ethnic mobilization of minorities. As a consequence, the theoretical focus inspired by POS considerations seems to lend itself to be applied to the case of nonterritorially bounded ethnic minorities in Central Europe.

However, we should be aware that the current studies that have applied POS theory as a point of departure for empirical research have not remained entirely without problems. Hassan Bousetta has shown that formal and informal organizational processes that take place *inside* an ethnic movement and give rise to certain strategic choices (a field which he calls "infra-politics") are often left out of sight when exclusive use of the POS perspective is employed (Bousetta 2001: 19–20). In other words, the internal organizational processes should be considered an integral part of the political mobilization of ethnic minorities, but remain hidden when importance is attached only to the "institutionalized" processes. Struggles surrounding strategic choices or questions of representation and group boundaries may take place between actors within the organizational realm of an ethnic movement. These may have a certain impact on how a movement will develop and will need to be conceptualized as an area of research. Furthermore, POS studies have also been criticized for overemphasizing the institutional political context as a causal variable and de-emphasizing other factors that may have contributed to the formation of opportunities. It must be realized that opportunities and constraints are not simply given. They have to be perceived as opportunities first before they will be able to function as such (Jenson 1998).

Framing Processes
Many authors on social movements agree that to some extent the problems associated with POS studies can be avoided when the POS perspective is integrated with insights that have been developed in the so-called "framing" literature (McAdam et al. 1996). In various types of research the term "frame" has been used to denote, in its most general sense, a schema of interpretation. The verb "to frame" refers then to a process through which meaning is reproduced in society. Most studies in social science that use the concept of framing offer a definition derived from the writings of Erving Goffman, in particular his book *Frame Analysis* (Goffman 1975). Goffman used the designation "primary framework" to refer to what he called a "conceptual structure" that organizes interpretation. Tom Burns reformulates Goffman's term as a "mental set" through which people understand and construct social events (Burns 1992: 250). This suggests that Goffman understood framing as cognition. As Goffman's work was mostly preoccupied with the production of primary frameworks through culture, he did not elaborate a fully worked-out definition of framing itself in his work (Burns 1992: 248). Nevertheless, the concept became an important source of inspiration for scholars interested in the development of social movements (McAdam et al. 1996). These scholars shifted the focus away from frames as pure cognition and started to concentrate on the power of deliberate framing within the organizational and collective processes that are part of mobilization (Johnston 1995: 217). For them, frames not only perform an interpretative function, as suggested by Goffman. They are also "made" by movement leaders with the specific intention "to mobilize potential adherents and constituents, to garner bystander support, and to demobilize antagonists" (Snow and Benford 1998: 198).

Social movement scholars in general have been interested in framing when understood as the way in which movement actors disseminate their understanding of social reality in order to appeal to a constituency. Different authors have often highlighted different aspects of the framing process, some emphasizing the individual control over framing processes. On this view, research has to focus on the ability of activists to actively assign meaning to social reality, promote a certain understanding of reality, and intentionally choose a frame for mobilization. They define framing as "the conscious strategic efforts by groups of people to fashion a shared understanding of the world and of themselves that legitimate and motivate collective action" (McAdam et al. 1996: 6). Others, however, have emphasized that the process of framing does not take place in a vacuum (Benford and Snow 2000: 628). For them, research should not discard the fact that framing is always negotiated and is to a certain degree shaped by the complex, multi-organizational, multi-institutional arenas in which it takes place. These authors have stressed that frame diffusion (how frames spread) and frame resonance (how frames become effective) is affected by the cultural and political environment. In this way, Robert D. Benford and David A. Snow have defined framing as the generation and diffusion by movement actors of mobilizing and countermobilizing ideas and meanings, a process which is facilitated or constrained by the cultural and political context, including the framing/counterframings of the elites in power (Benford and Snow 2000). Defined as such, the concept of "framing" creates an opportunity to examine both the element of *choice* in the construction of ethnic identity (the use of intentional frames) and the element of *designation* (the presence of countermobilizing frames or the (in)ability of a frame to resonate in a given context).

The concept of framing has offered a useful contribution to the study of ethnic mobilization. With regard to movement identity, it can be said that such an identity is created through framing. Constituencies do not exist until they are defined through an identity frame (Jenson 1998: 5). Identity frames are central to the process of ethnic minority mobilization, but it is likely that also other related frames will be employed during this process. Indeed, it is the contention of social movement scholars like Benford and Snow that different types of framing processes help to shape a social movement and its outcome. In their view, any movement has a number of core framing tasks: "diagnostic framing" (problem identification and attribution), "prognostic framing" (perspectives on how to remedy a certain problem), and "motivational framing" (providing a rationale for action) (Benford and Snow 2000).

Conclusion

This chapter has shown that a number of external observers have discerned a firm basis for Romani political mobilization in Central Europe. They have considered the Roma to be a group on the margins of society that is characterized by a strong feeling of ethnic identity. Although there is a certain amount of disagreement among academics about how exactly to understand the nature of Romani identity, almost all of them agree that this identity is a potentially powerful tool for mobilization. As I will argue later, feelings of group identity among Roma should not so much be seen as the basis of political mobilization but rather as its product. The academic studies about Romani identity are thus mainly important because they have contributed to the current general understanding of the Roma as one single group and thereby have provided activists with an important framework for political action. This framework has gained even more saliency with the publication of the results of an increasing number of independent research projects on the deplorable conditions in which many Roma have to live. By highlighting the problems of discrimination, poverty, unemployment, education, and housing, researchers have created a clear picture of the issues that should be at the heart of the Romani movement.

While the first part of the chapter has set the general context of descriptive literature in which the dynamics of Romani mobilization in Central Europe should be understood, the latter half of the chapter has laid out the general theoretical framework for the study of these patterns of mobilization. From the four theoretical perspectives on ethnic mobilization discussed in this chapter, this study is particularly interested in the "ethnic competition" and the "political process" perspectives. These perspectives pay attention to factors that are related to the strategic choices of ethnic leaders and factors that are related to the discursive and political environment.

One important strand of theoretical literature argues that processes of mobilization are to a large extent determined by changes in the formal and informal political environment. In order to find out if it is indeed true that the dynamics of Romani mobilization in Central Europe have been strongly influenced by the formal and informal political environment present in this region, it is logical to start in the following chapter with a close examination of how in recent times official policies towards the Roma in Hungary, the Czech Republic, and Slovakia have developed.

Chapter 2

The Development of Minority Policies in Central Europe

I spoke to Aladár Horváth for the first time in the spring of 1999. Since the late 1980s, Horváth has been one of the most prominent and one of the most controversial young Romani activists in Hungary. During the final months of the communist regime, he successfully led one of the first protest actions against the residential segregation of Roma (the Anti-Ghetto Committee in Miskolc) and co-founded the first independent Romani organization in Hungary (Phralipe). In 1990, at the age of twenty-six, he was elected as an MP for the Alliance of Free Democrats (SzDSz) and gained a seat in the first Hungarian postcommunist parliament. For a brief period he was also the president of an organization called Roma Parliament, which was the most ambitious attempt of the first half of the 1990s to unify all Romani organizations in Hungary. In the latter half of the decade, he established the Roma Civil Rights Foundation (*Roma Polgárjogi Alapítvány*), an organization that since then has sought to raise public awareness about anti-Romani discrimination and has actively supported victims of injustice.

I first met Horváth during a small music festival in one of the less inspiring districts of Budapest. The festival was not only an occasion to celebrate Romani culture, but also an opportunity for Romani activists to come together and talk politics. I asked Horváth how important he thought the self-government system was for the Romani movement. In 1993 the Hungarian parliament had created a new legal context for the cultural autonomy and political participation of national minorities (Act LXXVII on the Rights of National and Ethnic Minorities). Elections had been organized for minority "self-governments" on the municipal and national level, including "Gypsy self-governments." These self-governments had been tasked to represent minority constituencies in the field of culture and education and to act as consultative organs for the regular policy-making bodies. In the beginning of the 1990s, Horváth had spoken up in favor of minority autonomy; he had been part of the Minority Roundtable, a meeting between government representatives and minority activists negotiating a proposal for the new law. But he had also been among the very few MPs who, in 1993, voted against the law. Horváth had argued that in the final version of the Minorities Act the powers of the self-governments had been too reduced. The law, he had contended at the time, was at best a compromise between the dominant political parties; the voice of the minorities had influenced the outcome only marginally.

In 1999 the self-government system was entering its second term, and I wanted to know whether Horváth, with the passing of time, had changed his opinion and now perhaps would see benefits in the system. Was it not an opportunity for Hungarian Romani activists to find privileged access to policy-making debates? I discussed a number of topics with Horváth during this initial meeting, and I found him to be a soft-spoken man who carefully weighed his opinions. But with regard to the self-government system he sounded very definite. The only opportunity it offered, Horváth said, was for the government to further divide the Romani movement, as the authorities in the past always had done. In the months and years following, I met Horvath several times for more in-depth interviews. There always remained a considerable amount of ambiguity in his assessment of the self-government system. He argued that Roma should indeed have authority over their cultural affairs but, repeatedly, he called the current system an instrument of institutional segregation. In light of all this, it is perhaps surprising that he still found it worthwhile to campaign for the self-government elections. In March 2003, after an earlier election had been cancelled, Horváth led a political association called the Democratic Roma Coalition to a victory. It won forty-nine of the fifty-three seats in the National Gypsy Self-Government, routing its main competitor, Lungo Drom, which had dominated the body during the previous eight years. For a brief period, Horváth himself acted as the president of the National Gypsy Self-Government.[1]

This is an intriguing story in various perspectives, but the reason I have included it here is because it appears to illustrate the contention that political and institutional contexts play a crucial role in shaping mobilization. An existing institutional structure appears to have the power to persuade even principled opponents of specific political institutions to start acting within the confinements of these institutions. Is this also true for the Romani movement on a more general scale? Are movement dynamics among Roma strongly related to the opportunities offered by the political and institutional contexts in which Roma have to act? In order to find out whether this is indeed the case, it will be important to gain first a good insight in the development of these contexts. This will be the central task of this chapter: to examine the development of recent minority policies and their institutional expression over time. Although my main concern lies with contemporary policy developments, the first part of the chapter takes a few steps back in time and examines policy developments during the communist times. The examination of these older policies is mainly undertaken in order to provide a context for understanding the more recent policies which are discussed in the latter part the chapter.

Before starting with this discussion it is worth noting that policies targeted at a group defined as "Roma" or "Gypsies" in Central Europe are older than one might perhaps suppose. Most of the literature on the history of the Roma in Central Europe (Crowe 1995; Horváthová 1964; Nečas 1995) agrees that the first references to local measures aimed at groups called "Gypsies" in these areas appeared in sources from the fourteenth and fifteenth centuries. In that epoch this name was given to groups that were settling around castles in the Slovak portions of Hungary and were believed to be religious exiles (Crowe 1995: 69–70). In historical sources from the centuries following, references to "Gypsies" appear in Hungarian records, where they are referred to as castle musicians, metal workers, or soldiers. Anti-Gypsy sentiments and measures are first recorded in the sixteenth century—especially after the Turks had defeated the Hungarians in Mohács in 1526, and "Gypsies" were seen as a fifth column of the Ottoman Empire. Such conditions remained in place until the end of the seventeenth century, when Leopold I, Austrian emperor from 1657 to 1705, started to expand the Habsburg Empire into the south after the Turks had been pushed back from these regions. Decrees were then issued for a large-scale persecution: people who were identified as "Gypsies" were mutilated or executed. Attempts at driving particular populations out of the Austrian Empire continued until 1761, when Maria Theresia issued a decree aimed at full-scale assimilation: itinerant people were forced to settle; the use of the Romani language was forbidden; and even the name "Gypsies" was replaced by designations such as "new citizens" and "new Hungarians" (Crowe 1995: 69–74).

Various policies followed those of Maria Theresia and Joseph II, leading to the destruction of traditional lifestyles, but often without resulting in material equality or preventing discriminatory practices. This was felt more clearly with the advancement of industrialization at the end of the nineteenth century and on into the twentieth century. Measures aimed at "disciplining" the group were introduced in 1927 in the first Czechoslovak Republic—resulting in increasingly hostile reactions against them (Crowe 1995: 45–46). After the First World War, Hungary had become an ethnically more homogenous state, and a sometimes subtle but usually very powerful "Magyarization" campaign reduced opportunities for people to identify themselves publicly as members of an ethnic minority.

The Second World War strongly affected those known as "Gypsies" in Central Europe (Crowe 1995: 48–54, 90–91). There is still much uncertainty about the exact circumstances of what has become known as the

Romani Holocaust (or *Porajmos*, as it is called by many Roma) or the number of Roma who were murdered during that period. What is certain is that many Roma in German-occupied Central Europe were killed during round-ups or were brought to concentration camps (Barany 2002: 104). It is also clear that the impact of the *Porajmos* was particularly harsh on the Roma in the Protectorate of Bohemia and Moravia. A settlement campaign there in 1939 led to the detention of itinerant groups and eventually resulted in the opening of two "Gypsy camps," one in Lety and one in Hodonin. From there people were brought to the Auschwitz concentration camp or to the "Gypsy camp" in Birkenau. By 1943 groups of settled Roma in Bohemia, Moravia, and Sudetenland were imprisoned, and most of them were brought to Birkenau. This left the postwar Czech lands virtually without any Romani population. In Slovakia—during the war a Nazi-protected independent state under the leadership of Jozef Tiso—the destruction of the Roma had been more limited, and the overwhelming majority of them survived the war. Nevertheless, a large number of Roma in this area had been injured and traumatized by popular pogroms and stringent measures of apartheid. The situation was comparable in Hungary, where there was institutionalized discrimination but no systematic persecution before the 1944 take-over by the Arrow Cross Party (the Hungarian National Socialists) eventually leading to the deportation and murder of several thousand Roma.

It is not the purpose of this chapter to discuss the history of these older, pre-1945 regimes and their devastating impact. But it is important to realize that these were the historical circumstances that had colored the experiences of Romani communities at the beginning of the postwar era. It is not difficult to imagine that these experiences had a strong impact on many people's views of political authority in more recent periods.

Legacies: Communist Policies and Institutions

The attitude of the communist regimes in Central and Eastern Europe toward ethnic groups was characterized by a considerable degree of ambiguity. On the one hand, these regimes condemned all forms of national loyalty and regarded "ethnic nationality" as an epiphenomenon of the capitalist society. On the other hand, they reified nations and national minorities as "naturally" occurring entities, supported their cultural development, and institutionalized boundaries between them.

The way the Soviet Union dealt with these matters undoubtedly offers the clearest illustration. In the Soviet Union, power was centralized, and national entities could not engage in political activity. Nevertheless, the "blossoming of national cultures" was officially glorified, and the Soviet federation was structured in accordance with ethnic boundaries. Some administrative measures explicitly institutionalized national identities. Rogers Brubaker gives the example of the introduction of a new passport system in 1932 (Brubaker 1996: 32). Through this new regulation the USSR made ethnic nationality an official component of personal status. According to Brubaker, this showed that although Soviet policies were sold as anti-nationalist, they were not at all anti-national. They institutionalized territorial nationhood and ethnic nationality as fundamental social categories, and this, according to Brubaker, is at the root of today's post-Soviet nationalisms in the successor states (Brubaker 1996: 17, 23–54).

The ambivalence of communist state practice toward national groups has to be understood against the backdrop of Marxist-Leninist theorizing on nationalism.[2] The Marxist-Leninist argument was that class identity would transcend national consciousness. But it did not suppose that national identities would disappear immediately. It believed rather that this was to happen through a dialectical process in which the uniqueness of a nation had first to be nurtured by the state for a certain period in order to build trust among nations. The promotion of national autonomy was seen as a prerequisite for a higher stage in which such autonomy would no longer be legitimate. The idea was to encourage nations without simultaneously encouraging nationalism (Connor 1984: 583). The outcome of this encouragement had to be a voluntary and natural "rapprochement" of nations, resulting in the emergence of a single identity, that of a "socialist person" (Schöpflin 2000: 149).

The Soviet Union was one of the principal experimenters with ways to turn Marxist-Leninist theory into political practice. Policies toward nationalities designed by the Communist Party of the Soviet Union (KPSS) strongly influenced Moscow's allies in Central Europe. The Soviet Union wanted to maintain control over Central Europe by means of ideological influence. Imposing a particular policy on nationalities also served to reduce potential conflict between nationalities in the region. The Central European responses to Moscow's ideological pressure differed from country to country and over time. The only common element in the policies of the various Central European countries was the official discouragement of all forms of ethnic expression and national attachment, and the formal endorsement of the "internationalism" of socialism. In practice, however, the communist regimes in Central Europe often stimulated national consciousness to underpin the centralization of power, and sometimes they allowed a limited expression of ethnic and cultural diversity for short-term strategic reasons.

Hungarian Policy Strategies between 1949 and 1989: Automation, Assimilation, and Integration

In the period between the Nazi invasion in March 1944 and the official liberation of Budapest by the Soviet Red Army in April 1945, the Arrow

Cross Party launched an assault upon the country's Jewish and Romani populations, resulting in mass deportations to concentration camps.[3] After the war, Soviet rhetoric about combating nationalism, promoting proletarian internationalism, and setting right the Nazi persecution raised expectations about the introduction of comprehensive state protection against ethnic hatred.

Through its article 49, the 1949 Hungarian Constitution granted to all nationalities the "the possibility of education in their native tongue and the possibility of developing their native culture" (Küpper 1998: 83). Following this, a number of nationality associations were established (German, Slovak, Romanian, and Southern Slavic) that resided under the political direction of the Department of Party and Mass Movements, a division within the Central Leadership of the Hungarian Workers' Party (MDP). In practice, however, the establishment of the communist power monopoly in 1949 was accompanied by a less dialectical interpretation of the "nationality question."

Throughout most of the 1950s, the communists under Mátyás Rákosi addressed the nationality question in Hungary through the theory of "automation" (Küpper 1998: 84). This theory departed from the assumption that the antagonism between ethnic groups would disappear automatically with the establishment of socialism and the ongoing development of industrial modernization. Therefore, the promotion of Magyar national identity, and indeed any other ethnic identity in Hungary, was strongly discouraged. According to one author, nationalism was suppressed more in postwar Hungary than anywhere else in communist Central and Eastern Europe (Tőkés 1996: 120). In contrast to the Leninist theoretical prescription for achieving homogeneity through encouraging cultural diversity, the Hungarian authorities not only refrained from this sort of encouragement, but also expressly discouraged the articulation of ethnic interests.

In the case of the Roma, the policy was even taken one step further. According to Stalin in his 1913 tract, *Marxism and the National Question*, a nation was to be defined as a "historically constituted, stable community of people, formed on the basis of a common language, territory, economic life, and psychological make-up manifested in a common culture" (Stalin 1954: 307). Taking as their point of departure the observation that the Roma have neither a written language nor a territory, the Hungarian authorities refused to regard them as a nation or a nationality in the Stalinist sense, and believed that for the sake of achieving socialist unity it was better to omit the whole process of fostering their culture. The Roma were merely regarded as a group that had been oppressed in past capitalist societies, but now "along with other groups would disappear in the cauldron of the People's Republic" (Crowe 1995: 92). As a result there could be no policy initiatives targeted at this group.

Nevertheless, a significant number of Roma were singled out for unequal treatment. Michael Stewart has pointed out that those tacitly identified as Roma were systematically disadvantaged whenever something important was at stake (Stewart 2001). For example, the fact that the Roma had been persecuted by inter-war regimes and that thousands of them had been deported to German labor and death camps during the war was conspicuously disregarded by the communists, notwithstanding their avidity to present themselves as "liberators." No reparations were paid and no memorials were established until the mid-1980s (Stewart 2001: 74–75). At the same time, the communist state was not quite consistent in its attempt to let the Roma "disappear." On the contrary, certain administrative measures institutionalized a categorical division between Roma and others. For example, throughout the socialist period so-called "Gypsy crime" received a separate treatment. Moreover, between 1954 and 1963 Roma were provided with black passports, as opposed to red passports which were distributed among the other citizens (Stewart 2001: 75).

During the time that the communist party, the Hungarian Socialist Workers' Party (MSzMP), was led by János Kádár (1956–88), the attitude of the state toward minorities fluctuated with the state's position on freedom in civil society. After having eradicated all traces of the 1956 revolution, the MSzMP embraced a policy of relaxation in the 1960s, which led to the introduction of modest attempts at democratization and limited economic reform (Crampton 1994: 316–17). From the second half of the 1960s onwards, most Hungarians enjoyed more liberty than the citizens of neighboring countries. Most notably they gained the freedom of traveling abroad and had relatively easy access to foreign literature and *samizdat*. There were symbolic moments of political restriction in the 1970s. Generally, however, there emerged no pattern of increasing suppression of dissident initiatives, as was the case in some other countries. The MSzMP continued to portray state policy as an ideological struggle toward socialism, but in practice policy decisions were gradually more removed from ideology and increasingly a pragmatic way to maintain power. Juan J. Linz and Alfred Stepan categorize post-1956 Hungary as a post-totalitarian regime. Although the power was still monopolized by one party, the regime tolerated the attempts of dissident groups to create a very limited form of pluralism. Hungary between 1982 and 1988 has even been characterized as a "mature" post-totalitarian regime because of the strength of the emerging democratic opposition (Linz and Stepan 1996: 42–43).

The way in which the Hungarian state dealt with ethnic minorities mirrors this development quite accurately. In principle, the formation of private interest associations was forbidden, and the organization of a public discussion of issues pertaining to the political and socioeconomic situation of minority groups was highly restricted. This tight restriction was, however, gradually abandoned as a result of the growing public concern for the Magyar minorities abroad. During the Rákosi years, any discussion referring to the Magyar populations in the Carpathian basin had been taboo. It has been plausibly argued that one of the reasons for this was the Soviet interest in maintaining a territorial status quo in the region (Kende 1988: 276). After the events of 1956, however, the new stance toward national identity in Hungary—stimulated by anti-Russian sentiments—and toward the Magyar minorities outside Hungary brought with it the first shift in the state's attitude toward the Roma within Hungary. Indicative of this (limited) modification was the establishment of the Hungarian Gypsy Cultural Association (MCKSz) in the autumn of 1957. The idea to establish this organization had initially been put forth by a Romani woman called Máriá László who was able to receive backing from the Ministry of Culture (Sághy 1999; Stewart 2001: 76). The association was modeled after the existing cultural associations for the other nationalities, but this did not mean that the Roma were now regarded as a nationality. What had changed was the communist party's belief in the automation approach. A number of years of neglect had shown that automation had not worked, and that the position of the Roma was still problematic, especially in economic terms.

The very fact that it had been possible to set up the Hungarian Gypsy Cultural Association was indicative of the rising awareness among political leaders of a need for proactive policy measures. Not by accident, the ministry of labor began discussing what it called the "Gypsy question" and explicitly linked the Roma's class situation and ethnic status. The ministry stated that the "Gypsies" were "a post-tribal population among whom social classes had come into being but which still had not reached the stage of being able to form an autonomous nation-state" (Stewart 2001: 78). The Hungarian Gypsy Cultural Association was not as fully developed as other nationality associations, but functioned as a kind of service organization aimed, among other things, at offering economic and administrative help to cooperatives where Roma were employed. László's ambitions, however, were clearly higher. Her attempts to promote the use of the Romani language and her protest against the prejudice of the police forces against the Roma made clear that the ultimate aim was indeed nationality status. This ambition soon sealed her fate. In 1958 she was dismissed from her position. Less than two years later the association was abolished, a move that again announced a new policy shift (Stewart 2001).

In 1961 the Political Committee (*Politikai Bizottság* or Politburo) of the MSzMP adopted a decree ("Tasks in Relation to Improving the Circumstances of the Gypsy Population") that officially marked the end of the automation approach and promoted an active assimilationist "Gypsy policy." According to this resolution "the basic principle of policy is that Gypsies, in spite of the fact that they have certain ethnographic features, are not considered a nationality. In order to solve their problems, their special social position must be taken into account" (Central Committee of the Hungarian Socialist Workers' Party 1961). In terms of long-term goals the assimilation approach differed not that much from the automation approach. They were both aimed at the complete disappearance of the group's identity in such a way that it would no longer function as a point of reference for either the members of the group or those outside the group. In the short term, however, assimilation entailed purposeful action on the part of the state to reach this goal. Underlying this policy shift was the undeniable observation that the Roma found themselves in increasingly problematic circumstances. In the decree, a special concern was expressed for the social situation of the Roma, and a clear link was created between the observed social problems and Romani identity (the document mentioned that the Roma were characterized by "grave backwardness" and that a "cultural advancement" was needed). The Politburo recognized the problem of prejudice ("an almost irrational aversion to the Gypsies") and discrimination present in society (quoted in Crowe 1995: 93). But according to the decree, this problem was also fundamentally related to the persistence of Romani identity:

> Many still have incorrect views about the Gypsy question. Many people consider it a nationality question and suggest to develop the "Gypsy language", establish Gypsy language schools, colleges, Gypsy cooperatives etc. These views are not only incorrect, they are also harmful, because they perpetuate the separate position of the Gypsies and slow down their adaptation to society. (Central Committee of the Hungarian Socialist Workers' Party 1961)

Active denial of Romani ethnic identity was meant to change the position of the Roma in society, foster the disappearance of the "Gypsies as a socioeconomic class" and end problems of prejudice and discrimination.

Three policy areas were seen as crucial for realizing this aim: education, housing, and employment in regular labor. For example, through a housing program in 1964, an attempt was made to dismantle substandard housing and move Roma from isolated settlements into 2,500 new homes in cities or villages (Crowe 1995: 94). The campaign had only limited success, and renewed attempts at relocation had to be made in the 1970s. The policy of settlement liquidation did, however, have a strong impact on the material conditions of the Roma. A survey conducted in 1971 by the Sociological Research Institute of the Hungarian Academy of Sciences found that 65.1 percent of the Romani population lived in separate settlements (*cigánytelepek*), while in comparable surveys in 1993 and 1994, carried out by the same institution, this figure had declined to 13.7 percent (Havas et al. 1995: 74).[4] The policy of slum clearance in combination with access to public housing and low-cost building loans enabled Roma to enjoy more comfortable housing (Kovats 2001b: 338). Tens of thousands of Roma moved to urban areas and village centers.

It is debatable, however, whether it altered the problems of prejudice and discrimination. And also in more tangible areas the results were not encouraging. Employment percentages in the 1971 survey showed no significant difference between Romani and non-Romani men of working age. During the decade of the 1980s, however, there was a general fall in employment that disproportionately affected the Roma. Moreover, Roma continued to occupy flats that were generally smaller and of poorer quality than the national average (Kovats 2001b: 338). Concerning education, the authors of the 1971 survey called attention to the fact that in the 1950s and 1960s, the educational level of the non-Romani population had risen rapidly with the social distance between Roma and non-Roma widening (Havas et al. 1995: 69). The most important conclusion of the 1971 survey, however, was that a decade of active assimilation had not been enough to alter the situation in any radical way. As a result the legitimacy of a strong assimilation policy diminished.

Halfway through the 1970s the policy of assimilation was explicitly abandoned, and "integration" now became the new guiding principle. This followed a change in the constitution in 1972—article 61 paragraph 1 now described the right to the use of one's native language and the conservation of one's culture. The changing policy climate also led to the establishment of a new state institution for the Roma. In 1974 a so-called consultative Gypsy Council (*Cigányszövetség*) was created to highlight a modest recognition of the phenomenon of "Gypsy culture," by which was meant all kinds of art regarded as typical of the Roma. A famous Romani fiction writer, Menyhért Lakatos, became the head of this Gypsy Council. The experience was short-lived. By the end of the 1970s there was nothing to indicate that it still existed. Moreover, the direction that policy development concerning Roma had taken was not changed. As a temporary measure the Roma were in 1979 officially regarded as an "ethnic group" (Resolution 1019/1979). This had no legal consequences, but prepared the way for limited forms of independent organization in the 1980s.

The ambiguity with regard to the status of the Roma was in this period not only visible in the policy shifts, it was also reflected in the texts and speeches of those who wanted to make themselves known as Romani leaders. One striking example of ambiguity can be found in an interview with Menyhért Lakatos conducted in October 1981 by two Dutch journalists (Dedinszky 1997: 215–38). At various points during the interview Lakatos argued that the lifestyle of the Roma was primitive and uncivilized and needed therefore to be brought into conformity with the mainstream of society. In his opinion, the authorities bore the main responsibility. "Cries for 'tolerance,' talk about 'respect for the divergent culture of others' or 'respect for fundamental human rights' are often nothing else than other words for laziness," he argued (Dedinszky 1997: 218). What was needed, he believed, was not tolerance and direct financial support, but the active "instruction" of the Roma by non-Roma, attempts to raise them to a higher level of civilization (Dedinszky 1997: 221). Interestingly enough, at other moments in the interview Lakatos argued strongly *against* assimilation attempts and argued in favor of maintaining—at least temporarily—the segregation between Roma and non-Roma:

> In my opinion it is impossible and undesirable to take Gypsies away from their groups and, from one day to the next, put them alongside people with a totally different lifestyle; they have been together in close-knit communities for such a long time. Attempts to assimilate people are always counterproductive ... The right of a group to live in an isolated settlement, if that group wishes to do so, is a "human right." This has nothing to do with ghettos, discrimination or isolation. To the contrary! We have to realize that the enormous, age-old divide between Gypsy culture and lifestyle on the one hand and a much more modern society on the other cannot be bridged overnight. (Dedinszky 1997: 224)

And he even concluded at some point in the interview that any action by non-Roma to remedy the problems facing the Roma by assimilating them would in fact be pointless: "In order to really be able to help the Gypsies as a leader of a movement or as an organizer and mediator, you need to be of Gypsy origin yourself" (Dedinszky 1997: 219). By displaying this ambiguity, Lakatos presented himself as the perfect spokesman for the policy of integration as it was being promoted by the government at that time. In practice integration was a policy aimed at actively abolishing what were considered negative elements of culture and lifestyle, and encouraging at the same time a feeling of ethnic identity by financially supporting elements of culture that were regarded as more positive, such as language, music, and literature. In 1984 the Political Committee of the MSzMP stated the following:

> In order to put Gypsy ethnic traditions at the service of the integration of those Gypsies who are ready to adapt to society, it is necessary to support the development and promotion of Gypsy culture and establish appropriate institutions and facilities for its dissemination. (Department of Science, Education, and Culture of the Central Committee of the Hungarian Socialist Workers' Party 1984)

Although the 1979 decree remained the crucial point of reference during the first half of the 1980s, the active policy of integration was soon more or less suspended for two important reasons. First, an economic crisis and an ensuing austerity policy greatly restricted the possibilities for spending money on integration programs as they had been designed up to that point. Second, in an atmosphere of distancing itself further from Soviet views, the MSzMP turned away from ideological rigidity and pursued a policy of "new consensus" (Kovats 1998a: 116). In a 1984 document, the *Hazafias Népfront* (the Patriotic People's Front)—the communist organization that coordinated all non-party organizations in Hungary—explicitly referred to this policy of "new consensus" as a novel way of dealing with the Roma within the given economic circumstances. This "consensus" meant that a dialogue was to be fostered between the state and a selected group of "Romani intellectuals," in order to let them gain responsibility in solving the problems of the Roma and stimulating Romani cultural identity. Direct attempts at assimilation or the active stimulation of Romani culture disappeared into the background, and focus was now placed on the institutionalization of a Romani elite.

From that moment on, policy went in the direction of tolerating cultural and economic differences in society, while at the same time establishing and controlling the spokespersons of the Romani minority. Two new institutions were set up: in 1985 the National Gypsy Council (*Országos Cigánytanács*) and in June 1986 the Hungarian Gypsy Cultural Association (*Magyar Cigányok Kulturális Szövetség*, MCKSz).[5] The National Gypsy Council was founded as an advisory body to the *Hazafias Népfront*. Instead of having state bodies working directly on the integration of the Roma, preference was now given to deliberating policy with Romani "representatives." This also led to the establishment of a number of Gypsy Councils at the county level. In theory, Roma who wanted a policy change had now a legal channel through which they could pressure for this. In practice, however, there were very few, if any, new policy initiatives. But this development did make one thing clear: more than ever before the Roma were de facto treated as a nationality.

Policy Strategies in Czechoslovakia between 1948 and 1989: Equality, Assimilation, and Ambiguity

In the Czechoslovak Republic after the Second World War, little importance was attached to the cultural and political rights of national minorities, and certainly not to the position and status of the Roma. In 1945 President Edvard Beneš, the state's wartime leader in exile, had defined the Czechoslovak state as one of Czechs and Slovaks—a basic view that in essence remained unchanged during the whole communist period from 1948 to 1989. The position and rights of those who felt ethnically distinct from both Czechs and Slovaks had been important issues of political debate in the inter-war period, but after the war public discussion about these issues was suppressed.

This was to some extent related to the fact that the leverage of ethnic group activists had been greatly reduced as a consequence of the diminished demographic weight of minorities. Between 1945 and 1948 great numbers of Sudeten Germans from Northern Bohemia and the Magyar population in Southern Slovakia had fled or had been expelled.[6] Moreover, through border revisions Sub-Carpathian Ruthenia was transferred to Ukraine, while most of the Jews and almost all of the Roma who had lived in the Czech lands had been deported and murdered during the war. Although the postwar Czechoslovak Republic still contained ethnic minorities, it was a much more ethnically homogenous country than it had been prior to the war. This homogeneity was used as a pretext by politicians to promote the idea that Czechoslovak nationhood would only include Czech and Slovak identities and would considerably restrict the cultural rights of national minorities.

The position of the Czechoslovak leaders toward ethnic minorities was soon supported by an ideological argument. With the coming to power of the Czechoslovak Communist Party (KSČ) in 1948, a Stalinist-inspired approach to national groupings gained ground, and this gave minority activists little opportunity to express dissatisfaction with their status. The constitutions of 1948 and 1960 described Czechoslovakia as a unitary state encompassing two nations, with the emphasis firmly placed on the principle of unity. The campaign against "bourgeois nationalism" waged by the communist party primarily affected those politicians who demanded a special position for Slovakia (Rychlík 1995: 193). Slovak nationalism was strongly discouraged, while Slovakia received economic support that was supposed to lead to a reduction of material inequality and the disappearance of Slovak demands for autonomy. But Slovak discontent with the grave economic inequities between the Czechs and Slovaks persisted and prompted the communist leaders to promise Slovakia a limited form of autonomy. This autonomy was realized only in 1969, with the creation of a federal Czechoslovakia. And even then Slovak aspirations for parity did not vanish. Although the federalization was one of the few elements of reform that remained in place after the invasion of Czechoslovakia by Warsaw Pact troops and was symbolically important, its meaning was reduced because of the reduction of the powers of the republic governments that soon followed (Wolchik 1994: 163).

For the national minorities—in the first place for the Magyars in southern Slovakia—communist rule did not change much. To be sure, Soviet pressure to preserve state integrity in Czechoslovakia prevented further expulsions after 1948, but national minority activists were not given the opportunity to articulate demands on the basis of ethnicity. As in Hungary, the Roma in Czechoslovakia were not recognized as a nationality after the communist take-over, and no policies were designed to defend their position as a minority. The communist party was nonetheless concerned about the economic and social position of those who were called Gypsies. Their concern was stimulated by the ongoing migration. A considerable number of people, not exclusively Roma who had an itinerant lifestyle, went from Slovakia to the Czech lands in response to labor opportunities in the areas from where the Sudeten Germans had been expelled. In 1949 the government of Klement Gottwald created an inter-ministerial commission to examine how the Roma might be settled and integrated into the workers' class. In practice, however, the agencies responsible for this job had little success, a fact that was blamed on the phenomenon of migration and the nomadic lifestyle of the Roma. According to a 1959 handbook on this topic, migration was a problem because it could lead to concentrations of Roma and a perpetuation of "the backward Gypsy way of life" (quoted in Guy 1998: 26).

In 1958 the official concern about the segregation of the Roma and their lack of involvement in the labor process led to a firm policy campaign aimed at assimilation. In the understanding of the party, assimilation entailed control over migration and the denial of ethnic identity. The usual designation "Gypsy" was banned and replaced by the formulation "citizens of Gypsy origin" (*občany cikánského původu*). This was an attempt at specifying to whom policy was directed without, however, describing them as a "real" ethnic group. Control of migration was made concrete through legislation prohibiting nomadic life. Law 74/1958, "on the permanent settlement of nomads," was aimed not only at settling ambulant Vlach Roma, but also at controlling the employment of those Roma who had migrated from Slovakia to the Czech lands. The law appears to have been relatively effective in eliminating the transient lifestyle of Vlach Roma, but it did not succeed in dispersing the Roma to registered work places. According to Will Guy, the local authorities represented an important obstacle. They were usually unwilling to register Roma or provide them with jobs and accommodation (Guy 1998: 28).

The then current views on Romani policy received support from the academic world. In 1961 Jaroslav Sus published his *The Gypsy Question in ČSSR* (Sus 1961), a work in which he reduced the identity of the Roma to that of a socially underdeveloped class and argued in favor of measures to disperse the Romani population. Having observed that uncontrolled migration of otherwise settled Roma from Slovakia to the Czech lands was still taking place and led to concentrations of Roma in the Czech lands, the government issued a plan in 1965 which was meant to go further than the 1958 measures. Government decree 502/1965 introduced a far-reaching program for the transfer and dispersal (*přesun a rozptyl*) of Roma from settlements in the Slovak countryside to mostly industrial locations in the Czech lands. The idea was that migration would be allowed only if regulated by very strict quotas.

The plans failed for various reasons. Local authorities in the Czech lands were still not open to newcomers. Many Roma moved outside the control of the plan, in spontaneous response to economic opportunities. The Czech Ministry of Labor admitted that during the period from 1966 to 1968 there were "three times as many *recorded* unplanned moves by Gypsies [from Slovakia] into and within the Czech lands as there were [officially] planned moves" (quoted in Guy 2002: 59; emphasis in original).[7] The National Council for the Questions of the Gypsy Population, the state body in charge of executing these measures, was abolished in 1968 (Crowe 1995: 57; Guy 2001c: 291).

At the end of the 1960s a new democratic movement fostered ideas about the federalization of Czechoslovakia and led to the adoption of a new constitution in the spring of 1968. After the Soviet military incursion, the constitution was first aborted, but later, in January 1969, a federal structure was introduced anyway (Connor 1984: 232). This affected the Party's attitude toward nationalities. Sharon Wolchik notes that, through the federalization, Czechoslovakia became one of only three European communist states (joining the Soviet Union and Yugoslavia) to recognize ethnic divisions by formally incorporating them into the state structure (Wolchik 1991: 62). At the same time no form of autonomy was granted to ethnic groups other than Czechs or Slovaks.

It is in this context that the Czechoslovak authorities, quite surprisingly, allowed the establishment of a Romani cultural-social association with local branches; by so doing they accepted the Roma de facto (though not de jure) as a nationality. The organization was called the Association of Gypsies-Roma (*Sväz Cigánov-Rómov/Svaz Cikánů-Romů*). It was first formed in Slovakia, in 1968, and a year later complemented by the establishment of a Czech branch and regional offices. The Association of Gypsies-Roma was subsumed under the National Front (*Narodny front/Národní fronta*), the communist umbrella organization for civil associations, which supported and controlled its activities. The official purpose of the association was the fostering of both the cultural and economic activities of the Roma. This shows that, although the ultimate policy goal (the assimilation of the Roma into a socialist Czechoslovak identity) had not changed, the vision concerning short-term means had been radically altered. The communists now allowed the Roma to strive for socioeconomic equality by regarding Romani identity as a legitimate way of self-help. This might appear to be a return to the Marxist-Leninist belief in the effectiveness of a dialectical strategy. However, as the Roma were not de jure recognized as a nationality, it is possible that such a change in strategy had less to do with ideological reflections than with pragmatic decisions. This new experiment could have been prompted by the fact that political leaders realized that the programs of the past two decades had failed to come even near to the stated goals.

The abolishing of the Association of Gypsies-Roma followed shortly after the introduction of a new way of approaching the Roma, an approach that was labeled "acculturation" (Guy 2001c: 292). Scholars writing on the Association of Gypsies-Roma remain puzzled by the sudden closing-down of the organization and have come up with different interpretations, but they agree that it represents an unambiguous return to a policy that refrained from dealing with the Roma as an ethnic or a national minority. A 1975 publication by social scientists under the title *Gypsies in the ČSSR in the Process of Social Integration* publicly supported this shift by stating that, although Gypsies could be considered an "ethnic group," they would never be a "nationality," since in their current stage of development they were already too diffused among the ethnic majority (Mann 2000: 53).

It is important to note that this shift toward negation and assimilation did not mean that all earlier policies toward Roma ceased.[8] The authorities continued relocating people from illegal or dilapidated housing—an activity made necessary in part because of earlier planned and unplanned migration. However, an attempt was made to describe the problems facing Roma without any reference to demands for ethnic recognition. The efforts of the Association of Gypsies-Roma to achieve national minority status were followed by a period in which such ventures were not allowed. Despite the fact that this was protested against by dissident organizations in the 1970s, the Roma did not achieve the status of a national minority in Czechoslovakia before 1991. In the latter half of the 1980s, the World Romani Congress (WRC) made an appeal for Czech and Slovak Roma to be recognized as a national minority, but this was rejected (Guy 1998: 55). In 1987, a small number of people started organizing in a network that was meant to become a new national Romani association. Apparently, the Czechoslovak government became interested in starting up a dialogue with these loyal activists, but a plan that was proposed in 1988 to institutionalize a form of Romani "representation" was never realized.

The Impact of the Communist Past on More Recent Forms of Romani Mobilization

Both in Hungary and Czechoslovakia, the communist period was characterized by a tension between theory and practice. In theory, Romani identity was suppressed—in neither of the two countries did the communists grant the Roma the legal status of a national minority. Official discourse, inspired by elements of Marxist-Leninist argumentation, considered the Roma to be a group distinguishable merely in terms of its problematic social and economic position. Such an approach was also built upon certain traditional depictions of the Roma as a group characterized not by ethnicity but by lifestyle, marginality, and poverty. According to the logic of the communist argument, the state had to concentrate on, and endeavor to improve, the material circumstances of this group, while at the same time banning attempts to let them define their identity in ethnic terms. Therefore, if special institutions to implement these policies needed to be created, they had to be directed only toward groups that were defined in terms of socioeconomic class, not toward groups that were defined in ethnic terms. And they had to be temporary.

In practice, however, matters were more complicated. In both countries the state took initiatives that can be interpreted as steps in the direction of treating the Roma de facto as an ethnically defined group. In Hungary as well as Czechoslovakia, discussions pondering the possibility of granting nationality status to the Roma followed periods in which official policy had manifestly failed to lift ethnic differentiation through diminishing economic inequality. In Hungary, official policy shifted in response to experiences of failed equalization, and in the 1980s it gradually moved toward a controlled treatment of the Roma as a national minority. In Czechoslovakia, such an approach was restricted to a short period after the upsurge of a democratic movement at the end of the 1960s. In both countries, the tendency to recognize the Roma as a national minority coincided with the relative openness of the regime to dialogue with civic actors. This was clearest in Hungary, where authorities engaged in an official dialogue with a handful of party-loyal Romani personalities. They were placed in the position of "Romani leaders" and "Romani representatives." At the very end of the communist period, the idea of constructing and institutionalizing such a putative Romani representation also surfaced in Czechoslovakia, but in this country it was never put into effect.

In what way could this legacy have marked more current attempts at Romani mobilization? On the basis of the comments made by Romani activists during interviews, I argue that the institutional and political context of the communist past has left traces on more recent mobilization efforts in a number of ways. In Hungary, the period of the 1980s was considered by many of my interviewees to be a fulcrum for understanding more contemporary developments within the Romani movement. It was regarded as the period during which a significant part of the current Romani "elite" had made its first public appearance. A number of people who had become Romani political leaders at that time—some of them in communist-led institutions, others in independent networks—remained on the scene during the 1990s. Many of the Hungarian Romani activists whom I interviewed spontaneously referred to the latter half of the 1980s as the formative period of Romani politics. But they were very often also extremely critical of what had happened at the time. Aladár Horváth, whom I mentioned at the beginning of this chapter, wanted to be particularly clear on this. He called the organizations that had been set up in the mid-1980s examples of bogus representation; the members of these organizations, he argued, were appointed only because of their loyalty toward the communists. In his understanding, the Hungarian party-led institutions of the 1980s had brought to the fore a number of Romani leaders whose only quality was their expediency. At the same time, the end of the 1980s saw the first activists who deliberately refrained from aligning themselves with communist-led institutions. According to

Horváth, two groups of activists emerged, and the division between these two groups remained tangible throughout the 1990s.

Similar accounts of the communists as the principal architects of an entrenched divide between two groups of Romani activists were given by other progressive activists, such as Ágnes Daróczi, Béla Osztojkán, Blanka Kozma, and Antónia Hága. Almost ten years after the collapse of communism, Romani activists who originally came from party-led institutions, such as Menyhért Lakatos, Gyula Náday, and József Raduly, were still regarded as opportunistic and loyal to political power. Ágnes Dároczi called these activists "puppets in the hands of the politicians in power." Dároczi and Horváth also categorized Hungary's leading Romani activist and president of the National Gypsy Self-Government between 1995 and 2003, Flórian Farkas, as a product of the loyalist group. Indirectly the divide was also recognized by those activists who were deemed to be loyalists. For example, when I asked Gyula Náday to explain his current position in the Hungarian Romani movement, he started with an account of how he and his fellow activists were brought together by communist-led institutions in the 1980s. In an interview with a journalist, Flórian Farkas admitted that there was a basic tension within the Romani movement. He argued that this "rivalry syndrome was something the Hungarian Roma inherited from the Hungarian political elite." He added furthermore that the Roma would soon grow out of it (Kosztolányi 2001: 70).

In sum, former affiliation with the communists in Hungary became an important element in the construction of a divide between various brands of activists. It specifically figured in the formation of a strong division between those activists who have by some been labeled "opportunistic" and others who have often been seen as "radical." This divide was to some extent consolidated by the fact that a number of important civil servants and politicians who had been active in communist structures in the 1980s came to occupy important positions after 1989 in the field of minority policy. One example is János Báthory, who had been the government's head counselor on Romani affairs during the period of the changes between 1989 and 1990. He is usually considered as someone who had a strong personal influence on the development of policies toward the Roma between 1990 and 1995, the period during which he was deputy president of the government's Office of Ethnic and National Minorities (*Nemzeti és Etnikai Kissebségi Hivatal*) (Kovats 1998a: 118). From 2000 to 2002 he was the director of that same government body. These and other facts seem to indicate a level of continuity in the networks of contact between activists and the people working in the new government institutions. Whether these networks today still give certain activists privileged access to the policy-making process is difficult to ascertain. Báthory himself, for instance, argued in the interview I conducted with him that the only reason Horváth had more difficulties than others in communicating with state institutions and mainstream politicians was his "radicalism." Nonetheless, the suspicion among some activists that old informal ties persisted did create tension between activists. The nature of this divide and the profile of all the people mentioned above will be further discussed in Chapter 3.

In the Czech and Slovak cases there appears to have been little continuity of personnel (both within the Romani movement and in the realm of policy making on issues of concern to Romani activists). The reason seems to lie primarily in the fact that the only organization that had functioned under the label of Romani identity during communist times had already been abolished in 1973—thus too remote in time to be able to provide for any visible continuation in personnel. The result is that former affiliation is not seen today as a principal source of division between those engaging in protest against the authorities and those seeking access to government. References to the Association of Gypsies-Roma were as good as absent from the interviews I held with current activists in the Czech Republic and Slovakia. This does not mean that the Association of Gypsies-Roma has left no imprint at all on the situation of Romani activists in these countries. For some activists, most notably Karel Holomek, it may have been a source of inspiration for his dissident activism in the 1970s and 1980s (see Chapter 3). Holomek was the son of one of the Czech leaders of the Association. Since the beginning of the 1990s, he has been one of the most trusted Romani activists in the Czech Republic. What is, however, clear from my interviews, including those I conducted with Holomek, is that the communist policy to allow some form of Romani action in the period before 1973 is not seen as an important point of reference for explaining the current fault lines and positions within the movement.

The Domestic Political Context of Romani Mobilization: Institutions and Policies

Transition to democracy in the postcommunist part of Europe entailed the formation of a new general constitutional order, and thus it opened up the opportunity to introduce particular systemic responses to ethnic diversity. In the course of the 1990s the Central European states adopted various policies and introduced new institutions to manage minority-majority relations. In the following sections I will examine and map out the particular choices that the Czech Republic, Hungary, and Slovakia made in this field.

In order to produce a cartography of the general trends that have characterized this policy field, it is useful to determine first a number of essential analytic coordinates. To begin, I propose to distinguish between two dimensions of minority policy, a general and a specific one. During the 1990s the Central European states established institutions and introduced policies to deal with ethnic minorities in general, and they have at certain points in time introduced measures and institutions specifically directed at the Roma. I will explore both dimensions.

Then, with regard to policies toward minorities in general, a further basic distinction can be made between what can be called a "minority rights" model and a model of "undifferentiated citizenship." The former model endorses the strategy of granting members of national minorities special, group-differentiated rights with regard to culture, language, traditions, and participation in the social and economic domain. Minority rights can be very diverse, but according to Will Kymlicka—one of the principal advocates of this model within the framework of a liberal theory of rights—they have two important features in common: (a) they go beyond the familiar set of common civil and political rights of individual citizenship which are protected in all liberal democracies; and (b) they are adopted with the intention of recognizing and accommodating the distinctive identities and needs of ethnic groups (Kymlicka 2001a: 17 n1). As Kymlicka (1995, 2000, 2001a, 2001b) in his extensive discussions shows, the underlying logic of such an approach is that group-differentiated citizenship rights are legitimate in a liberal democracy because—in contrast to what classical liberal theorists have argued—the liberal state is never ethno-culturally neutral; through "nation-building" it inevitably promotes certain conceptions of a "societal culture" (certain languages, certain administrative boundaries between populations, certain forms of education, etc.). The unavoidability, and perhaps even necessity, of such nation-building processes must not, however, make states insensitive to the possible repercussions for the ethnic minorities living within their territories. To prevent nation-building processes from resulting in fundamental injustices for ethnic minorities, a state needs to construct special policies and rules of exemption for these minorities.

The "undifferentiated citizenship" model, on the other hand, is premised on the idea that there is no principle of justice mandating exemptions to generally applicable laws. The underlying logic here is that the problems that face ethnic minorities need to be disassociated from culture, since they are dependent on socioeconomic and class factors. It argues that the problems facing ethnic minorities do not necessarily derive from distinct cultural characteristics, but generate from poor educational, employment, social, or environmental records (see Barry 2001; Favell 1998). In the field of culture, this model stands for the idea that "the neutral attitude of the state will permit different cultures to coexist in a purifier society" (Entzinger 2000: 109). On this basis public intervention may take place to protect basic individual human and civil rights (for example, through anti-discrimination campaigns), but not to introduce special rights for minorities in the field of language, representation, self-government, or certain types of accommodation rights. In the economic field, it is assumed that the state should provide equality of opportunity: ethnic origin should be no obstacle to equal access to economic opportunities. This model embraces strategies that focus on creating equality of socioeconomic opportunities in society, while retaining conceptions of individual rights that are neutral with regard to features of cultural diversity. In this understanding, citizenship is a "forum where people transcend their differences, and think about the common good of all citizens" (Kymlicka 1995: 175).

The above distinction will allow us to contrast (a) policy approaches that emphasize the socioeconomic position of individual ethnic minority citizens and attempt to remedy socioeconomic inequality through broad-based egalitarian policies with (b) policy approaches that emphasize cultural differences between ethnic groups and attempt to ameliorate the position of ethnic minorities through the politics of cultural difference. Of course, the models as I describe them here represent ideal types; in reality, policy approaches will often find themselves on the continuum between the "minority rights" model and the model of "undifferentiated citizenship."

A final heuristic device in order to structure my examination of policy types is a division in subperiods according to a number of critical junctures. For each country I have divided the total period between 1989 and 2004 into the following subperiods, with each subperiod presenting a different "case." As will become clear in the description of these cases, beginnings and endings of the periods coincide with striking changes in a state's strategy of dealing with the Roma:

1. Hungary 1989–1995
2. Hungary 1995–2004
3. Czechoslovakia 1989–1992
4. Czech Republic 1993–1997
5. Czech Republic 1997–2004
6. Slovakia 1993–1998
7. Slovakia 1998–2004

1. Hungary between 1989 and 1995: The Minorities Act and the Emergence of a Policy of Differentiation

In the period between the collapse of communism in 1989 and the first elections of what became known as the "minority self-governments" in 1994 and 1995, the official attitude toward minorities in Hungary underwent a fundamental change. In the space of approximately five years, the country saw the emergence of a complex system of minority rights protection. Central to this undertaking was the adoption in July 1993 of Act LXXVII on the Rights of National and Ethnic Minorities (also known as the Minorities Act). This law, which was enacted by the Hungarian parliament by an overwhelming majority of 96 percent, recognized thirteen "historical" minorities: Armenians, Bulgarians, Croatians, Germans, Greeks, Poles, Romanians, Ruthenes, Serbs, Slovaks, Slovenes, Ukrainians, and Roma.[9] It guaranteed these minorities, among other things, the right to use minority languages, the right to organize their own educational activity, the right to achieve cultural autonomy through self-governmental bodies, the right to political representation, and the right to maintain contact with both institutions in their home state and minorities living in other countries. In essence, the introduction of the system signaled a complete rejection of policies of assimilation and a gradual endorsement of a policy of differentiation (the legal recognition and political institutionalization of ethnic difference). The idea was not simply to eschew the Marxist-Leninist-inspired position on ethnic difference, but to reverse it entirely. Minority languages were no longer meant to be suppressed, but preserved, and indeed actively revived. In the following paragraphs I will first discuss the general features of the main legal and institutional components of the minority protection system; then, I will turn to the historical and political context in which that system was developed; following this, I will briefly examine the position of the Roma in the new legal and institutional context.

What are the most important features of the minority self-government system as it took shape in the beginning of the 1990s? Particularly striking is the electoral basis of the system. Minority self-governments were clearly meant to be more than merely collections of minority activists; they were envisaged as the democratically elected representation of all minority citizens in Hungary. This is clear, for example, from the rules that were specified with regard to the election of these self-governments. The law stipulated that for a municipality with less than 10,000 inhabitants, a minority self-government could be established where a minority ballot list received at least fifty valid votes; in a municipality with more than 10,000 inhabitants, at least one hundred such votes needed to be cast. This was called the "direct" election of minority self-governments. The Minorities Act further stipulated that in cases where at least 30 percent of the elected representatives for a local council election were candidates of one and the same minority, these representatives would be regarded as an indirectly elected minority self-government. It also stated that if more than half the members of the local government were elected as candidates of one minority, the entire local government could declare itself a minority self-government. Finally, the act determined that within sixty days of the election of the local minority self-governments, the elected representatives in turn needed to elect a national minority self-government, consisting of between thirteen and fifty-three members.

The law assigned the minority self-governments rather restricted competencies; they did not gain the powers of regular authorities, but were, instead, appointed extensive consultation and consent rights. Local minority self-governments were endowed with the right of consent in issues having to do with local public education (e.g. the appointment of the head of a local school), local media, preservation of heritage, culture, and collective language use. The national minority self-governments acquired the right to decide independently on the establishment and maintenance of minority institutions that promote minority cultures (theaters, publishing houses, libraries etc.), and could express their opinion on bills of legislation affecting minorities (including county ordinances and those passed by the general council of the city of Budapest). Moreover, national self-governments obtained the right of consent in matters of legislation on the historical heritage of minorities and the establishment of the core material for minority education.

One of the main purposes of the minority self-government system was clearly the legitimatization of minority representation. The elected minority self-governments were placed within the public administration, and therefore became the official minority interlocutors for policy makers on the local and the national level. The system also became the framework within which minority representatives accepted responsibility for their own communities. A 1997 government report formulated the matter in this way: "In the medium and long-term, it is our goal that the Minority Self-Governments be the owners of the minority educational, cultural and other institutions" (Government of the Republic of Hungary 1997: 15). There was also a strong belief, held for example by the people who negotiated the system, that minority self-governments would have an "emancipating" effect, since they could bring people into public office who would never have been elected in the regular electoral system. According to Csaba Tabajdi (MSzP), State Secretary for Minority Affairs under the government led by Gyula Horn (1994–98), it is a form of political education: "a lot of people have appeared on the political scene thanks to this system ... And it also represents a constant opportunity to find new faces" (personal interview).

Where lie the roots of the 1993 Minorities Act? One would perhaps be inclined to assume that the introduction of cultural autonomy followed demands made by minority organizations at the end of the 1980s. Yet it is doubtful whether such demands were really made. Minority activists at that time did urge for a policy of recognition, but virtually none of them appear to have made claims to self-government rights. This leaves the impression that the motivations for introducing a far-reaching form of cultural differentiation were not merely related to the concerns of the minority organizations. To gain a better view on how internal and external factors interacted in the formation of the Minorities Act and the general minority policy in the period prior to 1995, it is worth having a closer look at some details of the political and historical context (Vermeersch 2004: 8–12).

In the latter half of the 1980s, at a time when the Hungarian state was beginning to undergo a process of economic and political transformation, a number of legal changes were introduced that enabled a fundamental shift toward minority rights. The first crucial action was the introduction of legislation in December 1988 and January 1989 establishing rights of association and assembly. Furthermore, through an amendment of the constitution in October 1989, minorities gained the right to their own culture, religion, and the use of their mother tongue. In 1990, Article 68 was added to the constitution. This article stated that ethnic and national minorities living in Hungary were "a constituent part of the State" (paragraph 1). The article also stipulated that the political representation of national and ethnic minorities was to be ensured (paragraph 3), and that these minorities had the "right to form local and national bodies for self-government" (paragraph 4). Moreover, Article 70/A recognized the illegal character of discrimination and the need to provide equal opportunities to all Hungarian citizens. The new constitution also contained a provision enabling the introduction of a Parliamentary Commissioner for Ethnic and National Minority Rights (article 32/B, paragraph 2), whose task it would be to assist minority citizens whose rights are abused.

That these legal changes foreshadowed nothing less than a general shift toward cultural autonomy became apparent in the political discussions in the Nationalities Board (*Nemzetiségi Kollégium*), a communist-led government office that was established in 1989 and was the predecessor of the postcommunist Office for Ethnic and National Minorities. Here it became clear that the choice for minority rights was strongly linked to matters of international politics and security. Within the discussions of the Nationalities Board the question of minority accommodation in Hungary was explicitly linked to a specific foreign policy concern. Hungary wanted to secure regional stability and peace, and at the same time create an opportunity to enhance the protection of the Magyar minorities in neighboring countries. A strong endorsement of minority rights served as a moral justification for its stance toward the Magyar minorities in neighboring Romania, Slovakia, Ukraine, and Yugoslavia, whose fate it wanted to influence positively (Schöpflin 2000: 375). It is therefore not surprising that in the final version of the Minorities Act an allusion to this motivation was included: "The peaceful co-existence of national and ethnic minorities with the nation in majority is a component of *international security*" (Minorities Act, preamble, emphasis added). In the bilateral treaties on "good neighborliness and friendly cooperation" that Hungary signed with Slovakia and Romania in the mid-1990s, Hungary managed to introduce a unambiguous reference to the view that minority protection does not constitute an exclusively domestic affair of individual states but is subject to the legitimate concern of the international community.

The Nationalities Board held meetings and sessions from June 1989 to March 1990 during which time it outlined the central characteristics of the minority protection system as it would take shape in the following years (Krizsán 2000: 250). The idea that gained ground was to work out a system that would aim at a maximal protection of cultural interests of minorities without linking this to territorial autonomy. This was a logical choice for internal reasons: policy makers at the end of the 1980s perceived Hungary as an ethnically homogenous country containing only small, territorially dispersed minority groups that were strongly assimilated by the previous regime.

After the changes of 1989 the establishment of a number of new institutions embodied the real shift toward a minority rights model. The first new institution for minority affairs to appear after the introduction of the multi-party system was the Office for Ethnic and National Minorities (*Nemzeti és Etnikai Kisebbségi Hivatal*). This was a governmental office responsible for coordinating and developing policy toward minorities and entrusted with mediating between minority interests and the executive power (established in June 1990; Government Decree 34/1990). One of its main tasks was the preparation of a law on minorities that would effectively regulate the requirements set out in the constitution, i.e., minority political representation and the formation of local and national bodies for self-government. To legitimize the preparation of the legislation, the Office for Ethnic and National Minorities started a dialogue with the Minorities Roundtable, a consensus-based, independent body that brought together representatives from all minorities in Hungary. Of crucial importance here is that the Minorities Roundtable brought together old and new political elites. Thus, in the case of the Roma, both members of the communist-led National Gypsy Council (*Országos Cigánytanács*) and representatives from newly established independent Romani organizations—in particular people from an umbrella organization called the Roma Parliament—sat around the table. The Minority Roundtable model had been inspired by the National Roundtable, the body that between June and September 1989 had negotiated the introduction of political pluralism (Tőkés 1996: 305–60). The main purpose was to break new ground in legislative work on minorities by letting the minorities themselves influence the drafting of the Minorities Act.

Besides the Office for Ethnic and National Minorities, another important state institution was introduced, the Parliamentary Commissioner for National and Ethnic Minority Rights (often called the Minority Ombudsman). After the adoption of the Minorities Act in 1993, the Office for Ethnic and National Minorities remained responsible for assessing and documenting its implementation, communicating with the actors involved, and preparing possible modifications. The tasks of the new Minority Ombudsman overlapped to some extent with this agenda, but in contrast to the Office for Ethnic and National Minorities, he or she was given the freedom to interpret minority legislation by taking into account principles of political morality. It was also decided that the Minority Ombudsman would be elected by the parliament and become exclusively accountable to this body. According to its mandate as regulated by Act LIX of 1993, the office of the Ombudsman was designed to take into account complaints by minority citizens vis-à-vis the public administration or any public body. In other words, the Ombudsman became responsible for the supervision of the implementation of minority legislation and could report on this to parliament and the government. But there was more: Andrea Krizsán has pointed out that because the Minority Ombudsman was allowed to investigate *abuses* of minority rights (Act LIX of 1993, section 1), and not only *violations*, he or she became now also authorized to evaluate decisions of the public administration that, although in accordance with the law, appeared to have an unjust effect on minority citizens (Krizsán 2000: 255). The Minority Ombudsman became one of the crucial institutions for minority protection, because he or she could shape the context of the system. The first Minority Ombudsman, Jenő Kaltenbach, was elected in 1995 for a once-renewable six-year term, and re-elected in 2001.

How have Hungarian policy makers viewed the position of the Roma within this institutional and legal context? In general, Hungarian policy makers in the period between 1989 and 1995 saw the system of cultural autonomy as the core element in the amelioration of the Roma's predicament. It is striking that during this period no initiatives were taken to develop a policy for dealing specifically with the Roma. Most political debates on minorities during the first half of the decade in Hungary were exclusively focused on the law and its institutional setting. Roma were increasingly seen as a subject within this general debate, a minority among the other minorities. A number of examples illustrate this.

Although they were not yet officially recognized, Romani activists were present next to other minority representatives at the discussions in the Nationalities Board in 1989 and 1990. Two influential independent Romani organizations—the Democratic Alliance of Hungarian Gypsies (MCDSz) and Phralipe—were allowed to participate. The fact that they were independent actors is important, but should, at the same time, be put into perspective. In reality the Democratic Association of Hungarian Gypsies was closely tied to the communist leadership and to the communist party's chief advisor on Romani issues, János Báthory. For its part, the Romani organization Phralipe had been founded with the support of members of the Democratic Opposition, with pro-reform intellectuals from the Alliance of Free Democrats (SzDSz) playing a primary role.[10] During the founding session of the Nationalities Board, the Democratic Association of Hungarian Gypsies strongly urged the government to grant the "Gypsies" the status of nationality (Győri Szabó 1998: 201).[11] On October 24, 1989, a large part of the session of the Nationalities Board was devoted to questions related to the Romani minority. The results, however, were minimal because most of the session time was taken up by a heated debate between Phralipe and the Democratic Association of Hungarian Gypsies about which of the two could claim to be the legitimate representative organ of the Roma. The details of this discussion are not essential here. What is important is that questions relating to the situation of the Romani minority in Hungary were discussed within the framework of the policy-making efforts that were meant to be targeted toward *all* minorities in Hungary.

From 1990 onwards the tendency to bring the Roma within a more general scope on minority treatment endured, although some difficulties surfaced. In the course of the preparation of the Minorities Act, two interesting controversies arose, both relating to the status of the Roma in relation to other minorities. The first controversy was whether there was a difference between "ethnic" and "national" minorities. In a draft dating from February 1992, a distinction was made between "national" (*nemzeti*) and "ethnic" (*etnikai*) minorities, it being stated that the Roma would be considered an "ethnic minority," and not a "national minority." According to the conceptualization in the draft, this would have entailed that some rights were not to be conferred on the Roma: in particular, the right to learn and use native languages in every area of public life (Helsinki Watch 1993: 16). I interviewed some of the former members of the Roma Parliament on the issue, and they argued that pressure was exerted by Aladár Horváth—who had participated in the Roundtable and was at that time already an MP for the SzDSz—to abolish the difference between ethnic and national minorities in the draft. The distinction was effectively deleted in June 1992.

The second controversy related to the question of how to secure minority representation in parliament. Minority representatives believed that the self-government system did not meet the requirements for a secured representation of the recognized minorities in parliament, as was set forth in the constitution. A demand arose for a law that would secure this representation. But the debate on the subject raised all kinds of practical difficulties. It was far from easy to determine the degree of disproportionate representation a minority should receive, there being one large minority (the Roma) and a series of smaller ones.[12] In addition, political leaders feared that introducing secured seats in a unicameral legislature would affect the well-functioning of the parliament (PER 2001a). During the preparation of the Minorities Act, it was decided to regulate the question of secured representation through separate legislation (article 20, paragraph 1 of the Minorities Act). The topic remained subject to protracted discussion throughout the 1990s (Győri Szabó 1998; Krizsán 2000: 258). Various proposals were issued over the years, but no agreement on this subject was reached.

In sum, between 1989 and 1995, minority identity, including that of the Roma, became a legitimate political identity, supported by an array of new institutions. Underpinning the development of the Minorities Act was the conviction that the right to free association would not be enough to ensure the full development of minority culture. As stated by the head of the Office for Ethnic and National Minorities in 1999, the objective of the system was to make local minority self-government fully responsible for minority educational and cultural institutions (Doncsev 1999). During the whole period, Hungarian policy makers were primarily concerned with the legal position of the Roma; they paid less attention to socioeconomic matters. After the Hungarian legislature in 1993 considered the Roma legally to be on an equal footing with the other twelve minorities recognized, no additional programs were developed to target the Roma specifically. This period was also characterized by a determination to provide for a legitimate representation of minorities through democratic elections. However, one sees that despite attempts at making Romani representation more democratic, the government continued to have dialogues with the same limited number of activists. The people who had attempted to represent the Roma in the late 1980s still functioned as the main negotiating partners for the government in the first half of the 1990s.

2. Hungary between 1995 and 2004

The first local and national minority self-governments were elected in 1994 and 1995. The second term began in 1998 and 1999. In the whole period prior to the implementation of the Minorities Act, Hungary found considerable support from the international community for its plans to protect its minorities through a new comprehensive legislation on cultural autonomy. In November 1992, for example, the Council of Europe's Parliamentary Assembly issued a favorable report on the draft bill (Liégeois 1996: 25). But after the system was put into effect it did not take long before the legislation also aroused serious criticism. A number of problems became apparent especially with regard to the "Gypsy self-governments." The main controversies related to the question of legitimate representation, the financial basis of the system, and the inability of the system to tackle the "real problems" of the Roma. In the following paragraphs I will first discuss these criticisms and then canvass the additional policy measures that were taken by subsequent Hungarian governments in response to new Romani demands.

The question of legitimacy was a prominent topic in many of the interviews I conducted in Hungary. In the local elections of December 1994 almost 900,000 people voted for Romani self-governments all over the country, while the number of Romani electors in even the most optimistic estimates was not higher than 200,000 (Kovats 1998a: 129). The fact that so many "additional voters" had participated in the election was officially explained by reference to "sympathy voters" (Doncsev 1999: 3). Many of the Romani activists and independent observers I interviewed felt that this explanation was implausible, or at least insufficient. In their view, the high voter turnout illustrated a major weakness of the system, namely, the lack of voter registration. According to the law, every voter in the "regular" local elections could decide to vote for a candidate on the list of the minority self-government, independently of whether that voter identified herself or himself as a member of a minority. The openness of the system made it vulnerable to manipulation, and led some Romani organizations to question the legitimacy of some of the elected candidates. Were they really elected by "the Roma"? When I inquired about this controversy, one activist said:

> The electoral system is ... absolutely ill-devised. Everyone can vote for the minority self-government. It is as if the prime minister [of Hungary] would be elected in Germany. How should a non-Roma who is not involved in the Romani communities be able to decide who is a good representative and who not?

Some even went as far as to question the value of the existence of the National Gypsy Minority Self-Government. This distrust was exacerbated by the fact that the first election for the National Gypsy Minority Self-Government had been held in Szolnok, stronghold and home base of one of the main Romani organizations contending in the elections, Lungo Drom. The success of the Lungo Drom coalition—it won all fifty-three seats in 1995 and in 1999—raised the suspicions of many Roma that its advancement had been patronized by the Hungarian government (Kovats 2001a: 9). Moreover, doubts about the legitimacy of the elected Romani candidates on the local level were further triggered by the fact that—as the Hungarian press pointed out—some of the elected candidates had no clear link to the local constituencies where they were elected. Some observers even reported problems with people standing as candidates for two minorities (Riba 1999). At the time of the 2002 local minority self-government elections, the results could be compared with recent census data. Such comparison revealed that there were some municipalities where minority elections had been initiated despite the fact that according to the census data nobody there had professed to be a member of a minority community (Kaltenbach 2003).

I talked to several Romani activists about this. Many argued that the only real solution to this problem was the introduction of some kind of ethnic registration of minority voters. Only voters who are registered as a minority member, they contended, should be allowed to cast a vote on a minority self-government list. This solution was always reluctantly contemplated by Hungarian politicians, since it was deemed to contradict one of the basic principles of the minority protection system, the freedom of choice for one's own ethnic identity. Minority Ombudsman Jenő Kaltenbach, however, argued repeatedly that a form of voluntary registration of minority voters would be compatible with the law (personal interview; Kaltenbach 2003). In June 2005, the Hungarian parliament eventually agreed with Kaltenbach and adopted a law which gave the right to vote on a minority self-government list only to those citizens who declared to be a member of a minority community and were registered as minority voters (Law T/9126 on the election of minority self-government representatives). The new law also stipulated a stricter regulation concerning the selection of electoral candidates: they were to be selected now exclusively by minority organizations.

A number of Romani interviewees argued that the problem of non-representative self-governments was mainly caused by the decision to hold the minority elections on the same day as the elections for the "regular" local councils and the fact that every voter, regardless of his or her identity, receives voting slips for the minority self-government elections as well as documents for the mainstream elections; this somehow leads people to vote for a minority candidate, it was asserted, even if they do not belong to a minority themselves. This problem too Hungarian lawmakers hoped to have solved with the new law of June 2005.

The second controversy mentioned by interviewees pertained to the way in which the financial basis for minority self-governments had been arranged. The local minority self-governments were, to a great extent, made dependent on funding offered by the "regular" local governments (Kállai and Törzsök 2001: 81). This was feared to become a source of conflict within municipalities, leading to the ethnicized competition for resources. Moreover, with regard to the national self-governments many complained about a high degree of dependency on external sources of funding. Here, the opportunities of the National Gypsy Self-Government were deemed more limited than those of the self-governments of other minorities. Unlike other minority self-governments, the Roma cannot be funded by a "homeland" government, it was argued. As a result, competition among Romani actors for public money intensified. From the first election onwards the National Gypsy Minority Self-Government sorely needed extra money to fulfill its tasks. It had to establish new administrative structures in order to secure the cultural autonomy it was granted and to deal with the many demands coming from Romani communities, most often for better housing and employment. According to Martin Kovats (2001a: 11), the first National Gypsy Minority Self-Government (1995–1999) was not able to gather enough resources to set up its own cultural institutions such as a theater or a library. In its ambition to be able to offer Romani communities economic support, and at the same time in its willingness to increase its own political power, the National Gypsy Minority Self-Government actively sought to attract as much as possible of the public money available for "Romani issues." Kovats has argued that the first National Gypsy Minority Self-Government continuously attempted to increase its control over the distribution of state financial support for Romani projects coming through the Public Foundation for Hungarian Gypsies (*Magyarországi Cigánykért Közalapítvány*) and the Public Foundation for Ethnic and National Minorities (*Nemzeti és Etnikai Kisebbségekért Közalapítvány*).

Arguably, the controversy about the way public funding should be used by minority self-governments was related to many people's lack of clarity concerning the ultimate purpose of the minority self-government system. This is the third problem. The minority self-government system allowed minorities to revive patterns of cultural life, such as language and tradition, but many Romani activists expected something more than that. Kaltenbach, for instance, has argued that cultural autonomy was simply not the primary concern of many Romani communities (Kaltenbach 1995). As some expected, after 1995 the government was increasingly faced with the demand for additional measures to deal with the socioeconomic position of this particular minority group. In a report published in 1997, the government admitted that the self-government system was not suited to alter economic predicaments (Government of the Republic of Hungary 1997). A combination of reasons was mentioned. On the one hand, the report pointed to the practical (and thus temporary) difficulties of implementing the ambitious self-government system (it referred to its novelty, the limited experience of the elected representatives, etc.). On the other hand, the report referred to the "special situation" to which the Gypsy self-governments had to respond:

> As a result of the special and serious problems of the Gypsies, the expectations placed on the Gypsy Minority Self-Governments are too great for the self-governments to be able to meet them under the present conditions. Most of the minority representatives have just begun to be active and many of them do not have the experience necessary for their public role. Many of the Minority Self-Governments rely exclusively on the central subsidy for their operation and do not take advantage of the other forms of support. The Gypsy Minority Self-Governments find themselves in a special situation. Whereas the self-governments of the national minorities are active mainly in the areas of education, culture and preserving traditions, the Gypsy self-governments have additional tasks which relate to social, health and employment questions. (Government of the Republic of Hungary 1997: 28)

The government could no longer ignore demands for additional measures. In the period between 1995 and 2004, a series of new plans and proposals were launched that increasingly conceptualized the Roma as a minority with specific needs, dissimilar from those of other minorities. Government report J/3670, prepared by the socialist-liberal (MSzP and SzDSz) coalition government led by Guyla Horn (1994–98), expressed this changing attitude.

The issue of the integration of the Gypsies into society is of great importance for the internal stability and economic well-being of the country and it is also one requiring the implementation of measures which are different from those of traditional minority policy. (Government of the Republic of Hungary 1997: 11)

In other words, the "traditional minority policy," in which the preservation and stimulation of cultural difference was seen as a way to integrate the minority, now became regarded as insufficient for the Roma. As the deputy president of the Office for National and Ethnic Minorities described the issue in 1999:

the situation of the Roma minority is in many respects quite different from other minorities. The problems they face are not only of linguistic or cultural character, therefore they cannot be solved within the framework of [the] minority law and need some other measures as well from the central, regional and local governments. (Heizer 1999: 4)

Already during his first year in power, Prime Minister Horn (MSzP) had apparently become aware of the need to develop group-specific strategies to tackle the problems facing the Roma. As part of his program of "creating a minority-friendly environment" (Government of the Republic of Hungary 1997: 22), Horn introduced a number of symbolic measures such as a national minority day and a yearly awarding of minority prizes. The establishment of a general Foundation for National and Ethnic Minorities (*Magyarországi Nemzeti és Etnikai Kisebbségekért Közalapítvány*) primarily served to support projects that aimed at "preserving the self-identity of the country's minorities, and to nurture and pass on their traditions, language, and culture" (Doncsev 1999: 3). Some additional initiatives were taken specifically for the Roma. The Foundation for the Hungarian Gypsies (*Magyarországi Cigányokért Közalapítvány*) was established and was, in contrast to the Foundation for National and Ethnic Minorities, tasked to make extra funds available for the Roma in the fields of vocational training, health support, and the development of small enterprises (Doncsev 1999: 3). In 1997, most of its budget (80 to 90 percent) was disbursed in grants for approved schemes aimed at encouraging agricultural production (Kállai and Törzsök 2001: 18).

The introduction of this foundation was only one of three new resolutions. Resolution 1125/1995 acknowledged the existence of "urgent tasks" related to the predicament of the Roma that could not be addressed through the existing legal system of minority protection, and state bodies competent in diverse fields were urged to communicate and coordinate their work as far as it concerned the Romani minority. Through Resolution 1120/1995 a council was established to bring representatives of the various state bodies together, in order to coordinate various activities relating to the position of the Roma. One of its tasks was to prepare a "medium- and long-term program" for reducing inequalities between Roma and other groups in society.

In the latter half of its term in office, the Horn government's focus on the Roma as a "disadvantaged sector of society" became increasingly apparent. The 1995 resolutions were, it seems, aimed in the first place at making financial resources available and coordinating existing initiatives. In 1997 new measures were introduced aimed specifically at "improving the living conditions of the Gypsies." These measures were the core texts of what became known as the "medium-term strategy."

In Resolution 1093/1997 ("on the medium-term action plan for the improvement of the living conditions of the Gypsy minority") the central question shifted from how to "protect the minority culture of the Roma" to how to achieve "social integration." Issues having to do with employment and education were given special attention. It has to be noted that this new concern for education differed greatly from the concerns usually associated with minority education, such as the instruction of minority languages or the preservation of cultural characteristics. This resolution was aimed at integrating Roma into the regular education system, and removing Romani children from the so-called "special schools." The resolution maintained that the situation of the Roma needed to be tackled through fostering their participation in education (tuition fees, child protection schemes for families with limited financial means), increasing employment, and introducing measures designed to handle possible crisis situations in settlements inhabited by Roma. Believing very strongly that political consensus existed on these matters, the government included in the medium-term action plan not only measures to be implemented in the remaining time of the government's term in office, but also guidelines for areas to be addressed at a later date (this became known as the "long-term strategy"). In general, however, the resolution was strongly focused on planning and researching this policy turn. At the end of the term, both activists and observers found that the effects of this new policy had been minimal (Kovats 2001a: 16). According to Kaltenbach, "it never really got off the ground" (Kosztolányi 2001: 204). Significant is that of all the Romani activists I interviewed in 1999, not one referred spontaneously to the "medium-term strategy" as a crucial policy development.

After the 1998 elections, which brought to power a government consisting of the right-wing liberal Fidesz-Hungarian Civic Party (Fidesz-MPP) and two coalition partners, the right-wing populist Independent Smallholders Party (FKGP) and the moderate nationalist Hungarian Democratic Forum (MDF), the position of the 1994–1998 government on minorities was largely maintained, at least in its general wording and conceptualization. On the one hand, the new government —led by Prime Minister Viktor Orbán—emphasized that the minority issue was to be regarded as a matter of protecting *cultural* diversity (Government of the Republic of Hungary 1998). On the other hand, "the social integration of the Roma" was seen as "both a question of minority policy and of social policy" (Hornung-Rauh and Fretyán 2000: 2). In the government program, the Roma were not included as a specific topic under the heading "Ethnic minorities in Hungary," where one would expect the topic to appear. They were mentioned by name in the paragraph entitled, "Those who need help." And they were the only ethnic minority group mentioned under that heading (Government of the Republic of Hungary 1998). The continuation of the approach initiated by the Horn government showed that a broad coalition of political parties could agree with the way Hungary was developing its Romani policy. Doncsev, as head of the Office for National and Ethnic Minorities, spoke in 1999 of a general "political consensus" (Doncsev 1999: 1). The specific concern for the Roma was illustrated by the appointment in the Office for National and Ethnic Minorities of a deputy director specifically responsible for coordinating all matters related to them (personal interview with Gabriella Varjú).

But the government's approach did not remain beyond criticism. Four criticisms in particular are worth mentioning. First, the Office for National and Ethnic Minorities was put under the Ministry of Justice instead of under the Prime Minister, a move that aroused criticism from the socialists of the MSzP. The socialists, who were now in opposition, began to doubt the independence of the Office for National and Ethnic Minorities. Secondly, many Romani activists found that the reformulation of Romani policy had been superfluous. In their view it had done little more than postpone the "real work." The resolutions and the medium-term action plan, which had been initiated by the MSzP-SzDSz government, were first reviewed by the new government and then replaced by a new resolution in May 1999 (Government of the Republic of Hungary 1999) "about medium-term measures to improve the living standards of the position of the Roma population." Although the content of the specific tasks was slightly adjusted, the document retained the basic approach and the same chapters as the previous resolution.

Thirdly, there was substantial debate about the spending of the financial resources (Kadét 2001; Kállai and Törzsök 2001: 85–86). The question often brought up was whether the financial resources that were nominally earmarked for spending on tackling the problems that face the Roma were actually utilized for that purpose (Kállai and Törzsök 2001: 85). The most important criticism, however, came from commentators who pointed to the problem that the general living conditions of many Roma did not appear to improve. A report published in cooperation with the ministry of foreign affairs stated that the measures had done "nothing to improve the fundamental life prospects of those in the Roma community in general; indeed, if anything, those prospects have gone on deteriorating" (Kállai and Törzsök 2001: 85). In response to reporting about this unchanging situation, the government ordered the Office for Ethnic and National Minorities to elaborate a discussion paper outlining a long-term strategy (this discussion paper was adopted by the government on August 13, 2001, through Resolution 1078/2001). The purpose of this paper was to offer arguments for initiating further action and generating financial means to tackle the problems facing the Romani population. Minister of Justice Ibolya Dávid (MDF), who supervised the Office for Ethnic and National Minorities at that time, wrote in a preface to the paper that one of its fundamental aims was to "establish and maintain a social consensus" on this matter that would exceed the current government's term in office. She mentioned the need to win the support of the "majority society" for the strategy, and the importance of the Hungarian strategy as an example for other countries in Europe.

When, after the parliamentary elections in the spring of 2002, power shifted again to a coalition of socialists and liberals (MSzP-SzDSz), the socialists tried to make a connection to their previous term in power (1994–1998) by alluding to the importance of the initial "medium-term" measures passed in 1997. Although there now clearly appeared to be a more or less general consensus between the parties in power and in opposition on the need to introduce separate policy initiatives toward the Roma, the socialists were eager to demonstrate their special concern for the issue. Besides the existing bodies, a number of new organs were established. Prime Minister Péter Medgyessy (MSzP) set up a state secretariat in his office to promote the social integration of the Roma and appointed Romani activist László Teleki, who had been elected to parliament from the MSzP list, as the head of this secretariat. Together with Teleki, Medgyessy also headed a newly established consultative body that was placed within the Prime Minister's Office, the Council for Romani Issues (*Romaügyi Tanács*). Interestingly, the establishment of the latter body suggests a decreasing concern for political representation (as in the self-government system) and a higher appreciation of expert consultation. The council brought the head of the National Gypsy Self-Government together with twenty-one appointed public figures from independent Romani organizations, mass media, and the academic world. In 2003, this council did not yet have much sway over the formation of government policies.

3. Minority Policy in Czechoslovakia between 1989 and 1992: Ending the Ambiguity?

After the Velvet Revolution and the end of the Czechoslovak Communist Party's (KSČ) dominance, new opportunities for ethnic political activity arose. A debate emerged about the relationship between the Slovak and Czech parts of the Czechoslovak Federal Republic. Ethnic claims became a topic of open public discussion. According to the logic of this development, there was less ambiguity than in earlier times as to whether the Roma should be recognized. In 1991, the Slovak republic-level government formally categorized them as a national minority through Government Resolution 153/1991 (Government of the Slovak Republic 1991). The Czech republic-level government followed later in that same year, although it did not devote a separate government resolution to the issue. In the 1991 Czechoslovak census, the name Roma was for the first time an official category for self-identification.

In the period between 1989 and 1992, the Czechoslovak policy on minorities in general and on Roma in particular was characterized by two main features. First of all, general minority policy was based on what became known as the "civic principle" (*občanský princip*). This means that the Czechoslovak state sought to maintain an undifferentiated citizenship status for all its citizens, and that the expression of ethnic difference was regarded as a private matter. Secondly, the Roma were regarded as subject to the general minority policy; they were placed on an equal footing with the other minorities.

Especially with regard to the first feature, the Czechoslovak position differed quite sharply from the Hungarian one. In contrast to Hungary's minority policy in the beginning of the 1990s, Czechoslovakia in this period did not grant cultural autonomy to its ethnic minorities. Ethnic minorities were recognized, but the recognition was based on a model of citizenship in which all citizens share a common set of individual rights. Recognition of ethnic diversity was not considered a legitimate basis for granting group-differentiated rights. Through its articles 24 and 25, the Charter of Fundamental Rights and Liberties, adopted by the Czechoslovak Federal Parliament in January 1991, provided everyone with the right to decide on her or his own ethnic identity and the right to form ethnic associations (Bugajski 1994: 299). According to this document, the protection of ethnic minorities was subsumed under the protection of the human, civil, and political rights of all citizens, and did not have to be guaranteed by group-specific rights or measures of exemption. The Roma in Czechoslovakia, in other words, were regarded as subject to a *general* minority policy, not as a special case. They fell under a regulation that had to protect all minorities, and that made no distinction between their position and those of the other minorities.

At certain points during this period, however, it was feared that the policy of undifferentiated citizenship would be unable to guarantee minority inclusion. It must have been this worry that inspired Vice Prime Minister Jan Mikloško and Minister of Labor and Social Affairs Petr Miller in 1991 to organize a series of roundtables on the question whether specific policy measures for Roma were needed (Sulitka 1999: 225). The result was a document that was later adopted as a federal government resolution, entitled "Principles of the government of the Czech and Slovak Federal Republic on a policy toward the Romani minority" (Government of the Czech and Slovak Federative Republic

1991). Its importance was mainly symbolic. The resolution made clear that current policies differed from the communist way of dealing with the Roma in that assimilation was now no longer the ultimate goal. To the contrary, the resolution stated, the development of Romani identity —and not its destruction—was a crucial element in equalizing the position of the Roma with the rest of society (Sulitka 1999: 226). The efficacy of the civic principle was, however, called into question by the Slovak republic-level government. In its Resolution 153/1991 (Government of the Slovak Republic 1991), Slovak leaders made a connection between Romani identity and social disadvantage— a view that could be interpreted as a first attempt at constructing a "Romani policy." Clearly, the need for group-specific measures for the protection of the Roma was felt more strongly in the Slovak part of the country.

4. and 5. The Czech Republic in the Periods 1993 to 1997 and 1997 to 2004

The new Czech Constitution, adopted in December 1992, reaffirmed the general acknowledgment of the rights and freedoms of individual citizens—including minority citizens—as stipulated by the Charter of Fundamental Rights and Freedoms. The Charter became a part of the constitutional order of the independent Czech Republic on January 1, 1993 (Government of the Czech Republic 1999a). The Roma in the Czech Republic were categorized as a national minority and were, just as the other minorities, granted "accommodation rights" in the field of culture.

Precisely what this meant became clear when in 1994 a new institution was established that was aimed at nurturing the cultural life of the recognized national minorities: the Council for National Minorities (*Rada pro národnosti vlády České republiky*). In this governmental body, a selection of people from the different recognized national minorities (Magyar, German, Polish, Romani, Slovak, and Ukrainian) who had been active in reputable minority organizations were brought together with delegates from the ministries, the parliament, and the office of the president. Together they acted as a consultative body for the government. The Council for National Minorities made summary reports about the state of affairs of the cultural situation of the minorities and put forward suggestions for policy improvement. In 1993, the government itself had promulgated a number of resolutions that ordered the various ministries to take into account the special position of the Roma in their activities. Nevertheless, the usual way of approaching the Roma was still to regard them as a "minority among the minorities." Dialogue between the government and Romani personalities about policy matters that affected the Roma could only take place within the Council for National Minorities, and not in any other separate institution.

Considering all this, it should come as no surprise that a number of (former) Romani members of the Council for National Minorities argued that they considered this an important body; it was for a long time the only channel for them to access the policy-making process. But they also admitted that in practice the Council was unable to do much more than secure financial support for minority press and cultural activities. A simple subject analysis of the official list of meetings of the Council for National Minorities between 1993 and 1997 shows that in 1993 and 1994 the situation of the Roma was usually discussed in connection with subsidies for Romani media and cultural events. The only politically sensitive topic that repeatedly appeared on the agenda was that of the building of a memorial on the site of the Second World War labor camp in the South Bohemian town of Lety u Pisku. Since 1974, an industrial pig farm had been operating on the terrain of this former concentration camp, where thousands of Czech Roma had been interned between 1939 and 1943, and several hundreds of them had died or been deported to Nazi extermination camps. The Council wanted to have the farm closed and the site commemorated.

In 1996, the Romani members of the Council (Ondřej Giňa, Stanislav Daniel, and Vladimír Oláh) began bringing up other topics that they felt had a more direct impact on the everyday circumstances of many Roma's lives, such as unemployment, discrimination, poverty, skinhead attacks, and the unfavorable effect of the Czech citizenship law on Roma, an issue to which I shall return in the next chapter. These were topics that had also began to attract increasing attention from the national and international press and from international human rights organizations. At the end of 1996, Romani Council member Ondřej Giňa took the initiative for establishing a special ad hoc working group within the Council of National Minorities in order to discuss issues that he believed to be specifically important for the Roma. The year 1997 then saw a conspicuous increase in the number of discussions at the level of the Council of National Minorities about the situation of the "specific problems" of the Roma. This increased attention eventually led to the establishment of new, separate institution and a modification in the way the government conceptualized and approached the group.

The year 1997 was a turbulent one in Czech politics and a crucial one in the run-up to a decisive shift in policy toward the Roma. In that year, Pavel Bratinka, President of the Council for National Minorities and Minister without Portfolio in the center-right government (ODS, KDU-ČSL, and ODA) under Václav Klaus, commissioned a group of experts to draw up a report on the situation of the Roma in the Czech Republic, taking into consideration the issues raised by the Romani members of the Council of National Minorities. An important role in the realization of this report was played by the head of Bratinka's office, Viktor Dobal, who had been a former MP for the Civic Forum (OF) and had worked with Romani communities in Prague's fifth district in the beginning of the 1990s. In 1997, Dobal considered it high time to draw the government's attention to the Roma and saw in the political controversy surrounding the wave of Czech asylum seekers a chance to rouse Bratinka's interest in the matter. The government's interest in a research report on the matter increased considerably after complaints reached the Czech Republic from countries that were receiving a growing number of Czech asylum seekers (in particular the United Kingdom and Canada). Bratinka's initiative also came at a time when reports by international human rights organizations such as Human Rights Watch elicited the attention of foreign governments, including the United States. In January 1997, a spokesman from the Ministry of the Interior and the Czech Ambassador to the United States had dismissed these reports and called them false accusations. In May and June, Minister without Portfolio Bratinka seized the opportunity and stated that there was indeed a problem of intolerance and discrimination in the Czech Republic, and that the most important reason for the persistence of this phenomenon was a lack of coordination at the policy-making level. Arguably, Bratinka wanted to use Dobal's report as strong evidence backing his statement because he knew the government was rather reluctant to design Roma-specific policies. Dobal recalled that, when he finally was able to present his study to the government, it was initially met with great indifference (personal interview).

Dobal's study, which later became known as the "Bratinka report," was completed at the end of August 1997. Reactions from the Romani members of the Council of National Minorities were mixed. On the one hand, they thought it was an important step forward, because this was the first time a ministerial document had gone so far as to identify anti-Romani discrimination as a crucial problem in the Czech Republic. On the other hand, they criticized the report for lacking clear policy proposals. The cabinet members for their part were not pleased with the report; they considered it too critical of past government initiatives. It was not until the end of October 1997 that the Bratinka report was finally adopted by the government (Government of the Czech Republic 1997). At that time there was a general fear that the asylum crisis would harm the international reputation of the Czech Republic. It eventually pushed the government to adopt the report without eliminating its critical tone.

The Bratinka Report was based on research that was meant to explore specifically the situation of the Roma, find out how this situation was related to the problem of discrimination, and evaluate the existing approaches. The importance of the report was not only that it represented the first modest attempt to publicize data on discrimination, unemployment, and poverty among Roma, but also that it criticized the government by suggesting that regular ethnic minority protection as provided by the law had failed to change the group's predicament. The solution the report hinted at was to make steps toward establishing institutions that would deal directly with the problems particular to the Roma. The report mentioned as an instructive example the ad hoc working group on Romani affairs of the Council of National Minorities, "whose members deal with specific cases of racially motivated violence and discrimination against Romani citizens" (Council for Nationalities of the Government of the Czech Republic 1997: Paragraph 2.3).

Shortly after the report was adopted as a government resolution, the Interdepartmental Commission for Romani Community Affairs (*Meziresortní komise pro záležitosti romské komunity*; hereafter Interdepartmental Commission) was formed. This was a new advisory body bringing selected "representative" Romani activists (first six, from 1998 onwards twelve, then, beginning in 2001, fourteen) together with an equal number of representatives from various ministries. The introduction of a new body within the government administration to prepare policy initiatives specifically aimed at ameliorating the situation of the Roma reflected the fact that the Roma had become a separate subject in public policy. From this time onwards the Roma were clearly treated as a minority group in need of special support on top of the existing support as provided to minorities in general.

The government implied that it accepted a deviation from the general rule for the Roma, but only on a temporary basis. A group-specific policy toward the Roma was not presented as an end in itself, but as a means to "deal with the current problems" and to compensate for "prior discrimination which now burdens the society as a whole" (Council for Nationalities of the Government of the Czech Republic 1997: introduction, paragraph ii). In other words, special treatment for members of one disadvantaged group was considered justifiable as a means to achieve greater equality in the society as a whole. Although the report did not make it explicit, this meant that such a special treatment was to last only as long as the inequality persisted, and that the objective of such measures was the disappearance of the need for such special measures. The report did not put forward a detailed proposal for how this sort of special treatment as a whole was to be conceived. It recommended that certain aspects of the legislation or government practice that were demonstrably pernicious to the Roma be changed, but it remained silent about how a temporary policy of special treatment should be designed in terms of institutions. It contained references to both the system of affirmative action in the United States and the Hungarian minority protection system, not so much as examples to be followed, but to provide context to a political debate.

In December 1997, the government led by Václav Klaus was forced to resign after a scandal about the financing of the Civic Democratic Party (ODS). The following January, a new six-month transitional government took office led by Prime Minister Josef Tošovský, an independent politician and former governor of the Czech National Bank. This period saw the beginning of the functioning of the Interdepartmental Commission. At first, Romani activists seemed satisfied with this institutional response. Soon, however, some confusion arose. After the resignation of the Klaus government, there appeared to be no complete clarity as to the tasks of the Interdepartmental Commission. An attempt to remedy this was made by the new Minister without Portfolio of the Tošovský government, Vladimír Mlynář (US), who was also the Chairman of both the Council of National Minorities and the Interdepartmental Commission. One of the ambiguities he faced pertained to the question of just how "representative" the Interdepartmental Commission had to be. In Mlynář's view, the commission's credibility depended on the participation of Romani activists. In addition to a number of "Romani representatives" who were consulted by the commission, he also insisted on having a Roma as Deputy Chair. Monika Horáková, a young Romani activist, was selected for this position.

The problem here was not so much that Roma were selected (and not elected) as members of the commission. Confusion arose, rather, from the lack of clarity that continued to plague the Interdepartmental Commission over whether its primary task was to develop a better policy or simply to *represent* the Roma. If the latter was true, Romani participants needed to act as representatives of their communities; in the former case, they would need to function as experts. The commission was criticized for being neither representative nor having sufficient expertise to assist in the formation of policy. A small number of well-known Romani personalities who were not selected to the commission seized the alleged democratic deficit to contest the appointment of both the deputy chair and the commission's Romani members. Although such criticism may have been based on personal rivalry among activists—as Mlynář suggested when I interviewed him on the matter—it could nevertheless not be warded off by the argument that the people in the commission were selected not because of their ethnic identity, but because of their expertise in the field. In an attempt to respond to the criticisms, Mlynář created a forum for well-known Romani personalities who had remained outside the Interdepartmental Commission and tried to achieve a consensus among the most vocal Romani activists. The most striking example of this strategy was the appointment of Emil Ščuka as Mlynář's personal advisor. Ščuka, a prominent figure in the international Romani movement, was at that time already a famous Romani activist in the Czech Republic but had not been selected for the Interdepartmental Commission.

With regard to the question of whether it was the task of the commission to prepare the government's "Romani policy," the commission was criticized for its apparent lack of power to exert real influence on the government. Mlynář attempted to tackle this criticism by focusing on highly symbolic issues. The first months of the Interdepartmental Commission will be best remembered for its lobbying for the establishment of a commemorative site for the Lety labor camp.[13] According to Mlynař, this was a crucial case for demonstrating that the government's attitude toward the Roma had changed. He also wanted to "change the attitude of the majority toward the Roma." He became a zealous advocate of introducing history on the Roma to children's textbooks. Having become focused on this matter, the Interdepartmental Commission soon became a symbol of the changing government attitude toward the Roma, rather than an instrument of policy preparation and deliberation.

After the 1998 parliamentary elections—which brought the Czech Social Democrat Party (ČSSD) under Prime Minister Miloš Zeman to power in a government that was based on an opposition agreement with the ODS of Klaus—the Interdepartmental Commission remained the central governmental institution for the Roma. This shows the growing agreement among mainstream politicians about the need to construct a policy toward the Roma that would diverge from the general minority policy. This view is clearly expressed in the programmatic statement the Zeman government issued at the beginning of its term in office:

> [The government] shall ... devote attention to all ethnic groups living in the Czech Republic, although the most serious, and undoubtedly most complex, issue is, in the Government's view, the coexistence of a part of the majority society with the Romany minority. The Government considers the Romany community a natural component of Czech society. The civic principle, as the basis for the solution of this problem, will be complemented by specific programs designed for the Romany minority in those cases where the hitherto existing handicaps cannot be overcome by measures aimed at the society as a whole. (Government of the Czech Republic 1998)

The new government understood the Interdepartmental Commission not so much as an instrument of policy making, but rather as a symbolic institution needed in order to embody the changing relationship between the state and the Roma. Although the government never stated it this way, this latter point of view became clear through the appointment of ex-dissident Petr Uhl to the position of chairman of the commission. There is little doubt that Uhl was appointed first and foremost because of his record as a celebrated human rights activist; for this reason he was seen as an ally of the Romani movement. However, in contrast to the situation under the Tošovský government, Uhl was not a member of the cabinet, and therefore Romani activists reckoned he would be unable to exert real influence on the government. In December 2001 the Interdepartmental Commission was renamed as the Government Council for Romani Community Affairs (*Rady vlády pro záležitosti romské komunity*) and came under the chairmanship of a cabinet member (Minister of Justice Pavel Rychetský), while at the same time two additional Romani members were appointed to make the body more representative. Nevertheless, some Romani activists still asked whether it was now really more representative and whether it was now more able to exert a stronger influence on policy development.

Other activists and observers whom I interviewed expressed moderately favorable opinions about some of the achievements of the Interdepartmental Commission. They were, for example, impressed by the attempts of the interior ministry to enhance feelings of security among Roma and to increase the opportunities for Roma to join the police. Suggestions made by the Interdepartmental Commission about possibilities to increase job opportunities were taken into consideration by the ministry of labor and social affairs. Most importantly, a number of Romani members of the Interdepartmental Commission felt they had been able to set the agenda of the government in the debate leading to the formulation of a "policy concept" on the Romani issue. In 1999 the Interdepartmental Commission finished a document presenting the concept of "Romani integration" (a policy which would be open to yearly revision by the Interdepartmental Commission). In April 2000 this concept was adopted by the government as the principal component of a new strategic "Romani policy" (Government of the Czech Republic 1999b; Parliament of the Czech Republic 2001).

The basic approach to Roma–state relations underlying this new policy initiative was tantamount to the idea that the Roma fall under a general framework of minority rights protection only as far as matters of communication, tradition, language, and cultural development are concerned. Regarding their socioeconomic situation, they were deemed to belong under a group-specific policy. In Uhl's words:

> The argument that the Roma problem is merely a social problem is generally the view of people who do not want to admit that the Roma are a national minority, thereby denying them the right to development. Yet, the social aspect must be solved. (Uhl 1998: 46)

Toward the end of the decade a more "multiculturalist" view on general minority policy gradually began to take shape (Vermeersch 2004: 14). This was, according to Uhl, primarily the result of the Czech Republic's adherence to the Council of Europe's Framework Convention for the Protection of National Minorities (personal interview). In July 2001, the Czech parliament adopted Act 273, "On the rights of members of national minorities," which was to some extent a further deviation from the earlier civic principle approach and the modest beginning of an approach of active protection of minority culture in public life, without, however, granting minorities self-government rights or far-reaching cultural autonomy. The general vision of the Czech government toward minorities was now that members of national minorities should be encouraged to develop their identity, and that in certain fields, such as education, official language use, and the promotion of minority culture, members of these minorities should be granted certain special rights. Together with the administrative reforms on the local level introduced in 2000, this law enabled the establishment of appointed local and regional advisory committees for national minorities in areas where minorities have a sufficient percentage according to the census (10 percent in municipalities, 5 percent in regions and in Prague). The law was clearly the result of a compromise between minority activists such as Petr Uhl who had advocated the introduction of special organs elected by members of minorities to govern their cultural affairs, and those who thought an extra law on minority protection was superfluous.[14]

6. The Slovak Republic between 1993 and 1998: Between Magyars and Slovaks

Ethnic politics in the independent Slovak Republic of the 1990s was dominated by the issue of the Magyar minority. The Magyars live rather compactly in three areas in the south of Slovakia, so after the break-up of Czechoslovakia they gained numerical and political weight in the independent Slovak Republic. Relations between Magyar activists and Slovak nationalist politicians became tense and had a strong impact on diplomatic contacts between the governments in Bratislava and Budapest. It should come as no surprise, therefore, that the manner in which the Slovak government addressed the Magyar issue differed slightly from the way it dealt with the Roma, even though both minorities were subject to the same legal framework. Political debate about the Magyar minority primarily concerned Magyar aspirations for regional autonomy and public usage of the Hungarian language. The Movement for a Democratic Slovakia (HZDS), Slovakia's most popular party throughout this period, used ethnic Slovak fears of Magyar autonomy to bolster populist election campaigns. The position of the Roma played a pivotal role in this conflict, since they were sometimes regarded as Magyars, sometimes as Slovaks, and sometimes as neither one nor the other. The government showed a tendency to treat them as a socioeconomic group from an uncertain ethnic background, rather than as a "regular" ethnic group.

An example of this can be found in the way the ministry of foreign affairs responded to a European Commission report in 1997. Contesting the numbers presented by the European Commission, the ministry claimed that:

> Of the almost 11% Hungarian minority, a large percentage belongs to the Romany minority. It is thought that within the Slovak Republic there are currently 280,000 persons of Romany ethnic origin, of which a large part currently claims affiliation to the Hungarian national minority and a smaller part to Slovak or Romany nationality. (Quoted in Henderson 1999: 146)

As Henderson notes quite accurately, the ministry did not offer any evidence in support of the argument that a large part of Slovakia's undeclared Roma had claimed to be of Magyar nationality in the censuses. Statistical uncertainty about Romani identity was thus strategically used as a way to question the numerical weight of the Magyar minority. More important in this context, however, is that the above-mentioned statement implies that Romani ethnicity can easily coincide with Slovak or Magyar ethnicity, while Magyar and Slovak ethnicity are apparently regarded as mutually exclusive. In other words, Romani identity was seen as not being of the same order as Slovak and Magyar identity. When looking at the policy initiatives taken by the government between 1993 and 1998, one quickly discerns that Slovak and Magyar identity were defined in terms of culture and language, while Romani identity was defined in terms of socioeconomic position. Although the Roma were legally acknowledged to be a "regular" national minority, in policy practice, it would appear, they were approached not as a national minority but as a socioeconomic group.

After the break-up of Czechoslovakia in 1993, the Slovak government issued three conceptual plans relating to the position of the Roma. The first was the 1996 "Activities and Measures in Order to Solve the Problems of Citizens in Need of Special Care," adopted in resolution 310/1996 (Government of the Slovak Republic 1996). This document described a number of problem areas (education, employment, housing, and health) and measures to be followed for their solution. Along the lines of the government's analysis that the situation was one of socioeconomic maladjustment, the document did not deliberate on possible external factors such as discrimination or human rights infringements as potential sources of socioeconomic decline. Consequently, no measures for remedying ethnic discrimination were included in this plan. The text largely laid the responsibility for the problems at the door of the Roma themselves—indeed, at some points it even pointed directly to the specific characteristics of Romani identity as the root of the problem. Illustrative hereof is the text's treatment of the phrase "citizens in need of special care" and the name "Roma" as synonymous concepts. While the title of the document ostensibly targeted all "citizens in need of special care," the text itself frequently mentioned simply "the Roma" as the target group, thereby suggesting that all Roma are citizens in need of special care and that there are no citizens in need of care who are not at the same time Roma.

In order to coordinate and implement the 1996 Resolution, the position of Government Commissioner for Citizens in Need of Special Care was created. Branislav Baláž, who never identified himself as a Roma but still became a member of a Romani political party (Romani Civic Initiative, ROI-SR), filled this position, and in November 1997 he tabled a document that led to the adoption of a new government resolution (Government of the Slovak Republic 1997; Commissioner of the Government of the Slovak Republic for Solutions of Problems of Citizens with Special Needs 1997). Although it was more detailed in its analysis and included more information on how to finance plans, the new resolution and the accompanying policy paper did not reframe the first plan's views of the Roma as being themselves the chief cause of the problems described. Neither did these government initiatives change the political and institutional context of Romani mobilization. Romani representatives remained rather confused about which institutions to align themselves with, which claims to stress, and what criticisms to cite in their protest activities.

The 1994–98 government—consisting of the populist Movement for a Democratic Slovakia (HZDS), the far-right Slovak National Party (SNS), and the radical leftist Association of Workers of Slovakia (ZRS)—had a strong nationalist imprint and was under a great deal of influence from its premier, Vladimír Mečiar (HZDS). Mečiar's authoritarian style, and his attempts to concentrate political power and aggressively promote Slovak nationhood were all heavily criticized both domestically and internationally, most clearly by NGOs (nongovernmental organizations) and European institutions (Bútora et al. 1999). However, realizing the potential size of the Romani electorate, the HZDS—and in particular its leader—more than once declared itself to be willing to "fight for the Roma." This, in combination with the influential rhetoric of the HZDS about a need for a strong social policy, attracted the attention of many Roma. In the run-up to the 1994 elections, for example, Mečiar publicly stated that financial loans would be made available to Romani politicians on condition that they would form a united party. He even offered financial and material support for the electoral campaigns of some Romani activists (Vašečka 1999a: 258).

These propositions aroused mixed reactions. Although some Roma were very pleased to see support coming from a mainstream political force, a number of them perceived Mečiar's initiatives and statements merely as cynical political tactics. Since Mečiar had made statements before that were clearly anti-Romani, some Roma thought it was obvious that his supposedly Roma-friendly discourse was driven not by a concern for the minority itself but by the will to obstruct the political advancement of the Hungarian minority. Moreover, by promoting Romani party formation, the HZDS could prevent other non-ethnically-based parties from drawing in Romani votes. In this sense HZDS support for a political Romani movement could be seen as a way to secure the party's own dominant position. Under these circumstances, a gap began to open up between those Romani activists who wanted to support Mečiar for tactical reasons and those activists who supported the international shaming campaign directed against Mečiar.

7. The Slovak Republic between 1998 and 2004: Introducing New Governmental Institutions for the Roma

The domestic political situation changed radically after the 1998 parliamentary elections. On the basis of a victory over the HZDS, the former opposition parties were able to agree on a grand coalition and established a new government dominated by the newly created Slovak Democratic Coalition (SDK, later SDKÚ) of Prime Minister Mikuláš Dzurinda. The new government immediately found support from the international community, not least because of its favorable attitude toward the Magyars. The Magyar Coalition Party (SMK) was one of the coalition partners in the new government. Political leaders in the West now openly argued for a re-examination of Slovakia's position toward the EU. The EU's criticism concerning the treatment of minorities in Slovakia became much less articulate, while the Slovak government regarded the Copenhagen political criteria for European Union accession as fulfilled.

In terms of its general minority policy, the new government program endorsed more clearly than ever before norms of minority rights protection. Illustrative of this turn was the fact that Magyar politician Pál Csáky of the SMK was able to fill the new post of deputy prime minister for human rights, minorities, and regional development. The formal legal recognition and implementation of this change of direction, however, did not follow smoothly. Magyar demands continued to cause heated debate within the ruling coalition, especially between the Party of the Democratic Left (SDĽ) and the SMK. Proposals by the SMK — for example the one proposing the creation of a separate administrative county in the regions predominantly inhabited by Magyars—also met with fierce protest from the opposition parties, HZDS and SNS, both of which easily found popular support simply by suggesting that the hidden agenda of the Magyar politicians was to return portions of Slovakia to Hungary. It took until January 2001 before Dzurinda's cabinet succeeded in taking a clear step in the announced direction by approving the European Charter of Regional and Minority Languages.

Regarding the Roma, the new government attempted to show its commitment by introducing a number of initiatives immediately after the beginning of its term in office. The most important ones were the establishment of a Government Council on National Minorities and Ethnic Groups (*Rada vlády SR pre národnostné menšiny a etnické skupiny*), which included a representative from a Romani organization (the Roma Civic Initiative, ROI-SR), and the appointment of a Government Commissioner for the Solution of the Problems of the Romani Minority (*Splnomocnec vlády Slovenskej republiky na riešenie problémov rómskej menšiny*). The earlier Government Commissioner for Citizens in Need of Special Care was abolished. The inclusion of some Romani activists in the Government Council on National Minorities and Ethnic Groups, which was primarily a government advisory body dealing with state support for minority cultural development, clearly represented a step in the direction of placing the Roma on an equal footing with other minorities. The other members in the council representing minority organizations were Magyar, Jewish, Czech, Moravian, Croatian, Bulgarian, Ukrainian, and Ruthenian. Selected for the position of the new Government Commissioner was former Slovak Helsinki Committee chairman and former MP, Vincent Danihel, himself a Romani activist—this latter point being vigorously emphasized by the government. Danihel's office, responsible for communicating Romani concerns with the government, completed a policy paper in June 1999 entitled "Strategy of the Government for the Solution of the Problems of the Roma," which was later adopted by the government (Government of the Slovak Republic 1999a). Both the introduction of the special government commissioner and the subsequent issuing of Resolution 821/1999 illustrated a tendency to consider the Roma as a group for which additional policy measures were needed.

This resolution was also underpinned by the idea that Romani organizations needed to be encouraged to participate in the implementation of the new plans. The government commissioner was most instrumental in this process. His office was to draft concrete projects, propose measures, and report to the government, and it became, to a large extent, responsible for the distribution of available funds. Romani activists were stimulated to found sociopolitical organizations and submit project proposals, and so they did. But two important problems remained.

First, although the resolution called upon Romani organizations to participate in policy formation and implementation, no clear structure was elaborated for achieving this. Danihel personally was to establish links with the Romani organizations. But very soon, many Romani activists saw in Danihel an obstacle rather than a facilitator. Danihel was branded as a political opportunist because he had supported the official government stance that Romani migration to the West was only economically driven, and not—as Romani activists and international human rights organizations saw the matter—the result of mounting discrimination. This led to a great deal of distrust, with many Roma believing that both Danihel's position and the whole strategy which he represented was merely aimed at enhancing Slovakia's standing in the international community and not to empower the Romani minority with a substantive voice in the policy-making process. An increasing number of Romani activists seemed to be convinced that policy change was designed specifically and narrowly to respond to external pressures. Danihel was pressed hard, since he was also criticized by the supervising minister, Csáky, for running the office in a not sufficiently professional way. In May 2001, after a two-year tenure in the post, he was dismissed, according to the government press conference, because of his lack of support among the Roma and, significantly, his inability to deal with international organizations. In July 2001, the position of government commissioner was filled by Klára Orgovánová, a renowned Slovak Romani activist and former director of an independent, internationally sponsored advocacy organization called Inforoma.

Secondly, some activists also questioned the utility of creating a specific ethnic institution to guarantee Romani influence in the decision-making process. The government argued that through the process of consultation there was now sufficient participation of Roma in the drafting and implementation of Roma-related policies. But this institutional mechanism did not at all facilitate Romani political involvement in the central institutions of mainstream politics. Even in the official explanatory text accompanying the resolution, there were no clear ideas of how to stimulate the presence of Roma in central political institutions or in mainstream political parties.

Converging Policies and Institutional Contexts

So far, this chapter has identified seven "cases" representing the various ways in which the Central European states have dealt with the Roma in the 1990s. In Table 2.1 I offer a summary of these cases.

It is more than obvious that of the three countries, it is Hungary that has adopted the fullest form of a "minority rights model" by granting aterritorial self-government rights to its national minorities at the beginning of the 1990s. It should be clear, however, that the Czech Republic and Slovakia also gradually moved in the direction of this model by adopting measures aimed at the special protection of minority languages and cultures.

Table 2.1 Summary of the seven cases.

	Domestic institutional and political context
(1) Hungary 1989–1995	Policy of ethnic differentiation; special institutions for all ethnic minorities. The Roma on equal footing with the other officially recognized minorities.
(2) Hungary 1995–2004	Ethnicization of Romani policy: introduction of additional measures and institutions specifically for the Roma.
(3) Czechoslovakia 1989–1992	Recognition of the Roma as a minority. The Roma on equal footing with the other minorities. Ethnic identity as a legitimate basis for political organization. No special Romani institutions.
(4) Czech Republic 1993–1997	A policy of socioeconomic homogenization targets all ethnic minorities. Roma on equal footing with the other recognized minorities.
(5) Czech Republic 1997–2004	Ethnicization of Romani policy: introduction of additional measures and institutions specifically for the Roma.
(6) Slovakia 1993–1998	A policy of socioeconomic homogenization to tackle the situation of the Roma. Legally the Roma have the same status as the other minorities, but in practice they are narrowly defined as "citizens in need of special care."
(7) Slovakia 1998–2004	Recognition of the Roma as a minority. The Roma on equal footing with the other recognized minorities. Ethnicization of Romani policy: the introduction of additional measures and institutions specifically for the Roma.

In the Slovak Republic, minority rights were primarily demanded by Magyar activists. Before 1998, these demands did not lead to any significant legal changes. More importantly, these demands were seized upon by the governing parties to stir up a highly charged political debate about what they regarded as perfidious attempts of the Magyars to harm Slovakia's territorial integrity. The post-1998 governments in Slovakia have had a different (although not uncontested) view on the issue of Magyar protection. The situation of the Roma was at first seen through the prism of the debate about the Magyar minority. Soon, however, the government formulated institutions and measures that again separated the issue of the Roma from the issue of Magyar minority protection.

In the Czech Republic the civic principle, which remained dominant during most of the 1990s, began to lose some of its credibility around 1997. The reasons for this can be found in the fact that at a certain point the government realized that the policies adopted up until that time had not been able to prevent the deterioration of the situation of the Roma. As a result, group-specific institutions for the Roma were established, while at the same time features of a general minority rights model became more prominent. This latter development is exemplified in the Czech ratification of the Framework Convention for the Protection of National Minorities at the end of 1997 and the law of July 2001 that among other things allowed the use of minority languages in some official documents. The strategy of targeting the Roma as a minority *and* as a socioeconomic group is rather similar to the strategies initiated by the Hungarian and Slovak governments. At the same time, the Czech approach to minority protection in general was less based on group differentiation than was the case in the two other countries.

Allies and Opponents

While institutions and policies are arguably crucial components of the political opportunity structure in which the mobilization of Roma takes place, the successes and failures of Romani ethnic activists may also to some extent be dependent on the presence or absence of strategic allies. Therefore, a few words still need to be said in this chapter about the relationship between Romani movement actors on the one hand and their political allies and opponents on the other. One expects the configuration of political power surrounding attempts at Romani mobilization to have had a strong influence on the shape and success of the ethnic movement. In order to provide a better view of whether this was indeed the case in the three countries under examination, this section offers a short description of the various areas where Romani movement actors experienced manifest support, and of those areas where they encountered strong opposition from other political actors. I will distinguish between two kinds of actors: (a) other domestic ethnic minority activists, and (b) political personalities, mainstream political parties in power or in opposition.

Other Minorities

It is easy to see why one would expect the case of Slovakia to be the most obvious example of a country where there is solidarity and alliance formation between various ethnic movements. Slovakia is the only country in the sample with a large, regionally concentrated national minority—a minority, moreover, that was able to mobilize rather successfully in national politics. Thus, one wonders whether the political claims and strategies of the Magyar organizations were indeed conducive to Romani activism in Slovakia.

A careful examination of this subject shows that the presence of a successful Magyar mobilization in Slovak politics was less important for the emergence of Romani action than one might perhaps expect. It appears that Romani movement actors did not perceive Magyar actors as good political allies, although they served as a source of inspiration for methods of political action. This latter contention is evidenced by the fact that, much more than in Hungary and the Czech Republic, Romani mobilization in Slovakia principally focused on elections and winning votes for parties that aimed at ethnic Romani representation. By so doing they hoped to achieve what the Magyars had been able to realize. From the beginning of the 1990s, the Magyar minority was quite successful in attracting Magyar voters for ethnically based Magyar parties, and became part and parcel of the Slovak political landscape, especially after the success of the Magyar Coalition Party (SMK) in 1998.

But even if they shared certain methods, there were no tangible forms of cooperation or alliance between Magyar and Romani parties—quite to the contrary, there was overt competition and fear that the issues of one group might overshadow those of the other. One exception was a very limited form of concerted action in parliament. Two MPs for the SMK, Imrich Tóth and László Nagy, attempted to create some form of Romani representation in parliament by inviting a couple of Romani activists to take seats in the Parliamentary Commission for the Roma, a subcommission of the Parliamentary Commission for Human Rights. Of the three Romani activists whom I interviewed and who were members of this commission, none attached much importance to the existence of this commission.

Moreover, there was little or no convergence between demands of the two groups. One could perhaps think that the demand of the SMK to change the first sentence of the Constitution's preamble from "We, the Slovak nation" to "We, the citizens of Slovakia" would also have interested Romani activists very much. This was not the case. Other demands, such as the establishment of a Hungarian-language university and the creation of a separate administrative county in the south of the country, were also of minimal concern to many Romani activists. Romani activists actively seeking the support of Hungarian speakers were usually seen in a negative light by the Magyar parties because it was believed that such activists would take away votes from them, thus making the Magyar community appear smaller in size.

The situation in the other two countries was in many ways radically different, but there, too, other ethnic minorities were not necessarily the most obvious allies for the Roma. Hungary had recognized a range of minorities but there were few similarities between their demands and those expressed by Romani activists. In my interviews, Hungarian Romani activists frequently emphasized the difference, both in content and scale, between the situation of the other minorities and the predicament of the Roma. According to both Romani and non-Romani interviewees, the challenges faced by the Roma were not comparable to the ones faced by the other minorities. Various crucial differences were referred to. For some the difference was primarily related to the fact that the Roma had been the "losers" in the economic transition and had to suffer unprecedented levels of poverty and unemployment. Others agreed with this to some extent, but added that the underlying cause of poverty and unemployment was the post-1989 growth of anti-Romani discrimination. Still others pointed to history and culture. In their opinion, the historical marginalization of the Roma had set the latter apart from other minorities. The absence of a standardized language and the lack of support by a home country was for some an important obstacle hindering the convergence of demands.

Romani activists in Hungary seldom felt that they could form a united front with other minority movement organizations. This is perhaps best illustrated by the frustrations of some of them about the advancement of certain other minority activists to important positions in institutions established to secure minority rights protection. One interviewee argued that it was problematic that the Minority Ombudsman had not been chosen from among Romani activists. The importance attached to the difference between the Roma and other minorities can also be evidenced by the way many Romani activists responded in 1995 to the selection of a Romani activist (Éva Orsós) for the position of head of the Office for Ethnic and National Minorities. In my interview with her, Orsós recounted how many Romani activists were supportive of her candidacy simply because she was Romani, even without knowing whether she had the appropriate skills for the position. She felt she had been maneuvered into the position of a political representative of an ethnic minority, while the position itself was in reality supposed to be that of a neutral public administrator. She also recalled that once she was appointed, many Romani activists contacted her, believing that through her they would gain privileged access to certain financial resources.

The situation in the Czech Republic was similar in the sense that there were few, if any, indications of solidarity between Romani movement actors and leaders of other ethnic minorities. As in Hungary, the Czech Republic saw the presence of only small minority groups, but in contrast to Hungary, they were never politically organized. The only political body in which delegates of minority organizations (Magyar, German, Polish, Romani, Slovak, and Ukrainian) met with one another was the Council for National Minorities. Within this body demands of the various minority delegates differed greatly. The German ethnic leaders, for instance, frequently demanded property restitution for people who had been affected by the Beneš Decrees, a demand that concerned other minorities to a much lesser extent. Other issues that were dealt with in the Council for National Minorities were usually related to financial support for the development of minority culture (primarily the media); the Romani delegates did not see these matters as being of primary importance. In turn, representatives of other minority organizations felt little affinity with what they regarded as the typical concerns of the Roma.

Domestic Elite Allies and Opponents: Political Personalities, Political Parties in Government or in Opposition

In general, Romani interests played only a marginal role in mainstream politics. Throughout the decade of the 1990s, topics related to the situation of the Roma were usually not at the heart of important political debates, and were usually given a minimal amount of attention in the political programs of the main political parties. Very few well-known politicians presented themselves as advocates of the Roma. Nor were there many successful political parties that mobilized voters exclusively on the basis of anti-Roma rhetoric.

Yet at times the issue of the Roma temporarily moved from the margins of political debate to the center. During these periods, certain politicians formulated clear anti- or pro-Romani statements. The events that led to these sudden changes, and the role of Romani activists in the politicization of these events, are matters I will discuss later. Here, I will focus on the political forces that acted as allies or opponents during those short periods in which the Roma became a central topic of public discussion.

One obvious observation with regard to alliance structure is that the most outspoken political opponents of the Roma were politicians from the radical right. At first sight the influence of these parties on mainstream politics might appear limited. The Slovak National Party (SNS) in Slovakia was for most of the decade not able to gain more than 10 percent of the votes and at one point barely passed the 5 percent parliamentary threshold. As a coalition partner of the HZDS in the three Mečiar governments, it was not able to escape HZDS dominance.[15]

The Assembly for the Republic-Czechoslovak Republican Party (SPR-RSČ), founded in 1989 by Miroslav Sládek, failed to gain admittance to the Slovak National Council in 1992, but did receive around 6 percent of the vote for the Czech National Council in that same year. After having received 8 percent in the 1996 Czech parliamentary elections, its support dwindled to 3.9 percent in 1998. In Hungary during the 1990s, the most vocal proponent of the radical right was the Hungarian Party of Justice and Life (MIÉP), led by writer István Csurka, who in 1993 left the center-right Hungarian Democratic Forum (MDF) to pursue a clear anti-Trianon course, and gained a dubious reputation by making overtly anti-Semitic statements. MIÉP did not manage to win any seats in 1994, gained fourteen seats (3.63 percent of the total) in 1998, but did not get into parliament after the 2002 elections.

Despite their lack of significance as regards electoral results, these parties indisputably played a considerable role in shaping public discourse on minorities in all three countries. There are several reasons. First, they appealed to various audiences. They attracted violent youth subcultures and were able to mobilize nationalist feelings among middle- and lower-class people confronted with the uncertainties of the political and economic transition (Cibulka 1999; Karsai 1999). Moreover, they had a significant influence on the discourse of center-right parties. In Slovakia, the HZDS and the SNS agreed with each other in their aversion to Magyar political demands. The SNS had first promulgated anti-Czech views in the beginning of the 1990s, but gradually began targeting the Magyar minority and the Roma. Former chairman of the SNS and mayor of the northern Slovak city of Žilina, Ján Slota, became known for his harsh, stigmatizing statements on "the Gypsies" as a threat to "the Slovaks" (Haughton 2001: 753). In 2000, the former chairman of the SNS, Vít'azoslav Moric, even argued in parliament that the Roma were "idiots" and that a humane way of dealing with them was to put them on reservations. Statements like this aroused great controversy among politicians (in this case, the Slovak parliament decided to strip Moric of the immunity from prosecution he normally enjoyed as an MP). Yet the construction of a basic contrast between Romani and Slovak identity soon became discernible in statements by mainstream politicians, particularly those from the HZDS. A telling example is that of MP Alojz Engliš (HZDS), who in an attack on Prime Minister Dzurinda during a vote of no confidence in the spring of 2000, labeled him an *"obyčajný cigán"* (an ordinary Gypsy) (Haughton 2001: 753).

MIÉP activists in Hungary, too, stressed the ethnic unity and purity of the people they sought to represent and openly branded the Roma as a foreign element within their "own" Magyar culture. The slightly more moderate right-wing politicians in Hungary were able to construct a much more acceptable image than that of MIÉP, but nevertheless copied some of the basic presuppositions of the radical party. An openly populist party such as the Independent Smallholders Party (FKGP), for example, invoked more than once a discrepancy between the borders of Hungary and the boundaries of Magyar identity. Fidesz-MPP formed a government coalition with the FKGP in 1998. Although staying away from overtly discriminatory language, politicians from the rightist "people's party," Hungarian Democratic Forum (MDF), and the right-wing liberal Fidesz-MPP tried to garner voter support by suggesting that the national interests were primarily those of the Magyars. By so doing they indirectly placed the interests of the Roma—a recognized minority and thus non-Magyar by definition—outside the national interests. However, the message sent by Fidesz-MPP at times also demonstrated its willingness to gain a more inclusive character. Before the 2002 elections, the Fidesz-MPP–MDF alliance signed a cooperation agreement with one of Hungary's largest Romani organizations, Lungo Drom.

In the Czech Republic, politicians of the Republican Party promoted the idea that the "Romani problem" was merely a consequence of what they saw as the biological inclination of the Roma toward antisocial behavior (Bugajski 1994: 305). Miroslav Sládek is famous for having claimed that "for Gypsies the age of criminal responsibility should be from the moment of birth because being born is, in fact, their biggest crime" (quoted in Fawn 2001: 1202). The Republican Party's electoral results were poor throughout the 1990s, but this did not prevent politicians from mainstream parties believing that expressing hostile sentiments toward the Roma would bring reward. Although official statements from mainstream political parties did not contain anti-Romani language, there were informal statements by ODS politicians that were at least precarious, especially regarding the refugee crisis and the Matiční affair in Ústí nad Labem (see next chapter for a detailed account of these two events). Often recalled examples are those of ODS senator Zdeněk Klausner, who proposed relocating Roma out of Prague, and Liana Janačková (ODS), mayor of Ostrava, who suggested using municipal funds to buy one-way air tickets for Roma who opted to leave for Canada (Fawn 2001: 1203). Negative political discourse was clearly not confined to the extreme right parties.

It goes without saying that Romani activists found no allies in radical right parties. But how did Romani activists regard the more moderate nationalist, populist, or center-right politicians? Interestingly, the attitude of some activists toward these politicians was more positive, and some limited forms of cooperation between Romani activists and these parties emerged. Interviews in Slovakia revealed that Romani activists looked upon SNS politicians in a much more negative light than those from the HZDS. However much Romani activists in Slovakia were divided on political strategy, they were more or less united on one thing, that SNS is anti-Roma. The HZDS did not have an immaculate image in the eyes of many Romani activists, but this apparently did not prevent some Romani activists from appearing on HZDS candidate lists during parliamentary elections. A similar phenomenon was observable in Hungary, where some Romani activists appeared on the Fidesz-MPP and the Socialist Party (MSzP) candidate lists in the 2002 parliamentary elections. This last case shows that Romani politicians may be able to gain access to mainstream parties more easily when the electoral competition is quite tight and when theoretically Romani voters can make the difference, as was the case between Fidesz-MPP and the MSzP in Hungary in 2002. Clearly, Hungary's main parties in these elections supported Romani candidates primarily because of the paper-thin electoral margin. A number of Romani activists were quite willing to accept a place on their lists—largely independently of whether they had given any previous attention to the Roma. It was only with the commencement of talks about a possible coalition between Fidesz-MPP and MIÉP that a discussion arose among Romani activists about whether indeed Fidesz-MPP would be a suitable ally for Romani politicians. In Slovakia, similar discussions occurred about the participation of Romani activists on the HZDS candidate list.

Where can one find examples of more genuine political allies? The Roma, as well as other minorities, usually found vocal support from a small number of politicians who tried to attract voters among intellectuals, mostly in the cities; they probably remained unknown among many local Romani communities. A number of them came from ex-dissident groups who strongly engaged in the "politics of moral conviction" (Tucker 1999). In the first place, these were political personalities with symbolic power, but less direct influence on politics. The most obvious example is, no doubt, President Václav Havel in the Czech Republic, who over the years made many statements condemning intolerance and negative attitudes toward the Roma (Fawn 2001: 1207). Czech Romani activists usually understood his statements as a strong support for their movement, although they considered the practical consequences rather minimal.

In Hungary, popular intellectuals who did not pursue political careers —examples are György Konrád and Péter Eszterházy—supported the claims of the Roma. The alliance between these intellectual ex-dissidents and the Romani movement was quite clear in both Hungary and Czechoslovakia right after 1989. In Hungary, Romani activists and activists from the "Democratic Opposition" joined forces in protest against the plans of the local government of the city of Miskolc to relocate the Roma in substandard housing. Aladár Horváth, who, as I mentioned, was the leading Romani protester in Miskolc, stated later that the people who supported the protest did this more "as an expression of their opposition to the Communist system than of their sympathy for the Roma" (quoted in Kosztolány 2001: 123). Later members of the Democratic Opposition, such as Gábor Havas and János Ladányi, participated in the founding of the first independent Romani organization in Hungary, Phralipe. In the early 1990s, the liberal SzDSz, the political party that emerged from the Democratic Opposition, strengthened its image as a vehement protector of minorities and supported Romani activists. After 1994, it placed its liberal and monetarist economic policies in the foreground, and less attention was devoted to minority issues (Körösényi 1999: 42). In Czechoslovakia, Romani activists found access to the Civic Forum (OF), which formed a broad-based opposition against the communists. Later on, however, no party sought to be the ethnic representatives of the Roma, or other minorities gained priority. Yet a limited number of individual Romani activists were still accepted as candidates for parties both on the left and the right side of the political spectrum.

Conclusion

In the decade after the collapse of communism in Central Europe, official attitudes toward minorities in the Czech Republic, Hungary, and Slovakia underwent a fundamental change. In this chapter, I have offered a detailed description of how in the course of the fifteen years following 1989 these states elaborated domestic minority policies and special policies on Roma, how institutions evolved, and in what way these developments were influenced by day-to-day politics. I have also attempted to place the evolution in its historical context by considering the importance of the pre-1989 period.

The main hypothesis of the "political process" explanation of ethnic minority mobilization is that mobilization is strongly determined by changes in the formal and informal political environment. On the basis of the explorations offered in this chapter, one may conclude that by the end of the 1980s the domestic political context in Central Europe offered an increasing number of opportunities to ethnic mobilizers. The change of most consequence may have been the introduction of the freedom of association under an ethnic label. At the same time, I have shown that the domestic opportunity structure for Romani mobilization in Central Europe did not remain undifferentiated. Divergent political traditions and specific national interests were pivotal in determining the different paths taken by the countries toward the adoption of a minority rights model.

It is now time to attend to the development of the Romani movement during the periods described. Into what structures did the Romani movement crystallize at particular points in time? What were the events around which Romani movement actors tried to mobilize support? This is what I will turn to in the next chapter.

Chapter 3

Ethnic Politics from Below

After 1989, the spectrum of potential sites for political action on the basis of Romani identity in Central Europe broadened considerably. One way in which activists hoped to find public support for their claims was through establishing ethnically based political parties. Romani political parties were seen by many as organizational sites that should be able gain a position at the forefront of the Romani movement; through party politics activists believed they could not only make unambiguous assertions about their ethnic basis—and, in this way, nurture solidarity among Romani communities—but could also make clear that their goals were inherently political.

Besides parties, however, all kinds of other organizations and groupings came into being. Sometimes these were registered and well-established associations with names and activities that suggested an unequivocal concern with the formulation and defense of Romani interests (such as information centers dealing with news on Roma, organizations seeking to develop contact between Roma through the Internet, organizations documenting the human rights situation of the Roma and offering legal support to Romani victims of injustice, and so forth); at other times these were more informal and episodic gatherings, not necessarily with political aims (such as ad hoc protest groups, religious gatherings, musical ensembles etc.). Of course, the boundaries between these categories are blurry: a grouping could find itself in the hybrid area between established and episodic, or it could easily shift from one category to another. A special position was occupied by those organizations that had a *supportive* agenda: they did not identify themselves as Romani, but their activities were almost exclusively directed at the Roma.

This chapter will not deal with this latter category of supportive organizations but is devoted to exploring and charting the organizations and actions of those Romani activists who have couched their activism clearly in terms of ethnic politics. The first part of the chapter discusses electoral forms of Romani political action (through Romani parties and mainstream parties). The latter part examines nonelectoral forms of political action, focusing on a number of particular events that were pivotal in generating increased collective action.

Before turning to these sections in detail, however, a brief note should be made on the methods used for the analysis in this chapter. One way of studying the emergence and development of Romani politics from below would be to count the number of organizations. The available literature on the Roma in Central Europe contains various numerical assessments of movement activity (Barany 2002: 207; Crowe 1995: 105; Klimová 2002; Šiklová 1999; Vašečka 2001: 179). Thus one finds authors reporting that, for example, in Czechoslovakia in 1990 there were more or less forty independent Romani organizations. In 1997 this figure had apparently risen to 113 in the Czech Republic alone. In 1999, the same authors tell us, Slovakia was home to ninety-two Romani organizations. Hungary in the beginning of the 1990s had eighteen of such organizations and the figure increased to about 250 in the latter half of the decade.

Ostensibly, the numbers present straightforward evidence of the expansion of the Central European Romani movement in the 1990s. In reality, however, this needs to be put in perspective. There is less general agreement on the available figures than may appear at first sight. Not only can one find authors who cite much lower figures; the overwhelming majority of the authors also remain extremely vague about the *kinds* of organizations they have counted or on what sources they have based their estimates. This clearly limits the evidential value of the available numerical assessments. But their major disadvantage is that they are not based on a common definition of the term "Romani organization." Some of the scores may easily include types of organizations that were excluded in others. Certain authors, for example, may not have counted Romani political parties, while others may not have included supportive organizations. Even from the lists of the officially registered membership organizations kept at the ministries of interior of the three countries, one cannot without problems identify the exact number of Romani organizations. The registered names do not always contain information about ethnic identification, and the lists are hardly a basis for gaining insight into the activities of the registered organizations, so it is not always possible to know whether their activities are directed towards the Roma. Moreover, it is impossible to know from the lists whether the organizations are indeed functioning, and to what extent their activities and actions have had any public impact. Some registered Romani organizations may have only existed on paper. Other organizations may have been active without having been officially registered (Crowe 1995: 105).

But even if we were to have reliable data at our disposal, it would be debatable whether the *number* of organizations would indeed constitute a good operational measure of the level of Romani movement activity. An increase in the number of organizations can as much point to fragmentation and diffusion of interest defense as to movement growth. At a certain point Romani political parties in Slovakia, for example, outnumbered the Magyar parties, but this did not mean that the success of the Magyar movement had waned and the Romani movement was flourishing.

For these reasons, this chapter will take into account more than mere numbers. It will attempt to offer insight into the heart of Romani activism between 1990 and 2004 by describing the positions that some of the important aspiring movement leaders found themselves in and the dilemmas they were faced with. In other words, instead of analyzing Romani organizational growth on the basis of numerical data, I will look in depth at a small selection of organizations, more precisely those organizations that have had a tangible impact on public life, be it in politics, media, or culture. The idea behind such an approach is that ultimately numbers are less important than public attention. A small group of people or a small number of organizations may be quite successful in setting a movement into motion, especially if they catch the attention of key public figures and media.

This approach also allows one to explore the broad range of factors — some of them rather difficult to express in numbers—that led to what many people see as the two main characteristics of the Romani movement: (a) its apparent lack of mass support, and (b) the fragmentation and diffusion of the movement, or at least, its apparent lack of unity. Usually, both phenomena are attributed to the "black box" of Romani culture. Many consider deep-seated, largely inexplicable, cultural divisions between various Romani groups to be a major factor hindering the formation of a unified Romani movement. The lack of mass mobilization is usually blamed on the supposedly typical attitudes of the Roma. I will argue that the story is more complex. One might find additional, if not more important factors by considering the available strategic choices Romani activists are faced with and the circumstances in which aspiring movement leaders have to decide on these choices. The Roma's belated, rather ineffective and remarkably slow development of minority nationalism is not simply the result of their supposedly unique and ingrained aversion to political mobilization. Much of it is in fact explicable by reference to the broader political context.

Romani Identity and Electoral Politics

How old is the Romani movement in Europe? Attempts to voice Romani concerns at the political level are older than one might perhaps expect. Anthropologists Elena Marushiakova and Vesselin Popov (2001b) locate some early roots of the Romani movement in the Balkans at the beginning of the twentieth century. They describe small-scale initiatives such as congresses, campaigns for voting rights, and Romani newspapers. Often mentioned in the literature is the endeavor of the Kwiek family in Poland in the course of the 1930s to find a territory in India or Africa in order to establish there a Romani state (Ficowski 1989: 37).

More successful attempts to organize an international political movement date back to the 1960s and 1970s, with the foundation of the Comité International Tzigane (CIT) in Paris in 1965, the establishment of local Romani organizations in the United Kingdom, Spain, France, and Czechoslovakia in the latter half of the 1960s, and the organization of the first World Romani Congress (WCR) in London in 1971, attended by representatives from at least eight countries (see e.g. Acton and Klímová 2001; Marushiakova and Popov 2001b; Puxon 2000). These were the first efforts in organizing an international movement in Europe (at that time predominantly in Western Europe) around a common Romani identity, raising demands on the state and publicly constructing and defending the interests of the group "as a whole."

In the individual Central European countries, one can discern at least a few early instances of domestic mobilization. Political opportunities for ethnic mobilization were no doubt restricted during the communist period, but at certain points, policies were implemented that allowed and institutionalized ethnic identification. Many instances of Romani mobilization in that period were responses to top-down political initiatives, and were state controlled. Yet not all Romani organizations that were established during communist times should be seen as state puppet organizations (Guy 2002). Sometimes personal initiatives by individuals within a state-controlled organization were able to strengthen that organization's independent character. Sometimes limited forms of Romani mobilization took place in informal and dissident networks, largely outside the realm of state control. Although one can definitely not speak of a large, independently organized Romani movement during the communist period, one sees at various points in time the emergence of a crucial division between those Romani activists who wanted to challenge the communist state institutions and those who thought working *within* those institutions would lead to more success. As I showed earlier, in Hungary traces of this division were perceptible in more recent discussions and mutual accusations between new and older generations of activists.

The importance of the older initiatives, however, pales before the impact of the events of the 1990s. It was only in the last decade of the twentieth century that Romani mobilization in Central Europe gained greater momentum. One of the most visible expressions thereof was the emergence of Romani political parties and Romani candidates participating in national elections. This development posed new challenges to mobilizers. Immediately two important discussions arose among Romani activists. The first discussion centered upon the question whether it was necessary and feasible to engage in electoral politics, or whether it was better to engage in nonpartisan mobilization. For those who agreed that involvement in electoral politics was a necessary step, there was still the question of what *kind* of party to align with. The fundamental choice that aspirant Romani politicians saw themselves faced with was between involvement in a mainstream political party and involvement in an ethnically based political party. I will discuss both realms of political action in turn.

Romani Candidates and Mainstream Political Parties

Czech and Slovak Republics

During the period from 1990 to 2002, several Romani candidates in Central Europe contested parliamentary elections for mainstream, non-ethnically based political parties. In some instances, Romani candidates were able to enter the central arenas of political power through participating in or forging alliances with such a political party. This was possible especially in the beginning of the 1990s in Czechoslovakia, where the formation of political parties was primarily based on the division between communists and anti-communists. In the 1990 elections, a total of eleven MPs who identified themselves as Roma were elected to the various parliamentary assemblies of the federation (twelve if one includes human rights lawyer Klára Samková, the one non-Romani candidate who was nevertheless regarded by many as a Romani representative because of her membership in a Romani political party). Six of them were candidates for one of the two large dissident movement organizations, Public Against Violence (VPN) and Civic Forum (OF). I interviewed some of the Romani activists who were then elected and these interviews revealed that they saw the political programs of these large parties as less important than the mere fact that they had been elected. The political influence of the elected Romani activists was no doubt quite small. Some of them claimed that due to their parliamentary work the Slovak republic-level government had adopted—as one of the first governments in the region—a resolution that formally recognized the Roma as a national minority. Slovak Romani activist Klára Orgovánová, who was at that time advisor to the Slovak government (the Čarnogurský government from 1991 to 1993), believed, however, that the passing of this resolution had been more related to the Slovak government's eagerness to demonstrate a progressive record on inter-ethnic relations, than to demands lodged by Romani activists in parliament.

Soon after the 1990 elections, divergent opinions about how the common goal of economic and political transition was to be realized led to the break-up of the two large reform movements (Mansfeldová 1998: 195–96). In the Czech part of the country, the Civic Forum disintegrated into the liberal-oriented Civic Movement (OH) and the free market-oriented Civic Democratic Party (ODS); while in the Slovak Republic VPN disintegrated into the left-oriented and nationalist-populist Movement for a Democratic Slovakia (HZDS) and the more right-oriented Civic Democratic Union (ODÚ). Within these more narrowly defined political formations, candidates who had campaigned primarily on the basis of Romani identity less easily found their own niche. Apart from Ladislav Body, who remained an MP for the Communist Party of Czechoslovakia (KSČ) in the Czech National Council, all the Romani activists disappeared from the legislatures after the 1992 elections. It was not until the elections of 1998 that another Romani activist was elected to the Czech parliament.

On the basis of the official reports of the election results and interviews with the candidates themselves, I drew up an exhaustive list of all the politicians who identified themselves publicly as Roma and were elected to national legislatures in the Czechoslovak Federation and the Czech and Slovak Republics between 1990 and 2002. Table 3.1 illustrates the modest level of success of Romani identity as a part of the developing party identity systems in both countries.

Table 3.1 Overview of elected Romani candidates in the national legislatures of the Czechoslovak Federation, the Czech Republic, and the Slovak Republic (1990–2002).

Czechoslovak Federation (1990–92)
1990 elections *Federal Assembly — Chamber of the People (Sněmovna lidu)*, Czech vote • No Romani candidates were elected on mainstream party lists. *Federal Assembly — Chamber of Nations (Sněmovny národů)*, Czech section • Klara Samková was elected as a Civic Forum (OF) representative with the profile of "Romani representative." In total, OF received 50 seats (66.7 %). Samková did not identify herself as Roma, but she publicly associated herself with the biggest Romani party, Romani Civic Initiative (ROI). *Czech National Council (Česka národní rada)* • Romani candidate Ladislav Body was elected for the Communist Party of Czechoslovakia (KSČ). • Romani candidates Dezider Balog, Ondřej Giňa, Karel Holomek, Zdeněk Guži, Milan Tatár were elected for the OF, which in total won 127 seats (63.5 %). • Romani candidate Vladimír Zeman was elected for the regional interest party, Selfgoverning Democracy Movement/Association for Moravia and Silesia (HSD/SMS), which in total won 19 seats (8.4 %). *Federal Assembly — Chamber of the People (Sněmovna lidu)*, Slovak vote • Romani candidate Gejza Adam was elected for the People against Violence (VPN), which in total won 19 seats (32.5 %). • Romani candidate Vincent Danihel was elected for the Communist Party of Czechoslovakia (KSČ), which in total won 8 seats (13.8 %). *Federal Assembly — Chamber of the Nations (Sněmovny národů)*, Slovak section • Romani candidate Karol Seman was elected for the KSČ, which in total received 12 seats (13.4 %).

Table 3.1 Continued.

Czechoslovak Federation (1990–92)

1990 elections cont.,

Slovak National Council (Slovenská národná rada)
- Romani candidate Anna Koptová was elected for VPN, which in total received 48 seats (29.3 %).

1992 elections
Federal Assembly — Chamber of the People, Czech vote
- No Romani candidates elected on mainstream party lists.

Federal Assembly — Chamber of Nations, Czech section
- No Romani candidates elected on mainstream party lists.

Czech National Council
- Romani candidate Ladislav Body was elected for the Levý blok (Left Bloc), a party that in total won 35 seats (17.5%). The Czech National Council ceased to exist at the end of 1992. The Chamber of Deputies of the Parliament of the Czech Republic then replaced it. Its composition remained as it was until the election of 1996. Ladislav Body remained in the Chamber of Deputies as a member of the Left Bloc faction.

Federal Assembly — Chamber of the People, Slovak vote
- No Romani candidates elected on mainstream party lists.

Federal Assembly — Chamber of Nations, Slovak section
- No Romani candidates elected on mainstream party list.

Slovak National Council
- No Romani candidates elected on mainstream party lists. The Slovak National Council of the Czechoslovak Federation became the National Council of the Slovak Republic after the split of Czechoslovakia. Its composition remained as it was until the elections of 1994.

Czech Republic (1993–2002)

1996 elections
Chamber of Deputies (Poslanecká Sněmovna)
- No Romani candidates were elected on mainstream party lists.

Senate (Senát)
- No Romani candidates were elected on mainstream party lists.

1998 elections
Chamber of Deputies
- Romani candidate Monika Horáková was elected for the Freedom Union (US). The US won a total of 19 seats (9.5 % of seats).

Senate
- No Romani candidates were elected on mainstream party lists.

2000 elections
Senate
- No Romani candidates were elected on mainstream party lists.

2002 elections
Chamber of Deputies
- No Romani candidates were elected on mainstream party lists.

Table 3.1 *Continued.*

Slovak Republic (1993–2002)
1994 elections
National Council of the Slovak Republic (Národná rada Slovenskej republiky)
• No Romani candidates were elected on mainstream party lists.
1998 elections
National Council of the Slovak Republic
• No Romani candidates were elected on mainstream party lists.
2002 elections
National Council of the Slovak Republic
• No Romani candidates were elected on mainstream party lists.

Sources: Interviews; Český Statistický Úřad (2002), <http://www.volby.cz>; Štatistický úrad Slovenskej republiky (2002), <http://www.statistics.sk/struk/volby.htm>; <http://www.essex.ac.uk/elections/>.

The failure of Romani electoral politics after the 1990 elections is also obvious from the decreasing number of Romani activists in mainstream party candidate lists. Even after obtaining a seat in parliament in the first elections, Romani candidates did not automatically run again in the elections following. When they did, the results were disappointing without exception. In the Czech Republic, the well-known Romani activist Karel Holomek appeared on the 1996 list of Free Democrats/ National Socialist Liberal Party (SD-LSNS) in the electoral district of South-Moravia, but this list did not manage to win a single seat. In the elections of 1996 and 1998, none of the leading political parties had well-known Romani activists on their lists: neither the Civic Democratic Party (ODS), the strongest party on the right side of the political spectrum, nor the Social Democrats (ČSSD), the party that succeeded in building a strong left-wing opposition between 1992 and 1996. In 1998, Monika Horáková was one of the few Romani candidates and was elected for the Freedom Union (US) to the Czech Chamber of Deputies. This was seen as a very important symbolic victory for the Romani movement in the Czech Republic, and also internationally she was considered an important exponent of a new generation of Romani political activists. She herself, however, claimed to be in the first place a representative of her party, and not a representative of the Roma.

In the 2002 Czech parliamentary elections, some smaller parties, such as the Party for Social Security (SŽJ) and Vote for the Future (VPB), had a small number of candidates on their lists who actively presented themselves as Romani candidates, but none of them were elected. None of the main contending parties in this election—the social-democratic ČSSD, the rightist-liberal ODS, and *Koalice* (or "Coalition," an alliance of the Christian Democrats of the KDU-ČSL and the Liberal Conservative

US-DEU)—had any Romani activists on their candidate lists. These parties emphasized their openness to all ethnicities, but declared at the same time that party campaigning and representation had to be founded on party identity and not on any ethnic identification.[1]

In the early Slovak parliamentary elections of 1994, which brought Vladimír Mečiar (HZDS) to power for the first time in an independent Slovakia, four Romani candidates appeared on the list of opposition party Democratic Union (DÚ), but none of them were elected (Vašečka 1999a: 258). Romani activists played as good as no role in this election. In the 1998 elections two well-known Romani activists, Jan Kompuš of the Romani Civic Initiative (ROI-SR) and József Ravasz of the Party for the Protection of the Rights of the Roma (SOPR) quit their respective Romani political parties to be able to run on the HZDS list. This development was quite remarkable since the HZDS was generally not known as a minority-friendly party and had even campaigned explicitly against the demands of the Magyar minority. The deal was to a certain extent understandable from the viewpoint of the HZDS, which clearly wanted to get rid of its anti-minority image. HZDS's leadership may also have been aware of the possibility that it would lose the elections to the newly formed SDK and wanted therefore to attract as many voters as possible from among the minorities. The choice of the Romani activists to run on the HZDS ballot seemed less obvious, especially in the case of Ravasz, a well-known Hungarian-speaking Rom. The ambition of the party of Ravasz had precisely been to attract and unite people from the Hungarian-speaking Romani communities around the southern city of Dunajská Streda. Arguably, both Kompuš and Ravasz had turned to the HZDS more because of the inevitable popularity of the party and its willingness to fund their pre-election campaigns, than for reasons related to the ideological stance of the HZDS or its policy objectives. According to Ravasz, he and Kompuš had been willing to be placed on any of the candidate lists of the major political parties, but the HZDS was the only party ready to offer them such places. My interview with Ravasz revealed that he had not been sure whether he would have stayed loyal to the HZDS, had he been elected to parliament. Knowing that the HZDS had the means to reach large segments of the population through its campaign, even in more isolated places, he saw the HZDS as a good vehicle for enhancing the visibility of Romani interest representation. The price for this was the potential alienation of a part of his electorate among the Hungarian speakers. Choosing for the HZDS positioned him firmly against the camp of those parties that aimed to represent the Magyar minorities.

In the end the whole operation was of no avail in electoral terms. Kompuš had a relatively favorable place on the list and would have had a chance of getting elected to parliament in the case of a massive HZDS victory, but weeks before the election he died in a car accident and was not replaced by another Romani candidate (Vašečka 1999a: 260). Ravasz received a little more than 3,000 preferential votes and was not able to secure one of the forty-three HZDS seats in the National Council. As a result, the most tangible and perhaps only real effect of the deal was that it made existing strategic divisions within the Romani movement even deeper. In contrast to ROI-SR and SOPR, a third Romani political party called the Romani Intelligentsia for Coexistence (RIZS) had forged an accord on pre-election and post-election cooperation with the major contender of the HZDS, the Slovak Democratic Coalition (SDK). The SDK had formed an anti-HZDS alliance with a number of other parties, among others the Party of the Magyar Coalition (SMK), which won the election and appointed the new prime minister (Mikuláš Dzurinda). However, here also the incentive of RIZS to sign an agreement with the SDK had less to do with party programs than with calculations about access to political power. RIZS activists had hoped that when the SDK came into power, some of them would be recruited for key positions in the government institutions responsible for implementing Romani policies. They were more than disappointed when this did not happen. After 1998, however, Romani activists continued to seek links with mainstream parties for the purpose of getting elected without paying too much attention to the incorporation of their demands in the programs of these main parties.

In the run-up to the 2002 parliamentary elections in Slovakia, politicians from a small Romani political party named the Slovak Romani Initiative (RIS)—a party that had originated from a split within RIZS in 1999—made clear it wanted to support opposition party HZDS. The president of RIS, Alexander Patkoló, found his way on to the HZDS list, but was not elected. Striking about these 2002 elections was that a number of other parties for the first time listed Romani candidates. This included the Party of the Magyar Coalition (SMK), which now clearly targeted those Roma who were part of the party's traditional electorate of Hungarian speakers. More surprisingly perhaps was the fact that two new parties, the right-wing liberal party Smer (Direction) and the center-liberal New Citizen's Alliance (ANO) fielded some Romani candidates. Two Roma also appeared on the list of the Slovak Communist Party (KSS) and the Slovak Christian Democratic Union (SDKÚ). None of these candidates, however, were on favorable places—a fact which indicates that none of the parties full-heartedly embraced the idea of Romani mobilization. Some parties, the SDKÚ in particular, officially rejected the idea that Romani candidates in their party lists should represent ethnically restricted interests. Unlike the situation in Hungary in 2002, parties did not actively engage in creating a Romani electorate in order to find the last necessary votes to effectuate a power shift. Although other parties, such as ANO, attempted to let the importance of Romani participation figure as a topic in the pre-election campaign, nowhere in Slovakia did the composition of the electoral lists reflect a radical choice for minority inclusion. But the development does at least suggest that the act of including Romani candidates in mainstream party lists slowly attained a certain symbolic importance.

Hungary

Between 1990 and 1994 the Hungarian National Assembly contained three MPs who were known to be Romani activists. Two Romani candidates (Antónia Hága and Aladár Horváth) had been elected from the list of the liberal party, Alliance of Free Democrats (SzDSz), and one Romani MP (Tamás Péli) had been a candidate of the Socialist Party (MSzP). Of these three, only Hága was able to keep a seat until 1998. There were no Romani activists in the National Assembly between 1998 and 2002. Antónia Hága and Ágnes Daróczi appeared on the national list of the SzDSz in 1998, but did not obtain mandates.

Although, later on, the MSzP took some pride in the fact that it had brought a Romani candidate to parliament, it is debatable whether, at the time, the party saw Péli as a representative of the Romani movement. The MSzP had been rather reluctant to support ethnic interest representation. The inclusion of minority candidates on the SzDsZ list fitted much more in the party's general moral commitment to human rights and minority rights. Strikingly, however, this is not necessarily how the minority MPs themselves viewed their position. After four years of parliamentary work for the SzDSz, Horváth found that he had not been able to express himself as a Romani activist within the structures of the SzDSz group in parliament. Hága, on the other hand, found that she was too often seen *merely* as a Romani activist—someone who had the right to speak only when the issue concerned the Roma. Whether or not ethnic interest representation in nonethnic parties was possible remained a moot point among Romani activists. It is significant that it was the struggle for votes, and not so much moral or programmatic principles on minority interest representation, that ultimately led to a marked increase of Romani candidates in mainstream lists.

In the run-up to the April 2002 parliamentary elections, it became clear that the tight race between the main contenders (the socialist MSzP, the right-wing liberal Fidesz, and the moderate nationalists of the MDF) increased competition for the so-called Romani vote. In December 2001, a large number of Romani organizations under the umbrella of the organization that dominated the National Gypsy Self-Government (Lungo Drom), pledged to support the government center-right coalition lists of Fidesz and MDF, in exchange for their granting three places to Romani candidates on its national list and seven places on their regional lists. The chairman of Lungo Drom and president of the National Gypsy Self-Government, Flórián Farkas, was listed among the top twenty candidates of the Fidesz–MDF national list and was elected to

Table 3.2 Overview of elected Romani candidates in the Hungarian parliament (1990–2002).

Hungary 1990–2002
1990 elections   *Hungarian National Assembly (Országgyűlés)*   • Romani candidates Aladár Horváth and Antónia Hága elected for the Alliance of Free Democrats (SzDSz). SzDSz received a total of 92 seats (23.8 %).   • Romani candidate Tamás Péli was elected for the Socialist Party (MSzP). The MSzP received a total 33 seats (8.5%).
1994 elections   *Hungarian National Assembly*   • Romani candidate Antónia Hága elected for the SzDSz. SzDSz received a total of 69 seats (17.8 %).   • Romani candidate Tamás Péli elected for the MSzP. MSzP received a total of 209 seats (54.1 %). Péli died in 1996.
1998 elections   *Hungarian National Assembly*   • No Romani candidates elected on mainstream party lists.
2002 elections   *Hungarian National Assembly*   • Romani candidates Flórián Farkas, József Varga, and Mihály Lukács elected for Fidesz-Hungarian Democratic Forum (MDF). Fidesz-MDF received 188 seats (48.7 %).   • Romani candidate László Teleki elected for the Socialist Party (MSzP). The MSzP received a total of 178 seats (46.11 %).

Sources: Interviews; Parliamentary Information Service, <http://www.mkogy.hu>; Ministry of Interior, Central Data Processing, Registration, and Election Office, <http://www.election.hu>; <http://www.essex.ac.uk/elections/>.

parliament together with two other Romani activists supported by Fidesz–MDF (József Varga and Mihály Lukács). At the same time the Socialist Party (MSzP) decided *not* to nominate two well-known Romani activists, Aladár Horváth and Éva Orsós, who had wanted to form a political alternative to Lungo Drom within the MSzP; but the party did field six other Romani candidates and brought László Teleki to the parliament, who was at the time the vice-chairman of the National Gypsy Self-Government and had the image of a less radical Romani activist. Romani activist Blanka Kozma was nominated as a candidate for the SzDSz in the district of Borsod-Abaúj-Zemplén, but was not elected. (See Table 3.2 for a summary.)

As these overviews suggest, the total number of Romani activists elected to national legislatures on mainstream party tickets remained very low throughout the decade, leading to the situation in 2003 that only in Hungary some of them had managed to get elected. The proportion of Roma included in mainstream party lists also remained low, even in the cases of Hungary and Slovakia, where there was a slight increase in the run-up to the 2002 elections. This is striking in the context of the electoral competition in the region. In Hungary and Slovakia, a party could in theory secure or tilt power balances simply by attracting large parts of the Romani voters. Nonetheless, mainstream parties in general did not deeply engage in such attempts. They usually argued that good Romani politicians were few and far between and that putting Romani politicians on the list would not necessarily mean that Roma would vote for them. In the Czech Republic, where the demographic weight of the potential Romani electorate is too small to have any political influence, parties most clearly stated that if Romani candidates were to appear on their lists, they should not be seen as Romani activists any more but as representatives of the party. Their Romani identity was seen as a private affair, not as an expression of their political identity.

Seeking access to mainstream parties was thus for many Romani activists a far from obvious choice. Those who did make that choice and sought to find a place for Romani politics within the landscape of mainstream political parties had to face a number of crucial difficulties. Not only did they run the risk of being completely marginalized within the parties they were campaigning for; in some cases the identity they intended to represent could not find expression within those parties. On the other hand, many believed that campaigning for a mainstream party was the only realistic way of mobilizing people into a Romani electorate. Many Romani activists argued that without the resources and logistic support of well-established mainstream parties it would be impossible to become known in the dispersed and economically isolated communities they sought to mobilize. That the overwhelming majority of the Roma who appeared on mainstream party lists also had been involved in attempts to form ethnically based political parties shows that their participation in mainstream parties was usually motivated by political calculation and not by the specific content of political programs of the parties in question.

This latter argument is supported by evidence from the first Hungarian elections for the European Parliament. In 2004, Hungary hit international news headlines for being the country with the first two Romani MEPs. In December 2004, Viktória Mohácsi, former ministerial commissioner responsible for Romani integration at the Hungarian ministry of education, took the place of Gábor Demszky, mayor of Budapest, in the delegation of the Free Democrats (SzDSz). A few months before, in June 2004, Lívia Járóka had already become an MEP for Fidesz. This latter case is especially interesting. Although not a member of the party she represents, Romani activist and anthropologist Lívia Járóka was elected directly from the list of the right-wing liberal party Fidesz to the European Parliament. Interestingly enough, before Fidesz asked her to figure on the list, Járóka had been very critical of the party's stance towards the Roma. When she was asked to join the list, however, she agreed. She insisted that she was not being used just to attract the votes of the Roma and argued that it was her moral duty to seize the opportunity to represent the Roma at a high political level.[2] This is arguably a good illustration of how even mainstream parties that do not have an outspoken minority-friendly image can figure as important vehicles for Romani mobilization. Járóka's electoral success has also highlighted the fact that the usual channels for Romani mobilization in Hungary should not necessarily be seen as the most effective ones. Járóka had been an unknown face in Hungarian minority politics before 2004; she had not been a prominent Romani activist, had never belonged to a Romani political party, and she had not participated as a candidate in any of the minority self-government elections.

Romani Political Parties

In the three countries under study, the 1990s saw a profusion of ethnically based Romani parties, all with the aim of creating and representing a Romani constituency. In Hungary, the number of Romani parties increased steadily during the course of the decade. According to the registration list of the Hungarian Central Registration and Election Office, just one Romani party was registered in 1989; at the end 1995 this figure first rose to five, in 1998 to seven, and finally, in 2001, another one was added to the list.[3] Not all of these parties participated in national elections, but of those that did take part none ever managed to gain mandates in parliament. In 1990, the Hungarian Gypsy Social Democratic Party (MCSzDP) participated but foundered at 0.01 percent of the votes in one single-member district in the first round. In 1994 the Hungarian Gypsy Solidarity Party (CMSP) was the only Romani party to participate in the elections, but its single-member candidate received merely 0.06 percent in the first round. The 1998 elections saw the participation of the Democratic Party of the Hungarian Gypsies (MCDP), which polled 0.01 percent single-member district votes in the first and the second round. The 1998 elections furthermore saw the participation of a party that sought to represent all national and ethnic minorities in Hungary. The party was named Nationality Forum (*Nemzetiségi Fórum*) and fielded a few Romani candidates. But once again the initiative was not a success. For the 2002 elections a number of newly established Romani parties with similar names announced their participation, among them parties such as the Hungarian Romani Party, the Democratic Romani Party, the Democratic Party of the Hungarian Gypsies, and the Democratic Party of Hungarian Roma. All claimed a large support from among the Roma, but none of them achieved better results than any Romani party in previous attempts.

In the Czech Republic, too, Romani parties failed to be significant in electoral terms. In contrast to Hungary, however, the number of Romani political parties decreased during recent years. In 1998, there were five officially registered Romani political parties, a number that according to the Ministry of the Interior dropped to three in 2000. The only Romani party that ever ran on its own in Czech national elections was the Romani Civic Initiative (ROI). It stood in the 1992 elections for the Federal Assembly and the Czech National Council, in the 1996 Senate elections, and in the 2002 elections for the Chamber of Deputies. The results were low in all these cases. In the 2002 parliamentary elections ROI foundered at a total of 523 votes—barely 0.01 percent.[4]

The Slovak Republic differs from the Czech Republic and Hungary in the sense that the number of registered Romani-based political parties was even higher, and that there were several attempts over the years to form larger coalitions. In 1999, the Slovak authorities registered fifteen ethnically based Romani political parties, a list that was even extended to eighteen in 2000, and to twenty in 2002 (Šebesta 2003: 209). Many of these parties never participated in national elections, and when they did, they never managed to fulfill promises of attracting large constituencies and never passed the electoral thresholds for representation. During the 1990 elections for the Federal Assembly, voters had the possibility to vote a coalition of the Democratic Union of Roma and the Party for the Integration of Roma in Slovakia (DÚRS) to the Federal Assembly and the Slovak National Council. But with only 0.73 percent of the vote this coalition failed spectacularly. The Romani parties Roma Civic Initiative (ROI-SR) and the Party for Labor and Security (SPI) stood separately in the 1992 elections, but reached no more than 0.6 percent and 0.97 percent of the vote—far below the 5 percent threshold. In the 1994 elections, ROI–SR enjoyed support from the HZDS, but again did not manage to attract enough votes (0.67 percent). No separate Romani parties took part in the 1998 elections.

The bad experiences of Romani activists in Slovakia with giving up their membership in an ethnic party in order to run for a mainstream party renewed an interest in ethnically based Romani politics in the beginning of the 2000s. A number of Romani parties in Slovakia, most notably the Romani Civic Initiative (ROI-SR), were in the autumn of 2000 involved in a rather ambitious attempt to unite Romani politicians in an electoral platform for the parliamentary elections of September 2002. The attempt led to the establishment of an umbrella organization called the Romani Parliament (*Rómsky Parlament*), which included thirteen Romani political parties and twenty-five nonpartisan civic associations.[5] Although this was perhaps a useful exercise in fostering communication among Slovak Romani activists and parties, it did not lead to the establishment of an electoral coalition. Already in the autumn of 2001 strong divisions emerged within the *Rómsky Parlament*.

Meanwhile, as was mentioned in the previous section, the Slovak Romani Initiative (RIS)—the sole Romani party that had not entered the *Rómsky Parlament*—placed its bet on electoral cooperation with the HZDS of former prime minister Mečiar. This seemed to announce a repetition of some of the peculiar earlier strategies employed by both Romani activists and the HZDS. The standing of the HZDS in matters of minority protection had not in any particular way improved over the years, but thanks to its popularity among Slovak voters it nevertheless continued to appeal to Romani politicians in search of votes. But again, coalitions did not further the case of the individual Romani politicians. Whatever the Roma claimed was to be gained from these coalitions, it had no lasting effect on people's willingness to vote for them. In the country's first-ever elections to regional parliaments in December 2001, the HZDS won the majority of seats, but none of the fourteen RIS candidates who appeared in lists in six regions were elected. Perhaps even more telling for the general situation of Romani parties in Slovakia is that in these same elections ROI-SR did not succeed in getting even one of its candidates elected, although it had listed a total of sixty candidates in four regions (forty candidates alone in the Košice region).[6] These results made clear that the chances of Romani parties in the 2002 Slovak parliamentary elections would be quite limited. Two Romani parties participated in these elections. ROI-SR in the end did not do better than 0.29 percent of the votes; even in the district of Spišská Nová Ves, where the party received most of its votes, they only managed to attract 1.83 percent. The Political Movement of the Roma in Slovakia (also known as ROMA), a new Romani political party at the 2002 elections, scored in general a mere 0.21 percent; only in the district of Rimavská Sobota did they manage to attract the marginally better score of 1,354 votes (3.27 percent).

Why did Romani ethnically based political parties in the three countries perform so badly? The success of political parties of ethnic minorities is in general dependent on a number of *structural* and *systemic* factors. One structural factor that is often mentioned is the composition of the potential electorate of these parties. The fact that Romani communities have a younger age structure means that a smaller share of their population is of voting age.[7] This may be a part of the explanation, especially in the Czech Republic, where the potential Romani electorate is rather small: given the low census score for the Romani population, it is unrealistic to expect high electoral support for ethnic Romani parties. But this reason is not entirely valid in the Hungarian and Slovak cases. If all the people who officially identified themselves as Roma in these countries had voted for a Romani party, such a party would have been relatively successful. It would, perhaps, not immediately have helped them to find access to national parliaments, but it might at least have put these parties on the map as the political wing of the Romani movement, both locally and nationally.

There is another structural reason that needs to be considered. In all three countries Romani activists primarily tried to mobilize people who find themselves in situations of poverty and marginality. As a result, they had to deal with a phenomenon that is sometimes believed to characterize poor populations in general: the acquiescence of these populations in their situation, the disbelief among them that political participation will remedy their problems. In the literature on social reform, much has been said about the theory of the socialization of poverty, the idea that poor populations learn to adapt to exclusion and oppression to such an extent that they do no longer feel the desire to organize and participate in combating marginality.[8] According to some of the authors in this field, the root cause of this lies not with these populations per se (although some are clearly not averse to a "blame the victim" approach), but with the situation of poverty that has driven them to passivity and political apathy (see, e.g., Patterson 2000). Because of the conditions in which they live, they may find the costs of participating in mainstream society higher than the costs of retreating into a position of sustained marginality, where there might be individual gains in the informal economy.

This theory, although highly controversial, may perhaps to some extent be considered helpful in explaining the persistence of economic marginality among a number of Romani communities—consider for example Michael Stewart's descriptions of the particular advantages that people find in participating in "Gypsy work" (Stewart 1997)—but with regard to explaining patterns of political participation it is not very useful. The explanation is premised on the idea that marginalized populations such as the Roma are not interested in general politics. Various research projects, however, have suggested that among Roma the potential for mobilization in domestic politics is not universally low—at least, it is not always much lower than the average among the total population. From survey results in Hungary collected by Ipsos-Szonda between May 1999 and June 2000, and the results of a survey on poverty and ethnicity in Central Europe, Hungarian sociologist János Ladányi concludes that among those identified as Roma the percentage of people who are willing to participate in elections is as high as 54 percent, and that is not much lower than the 60 percent self-identified confident electoral participants among the non-Romani populations in Hungary (Ladányi 2002). Looking at voter turnouts during the 2002 parliamentary elections in Slovakia, it is clear that results are lower in the eastern districts, and sometimes quite low in municipalities that are known to have large poor populations. But at the same time, on the district level the turnout never dropped below 58 percent. Even more telling are the results from a UNDP/ILO survey carried out in the Czech Republic, Hungary, and Slovakia between November 2001 and January 2002 among a sample of about 1,000 people in areas where according to the census there are concentrations of Roma (UNDP 2002). In this survey 63.3 percent of the respondents in Hungary reported that they had voted in the last elections. In Slovakia 64.2 percent of the respondents reported that they had done so. Only in the Czech Republic was the Romani turnout conspicuously lower (29.13 percent). On the basis of these crude measures, one may conclude that at least in Hungary and Slovakia the poor results of Romani candidates and parties during national elections are not necessarily linked to general political apathy among the Roma.

Are there other reasons, and where should we find them? It is worth considering some elements related to the way the political system is organized. In the three countries there were electoral thresholds that prevented smaller parties from entering the legislature. This made it more difficult for parties that wanted to attract voters on the principle of minority membership. For Romani parties in the Czech Republic, for example, the electoral threshold of 5 percent was higher than the highest estimates of the proportion of Roma among the total number of citizens. As a result, even Romani activists themselves knew that the chances of getting into parliament through an ethnic political party were as good as nonexistent. Instead of engaging into difficult attempts at broadening their electorate to those who do not necessarily identify themselves as Roma, a good deal of these activists preferred safer options outside electoral politics. The fact that Romani parties could not gain much visibility as long as they attracted less than 5 percent of the votes made it difficult for them to get their message communicated with their potential electorates. Electoral campaigning becomes easier as one becomes bigger and gains visibility. Romani parties never had a chance to attract the initial percentage of the votes necessary to support more successful campaigns.

This brings us to the factor of electoral competition. The previous chapter has shown that Romani political parties could not find powerful allies or inspiring models in the political parties of other ethnic groups, not even in Slovakia where there was a relatively effective Magyar mobilization. One of the reasons is that none of the three countries had an unambiguous ethnic party system. Some political parties derived their support from a single ethnic group, but the most important lines of political division were never related to ethnicity. This is most clearly the case for the Czech Republic and Hungary. There is relatively broad agreement among analysts that in these countries ethnic divisions were not crucial in the formation of political cleavages. In Hungary, political scientists have usually emphasized the existence of dichotomies tied to religion, the communist elites, and the division between urban and rural interests (Körösényi 1999: 59–70; Tóka 1998). In the Czech Republic the political cleavage structure in the first half of the 1990s was dominated by conflicting attitudes towards the federal state and towards the political and economic transition. Later on socioeconomic divisions became more important (Mansfeldová 1998). Zdenka Mansfeldová further argues that traditional conflict structures, such as state versus church, rural versus urban, or ethnic antagonism, were not articulated in Czech politics (Mansfeldová 1998: 205). Although some authors observed an ethnic dimension (Slovak versus Magyar and Slovak versus Czech) in Slovak electoral politics in the period before 1998 (Mesežnikov 1999: 57; Wolchik 1994), political scientists generally agree that this cleavage was never predominant, and that by 1998 it was completely overshadowed by the need for joint action against the authoritarianism of the Mečiar governments. As a result, most political parties in Slovakia defined themselves less by their ethnic affiliation than by their stance with respect to the HZDS (Friedman 2002: 305). Within such a party system, it was difficult for Romani parties to find a distinct and united ethnopolitical profile.

Another factor that helps to explain the failure of Romani parties might be discerned in the often turbid content of the political demands made by Romani politicians. I frequently had the impression from my interviews with activists who engaged in electoral politics that their motivation to do so was largely restricted to the *symbolic* value of ethnically based Romani representation. In other words, their political campaigns were to a large extent aimed at the Roma; they were aimed at "making" a unified group, expressing a coherent group identity, gaining control over the representation of the group. Rarely were they aimed, or so it seemed, at influencing policy. This strategy, however, brought them into trouble when more particular issues, for example the question of whether the Roma should be targeted by group-specific measures, were at the center of the debate. While in the beginning of the 1990s, the recognition of the Roma as a national minority emerged as a political demand, in more recent years Romani politicians usually came up with programs that contained just a handful of loose descriptions relating to the need to prevent discrimination and enforce human rights protection. Rarely aspirant Romani politicians made unambiguous statements about whether they were in favor of education in the Romani language or the recognition of Romani language as a minority language. Very often they also remained ambiguous about the ideological background of their statements.

This could also be linked to the intrinsic difficulty of developing a party program that is concrete enough to be mobilizing, but at the same time broad enough to appeal to the widely diverse demands and concerns springing from the heterogeneous circumstances in which Roma live. Furthermore, writing a program is not enough; it must also be distributed. Romani activists often mentioned the difficulty of communicating their programs to potential voters who live dispersed throughout the country in sometimes isolated areas with limited access to mass media and poor educational resources. This was especially problematic in combination with the lack of experience of most of the aspirant politicians in poorly funded parties.

The low importance attached to the development of a political program and influencing policy, the great importance attached to the symbolic value of Romani parties, and the focus on finding financial sources to assist Romani communities, no doubt constitute factors that also help to explain the divisions among Romani political parties. All the activists in such parties had more or less similar concerns and ideas, but differed in their calculations about how best to gain access to politics.

The Minority Self-government System in Hungary: Toward Ethnic Mobilization in Mainstream Politics?

The conclusions made above hold for Hungary as well as for the Czech and Slovak cases. The difference between Hungary and the two latter cases, however, is that Hungary has seen a spectacular increase in the involvement of Roma in public life through a separate institutional channel. Interestingly, the special rules for the construction of Romani representation through the self-government system did not lead to greater success for ethnically based Romani parties within the general political system. Why did this not happen?

When one compares election results, it is difficult to find an answer to this question. The figures merely show that many more people voted for Romani candidates to the minority self-governments than for Romani parties in the national elections. They also illustrate the continual growth of the number of Romani self-governments in absolute figures. In 1994, a total of 415 local Romani self-governments were elected and a further 61 in 1995. The majority of all minority self-governments in Hungary were Romani, even after the dissolution of a number of them during the first term. After the October 1998 self-government elections the number of the local Gypsy self-governments increased to 759. In 1999, the deputy president of the Office for Ethnic and National Minorities estimated that more than 3,000 Roma were taking part in local public life through the activities of the minority self-governments (Heizer 1999: 4). In the elections of October 2002, 1,003 local Romani self-governments were elected.

Their position as public figures might have helped some politicians from the National Gypsy Self-Government to get elected into parliament from mainstream party lists, but the self-government system as a whole clearly did not lead to a greater general success for Romani parties in parliamentary elections. Apart from the constraints of the electoral system and the fact that Hungary does not have an ethnic party system, additional reasons might be connected to the way voters evaluated the role of the minority self-governments. Two issues in particular are important here.

First, there is evidence suggesting that the potential Romani electorate did not see a close connection between the Romani self-governments and ethnic interest representation in mainstream politics. Local minority politics and mainstream politics were simply seen as two entirely different arenas. The above-mentioned UNDP/ILO survey found that in Hungary the overwhelming majority of the Roma interviewed (91.6 percent) could not name a Romani political party they would trust. This is consistent with the low scores attained by Romani parties in national elections. The broad participation in self-government elections, however, suggests that in the local arena trust in Romani representatives was much higher.

Second, some of my interviewees pointed out that those who had managed to get elected in the self-government system owed their support mainly to their profile as civil society actors, not to their actions in a political party. Romani organizations that were successful in the self-government elections acted very much like service organizations; they focused on strengthening ethnic communities and finding financial resources to fund projects aimed at directly assisting Romani communities. Lungo Drom is a case in point. Lungo Drom was very successful in the minority self-government system, but did not find in this an incentive to develop a separate program as a political party in mainstream elections. As a dominant force in the National Gypsy Self-Government, Lungo Drom was nevertheless able to gain a relatively strong profile among Roma as an organization with privileged access to state funding. The National Gypsy Self-Government's own resources were limited, but it enjoyed a degree of influence over significant sums of public money allocated for Romani programs and initiatives through its representation on the board of trustees of the public foundations responsible for funding minority projects (Kovats 2001a: 12). It is plausible that the self-governments enjoyed more support than the ethnic candidates in national elections precisely because self-governments were generally seen as bodies that were able to offer direct patronage to their supporters. Romani parties and candidates in mainstream elections could not realistically offer such prospects.

One example that illustrates this theory is that of the Romani activist László Teleki. Teleki led a local minority self-government in Nagykanizsa and managed to organize a relatively dense service network around it, including a weekend boarding school, a linguistic study group for Romani language, a youth teahouse, a traditional folk ensemble, a poetry group, and a legal aid service. His local success made Teleki so well known that he was elected deputy chair of the National Gypsy Self-Government in 1999 (Forray and Mohácsi 2002). His career in mainstream politics, however, did not lead through a Romani party. As indicated earlier, it was the Socialist Party (MSzP) that brought him into parliament in 2002 by offering him a favorable position on its list.

Nonelectoral Romani Mobilization in Hungary: Actors and Issues

Having detailed the various ways in which Romani activists have attempted to mobilize through electoral politics (either in Romani or mainstream parties), it is now time to explore the instances of Romani mobilization that have developed outside the arena of electoral politics. I examine Hungary first; in the last sections of this chapter I turn to the Czech and Slovak cases.

Nonelectoral politics is, of course, a broad terrain that cannot in any way be fully covered in a couple of sections. My main aim in the remainder of this chapter is not to tell the story of all movement activity, but rather to select a number of particular events that in my view have been key in generating episodes of increased movement activity in that part of the Romani movement that remained outside the realm of electoral competition. I am not primarily interested in the historical details of these key events but in deriving from the stories activists tell a map of the strategic divisions within the Romani movement. More specifically, I focus on some of the crucial tactical decisions that Romani activists had to make in response to these key events. The result is not a full-scale historical narrative of nonelectoral Romani movement activity in Central Europe, but it should at least give a good overview of the crucial defining moments in that history.

From Phralipe to the Roma Parliament: Attempts at Unification

In contrast to other countries in the region, Hungary at the end of the 1980s did not see the emergence of a unified opposition demanding a fundamental revision of the political system (Jenkins 1998: 1). One of the reasons was that the ruling elite itself was not unified. After the replacement of Kádár as the first secretary of the MSzMP in the spring of 1988, influential party officials were allowed to express divergent opinions about the state of affairs in Hungary. Since some of the politicians within the MSzMP were even amenable to the idea of changing the political system quite radically, opposition forces gained many opportunities for negotiation. Hence, more than in other countries in Central and Eastern Europe, there was space for strategic maneuvering within the opposition.

This clearly affected Romani mobilization. In contrast to earlier periods, Romani activists could now choose from a variety of potential political allies. As a result, in the spring of 1989 a significant division grew within the Hungarian Romani movement. A number of Romani activists decided to support new party initiatives. In particular, they applauded a plan launched by János Báthory, the MSzMP's principal advisor on Romani affairs. Benefiting from the fact that by 1988 informal, independent political organizations could be set up without official sanction, Báthory urged that a new *independent* Romani organization be created. In his view, this new organization needed to bring together *all* Romani activists in Hungary in order to become the government's negotiating partner on issues having to do with the Roma. The activists who agreed with Báthory's plans thought that such a new organization would have the potential of becoming a reasonable alternative to the rigidly state-led National Gypsy Council (*Országos Cigánytanács*). In February 1989, Báthory put his plan into effect: the Democratic Alliance of Hungarian Gypsies (MCDSz) was established, and Gyula Náday, a Romani activist and high school teacher, was made the president of this first-ever independent Romani organization in Hungary. There was one problem: the organization was not nearly as independent as it was portrayed to be. Báthory argued that the expansion of Romani political activity—which he believed would inevitably take place in the course of 1989—needed to be controlled as much as possible in order to avoid a violent ethnic upsurge by Romani "radicals." He therefore suggested that exclusive state support be offered to the MCDSz as a "bulwark against radicalization" (Kovats 1998a: 120). In other words, although the MCDSz was established on the basis of a new law legalizing freedom of association, its roots were firmly connected to the preferences of the ruling elite.

A number of Romani activists—the most prominent ones being Ágnes Daróczi, Aladár Horváth, Béla Osztojkán, and Jenő Zsigó—did not agree with the MSzMP's plan of establishing a single official organization that would be led by "moderate" Romani activists. In their view the MCDSz was merely a continuation of the National Gypsy Council. In April 1989, these activists managed to bring together forty-seven people, and, benefiting from the same new law on association, they established an alternative Romani organization, which they called Phralipe (meaning "Brotherhood" in Romani). Phralipe was the primary example of a "new style" of Romani organizations and was considered a model for Romani activists in other countries. The organization aimed to be truly independent. It was the initiative of a small group of people who had refused to bow to pressure from above, and it had to survive without financial support from the state. Moreover, in contrast to the state-controlled Romani organizations, Phralipe did *not* claim to represent all Roma in Hungary, only its members.

Phralipe's founding meeting took place at the Eötvös Loránd University in Budapest. This fact alone quite strongly shaped Phralipe's reputation of an organization close to the critical intelligentsia of

Hungary's democratic opposition. Phralipe's natural partner in the mainstream political negotiations was the Alliance of Free Democrats (SzDSz)—the political party that was born out of the "cosmopolitan" side of a decade-old, informal, anti-communist opposition network that had emphasized notions of individual liberalism and human rights. Phralipe's close connection to the SzDSz was also evidenced by the fact that non-Romani SzDSz members (Gábor Havas, Ottilia Solt) and Romani candidates for the SzDSz (Antónia Hága, Aladár Horváth) became members of Phralipe's executive board. The intimate link between the founding members of Phralipe and the SzDSz became further visible after the first parliamentary elections in 1990, when five founding members of Phralipe (among them Antonia Hága and Aladár Horváth) were elected as SzDSz deputies to the Hungarian National Assembly. According to Osztojkán, the fact that precisely these people were involved illustrated "that we were close to SzDSz. We were not politically dependent on these people or on the political party. But we were strongly linked to them on the basis of friendship and respect" (personal interview).

Many of these friendship ties had been forged during a successful protest campaign in February 1989, led by Aladár Horváth. This campaign involved public demonstrations and petitions and was meant to halt the planned expulsion of Romani residents from a social housing estate in Miskolc. This so-called Anti-ghetto Committee (*Gettóellenes Bizottság*) can be seen as one of the first successful Romani protest campaigns in Hungary, and it appealed not only to Romani activists, but also to several anti-communist intellectuals. As one Romani participant recalled the events:

> [the Anti-ghetto Committee in Miskolc] was not an organization in the strict sense of the word ... In the period from February 2 to March 2, 1989, we were able to change the minds of the members of the local government [in Miskolc]. On February 2, the members of the local government were all in favor of this ghetto, on March 2, they were all against it. This was our first attack on communism. It was an independent action, not linked to any political party. It involved a lot of coordination among activists. It was the first step in the development of the democratic [Romani] movement. (Personal interview)

In 1989 and 1990, both Phralipe and the MCDSz were allowed to participate in the discussions leading to the development of new minority policies, and often they represented opposite standpoints. This was most obvious during some of the sessions of the Nationalities Board—the dialogue body that met several times between June 1989 and March 1990 to discuss the contours of Hungary's minority policies. Both Phralipe and the MCDSz were represented in this body, but they never functioned as allies. In one session the Phralipe representative even questioned the legitimacy of the board, since, he argued, it contained for the most part members from the Romani organizations of the old era. He also argued that the SzDSz was the only party that *really* represented the Hungarian Roma (Győri Szabó 1998: 203–4).

After the introduction of the Law on Associations, other independent Romani-based organizations came into being, although none was as articulate in its protest as Phralipe. On the basis of its initial success, Phralipe sought to extend its membership and to prevent as far as possible the new Romani organizations from cooperating with Náday's MCDSz. In order to foster Romani self-organization and marginalize state-controlled Romani organizations, the Phralipe leadership launched a plan to set up an "umbrella" Romani association. In December 1990 and January 1991, such an umbrella organization was created, initially for fourteen Romani organizations; it was named the Roma Parliament. The Roma Parliament saw as its role, to "represent and realize the interests of its member organizations at the highest legislative and executive fora in the Hungarian Republic" (quoted in Kovats 1998a: 141).

What one observes is thus a tactical shift among Phralipe activists: although they initially sought to form an elite-led movement representing only those people expressly supporting the ideas of the Phralipe leadership, they soon wanted to attract a broader constituency and attempted to form some kind of national Romani organization that would be more representative, even if this involved toning down their claims and protests. Phralipe activists, who naturally took the lead in the Roma Parliament, aimed at constructing a coalition sufficiently broad to bring aboard even those Romani activists who had earlier pursued careers in state-supported Romani bodies. Thus, perhaps surprisingly, Phralipe activists allowed the participation of Gyula Náday (MCDSz) in the Roma Parliament, along with a number of people who had been associated with the National Gypsy Council, such as József Raduly. An important young activist who joined the Roma Parliament was Flórián Farkas, head of the organization Lungo Drom, who had managed to gather a large following from the Szolnok region. As I mentioned, Farkas would soon become *the* crucial figure in the Hungarian Romani movement. The elite-oriented members of the Roma Parliament decided to support Farkas. Although they realized he maintained close ties with the people from the communist Romani institutions, they could not ignore the fact that his organization enjoyed much more popular support from "ordinary" Roma than did Phralipe.

Between 1990 and 1992, the Roma Parliament appeared to be working rather effectively (Kovats 1998a: 142–44). It fostered Romani activism and organizational growth within Romani communities. The state financial support for minority organizations was stepped up in the course of 1990, and the Roma Parliament was assigned the task of monitoring the distribution of that state support among its member organizations. As a result, the number of member organizations rapidly increased during these years. Moreover, the Roma Parliament managed to improve the political reputation of the Roma in Hungary. Since it was soon considered the principal Romani interest organization, the Roma Parliament was able to send a delegation to the Minorities Roundtable, the body that sought to represent all the minority groups and protect their interests during the discussions on the Minorities Act. Furthermore, the Roma Parliament organized protest campaigns calling upon the government to initiate measures to prevent discriminatory practices. At the same time, however, the Roma Parliament had to face serious obstacles. Most importantly, the fact that there was now an umbrella organization had not diminished personal and strategic conflicts between some member organizations. Even in its most successful period, in 1991, there were Romani activists who continued to disagree with the leading role of Phralipe in the Roma Parliament.

It comes as no surprise, then, that the Roma Parliament soon fragmented. Gyula Náday—the first vice-president of the Roma Parliament —and his MCDSz left the umbrella organization shortly after its establishment, due to a conflict with the president of Phralipe, Béla Osztojkán. Phralipe's informal connection to the SzDSz caused several newly established Romani organizations to be suspicious of full cooperation with the leadership of the Roma Parliament. György Rostás-Farkas, who was oriented towards the Hungarian Democratic Forum (MDF), and Attila Móhacs, who was close to the Socialist Party (MSzP), founded rival Romani umbrella organizations. This fragmentation also affected the Phralipe leadership itself: Ágnes Daróczi—one of the founding members of Phralipe and later an electoral candidate for the SzDSz—broke with the Roma Parliament because the organization was, in her eyes, too open to the "compromised" activists of the MCDSz and the National Gypsy Council (personal interview). In 1992, József Raduly and Flórián Farkas also left the Roma Parliament and established a third rival umbrella organization (The Coexistence Alliance). Their motivation was to avoid being associated with Phralipe's reputation as a protest organization. They believed it would be easier to develop good relations with the Antall government and the Office for Ethnic and National Minorities if they did not cooperate with those known as more radical activists, such as Aladár Horváth. Flórián Farkas's decision to leave the umbrella organization had an especially important effect on the general situation, since a great number of organizations left with him. In 1993, the membership of the Roma Parliament dwindled to only a fraction of what it had been the year before. The basic choice between closer cooperation with the bulk of the member organizations or holding on to a more antagonistic strategy increasingly became a topic for discussion within the Roma Parliament. Osztojkán seriously considered steering a more "moderate" course and taking the viewpoints of the member organizations much more into account, instead of automatically adopting the rigid line of the leading Romani intellectuals. But his appeal did not meet with a positive response from Horváth and Zsigó; in 1993 this led to a break between the Roma Parliament and Phralipe (Kovats 1998a: 150).

What was left of the Roma Parliament after Phralipe had left was a rump organization that lacked popular backing but was still an assiduous critic of the government. One of its most critical voices was Aladár Horváth. As a well-known Romani activist and MP for the SzDSz, his statements were more widely distributed among Romani populations and the general public than those made by other activists. But instead of becoming a successful and charismatic movement leader, his position in the Romani movement became quite problematic because of the fragmentation of the Roma Parliament. His criticism was not endorsed by other Romani organizations and did not receive a great deal of popular support. Moreover, his image as a radical Romani activist soon complicated his relationship with an important ally, the SzDSz. In the run-up to the 1994 elections, the SzDSz became less inclined to support Horváth's critical statements. Horváth broke with the SzDSz, leaving a gulf between the Roma Parliament and mainstream politics. By 1995, the Roma Parliament had become a relatively small organization that focused on cultural and societal development within local Romani communities and published an independent Romani magazine, *Amaro Drom* (Our Way). The organization never again succeeded in uniting the whole spectrum of Romani organizations. Even Aladár Horváth left the former umbrella organization after a while and chose to set up a human rights and legal defense bureau that was not dependent on membership.

In sum, the first years of postcommunist Romani mobilization in Hungary yielded not much more than sharp divisions. On the one hand, there were those Romani activists who had chosen to follow a strategy of elite-driven protest and criticism. They were opposed, on the other hand, by those who opted for cooperation with the government administration and focused on attracting a mass Romani constituency. With the first election of the local Gypsy minority self-governments (December 1994) and the establishment of the first National Gypsy Minority Self-Government (April 1995), the division between those two currents of Romani activism became even more obvious. Through the minority elections the activists who had endorsed the strategy of cooperation were able to consolidate their position and began to dominate the arena of official Romani politics. Although there were attempts at unifying the Romani activists who had been close to the SzDSz with those close to the MSzP—especially since the two parties formed a new coalition government in 1994—the Roma Parliament did not succeed in organizing a viable electoral group of candidates for the minority elections. This sealed the organization's fate. Lungo Drom succeeded in setting up a more or less successful electoral campaign in the eastern counties of Hungary and managed to attract the majority of voters in these communities.

By 1995, the 53-member National Gypsy Minority Self-Government had become the centerpiece of the Hungarian Romani movement. The government considered this body to be the "legitimate" representative organization of the Roma. Other Romani pressure groups were deemed "nonrepresentative." From that time, the National Gypsy Minority Self-Government was able to participate in policy deliberation, first through the Office for Ethnic and National Minorities, and later through the Interdepartmental Committee for Gypsy Affairs. Independent Romani organizations with no electoral basis were permitted to take part in particular meetings organized by the Office for Ethnic and National Minorities, but there was less pressure on the government to take opinions of these independent organizations into account. This was another factor consolidating the fundamental division within the Hungarian Romani movement. Moreover, a large number of activists argued that there were fundamental problems with the way the National Gypsy Minority Self-Government claimed to represent the interests of the Roma. One allegation, made chiefly by nonelected activists, was that the National Gypsy Minority Self-Government did not really reflect the diversity of Romani interests since the body was dominated by candidates from only one party.

The choice between acting within or outside the National Gypsy Minority Self-Government was perceived as a fundamental choice between critical and loyal activism. That this became an important division in the movement could be seen in the strenuous attempts by some activists to form an opposition *against* Lungo Drom in the run-up to the minority elections in 1999. In 1998, Aladár Horváth called upon Béla Osztojkán to gather together nineteen Romani organizations and establish an alternative coalition in order to defeat Lungo Drom. After months of working on such a coalition, Osztojkán understood that chances of success were not increasing. He believed that an alternative coalition would not be sustainable without gaining at least a part of the Lungo Drom electorate. At the same time, he knew that the new coalition lacked the means to set up a successful campaign to mobilize Romani communities. In January 1999, Osztojkán changed his tack quite radically and decided that his organization, Phralipe, would join the Lungo Drom coalition. As a result, Horváth's position became weaker, and the alternative coalition failed. The results of the 1999 election for the National Gypsy Self-Government clearly showed the deep division within the Hungarian Romani movement between a moderate and a more radical style of Romani activism.

Symbolic Cases of Contentious Politics: The Example of the "Zámoly Affair"

Throughout the 1990s, the noninstitutionalized wing of the Romani movement in Hungary attempted to continue its protest activities and attracted growing media attention. One of the most prominent and most divisive issues was that of Romani migration. Romani migration is, of course, a field of study in itself (see, e.g., Braham and Braham 2003; Castle-Kaněrová 2003; Crowe 2003; Guy 2003; Vašečka and Vašečka 2003) and should therefore ideally be examined in the context of more general study projects on contemporary East–West migration. It cannot be the purpose of the following sections to carry out such an examination. What is a more appropriate and more realistic aim, however, is to explore the issue of Romani migration briefly in order to illustrate its importance as a factor influencing movement activity. In Hungary much of the debate has revolved around the "Zámoly affair."

In 1997, a number of Hungarian citizens applied for political asylum in Canada and EU member states. According to figures of the UN High Commissioner for Refugees (UNHCR), the total number of Hungarian asylum applicants in 1998 was 1,033. This figure rose to 1,532 new applications in 1999, 2,612 in 2000, and 4,022 in the year 2001. In 2002, this development made Hungary, after Colombia and Mexico, the country with the highest relative increase of asylum seekers (UNHCR 2002: 5). The facts were noticeable especially in Canada, where Hungarians formed the largest group of refugee claimants—most of them identifying themselves as Roma and claiming that they were discriminated against in their home country. The year 1997 can clearly be identified as the year that set the trend for the spectacular increase. In 1996, the total number of Hungarian applicants for Canada was 64; in 1997 the number rose to 294, in 1998 to 977, in 1999 to 1,581 (UNHCR 2001: 168), in 2000 to 2,474, and in 2001 to 3,812 (UNHCR 2002: 25). As will be discussed, Hungarian Romani organizations did not at all agree among themselves on the question of whether the situation in Hungary justified the Roma's claims for asylum. Nevertheless, some pressure groups were able to use the controversy about the wave of asylum seekers in their much wider protest campaigns against the Hungarian government.

One case that merits attention in this context is that of a group of twelve Romani families from the town of Zámoly who, in July 2000, applied for political asylum in France. József Krasznai, president of a local Romani organization (the Fejér County Romani Association), member of the National Gypsy Self-Government and vice-president of the Roma Parliament, acted as a spokesman for these families both before and during their migration to Strasbourg. He immediately attracted the attention of domestic and international politicians and journalists. It seems useful to recount here the details of this case, since it offers a good view of the various sides of the Hungarian Romani movement. It also illustrates quite well how other actors, such as the government, the opposition parties, and human rights organizations, have responded to such episodes of increased Romani movement activity.

The origins of the case date back to 1997. In that year a storm damaged one of the buildings in which a number of Romani families were living. The local authorities tore down the entire set of houses but failed to provide viable alternative accommodation. In response, the National Gypsy Self-Government used funds to erect temporary housing. Meanwhile tensions rose within the community. Non-Romani inhabitants of the village began to reproach the Roma for having occupied the local community center for too long a period. In 1999, a fight broke out in which one of the non-Roma involved was severely injured and died. According to József Krasznai, this event polarized the community, and the Roma received death threats. Believing that, in case of an attack, they would not be able to count on protection from the police, the Romani families decided to travel to Strasbourg and claim political asylum. In March 2001, fifteen of the forty-six people who had originally left Hungary were granted political asylum by the French Office for the Protection of Refugees.

Gradually the case assumed a meaning that was larger than that of the concrete realities of the case. Spokesman Krasznai was able to attract domestic and international media attention not only to these specific Roma but also to the situation of the Roma in Hungary in general. He attempted to turn his work on this specific case into a general protest action against the Hungarian government's treatment of the Roma. Several features of the case contributed to this. First, even before the departure of the Romani families to France, Krasznai had argued that the Hungarian government was responsible for finding a solution for them. Before leaving Budapest he had organized a press conference and had warned the government that if it did not take measures, he would leave the country. Secondly, by choosing Strasbourg as a destination, Krasznai placed the whole case in a European context. He told the press that he had written complaints to the European Court of Human Rights, the Council of Europe, and the European Parliament. Upon arriving in France he also sent a letter to the French President, Jacques Chirac, requesting his support for the asylum application and asking him to use his influence to persuade the Hungarian government to improve the conditions of the Romani communities. By so doing Krasznai managed to touch upon an important foreign policy concern of the Hungarian government: its reputation among the EU countries. The Hungarian government was brought into a position where it was forced to respond. When I asked Krasznai in October 2001 whether he considered Romani migration an effective method of protesting, he stated the following:

> Yes, I think so. Everyone was talking about it. Never before could the Roma attract so much attention to their situation. During the first three months in France, the government didn't take our demands seriously. But after the stay was extended and a couple of them received political asylum, the government began to take the case seriously. (Personal interview)

Significant, too, is that Krasznai's protest letters received backing from a number of well-known intellectuals in Hungary, most of them close to the opposition party SzDSz. In March 2001, a letter signed by, among others, the internationally renowned authors Péter Esterházy and György Konrád was sent to the French Prime Minister, Lionel Jospin, thanking France for granting political asylum to the Roma from Zámoly. The letter compared the decision of the French authorities with the "protection [that] has been given to many Hungarians during various centuries, most recently during the 1956 Hungarian revolution." It also stated that "the decision of the French authorities will serve as a moral lesson for Hungarian society." [9]

One can summarize Krasznai's view of the Zámoly case in three general points: (a) the case of the Zámoly Roma is indicative of the situation of the Roma in Hungary in general; (b) the Roma in Hungary are threatened by racist violence, lack protection from the authorities, and suffer from a general climate of discrimination by the authorities; (c) current policies and minority rights protection systems initiated by the government have failed to change this situation, and this is why so many Roma resort to seeking asylum in what they regard as safer countries. In their discussion of the case, government officials and mainstream politicians emphasized other elements. According to the official government view, the Roma were not leaving for reasons of discrimination, but to escape socioeconomic marginality. The Hungarian government claimed that it had already invested unprecedented amounts of money into programs aimed at alleviating the Roma's socioeconomic predicament; therefore, it argued, Romani activists should now help the government to implement these programs. The government also argued that Romani migration was incited by individuals who had no other aim than to discredit Hungary's reputation among the EU countries; according to the government, it was not driven by a genuine concern for the Roma.

With regard to the first element in the government's counterframing, it has to be noted that the government was not able to avoid talking about the existence of ethnic discrimination in Hungary. It admitted the existence of discrimination but argued that it did not constitute a legitimate reason for the Roma to claim asylum, since measures had been implemented to remedy such problems. To buttress this reasoning, government officials referred to the fact that in the overwhelming majority of earlier cases Romani asylum claims had been refused on the grounds that the claimants were clearly not persecuted by state authorities and did not lack protection against discriminatory practices. In this way the government took the edge off the main argument of those who argued that the government was responsible for causing the Romani migration; at the same time it expressed an opinion that was perfectly acceptable to a large part of the Romani movement.

The government's argument that Romani migration was deliberately organized by individuals to discredit both the Hungarian government and the Hungarian Roma persuaded many of the Romani activists into criticizing the asylum seekers.[10] A large number of Romani activists did not want to see the Roma blamed for blocking Hungary's entrance to the EU. In response to the government's point of view, the president of the National Gypsy Self-Government, Flórián Farkas, declared that he was opposed to Roma seeking asylum abroad, since this in his view caused "damage to Hungary's reputation."[11] For this reason he also tried to dissociate the Zámoly affair from the general situation in Hungary.

> The Zámoly affair cannot be lumped together or mixed up with the situation of the Roma in Hungary in general. The Zámoly affair is a quite particular one, a peculiar internal concern, an internal problem, which I am not delighted about. I do not agree with this particular act of emigration even though I identify myself emotionally with the families concerned. Leaving this country is not a viable solution. (quoted in Kosztolányi 2001: 67)

It is interesting—and perhaps telling for the persistence of the division within the Hungarian Romani movement—that the National Gypsy Self-Government and the Romani activists affiliated to it stood uncritically by the government's opinion on the Zámoly case even when government officials, on the basis of that case made questionable statements about the Roma *in general*, alleging that the Roma themselves had been in large part responsible for creating the problems that faced them. For example, in August 2000, the minister of social and family affairs stated with regard to the Zámoly case that the government, "had done more to help the Roma than the Roma had done to help themselves," a statement to which Prime Minister Viktor Orbán reportedly added that, "Hungarian Roma should try to learn and work more."[12]

Nonelectoral Romani Mobilization in the Czech and Slovak Republics: Actors and Issues

In contrast to the situation in Hungary, Romani activism in Czechoslovakia at the end of the 1980s was not channeled through communist-led government institutions. This largely confined ethnic mobilization to fragmented, informal networks, such as extended families and musical bands. Emil Ščuka and Ondřej Giňa, who already in the 1980s had entertained ambitions to develop a large Romani movement, stated in my interviews with them that within some of the informal networks important preparatory work was done for the establishment of the present-day Romani organizations. But despite such groundwork, a unified Romani movement did not arise.

During the months and years after the Velvet Revolution—the popular demonstrations in November and December 1989 that had forced the Communists to give up their power monopoly—a plurality of Romani initiatives came into being. The most successful activists were clearly those who were able to join the dissident organizations of that time. During the formative days of the Civic Forum (*Občanské Fórum*), a small group of Romani activists took the initiative of joining the organization in the hope that they would be able to play a crucial role in the new political system. The post-Velvet euphoria led to a rather successful attempt by Romani activists at turning Romani identity into a new political identity (Holomek 1999: 302). Among the large number of new Romani associations and Romani political parties that were established in 1990, the Romani Civic Initiative (ROI) was clearly the most successful. According to the accounts of its leaders, ROI was able to attract a large membership, numbering some thousands (Crowe 1995: 63). Its most tangible success was in bringing the issue of Romani political representation into the anti-communist movement. Some Romani activists were placed in winnable positions on the Civic Forum's candidate lists.

In contrast to Hungary in that period, Czechoslovakia did not see any meaningful attempts at unifying the newly established Romani associations. Neither were there any key issues around which Romani-based organizations were able to mobilize political protest. The new Romani associations devoted most of their attention to the promotion of Romani culture (music and literature), to self-help actions in poor communities, and to the development of Romani minority media. It is in this period that Romani newspapers and magazines began to be published and distributed on a relatively wide scale. There were few, if any, public protest campaigns.

Mobilizing Issues in the Czech Republic between 1993 and 2004

This situation changed in 1993. Romani organizational life was deeply affected by the break-up of Czechoslovakia in that year. This was mostly felt within the new independent Czech Republic, where Romani organizations were faced with the task of attracting activists from among a group of people that was suddenly much smaller. Although Romani cultural associations and political parties continued to function during this period, they did not seem to be able to make strong claims for change or communicate these claims to a broad public. Former key members of ROI, still the most successful Romani organization at the time, painted a rather pessimistic picture of Romani mobilization after the break-up. According to Ondřej Giňa, ROI began to disintegrate after 1993, and people stopped working for it.

Notwithstanding this rather bleak picture, there were other organizations (support and advocacy organizations) that did find new issues around which to organize small-scale protest. They managed to foment a modest revival of Romani activism in the latter half of the 1990s. These support and advocacy organizations rallied around a campaign that centered first and foremost on the new citizenship law (Law No. 40/1993) and its disproportionate effect on many Roma.

Romani protest against violent attacks increased after 1993, especially in the aftermath of the death of a young Romani man, Tibor Danihel, who drowned after having been chased into a river by a group of skinheads in the South Bohemian town of Písek. Another deadly attack on a Romani man in May 1995 incited further public debate about racist violence in the Czech Republic and led the government to introduce a special department within the police force to deal with violent groups such as the skinheads. Human Rights Watch wrote in 1996 that the May 1995 attack brought the number of Roma murdered in the Czech Republic since 1989 to an estimated twenty-seven. In 1995 alone, the organization wrote, "there were at least 181 reported attacks against Roma or foreigners in the country" (HRW 1996).

The Czech Citizenship Law

Given the rather poor state of Romani political life after 1993, it should not be surprising that the first response to the citizenship law did not come from Romani activists. It came rather from international advocacy organizations (human rights groups) and politicians from abroad. Independent organizations such as Human Rights Watch denounced the citizenship law in their international publications (HRW 1996). The law was also condemned by international governmental actors—most notably by the Council of Europe, the OSCE's High Commissioner on National Minorities (HCNM 1993), and the United Nations High Commissioner for Refugees. It was also criticized quite sharply by the State Department of the US Congress and the US Commission on Security and Cooperation in Europe (the Helsinki Commission) (CSCE 1994; CSCE 1996). Only in the wake of this criticism did a number of individual Romani activists begin to voice their concerns.

One must see the citizenship problem against the backdrop of the federalization process in Czechoslovakia. From the time of the creation of the first Czechoslovak Republic in 1918 to the Prague Spring in 1968, Czechoslovakia recognized only *one* form of citizenship—that of "Czechoslovak" citizenship. However, during this whole period there had been numerous Slovak demands for some form of political autonomy. The topic figured prominently in debates at the end of the 1960s about democratization and the reform of socialism, both of which led to the Prague Spring. One of the few lasting results of the Prague Spring was the federalization of the state in 1969. The Czech and Slovak republics received autonomy over local affairs, with the federal government and federal assembly being responsible for foreign relations, defense, and finance. After Warsaw Pact troops crushed the reform movement, the Czechoslovak communists unanimously condemned the entire program of the Prague Spring, but they nevertheless retained the idea of federalism. It has been pointed out that the reason for this presumably lay in the fact that the decentralization of power was seen as a way to make unified attempts at political resistance less likely (Pithart 1995: 204). The practical results of the federalization process must not be overestimated: the Czechoslovak Socialist Federal Republic during the following years remained under the firm power of the Czechoslovak Communist Party.

What is important here is that the establishment of the federal state involved a new regulation concerning citizenship. Under Law No. 206 (1968) of the Slovak National Council and Law No. 39 (1969) of the Czech National Council, all Czechoslovak citizens were deemed "Czechs" or "Slovaks" according to their place of birth (*jus soli*). Many Czechoslovak citizens who were born in the Slovak Republic but now lived in the Czech Republic were, according to these laws, "Czechoslovak citizens" with official "Slovak nationality." For people born after 1954, the principle of *jus sanguinis* (citizenship of the parents) was used to determine their republic-level nationality. For example, children of Slovak nationals living in the Czech Republic would continue to be considered "Slovaks," even if they had never set foot in the Slovak Republic. For a certain period after the introduction of this new legislation, one had the option of changing one's republic-level nationality. However, as Jiřina Šiklová and Marta Miklušáková have pointed out, very few people actually made use of it, probably because this nationality designation—in contrast to one's Czechoslovak citizenship—had no practical implications: "it was not found on any identity documents, and all rights (including the right to education, social benefits, housing, and the right to vote) were established according to one's permanent residence" (Šiklová and Miklušáková 1998). After the breakdown of one-party rule in 1989, republic-level nationality had no impact on the civil, political, or social rights of Czechoslovak citizens. For example, in the 1992 parliamentary elections, constituencies were based on permanent residence; those who lived in the Czech Republic could not vote for the Slovak National Council, even if they had Slovak republic-level citizenship.

With the break-up of the country, both the Slovak and Czech Republics adopted new citizenship laws. Slovakia adopted a rather inclusive law that made citizenship available to all former Czechoslovak citizens, while the Czech Republic opted for a more restrictive law that gave citizenship to a more limited category of Czech residents (CSCE 1996: 3). This category comprised those with Czech republic-level citizenship under the 1969 law. Residents who did not have Czech republic-level citizenship had to submit an application. In order to be eligible they had to fulfill two preconditions: they needed to have been a permanent resident in the Czech Republic for at least two years, and they were required to have had a clean criminal record for five years. This latter requirement in particular was subject to much criticism. Many considered it an *ex post facto* increase of a criminal sanction (CSCE 1996: 4). Moreover, it was believed to have a disproportionate effect on Romani populations in the Czech Republic.[13]

The latter criticism was based on the observation that among the people who had moved between the Slovak and Czech republics in the period before 1992 there were a considerable number of Roma. Some of them had moved within the framework of earlier dispersal plans initiated by the government, while others had responded to economic opportunities in the Czech lands. In 1993, it was obvious that many of the "Slovak" Roma who lived permanently in the Czech Republic did not possess republic-level citizenship under the 1969 law and were obliged to submit applications for citizenship in what they regarded as their own country. This obligation came at a time when many of them faced growing socioeconomic problems. As a result, those who found themselves in this situation did not always know that they had to apply for Czech citizenship. When they found out, they could not always provide the right documents. Some had been living for decades in Czech factory dormitories; some were even born there; officially, they continued to be temporary residents (Šiklová and Miklušáková 1998). It is not at all clear how many people the new citizenship law affected, and neither is a clear picture available of what percentage of the population was obliged to undergo the application procedure. It is clear, however, that there were enough cases for organizations to be almost permanently busy assisting Romani applicants.[14] In response to the growing protest, the law was amended in 1996 (Law No. 139) to allow the Interior Ministry to waive the clean criminal record requirement. Law No. 193 (1999) further amended the law in such a way that former citizens of the Czechoslovak Federal Republic who were not citizens of the Czech Republic, but were living within its borders at the end of 1992, could now acquire citizenship by declaration.

What is important here are not so much the technical and legal details of the citizenship law, but the way it became both a central focus of domestic and international criticism and a crucial mobilizing issue for civil activism in the years between 1993 and 1997. The most prominent protesters during those years were the Tolerance Foundation (Nadace Tolerance) and the Counseling Center for Citizenship of former Citizens of the Czechoslovak Federation (after 1999 renamed as *Právní poradna pro občanství, občanská a lidská práva* or the Counseling Center for Citizenship and Civil and Human Rights). The activities of both organizations were linked to and supported by international advocacy networks. Ethnically based Romani organizations engaged less in coordinated action. Nevertheless, certain individual Romani activists seized the opportunity to conduct a more general protest campaign against the climate of exclusion and discrimination that they argued existed in Czech society and was promoted by Czech authorities. One example is Ladislav Body, who, as has been mentioned, was a member of the Communist Party of Czechoslovakia (KSČ) and the only Romani activist who was an MP in the Czech National Council. He protested against the law in 1992 by abstaining from voting and leaving the room while the other members of his parliamentary group voted in favor of the law. Although he did not set up a real protest campaign, he is known to have "warned" Roma about the effects of the law by writing on the issue in Romani magazines. During 1994, other Romani activists protested in the press, but there was no sign of any organized action.

However, in more recent accounts by Romani activists, the protest against the citizenship law is seen a crucial turning point in the Romani movement. Some of the Romani activists I interviewed argued that the citizenship law evidenced the tendency of the political elite to introduce measures that exclude the Roma from Czech society. Many of them began to argue that the citizenship law had been very much in line with the expulsion policies that certain local authorities in Bohemia had attempted to carry out in the period before the Velvet Divorce (the dissolution of Czechoslovakia in January 1993). They directed their criticism not only against the law itself but also against the whole societal climate and the general attitudes of ignorance and discrimination among politicians that, according to them, had made this law possible.

The Migration Debate in the Czech Republic

When I asked Romani interviewees in the Czech Republic to describe the issues that had worried them most in the early 1990s, they frequently mentioned the problem of violent anti-Roma attacks. The occurrence of such violence was, according to many activists, a clear illustration of the then current atmosphere of encroaching prejudice. Particular attention was given to attacks that were carried out or supported by members of the skinhead movement. Individual Romani activists had voiced their concerns at the time, and their complaints reached the international press. But they were not able to mobilize large-scale domestic protests. A lot of the protest work was again done on the initiative of non-ethnically based advocacy organizations (HRW 1996). The Roma in the Council of Nationalities were able to place the issue on the political agenda, and this resulted in the establishment of an ad hoc working group within the council. However, at that point there was no firm backing from any of the ministries. The Romani members of the Council of Nationalities felt that their concerns had not been taken seriously (personal interviews).

This changed quite abruptly in 1997. In that year the complaints were taken more seriously, and this was, according to a large number of my interviewees, due to one particular phenomenon: the sudden increase in the number of Czech asylum seekers leaving the country. According to UNHCR statistics the total amount of new asylum applications from the Czech Republic in 1998 was 794 (UNHCR 1999), and in 1999 a total of 807 new applications were submitted (UNHCR 2000). In absolute figures the number of Czech asylum applicants remained far below the total numbers of the Hungarian and Slovak applications, but the phenomenon nevertheless incited a strong debate in the Czech media and in politics about the position of the Roma within the country. Interpretations of the events differed among observers as well as among Romani activists, but from the beginning there was more or less a consensus about what triggered the first massive departure of Czech citizens to Canada in the summer of 1997. Czech citizens had begun lodging asylum claims in Canada in the spring of 1997, when the Canadian authorities lifted visa restrictions; many agree that a controversial television program stepped up the process later that year. In August, a Czech commercial television station devoted its weekly documentary program to the circumstances in which Czech Roma lived while waiting for their asylum cases to be heard. Word spread rapidly that the documentary had painted a positive picture of the situation, that Canadian asylum-granting authorities were flexible, and Canada itself a haven of security and financial support (Chirico 1997).

What is essential here is the way in which Romani and non-Romani activists responded to the controversy. Non-ethnically based organizations were able to seize upon the refugee crisis as an opportunity for protest. They framed Romani migration as a symptom of a larger, underlying problem and substantiated that argument by referring to the anti-Romani statements made by certain politicians shortly after the news hit the headlines that thousands of Roma were inquiring about entry procedures at Canadian embassies (Chirico 1997). Czech human rights organizations referred, for example, to the mayor of Marianské Hory, who had declared on television that she intended to recommend that Roma who wanted to move to Canada receive two-thirds of the cost of their flight, provided that they give up their flats and their official residence (Chiciro 1997). Politicians from the extreme rightist Czech Republican Party set forth similar proposals, which built both on the idea that an unbridgeable Roma/non-Roma divide existed in the Czech Republic and the belief that the "Romani problem" was best "resolved" by "moderate" forms of expulsion (see, e.g., Fawn 2001: 1202).

Romani activists protested against such statements and felt encouraged by the fact that in April 1998 a family of Czech Roma was indeed granted asylum in Canada. Nevertheless, stimulating the growth of a stronger Romani protest movement was not as easy as it appeared at first sight. That handful of Romani activists who aspired to become Romani representatives still did not find a way to stir up support from "ordinary" Roma. Moreover, Romani activists were far from always being in agreement. Different Romani activists came up with different responses to the refugee crisis. Some of them opposed the decision of the Roma to leave the country. They feared that the whole migration issue would hinder their attempts at finding access to the Czech policy-making process. Some of them, most notably ROI leader Emil Ščuka, supported the government's opposition to the Romani refugee crisis (personal interview). In a press conference on August 14, 1997, Ščuka supported the statement made by premier Václav Klaus that the Czech government was indeed taking Romani issues to heart, and that emigration was hence not legitimate. This came at a time when a government report that was rather critical about the way the Czech Republic dealt with the situation of the Roma was being prepared for the Minister without Portfolio. Viktor Dobal, one of the main authors of the report, expressed his surprise at the uncritical viewpoint expressed by Ščuka in August 1997 and explained it as a reflection of Ščuka's hope of being included in the new government institutions for dealing with Romani issues (personal interview).

In 2001, the issue of migration came to the fore again and continued to divide opinions within the Romani movement. In the summer of that year, British customs administrators were placed at Prague's Ružyne Airport to conduct pre-clearance controls. The initiative was the result of an agreement between the Czech and British governments and represented an effort to curb the influx of large numbers of asylum seekers in the United Kingdom without introducing visa obligations for Czech citizens. Well-known Romani individuals immediately opposed this practice and quite readily found a forum in the press. However, in this case, too, there were few if any signs of a strong ethnic protest movement. At the beginning of August of 2001, Romani groups organized small-scale protests at British embassies in London, Bucharest, and Warsaw, and at the Czech consulate in Slovakia.[15] The lead, however, was again clearly taken by human rights and advocacy organizations (most notably the Czech Helsinki Committee and the European Roma Rights Center), which criticized the controls as being ethnically biased. Doubts about the appropriateness of the British measures were also voiced by the chairman of the Czech Senate at the time, Petr Pithart, and the president, Václav Havel.[16] In December 2004, the Appellate Committee of the House of Lords found the government of the UK indeed to have acted unlawfully against Czech Roma in preventing them from traveling in order to stop them from claiming asylum upon arrival.[17]

Protesting Residential Segregation: Ústí nad Labem
Another event around which the Romani movement attempted to rally, and which rendered the characteristics of the Czech Romani movement more visible at the end of the 1990s, was the attempt of the local government in the north Bohemian town Ústí nad Labem to fence off a block of flats inhabited mostly by Romani families.

The controversy surrounding the local government's attempt to build a "wall" in the middle of a street in the district of Neštěmice in Ústí nad Labem illustrates very well both the strengths and weaknesses of Romani mobilization at that time in the Czech Republic. The controversy began in early 1998 when the municipal government issued plans to build a four-meter-high wall around two apartment blocks to protect the surrounding residents from the garbage and noise produced by the inhabitants of the two complexes. The plans were a response to a petition that a number of the neighboring tenants had filed with the district authorities of Neštěmice. According to newspaper reporting from that period, the residents of the neighborhood did not necessarily see the wall as a solution to the problem, but rather as a way of not having to see any more the conditions in which their neighbors lived.[18] The project of building a wall between Roma and non-Roma—with all its powerful reminiscences of the Berlin Wall and the Jewish ghetto walls—was quickly referred to by a number of Romani activists as the embodiment of Czech anti-Roma discrimination at the level of the local authorities. According to them, the plan to build the wall was just one example of the general tendency of the authorities to concentrate Roma in ghettos and force them into marginality. Ondřej Giňa gathered a number of Romani protesters in an organization called the Gremium of Regional Romani Representatives and stated in the press that blocking the construction of the wall was simply a matter of self-defense.

The issue soon reached international news headlines. It provoked criticism from, among others, the US Congress, the Secretary General of the Council of Europe, Walter Schwimmer, and the president of the European Commission, Romano Prodi. The latter made a direct reference to the Berlin Wall when saying: "Europe will never accept new walls separating European citizens from one another."[19] When in October 1999 the building of the wall started—in reality more a fence than a real wall—Romani activists and inhabitants were present and attempted to raze the structure virtually at the same time as it was being built. Only because of massive police presence did the construction works go ahead. But international criticism persisted.[20] Six weeks later the Chamber of Deputies decided that the fence needed to be removed.

Although the protests against the wall in Matiční Street had their effects, they were not entirely successful in unifying the Romani movement. All Romani activists felt, of course, equally scandalized by statements made by those who were in favor of the construction, especially when the argument was made that the whole problem was essentially the Roma living there. But what confused many local Romani activists was that some of the people in favor of fencing of the Roma argued that this would not go against the interests of the Roma living there, but that it was a practical way of easing the growing tensions in the neighborhood. Protest against the fence was to be avoided because, some of the local actors argued, it was nothing else than an additional source of trouble and instability.

Mayor Ladislav Hruska, for example, stated that the protests of "would-be human-rights protectors ... only enhance the disquiet."[21] These kinds of arguments prevented at least some Romani activists from participating in protest activities. A number of local Roma did not want to see tensions increased in the area and consented to the building of a fence as a practical solution. Some of the activists with whom I spoke also argued that mass support from the Romani communities for the protest against the Matiční fence was to some extent hindered by the fact that many potential participants did not want to be associated with the lifestyle of the inhabitants in the two blocks in question.

The Roma's Contentious Politics in Slovakia between 1993 and 2004

As was mentioned earlier, Romani activism in the Slovak Republic after 1993 was nurtured mainly by Romani political parties. Although these ethnic parties manifestly failed to attract voters, they still formed the most vocal part of the Slovak Romani movement. More than other Romani organizations they were able to draw media attention and represent the Roma in public debates. One reason underpinning the choice to organize primarily in the form of national political parties is arguably related to the role played by NGOs in Slovak politics. Rather paradoxically, during most of the 1990s NGOs were seen as less politically neutral than ethnically based Romani political parties. Romani activists who wanted to dissociate themselves from the anti-Mečiar "camp" of the Slovak civic associations found a safer option in starting what they called a political party.

Between 1993 and 1998, the HZDS-led government assumed a restrictive attitude towards independent civic organizations. By establishing Romani political parties, activists wanted to keep open the possibility of cooperating with the HZDS. In the run-up to the 1998 elections, however, the choice for or against Mečiar polarized the Romani movement. At that time, it became clear that a number of NGOs had become crucial partners for the political parties of the opposition. During the successful OK '98 campaign for fair and free elections in the early autumn of 1998, a range of civic initiatives was set up to make voters aware of the value of democracy and elections (Demeš 1999: 348). This campaign included a call for a greater recognition of minority rights. At that time, Romani activism was divided between keeping the option of participating with political parties such as the HZDS open, or joining the side of the NGOs, which increasingly gained the reputation of being close to the opposition parties.

The change of government in 1998 did not push such strategic issues to the background. The fragmentation among the Romani political parties remained in place, and although a need was felt to unite, there were still many doubts about whether such a unified movement would be able to find support from below. Moreover, the relationship between ethnically based Romani organizations and the growing number of non-ethnically based organizations that carried out projects for Romani communities was becoming ever tenser. As larger amounts of financial support became available from both international and domestic sources, competition for financial support increased among these organizations. In 2000, I had an interview with the well-known Romani activist Klára Orgovánová on this subject. She stated the following:

> Romani NGOs have fewer chances of receiving money, because other foundations have people who are fluent in English. ... Romani NGOs have become more aggressive. ... And they are right. I work with the Open Society Foundation and with Soros, so we don't have a problem with [getting] money and we can conduct interesting projects. But if I worked in a small NGO, my resources would be reduced. And when you see that other organizations are getting the money, then of course you become nervous about it. (Personal interview)

This tension was reflected in the attempts of a number of Romani NGOs to form the Romani Third Sector Gremium, which was intended to be an "umbrella" group of elected leaders from Romani organizations. According to Jozef Červeňák, one of the activists who launched this plan, such an umbrella organization was to resemble the Third Sector Gremium, an elected body of NGO representatives in Slovakia which had been in operation since 1994 and whose task it had been to negotiate with state representatives, local governments, firms, and international organizations (Vašečka 2001: 19, n63). Romani organizations were never a part of this Third Sector Gremium, an anomaly that, according to Červeňák, had to be compensated by establishing an alternative, ethnically based Third Sector Gremium exclusively for Romani organizations (personal interview). In October and November 2000, the ambition of Romani-based NGOs to form a united front was clearly visible: twenty-five of these organizations cooperated in an agreement initiated by thirteen registered Romani organizations and formed a "Romani Parliament."[22]

The most important point to be made here is that the Romani activists had an ambiguous relationship with both the government and the NGOs that were critical of the government. Some Romani activists opted for cooperation with one of the governing political parties, others with opposition parties. Some Romani activists chose to cooperate with non-ethnically based civic associations, while others opted for more restrictive ethnically based activism, even though they often depended on external resources.

Romani migration, once again

The centrality of the issue of migration within the Slovak Romani movement is far from surprising. The number of Slovak citizens who lodged asylum claims in other countries was even higher than the number of Czech and Hungarian asylum seekers, both in absolute and relative figures. According to UNHCR statistics there were 620 Slovak refugee-status applications in 1997, while in 1998 the number rose to 1,682. In 2000 and 2001, the number of asylum seekers peaked with 4,977 and 4,543 applications, respectively (UNHCR 1999: 62; UNHCR 2000: 95; UNHCR 2002: 9).[23] There have been a number of "waves," or periods during which large groups of people—mostly from the same localities in Slovakia—traveled to the same countries. For example, in the first half of 1998, 472 applications for asylum were lodged in the United Kingdom (representing about 1,256 Slovak citizens) (Vašečka 1999b: 407). In 1999, Finland and Belgium received by far the most Slovak asylum claims (1,175 in Belgium and 1,516 in Finland). In 2000, Belgium was the prime receiver of Slovak asylum claims (1,392 applications).

As in Hungary and the Czech Republic, the growing number of Slovak claims for political asylum outside Slovakia sparked off a protracted domestic debate among government officials, politicians from the opposition, civic associations, and journalists. Romani activists were forced to take a position in the discussion. As in Hungary and the Czech Republic, even those Romani activists who could successfully propagate their view on the matter found themselves faced with more powerful voices outside the movement who set the tone of the debate. More specifically, most politicians in parliament and government, who generally had much better access to mainstream written and spoken media than Romani activists, linked the issue of Romani migration to the debate about Slovakia's standing in the international community, and, in particular, to the country's reputation in the EU (Vermeersch 2002: 96–97). At first, many Slovak Romani activists welcomed this. They could utilize the international scrutiny to buttress their complaints against the government. The idea of building a protest movement in this way seemed a logical strategy, since Slovakia's treatment of the Roma was more than ever before evoking comment and reporting in the international mass media. However, not all voices in the debate agreed that the Slovak government needed to assume responsibility. As a result of the growing international attention, some Slovak daily newspapers began suggesting to their readers that the problem lay not so much with the treatment of the Roma, but with the attitudes of the Roma themselves, whom they believed were merely involved in an "asylum adventure" (IOM 2000: 139).

Moreover, the Slovak government asserted that Romani migration was not the result of a political problem in Slovakia, but on the contrary needed to be seen as a purely "economic" migration, involving people who were abusing asylum procedures and welfare systems in EU member states. For example, in July 1999, Minister Csáky appealed to the media to stop using the word "exodus"—as the refugee crisis had frequently been labeled in the press—on the grounds that this implied a violent act of forced eviction. Csáky preferred to describe the phenomenon as "ethnobusiness."[24] In this way migration was portrayed as the logical continuation of what was regarded as "typical" Romani behavior: abuse of a state's welfare resources. Tellingly, MP Róbert Fico—one of the country's most trusted politicians—tried in January 2000 to find popular support for his newly established political party, Smer (Direction), by proposing that social benefit payments would not be given to asylum seekers for a period of twelve months after their return to Slovakia.[25] In general, various politicians suggested that the Romani migration needed to be set against the broader picture of European integration. They argued that Slovakia's responsibility for the problem was limited and that emphasis needed be placed on the "pull factors" in the countries of asylum (for example, the fact that candidate asylum seekers received a considerable subsistence allowance while going through the asylum procedure). Moreover, the Slovak government frequently argued that the international and European levels had to assume responsibility for "solving the Romani problem." During the summer of 1999, Romani migration elicited suspicion, since speculations arose that the opposition party HZDS was involved in the financial organization of a migration wave to Sweden, at that moment president of the EU, for the purpose of discrediting the Slovak government.[26]

Romani protest was further hampered by the fact that only a very limited number of Roma were indeed granted asylum, and that in many cases EU governments used ad hoc measures to stem the flow of Slovak asylum seekers. For example, in October 1999, Belgium carried out a controversial collective repatriation, which was apparently specifically aimed at discouraging this group from seeking asylum (Cahn and Vermeersch 2000). Later, Belgium—like the United Kingdom, Finland, Ireland, Denmark, and Norway—introduced visa requirements for Slovak citizens. This latter measure caused additional pressure on the diplomatic relations between Slovakia and the EU countries. Particularly symbolic for many Slovaks was that, in spite of Slovakia's recent admission to the first group of candidate states to hold detailed negotiations on EU membership, they now had to possess a visa for traveling to the European institutions in Brussels. The blame for damaging Slovakia's relations with Europe was easily put on the Roma. The widespread conviction that "Romani culture" is characterized by negative traits produced a difficult situation for those activists who wanted to contest government policy from the Romani perspective.

Within this context, Romani activists were unable to agree on a single way of dealing with the refugee question. A large number of the Slovak

Romani activists whom I interviewed deemed this a crucial question. Within this group of activists very diverse and sometimes contradictory aspects of the issue were emphasized. A number of interviewees emphatically referred to discrimination as the root cause of Romani migration. Some of these, especially those activists connected to the political party RIS, spoke about their attempts to use the migration issue to put pressure on the government. Some of them had even published articles in newspapers or appeared on television, threatening that more Roma would leave Slovakia if no serious endeavors were made to improve the situation of the Roma. Others, however, argued that the rise in the number of asylum seekers was not necessarily a positive development for the Romani movement. Some expressed concern over the general image of Romani political parties, especially after there had been public speculation about deliberate attempts by Romani political parties to organize the migration.[27] Still others expressed concern about the negative impact of the responses of certain receiving countries (the introduction of visa requirements, for example) on the position of the Roma in Slovakia. One Romani activist said:

> the migration issue made our job [as activists] harder. The [non-Romani] majority acts more negatively towards us. They blame every Roma for the whole situation. It's an obstacle for our communication [with the majority]. For this reason, I made a statement on television asking the Roma not to leave the country. (Personal interview)

Two Slovak Romani activists whom I interviewed even stated quite clearly that they doubted that discrimination was the real reason for Roma to flee the country. They referred to unemployment and poverty as the main incentives. Another Romani activist argued that a *few* of the Romani asylum applicants were perhaps not "real" refugees, but that most of them were. He claimed that the Slovak government and the receiving countries had discriminated against the Roma by regarding them *all* as economic refugees.

In sum, one should conclude that the migration issue did not lead to unified strategies within the Romani movement. From the arguments offered by the activists themselves, one is led to consider several possible reasons for this. The first reason relates to the position of the Romani activists in relation to the institutions created for executing Romani policies. The Romani activists who cooperated with these government institutions disagreed with the argument that the Roma were really fleeing persecution. By doing so, however, they undermined the legitimacy of the claims of those who wanted to pressure the government by referring to the waves of migration.

The second reason is related to the views of the activists on how to combat the stigmatizing of Romani identity. Those activists who utilized the migration crisis to buttress their protests argued that the tendency of the public officials and the media to blame the Roma for the recent discrediting of Slovakia's bid for EU accession was a clear illustration of the racist character of Slovak society. Other activists, however, opposed Romani migration since they reasoned that it had done nothing but intensify prejudice against the Roma. Their primary concern was to prevent the Roma from being considered the factor responsible for blocking Slovakia's entrance to the EU.

Thirdly, the positions of the activists on the refugee crisis were dependent on how the problems facing the Roma were defined. Those activists who considered discrimination and persecution the fundamental reasons for the Roma's exit strategies blamed the authorities for failing to offer Roma the appropriate protection. Others, however, saw the Roma's economic position as the real reason. These activists were critical of the government's failure to address economic problems. However, their criticism was to some extent problematic in the refugee debate since one's economic position is not considered a legitimate reason to seek asylum.

Welfare Rules and Civil Unrest in Eastern Slovakia
It was far from easy for Romani activists in Slovakia to turn migration into an issue around which to organize a unified Romani movement. The fear of provoking an anti-Romani backlash clearly prevented some of the activists from publicly pointing to Romani migration as an expression of protest against maltreatment at home. That such fears are a more general problem undercutting Romani movement activity was illustrated by the way activists responded to the civil unrest that broke out in a number of Romani communities in central and eastern Slovakia in February 2004 (Tancerova 2004).

The story of the Roma rioting against poverty attracted the full attention of national and international media at the time, but the details of how this outburst had occurred remain today, to a certain extent, still unclear. What is clear, however, is that at the beginning of 2004, the government's decision to introduce a change in the system of welfare support that would reduce direct social payments began causing great concern in some of the poorest communities in Slovakia. It had become clear that these welfare reforms would have a severe impact on families that were dependent on social benefits. By the end of February, as the news about this reform spread, people began rioting and stealing food from shops. Romani activists were calling upon people to protest against the measure. The government, in turn, sent out more than 2,000 policemen and armed soldiers to various villages and towns in order to quell the unrest and to prevent people from further looting and damaging local shops and supermarkets. In some places, for example in the town of Trebišov, fierce fighting broke out between police forces and the protesters.

For many Slovak Romani activists this must have been a moment between hope and despair. They responded to the events in contrasting ways. Some activists saw in these events an important opportunity to galvanize Roma into unified protest action. They argued that it was a good moment to demand new governmental measures for the Roma by keeping up the momentum of protest and channeling the anger of the populations involved into a mass collective strike. Ladislav Fízik was one of the most vocal activists on this issue; he argued that it was time for a "strike alert" for "all Slovak citizens dependent on social aid."[28] He called upon the Roma to assemble for a large-scale peaceful protest demonstration.[29] Meanwhile, other activists appealed directly to the Roma with quite a different message. They launched a call that emphasized the need to stop looting, go back home, and demonstrate willingness to work. According to the activist František Guľaš, for example, the clashes that had appeared in the town of Trebišov were actually to be blamed on the calls for protest launched by Fízik. The Romani political party ROI-SR publicly distanced itself from activists who supported the protests.[30]

These two latter responses may seem slightly bizarre, especially when seen in light of Fízik's statements to Slovak press agencies that the Roma were not interested in creating unrest but rather wanted to show to the wider public that they were the victims of structural unemployment. "We don't want to steal and rob," he said, "we only want to work"[31]—a statement that was remarkably consistent with the views promulgated by activists like Guľaš. But the disagreements between activists are more understandable when seen against the background of the highly charged context in which their statements were made. While minority rights organizations, such as the European Roma Rights Center (ERRC), had argued from the outset that the new social provisions were discriminatory in nature and had been designed specifically to cut the number of Roma on the welfare rolls, government officials deflected that criticism by arguing that it was not the welfare cutbacks that were to blame but rather the illegal moneylenders who operate within Romani communities. These loan sharks, the Dzurinda government argued, were the ones who had urged the rioters. Meanwhile, other politicians who had been in favor of benefit cuts, such as Róbert Fico, publicly threatened the Roma by arguing that these riots could easily provoke extremist responses from "Slovaks." The ERRC noted that responses by local officials and security forces to the rioting were "primarily collectively punitive, further deeply alienating Romani communities."[32]

In sum, Romani activists found themselves maneuvering in the narrow space between, on the hand, criticizing the government and, on the other hand, avoiding being seen as responsible for defending illegal moneylenders and stimulating welfare dependency. Unfortunately, they did not manage to find a unified position in that narrow discursive space.

Nevertheless, the episode of increased tension did have a certain impact on Romani movement action and government policy. On February 25, international news agencies reported that thousands of Roma were peacefully demonstrating in eastern and western Slovakia, without any signs of people rioting or looting. Radio Free Europe Newsline noted that demonstrators carried banners expressing their willingness to work. Meanwhile the cabinet of Prime Minister Dzurinda decided to increase community-service wages and funding for a number of social programs to soften the impact of the welfare reforms.

Conclusion

The primary purpose of this chapter has been to describe the emergence and development of domestic Romani movement activity in Hungary, Slovakia, and the Czech Republic. I have analyzed recent developments in this area by examining the initiatives of Romani activists and organizations. The chapter has also explored some of the most important strategic choices that Romani activists were faced with. I have argued that these various choices, located either inside or outside electoral politics, were all characterized by their own specific complexities.

One overall conclusion made on the basis of the material reviewed in this chapter relates to the fragmentation of the Romani movement. In the three countries under study fragmentation followed both competition among actors for symbolic and material resources, and disagreement about strategies. The stakes involved were, among others, state funding for certain types of organizations (e.g. the minority self-government system in Hungary) or appointed positions in governmental bodies (e.g. the advisory bodies in the Czech Republic and Slovakia). Strategic preferences were related to decisions about whether or not to engage in electoral politics, to cooperate with government institutions, and to agree with the interpretations of events promulgated by politicians in power and prominent media. This last aspect should be seen in the more general field of discourse politics and the politics of interpretation that played an important role in the development of the Romani movement. I focus on the power of interpretation in the next chapter.

Chapter 4

The Power of Framing

"In a provocative formulation," writes Jane Jenson, "we might say that opportunities do not exist until perceived, interests do not exist until defined, and constituencies do not exist until named" (Jenson 1998: 5). Also other movement scholars have recently pointed out that opportunities, interests, discontent, resources, etc. are not simply "out there" in the external world, but have to be cognitively perceived, constructed, defined, communicated, and mediated into public discourses, that is, "framed," to become a basis for collective action (Koopmans and Statham 2000: 35).

When activists want to form a movement they have to deal with matters connected to interpretation and signification. A large part of social movement activity, in fact, consists of attempts by activists to invest situations and symbols with meaning. Before a movement can be successful activists must point to opportunities, define interests, and name constituencies in order to shape the public's understanding, and to persuade people to join or support their movement. In the words of Donatella della Porta and Mario Diani, collective action is facilitated by processes of "interpretative frame alignment," that is, by the "convergence of models of interpretation of reality adopted by movement leaders and those of the population which they intend to mobilize" (della Porta and Diani 1999: 82). This chapter examines more closely the role that these framing processes have played for Romani mobilization.

How should empirical research identify processes of frame alignment? Robert Benford and David Snow (2000) have propounded a number of useful heuristic concepts for analyzing frames. They propose to distinguish between two core framing tasks that social movement leaders need to carry out. The first task is "identity framing." Activists need to define the group they want to mobilize. More specifically, they need to do so by promoting particular views on the group's collective identity, and by defining the boundaries of that identity. Their second task is "problem framing." This is closely linked to the concept of "problem definition" as it has regularly been used in the study of policy making, and especially in research on how policy-making agendas are set (Anderson 2000; Stone 1998). Benford and Snow's innovation is that they consider "problem framing" to be not only the work of policy makers. Other social actors, too, such as movement leaders or the media promulgate perceptions of reality that are "constitutive." In order to mobilize a group, activists need to draw the attention of potential group members to a particular problem, and explain that problem in such a way that it warrants collective action. This can be done through "diagnostic framing" (identifying the cause of the problem) and "prognostic framing" (identifying remedies for the perceived problem).

But this is not all. Framing attempts by movement leaders do not take place in a vacuum. Mainstream political actors (allies and opponents), too, frame reality for political purposes. It is what some authors have called "counterframing." Counterframing is likely to be powerful, since politicians often have better access to mass media than movement leaders. Moreover, movement frames are likely to be influenced by the "cultural setting" of a given society, i.e. the particular understandings of reality that circulate within a society and are more often than not supported and promulgated by politicians and the mass media (Benford and Snow 2000: 628). According to Sidney Tarrow, framing by movement leaders involves setting a strategic course between the counterframing by political allies and opponents, the opinions of the ordinary citizens whose support is needed, and the cultural setting (Tarrow 1996: 123).

This chapter is divided into four sections. Drawing on interviews with Romani activists, I first explore aspects of *problem definition*, that is, the divergent ways in which Romani movement leaders have understood and framed the Romani issue. Secondly, I turn to aspects of *subject definition* as it appears in these same interviews. This section will focus on the various ways in which movement leaders have framed Romani identity. Then, the chapter takes us out of the Romani movement and concentrates on the *dominant political discourses*. On the basis of statements by politicians and civil servants, and drawing on the analysis of government reports about the situation of the Roma, this section will discuss some of the ways in which policy makers have framed the Romani issue. In concluding this chapter, I will briefly deal with the cultural setting and the *effectiveness* of Romani movement frames.

Problem Definition in the Accounts of the Activists

Ethnic Discrimination

In the previous chapter I showed how, in response to the refugee crisis, Romani activists, governments, and media offered divergent accounts of the same events. This section goes one step further and attempts to see the basic framing strategies of Romani activists with regard to what in the most general sense can be labeled the "Romani issue." What, according to these activists, is the issue? No doubt the most prominent explanation was ethnic discrimination. Many of the Romani activists I interviewed based their arguments on the premise that wherever Roma find themselves, they are inherently connected to each other because of the shared experience of discrimination. Arguably, this frame constitutes one of the core motivations of the movement. Most Romani activists believed that in order to create a Romani movement, one has to make people conscious of the fact that the Roma are discriminated against because of their ethnic identity (and not because of their personal capacities). Other problems, such as poverty, unemployment, illiteracy, and ill health must in this view be considered as by-products of discrimination.

My interviews revealed that the discrimination frame was relatively uniform in its direction of attribution. Anti-Romani bias was seen as an entrenched characteristic of non-Romani groups in society. Usually it appeared as a "narrow" discrimination frame; this means that activists emphasized the existence of patterns of *intentional* discrimination by non-Romani citizens and, especially, by authorities. When asked about what prompted their engagement in the Romani movement, the overwhelming majority of activists referred to the negative intentions of non-Roma. They talked about the image of the Roma in public opinion, the discrimination in public institutions, the attacks of extremist groups on Romani families, the deliberate targeting of Roma by the police, and the lack of protection offered by the authorities. A few Romani activists argued that anti-Romani discrimination should not necessarily be seen as deliberate. This "broad" understanding of discrimination allowed seeing it as the *unintended* effect of otherwise neutral practices and developments, such as economic restructuring or political transformation. Although this latter, more moderate view was put forward by a number of activists, materials published by activists suggest that it was rarely employed to attract movement participants.

The discrimination frame was most clearly in evidence during instances of successful Romani mobilization. One example from Hungary is the foundation of Phralipe in the wake of the protests in Miskolc in 1989. The founding documents of Phralipe show that discrimination by authorities and the population at large was considered to be nothing less than the principal cause of the problematic situation of the Roma in general. The founding declaration argues that the Roma were deliberately forced to the margins of society because of "popular prejudice" and deliberate ignorance on the part of policy makers (Phralipe 1989: 3).

There was a less overt use of the narrow discrimination frame in the Czech and Slovak Republics at the beginning of the 1990s. Most Czech and Slovak Romani activists referred to this period in terms of the need to gain better Romani representation in politics so as to overcome the discrimination of the past. ROI-SR, for example, demanded that the Roma be recognized as a national minority and aimed for an increase of Romani representatives in politics. The underrepresentation was not seen as caused by deliberate discrimination on the part of the new political leaders. Later, this view changed sharply. During the second half of the 1990s, there was clearly an increased use of a narrow discrimination frame in both the Czech Republic and Slovakia. In the Czech Republic the promotion of this perspective was closely linked to the increased number of attacks on Roma, the problems posed by the citizenship law, and the refugee crisis. Political representation was still deemed a problem, but the prime cause of the "Romani problem" was now clearly found in the high levels of intolerance, the unprecedented levels of anti-Roma violence, and the unwillingness of the government to address these issues. Increasing Romani political representation, pushing back poverty, and creating a better position for the Roma generally were all seen as tasks secondary in importance to addressing anti-Romani discrimination.

In Slovakia, this development was reflected in the emergence of new political entities alongside ROI-SR after 1996. As discussed in the previous chapter, for the purpose of gaining Romani representation in parliament, some of the activists associated with ROI-SR at certain times supported cooperation with Mečiar's HZDS and for this reason shifted their focus away from discrimination. In 1996, RIS—at the time a new Romani political party—tried to change this agenda and framed Romani activism more clearly within the context of the fight against discrimination. Interviews in 2000 revealed that many ROI-SR activists had also adopted this frame by that time and began accusing the authorities and main political actors of deliberate discrimination. But even at the end of the decade, Romani activists still held divergent opinions on how the problem should be framed. The spokesman of the Romani Parliament (*Rómsky parlament*) argued that the most important political demand of his group was for an increase in the number of Roma in "government, municipalities, and political decision-making processes" (personal interview). Therefore, he believed, activists should be open to the interpretations of the major political parties. At a working seminar organized by RIS in 1999, one participant clearly abandoned the discrimination frame by stating: "the Roma should first fix their own problems, before blaming others. The biggest enemy of the Roma are the Roma themselves" (quoted in Young 1999: 1). Other activists at this meeting argued that protest against discrimination should remain the main focus. It was thus possible to observe shifting positions and continuing disagreement. However, the amount of disagreement between Romani activists with regard to problem interpretation was, according to some of the interviewees at least, not to be overestimated. In 2001, the Government Commissioner for the Solution of the Problems of the Romani Minority, Klára Orgovánova, argued that Romani parties such as RIS, RIZS, and ROI-SR actually had a very similar understanding of the problem. Disagreement in problem analysis stemmed mostly from their strategic choices. All were quick to moderate their views when opportunities arose to cooperate with mainstream political parties.

Poverty and Social Behavior

However general, widespread, and prominent the ethnic discrimination frame may seem, not all Romani activists agreed with it. A small number of Romani activists attached less importance to the role of ethnicity, and alluded instead to the Roma's socioeconomic position as the main cause of discrimination. In their view not *all* Roma were always discriminated against. Rather, discrimination was linked to lifestyle and economic status: those who found themselves in impoverished circumstances tended to be subject to it. The main issue was thus poverty and the associated attitudes of the poor Roma.

In contrast to the ethnic discrimination frame the direction of attribution was less clear in this case. Some activists apportioned blame not only to the prejudiced attitudes of non-Roma, but sometimes also to the personal choices and actions of Romani individuals. A good example is Emil Ščuka's interpretation of the problem of segregated education in the Czech Republic. After his election as president of the International Romani Union (IRU) in 2000, the Slovak-born former leader of ROI became an internationally well-known Czech Romani activist. At a workshop organized in the framework of the Khamoro World Roma Festival in Prague in May 2003, Ščuka said that he had slightly revised his opinions on why Roma in the Czech Republic were generally not well educated. While earlier he had pointed to the mechanisms of discrimination that had put many Romani children in substandard schooling and in schools for the mentally disabled, he now argued that Romani parents were also in part responsible for the state of affairs by keeping their children deliberately away from education. He pleaded with the government to increase its fight against poverty but at the same time asked the Roma to break with attitudes that keep them isolated in their abject material conditions (personal interview).

This frame was clearly less successful in attracting support from Romani communities. Several reasons stand out. First, activists propagating this frame were usually unable to find powerful allies. Advocacy organizations in the three countries mostly emphasized ethnic discrimination. By pointing to impoverishment as a consequence of failing social policies, Romani activists could in theory form coalitions with organizations that attempt to support and represent the poor. In practice, however, few such political links were forged.

Secondly, activists were rather reluctant to frame poverty and social behavior as the core of the problem because such framing was often understood as stigmatizing. Some activists feared that focusing on this issue could convey the message that the cause of the problem was located within the Romani minority itself. Poverty would then be seen as the consequence of "unadjusted" social behavior (stealing, begging, loansharking, etc.). In such a view, it would be the Roma's alleged inability to create better living conditions for themselves that stood at the core of the problem. In an even more accusatory version, *their* supposed unwillingness to engage in social integration would be blamed. It is obvious that such framing is not very different from the blatant "blame the victim" rhetoric often used by individuals and organizations who directly oppose Romani movement formation. Some Romani activists felt reluctant to expose situations of poverty in their mobilization attempts, precisely because they feared it would force them to talk about problematic social behavior and the inability of some to escape the vicious circle of poverty.

A good illustration is the views of activists about the situation in Luník IX in eastern Slovakia. Luník IX is a housing estate in the outskirts of Slovakia's second most populous city, Košice, where around 4,000 Romani inhabitants live. It was built at the beginning of the 1980s as a residential area for dignitaries of the city of Košice, but was soon changed into a social housing project (Bačová and Bača 1994). In the 1990s the quality of the housing deteriorated quickly, and it became the location where the city's poorest population was placed. In 1995, in the course of an urban renewal project, the city of Košice approved a resolution that designated Luník IX as a housing estate for the "socially problematic." In practice, the area became a ghetto for poor Roma. Luník IX attracted foreign journalists and politicians, especially after it had become clear that a considerable number of Romani asylum seekers who came to EU countries from Slovakia were from this housing estate. Although the situation in Luník IX has its own historical particularities, it nevertheless began to function as a symbol of the plight of the Roma in the whole of Slovakia, this being perhaps best illustrated by the decision of the European Commissioner responsible for enlargement, Günter Verheugen, to visit Luník IX during an official visit to Slovakia in February 2001.

It is interesting to consider the way in which activists framed the problem. International activists and Roma in Bratislava tended to see Luník IX as caused by ethnic discrimination, in keeping with the view of supportive organizations such as the European Roma Rights Center (ERRC). They referred to Luník IX as a symbol, representative of the general situation of the Roma in Slovakia. Within Luník IX, however, there were local activists who felt reluctant to publicize the concrete situations that occurred within the housing estate, since they were afraid that they themselves would be held responsible for what they regarded as the inability of the inhabitants to change their predicament. In other words, the activists feared that they would not succeed in persuading anyone of the interpretation that what was generally perceived as the abject social behavior inherent to the Roma was in fact caused by external circumstances. Many of the references to Luník IX in the dominant political discourse and the media did indeed accuse the Roma of creating the trouble. Descriptions of Luník IX often served to "evidence" that it was not discrimination but the ignorant lifestyles of the Roma that were at the root of the problem. When housing is offered to them, they simply do not appreciate it and do not take care of it, so the argument went. In 1996, Alexander Weber (HZDS), at that time mayor of Luník IX, told a research mission led by the Slovak Helsinki Committee that it was one of the ideas from totalitarian times to "civilize the Roma," but that history had shown this to be impossible (Young 1996: 3). Some Romani activists in Slovakia feared that a movement campaign focusing on the poverty and material conditions in Luník IX would be counterproductive and induce further negative stereotyping.

In Hungary, some Romani activists expressly referred to problematic behavior as a feature of the "Romani problem." Sometimes this problematic behavior was seen as closely tied to traditions and habits. Most often, however, it was explained as the result of the Roma's general lack of education, and their current unwillingness to be educated. Just as Hungarian Romani Menyhért Lakatos talked at the beginning of the 1980s about the need to "civilize" the Roma, a number of activists at the end of the 1990s pleaded for a policy of actively "developing" them. Organizations such as the Democratic Alliance of Hungarian Gypsies (MCDSz), the Federation of Roma in Hungary for the Safeguarding of Interests (MCESz), and even Phralipe focused on the need to change the general behavior of the Roma. It is far from being the case that this point of view was always presented as a way to "culturally adapt" the Roma to such an extent that they would become assimilated in the dominant society. It is striking that the same people who seemingly argued in favor of cultural adjustment often stood up in their accounts for the protection of Romani cultural traditions and the use of the Romani language. Arguably, this should not be seen as a contradiction. Closer reading of their statements reveals that most of the activists talked about the socioeconomic adaptation of the Roma (the abolishment of certain objectionable aspects associated with the socioeconomic position of the Roma in society) and the promotion of certain other, more positively viewed aspects of their culture (such as language, music, etc.).

Prognostic Framing: Employing the Minority Rights Discourse

When I asked Romani activists about what they considered their most important demands, the word "rights" frequently surfaced. The 1990s saw a growing consensus among Romani activists that the situation of the Roma could not be ameliorated as long as their rights were not sufficiently protected. An increasing number of Romani activists applied a rights frame, making various more specific frames subordinate to that.

The word "rights" was usually applied in a metaphorical and broad normative sense, and did not always imply litigation or demands for legal change. That was arguably one of the strengths of the frame. The rights discourse was able to unite divergent opinions and varied strategies, it was applicable to very different contexts, and it could draw inspiration from the documents of a broad range of international advocacy organizations. Complaints about both deliberate and indirect discrimination could be included in the larger frame of lack of respect for human rights. Demands for political representation were placed within a frame of civil and political rights. Demands for special measures to tackle poverty and unemployment could be framed in terms of social and economic rights. There were even, although to a lesser extent, demands for cultural rights, in the sense of the right to education in the Romani language or the support of a nomadic lifestyle. The rights frame was able to bridge seemingly contradictory perceptions of a given problem. Whether the problem was to be seen as related to discrimination, poverty, or to a lack of social skills, in all cases the perspective of rights protection offered a useful vocabulary to demand action and stimulate mass support.

Employing a rights frame also enabled alliances with other actors. Again Phralipe serves as a good example. As was mentioned earlier, Phralipe managed to bring together both identity-oriented Romani activists and reform-oriented liberals by emphasizing Hungary's obligation to protect the basic human rights of *all* its citizens. In order to achieve this, Phralipe argued that Roma needed to be recognized as a nationality and protected in a legal framework that granted them minority rights. As Phralipe's founding document summarized the matter,

> This political movement is founded on the alliance of an independent Gypsy intelligentsia concerned [with] the common future of [the] Gypsies and Hungarians with intellectuals and other groups in society, both Gypsy and non-Gypsy, who are increasingly aware of their shared interests. (Phralipe 1989: 2)

In the Czech republic the issue of citizenship rights was a crucial issue fostering demands for appropriate human rights protection. In Slovakia, some Romani activists jumped on the bandwagon of protest against Mečiar by the Magyar minority and by NGOs supporting democracy and human rights.

The circumstances in which this frame proved successful were clearly linked to the international environment. The growing presence of international advocacy organizations in the three countries under consideration, and the increasing need for Central European countries to comply with international norms, was no doubt part of the reason for the success of the discourse of rights among Romani activists. Illustrative of this trend was the establishment in 1996 of an international public-interest law organization called the European Roma Rights Center (ERRC). The organization stated that its purpose was to act as a public advocate on behalf of the Roma. In a short period of time, this Budapest-based advocacy group, although not uncontested, was able to become one of the central supportive organizations for the Romani movement.

Interestingly, however, in terms of mass mobilization, this frame proved less effective. It did not attract a large and persistent following, not even the kind of support many of the more pessimistic activists had hoped for. Arguably, part of the reason was connected to the fact that many saw the rights discourse as a plea for *minority* rights. Although the demand for minority rights—in the sense of rules of exemption and special policies directed at ethnic minority groups—was picked up in domestic policy, as well as by NGOs in the three countries under consideration, it lacked the unanimous support of the Roma. There was no consensus among Romani activists about the usefulness of minority rights as an appropriate answer to their concerns. My interviews seem to suggest that this had to do, first of all, with the lack of clarity about what minority rights were supposed to mean in the case of the Roma. Especially in the Czech Republic and Slovakia, there were many Romani activists who strongly emphasized the need for minority rights, but few had concrete proposals for exemption measures or special positive regulations. The debates on this topic soon narrowed down to the question of whether it was advisable to produce handbooks on Romani history and organize education in the Romani language, issues that appeared to have little mobilizing potential.

More fundamentally, the lack of success of the minority rights discourse probably also related to the interpretations of many Roma that minority rights were not the appropriate answer to the problems they were facing. The most obvious example pertains to the status of the Romani language in education, about which there were mixed opinions. Some of the Roma to whom I talked expressed doubts about the usefulness of providing education in the Romani language. Even if they agreed in principle that language protection was important, from a more practical point of view they argued that participation in mainstream education was their greatest concern, and that teaching in Romani would not help to foster their acceptance in mainstream education.

The feeling that the granting of specific types of minority rights, such as self-government rights and cultural autonomy, were not a suitable answer to the problems facing the Roma was clearly detectable among Hungarian Romani activists. As was mentioned at the beginning of Chapter 2, one of the people doubting the merits of the self-government system was one of Hungary's best-known Romani activists, Aladár Horváth. At the time of my interviews with him in 1999 and 2000, Horváth had already been outside Phralipe for several years, and his opinion on what should be done to change the Roma's predicament had changed considerably in this period. At the beginning of the 1990s, Horváth had vigorously campaigned in favor of the minority rights system. More specifically, he had demanded self-government powers and the possibility of organizing educational and political institutions specifically for the Roma. His argument had been that the protection of individual rights could not guarantee that the situation of the Roma would soon change. In his view, then, minority rights were a necessary supplement to individual rights, needed to assure that the rights of the Roma were sufficiently protected. However, even before the introduction of the system of minority self-governments, Horváth began to doubt whether cultural autonomy and self-government rights were really what Roma needed. Soon he concluded that the minority self-government system was not able to ensure even a minimal form of what Will Kymlicka has called "ethnocultural justice" (Kymlicka 2001b: 72). Horváth believed the system would not be able to diminish discrimination. Moreover, he argued that the self-government system would create increasing competition and conflict for public office and resources among minority activists. In 2001, Horváth claimed that the whole system was "well suited to the purpose of institutionalizing segregation" (Kosztolányi 2001: 147). Minority rights, at least the minority rights protection system as it had been devised in Hungary, seemed to him deficient. To be sure, Horváth continued to be sympathetic towards minority rights as a principle, and lobbied for both the protection of Romani language and Romani language education. However, for the purposes of political action, he contended that Romani activism in Hungary primarily needed to be aimed at securing respect for *individual* human rights, since, he argued, "minority rights mean nothing if you don't even have basic human rights" (personal interview).

Subject Definition within the Romani Movement

Within Romani communities one often hears both "Roma" and "Gypsies" used as self-designations. Strikingly, these names are often treated as synonyms. There is, however, some anecdotal evidence to support the assertion that the word "Gypsy" is frequently used by Roma (as by non-Roma) to refer to someone who maintains a condemnable lifestyle. Michael Stewart, for example, encountered during fieldwork in a Hungarian Romani ghetto someone who asserted that he would like to stop being "*cigány*," while having no intentions of ceasing to be "Romani" (Stewart 1997: 114). In the Czech Republic and Slovakia as well, as I mentioned earlier, the term Gypsy has strong negative overtones among Roma, although it has to some extent continued to be used by "ordinary" Roma as a self-designation. In the language of activists, the usage of the term Roma (and the refusal of the term Gypsy) had manifest political purposes, and articulated new conceptions of Romani identity. The question I now want to turn to is: What conceptions of Romani identity did Romani movement actors use to mobilize a constituency? I contend that in Central Europe three main types of Romani identity frames were used to describe and underpin Romani collective action (Vermeersch 2003).

A Nonterritorial Nation

The first way in which activists described their constituency was as a nonterritorial nation. The Romani activists who subscribed to this perspective emphasized the view that all Roma in Europe possess a common history and, especially, a common origin. The apparent fragmentation of the different groups was in their view caused by assimilation attempts and repressive policies. They argued furthermore that all Romani communities are somehow deeply connected, not through territory but through blood ties, common history, and culture; and that therefore they should be granted a special European legal status—although there were usually no precise descriptions of what such a regulation should exactly mean in legal and practical terms.

This frame is clearly based on ideas promoted by international Romani activists in the 1960s and 1970s. I referred earlier to the first World Romani Congress (WRC), organized in London in 1971. At this first WRC, a flag and anthem were chosen and a unifying principle was promoted: "our state is everywhere where there are Roma, because Romanestan is in our hearts" (Marushiakova and Popov 2001b). Similar views were formulated by more recent organizations that claim to represent a cross-border Romani constituency, such as the German-based Roma National Congress (RNC) and the short-lived Europe-wide Romani organization EUROM (PER 2001b: 35). In both organizations Czech, Slovak, and Hungarian Romani activists participated. The RNC was the most vocal in demanding a special status for the Roma in Europe, and even drew up a European Charter on Romani Rights, which they demanded be adopted by European governments.[1] The idea of the Roma as a special European group was also promoted by the International Romani Union (IRU), an NGO that, after its foundation as the executive branch of the WRC in 1977, attempted to become the predominant forum for international Romani activism. Living up to this ambition proved not to be easy. The IRU spent most of its time searching for a clearer status and a larger constituency. In the 1990s, it was plagued by internal dissidence and leadership struggles (Acton and Klímová 2001: 162). In 2000, activists revived the IRU through a new congress held in Prague, an initiative that had been instigated by calls from international organizations such as the Council of Europe and the OSCE. There had also been a need for a legitimate international Romani agency to put forward a restitution claim for prewar financial deposits of Roma that were now made available by Swiss banks.

The fifth WRC in Prague and the project proposing that the Roma be considered an "a-territorial European nation" attracted massive attention from the media in the Czech Republic, as well as in a host of other European countries. Among domestic Romani activists in the Czech Republic, Slovakia, and Hungary, however, the response was often ambivalent. My interviews with Romani activists in Hungary revealed that the way in which the IRU sought to frame Romani identity had only a marginal impact on their activities within the Hungarian context. Although some activists pointed to the symbolic importance of the idea of the Roma as a transnational people, most of them primarily wanted to defend their position as a national minority within the Hungarian minority protection system. I was not able to find a single Hungarian Romani activist who was keen to support the idea of a special legal status for the Roma as a European nation without a state. The lack of Hungarian participation in the 2000 WRC clearly evidenced this lack of support.[2] However, there was still a belief detectable among certain activists that some kind of international cooperation among Roma was needed. They argued that this represented the best way to communicate with international organizations. Although ideas were never concrete, some Hungarian Romani activists believed that organizing an international lobby was useful for the purpose of gaining the attention of EU bodies and politicians, within the context of the process of European integration. Outside the context of European politics at the supranational level, they believed that the idea of a special "transnational" status for the Roma would be meaningless:

> Without European integration special transnational rights are meaningless. Gypsy politicians are discussing it, and four or five Romani intellectuals ... but the Roma themselves don't know anything about these discussions. So how could a Gypsy, who lives isolated, understand what these transnational rights mean? The only interest of these Roma is survival. If it is needed to be a Romani nation to survive, well, than they will choose to be Roma. If it is needed to be Hungarian, than they will be Hungarian. ... Few of them understand that it is very important to have the same rights as the Hungarians. No more, no less. There should be no segregation. And it is clear that a transnational status could mean segregation. (Personal interview)

In the Czech and Slovak Republics the IRU's current promotion of the idea of the Roma as a nonterritorial European nation had a much deeper influence on the discourse of Romani leaders. Part of the explanation is no doubt related to the specific strategic interest of the Czech and Slovak governments in promoting a view of the Roma as a transnational minority. I will return to this later. Here I want to focus on the fact that domestic Romani leaders in both countries saw the international Romani movement as the ideal way to enhance their position in domestic politics. Clearly, the election of Emil Ščuka to the presidency of the IRU at the fifth WRC in Prague in July 2000 played a significant role in the promotion of this frame in both Czech and Slovak Republics. In the first half of the 1990s, Ščuka had been the leader of the Czech part of the Romani political party ROI and later maintained a crucial figure in the Czech and Slovak Romani movements. During the latest WRC a declaration was adopted that conceptualized the Roma as nation on the basis of their common culture, language, and origin. Ščuka had been one of the main architects of the view that was propagated by this declaration. The IRU now claimed to be not just an international Romani organization, but also *the* representative organization for "all the Roma in the world" (Article 1 of the IRU Charter; Acton and Klimová 2001: 201). As Acton and Klimová note, the language of the WRC was that of a national liberation movement, although dissimilar to many other national liberation movements since it explicitly excluded *territorial* liberation as a goal.

Ščuka's ideas were widely distributed among Czech and Slovak Romani activists; not a single activist I talked to was unaware of the existence of the IRU. In particular, activists who had been present at the fifth WRC recognized its symbolic importance. Other Czech Romani activists who had advocated the nonterritorial nation frame usually maintained connections with the IRU or the Roma National Congress (RNC), although their knowledge of Romani activism in other countries was usually quite limited. For all these activists the nation frame primarily represented a useful tool for activism towards international organizations. In their view, direct lobbying of the Council of Europe and the OSCE had proven its worth; both organizations in recent times established special institutions to raise the level of awareness about the problems facing the Roma within the respective member states. Moreover, thanks to the good contacts of the IRU's Commissar for Foreign Policy (Paolo Pietrosanti) with the Transnational Radical Party and the Lista Emma Bonino in the European Parliament, the IRU was able to establish an office in the European Parliament buildings in Brussels.[3] This strategy also contributed indirectly to higher levels of external pressure and scrutiny on both the Czech and Slovak Republics. For this reason Romani activists often formulated their criticism in a language that referred to international standards such as human rights. One could perhaps argue that this strategy to some extent reflects the experience of what Yasemin Soysal (1996) has called "postnational citizenship," the idea of a citizenship that is increasingly defined according to entitlements emerging from the transnational discourse and the practice of international human rights protection. Arguably, the growing attention during the last decade of human rights organizations to the position of the Roma in both countries stimulated the development of this strategy.

Besides this symbolic importance, the concrete implications of the nation frame for domestic mobilization activity in the Czech Republic and Slovakia were quite limited. Some concrete influence of the fifth WRC could be detected in Slovakia during attempts of Romani political parties in October 2000 to unite in an electoral platform. Ščuka in his capacity as president of the IRU was present at the meeting in Košice where thirteen Romani political parties and twenty-five nonpolitical Romani organizations decided to join together in a unified Romani electoral platform for the parliamentary elections of 2002. However, the international aspect should not be seen as highly important, since the debates had been initiated by ROI-SR, a Romani political party with no clear international goals, and was unambiguously formulated as an attempt to stimulate Romani participation in the Slovak political arena.

If framing the Roma as a nonterritorial nation had any concrete relevance, it was mainly in the context of international Romani conferences. International governmental organizations became increasingly interested in these meetings; they appeared regularly, attracted more participants, and opened up new opportunities for finding financial support. One important example was the conference in July 2003 that brought governments from Central and Eastern Europe together with NGO representatives and that would lead to the "Decade of Roma inclusion" (2005–2015), an initiative sponsored in large part by George Soros's Open Society Institute and the World Bank and meant to instigate new policy strategies targeted specifically at the Roma.

The nation frame produced a number of contentions. The connection between the international level and the local needs of Romani communities was sometimes questioned. One activist argued that "Indian origin" and "trans-border cooperation" were very academic notions and thus poor tools for effective mobilization. The frame was in many cases regarded as purely symbolic. As one Czech Romani activist stated,

> We are a national minority ... The fact that the Roma are a world-wide and a European nation is only important to stress towards other countries where the Roma are not yet acknowledged as a national minority. (Personal interview)

Another contention related to the symbolic consequences of considering the Roma a separate nation. Some wondered what it would mean to be treated as a nation *within* another nation. One activist deemed this a serious problem: "Would this mean that, in the Czech Republic, for example, the Roma are no longer Czechs?" (PER 2001b: 37). One Czech activist even claimed that "ordinary" Roma were not interested in being regarded as a nation. According to him, they did not want Romani schools; they wanted to be regarded as Czechs with Havel as *their* President, too (personal interview).

Several Romani activists were also deeply suspicious of the strong verbal support the Slovak and Czech governments displayed for the WRC and the IRU Charter. Although many knew that the IRU had actively sought support from those governments, they feared that the whole process of promoting the Roma as a nonterritorial nation was primarily in the interest of individual states and not of the Roma. Such conceptualization "freed" the individual states of "their responsibility to address the problems of Romani citizens" in a domestic context, they argued (PER 2001b: 39). Thus a number of Czech and Slovak Romani activists perceived the strategy of the IRU as potentially undermining the position of the Roma as a national minority in the domestic context.

The Roma as a National Minority

The second way in which activists presented the Roma was as a national minority. Although in this case activists emphasized the difference between the Roma and the ethnic majority, they did not demand a special European status for the Roma. As the leader of ROI, Emil Ščuka had promoted this frame for most of the 1990s. At the end of the decade, however, he increasingly tried to distance himself from the view that the Roma were a minority.[4] His speech at the 2000 WRC in Prague succinctly explained why. According to Ščuka the *gadje* (non-Roma) always saw the Roma as "a minority group, a social group or even a criminal group ... Roma should not let themselves be defined in that way by outsiders" (Acton and Klímová 2001: 172). For Ščuka, promoting the frame of the Roma as a nation was a way to get rid of external control over the construction of Romani identity.

Romani activists who promoted the "national minority frame" did so primarily for two reasons. First, they tried to provide an alternative to the nonterritorial nation frame. A number of the Slovak and Czech activists to whom I talked were hesitant about giving full support to Ščuka's views, especially the view that the Roma should not be seen as a minority. In contrast to Ščuka they sought to emphasize the need for the protection of minority rights within the framework of the national state. For these activists the Czech and Slovak Republics themselves were to be understood as the homelands of the Czech and Slovak Roma; the factors determining the treatment of the Roma were believed to be in the hands of the national state. Activists who reasoned within this frame mostly lobbied for a stricter anti-discrimination policy.

Secondly, they hoped to find new allies for their projects. They looked for opportunities to form a bridge between the movement's main target audience and non-Romani supporters of minority rights. These could, for example, be other national minorities. This made sense especially in Slovakia. More than once the political success of the Magyar minority was referred to as an example. One Slovak Romani activist mentioned demands for cultural rights similar to the demands of the Magyar minority.

> Not far from Dunajská Streda there is a kindergarten only for Romani children. Some Romani parents there were angry about this, because according to them putting the

Roma in separate education is a form of discrimination. They are ashamed of being Roma. I say: the Magyar minority has its own schools where they teach their children Hungarian, so why should we be ashamed of creating a Romani school? (Personal interview)

The national minority frame was reflected in attempts by Roma in Slovakia to become involved in mainstream politics as an ethnically based political party. As mentioned, the attempts of ROI-SR in October 2000 to unite Romani political parties in an electoral platform can clearly be read as an attempt to strengthen the position of the Roma as a Slovak minority and bring it to the level of that of the Magyar minority.

However, there was no consensus among Romani activists. Some found this frame highly problematic, and this for a number of reasons. First, the experiences of the Roma were very different from that of other national minorities. In contrast to other national minorities, for example, the Roma had never had the intention to voice demands for political autonomy or territorial self-determination. This was the case not only in Slovakia, but also in the Czech Republic and Hungary. When in 1993 the Roma in Hungary were legally recognized as a national minority, Romani activists had been pleased as well as worried. Some of them had immediately voiced their doubt as to whether the Hungarian system of national minority rights protection (primarily the self-government system) was the right response to the problems the Roma were facing.

Secondly, parties and interest groups from other national minorities often distanced themselves from the Romani perspective. Slovak Romani activists, for example, estimated that only a small portion of the Magyars would fully identify itself with the plight of the Roma. Publications by Magyar organizations confirm this. For example, in 1997 the Magyar Coalition in Slovakia stated the following in one of its information books:

> Recently, the government has been trying to pretend that the Gypsy question is the most important minority issue in Slovakia. The condition of the Roma minority does indeed represent a very serious problem; however, the issues involved are very different from the unresolved issues of the Hungarians. The problems of the Roma minority are rooted in questions of a cultural, social and psychological nature, and the resolution of these problems requires a different approach to be made. (Information Center of the Hungarian Coalition in Slovakia 1997: 18)

In the Czech Republic there was even less opportunity to ally with other national minorities. The Roma did not feel any affiliation with the demands for self-government rights sometimes voiced by Moravian and Silesian political parties and civic organizations. Precisely for this reason, Karel Holomek, one of the Czech Republic's best-known activists, doubted whether establishing ethnic Romani political parties was a good idea. In his opinion a party such as ROI could not possibly be successful because it exclusively represented "minority views, which cannot be shared by others" (Holomek 1998).

There is also a third reason. Some Romani activists were concerned about conceptualizing the Roma as a national minority, because they feared that national minority rights would not primarily reflect Romani interests, but rather the interests of the authorities. According to this argument the issue of national minority rights played a fundamental role in the negotiation of the relationship between the EU states and the postcommunist candidate countries, and was therefore not driven by a real concern for the Roma. Although this criticism was only implicitly present in the interviews I conducted, it was most clearly expressed in other places. In 1997 Nicolae Gheorghe, a Romanian Romani activist and currently head of the Contact Point for Roma and Sinti Issues (CPRSI)—linked to the OSCE's Office for Democratic Institutions and Human Rights (ODIHR)—formulated the matter as follows:

> I personally am critical towards this trend in the Romani movement which seeks to fashion Romanies as a national minority because I consider that in reality, the true concept of national minority is only a by-product of nation-state building ... Ethnic minority policies are exhibited as if in a display cabinet, like a showcase in international politics to make sure that the Council of Europe and the western democracies think that things are good in eastern Europe. (Gheorghe 1997: 160)

The Roma as an Ethnoclass

The third frame conceptualizes the Roma as what could be called an "ethnoclass." I borrow the term from Ted Robert Gurr and Barbara Harff (1994), who have defined an ethnoclass as an ethnic group that resembles a class. Members of ethnoclasses are disproportionately concentrated in occupations at or near the bottom of the economic and social hierarchy (Gurr and Harff 1994: 23). Those who framed Romani identity in this way emphasized especially the detrimental social circumstances of Romani life. Romani identity, they argued, is characterized by a position at the bottom of the socioeconomic ladder. Their descriptions centered on topics in the sphere of social rights, such as the need for education, better housing, and employment. The protection of cultural aspects of Romani identity played a less prominent role; these matters were mostly regarded as strictly private. In general, activists advocated a certain degree of ethnic anonymity, while retaining the understanding that the social disadvantage of the Roma as an ethnic group has historical roots. This view was expressed, among others, by a Slovak Romani activist who in the beginning of the 1990s was involved in the establishment of a Romani party called the Party for Labor and Security (SPI):

> We disagreed with ROI-SR because we saw that they didn't manage to make any progress in integrating the Roma ... We wanted a party that would not represent only the Roma living in the East of the country [where the main support for ROI-SR is

located]. We wanted to focus on social issues in general, and most importantly, on unemployment. (Personal interview)

Another Romani activist formulated a similar perspective as follows:

> For at least two decades now, the IRU agenda has been packed with such ideas as developing a "Roma codex," codifying the language, and "renewing" old traditions and values—ideas the Romani masses really didn't care all that much about. The Romani leadership bears a responsibility to address the central problem of providing Roma with security. How the Roma will live their lives is a secondary concern. This is a matter of individual choice. (PER 2001b: 38)

There were even more extreme versions of this frame. Some activists argued in favor of the *disappearance* of Romani identity as an ethnic identity, and sought to mobilize on the basis of a demand for economic homogenization. For them, elements of ethnic culture, such as the Romani language, were nothing more than an obstacle. Slovak anthropologist Arne Mann refers to the existence of a Romani political party in Slovakia at the beginning of the 1990s (the Romani Integration Party) that had a plan of action for rejecting the legal acceptance of Romani nationality and achieving "faster assimilation of the Romany ethnic group" (Mann 1992: 264; Mann 2000: 66).[5] More moderate versions of this frame had a certain appeal for people who experienced that receiving attention as a national minority did not necessarily diminish levels of stereotyping. Romani activists who emphasized ethnoclass identity were well aware of this and wanted to avoid presenting themselves as too closely associated with Romani identity. They considered it unbeneficial to stress a form of identity that was generally perceived as pathological. Instead, they tried to mobilize on the basis of their social situation as poor or disadvantaged citizens.

Many Roma who advocated such a way of framing their movement identity had positive memories about the communist period. For them postcommunism had brought only a substantial decline in living standards and exclusion from economic opportunity. It is no doubt true that many Roma in the three countries under consideration had been in a better economic position during communist rule (and certainly in a situation where the relative deprivation was not as high). Nevertheless, none of the attempts by Romani movement actors to capitalize upon such feelings of nostalgia proved to be successful. Those Roma who favored diminishing the importance attached to ethnic differences, and chose instead to demand economic support for poor communities in general, hoped to find more successful lobby groups outside the Romani movement.

Policy Perspectives: Top-down Problem and Subject Definitions

It is now time to consider some of the policy documents (government reports and resolutions) of the latter half of the 1990s and the beginning of the 2000s and investigate the ways in which governments framed the "Romani problem." I will argue that policy makers in Central Europe mainly utilized four basic reccurring problem definitions. They focused on (a) the social behavior of the Roma, (b) patterns of discrimination by the ethnic majority or the state, (c) the failure of economic and social integration due to the unwillingness of the Roma or the lack of adequate policies in the past, and (d) the current lack of state protection.

These problem frames differed in scope and basic style of argumentation, and corresponded to various models for solution. They also varied with regard to whom or what they regarded as the culpable agents and the causal factors—what Benford and Snow (2000: 618) have called the "locus of attribution." Within the "social behavior" frame and also, in part, in the "failure of social or economic integration" frame, the Roma themselves were usually blamed for causing the problem. The "failure of social or economic integration" frame generally devoted less attention to the social behavior of the Roma, but rather emphasized material circumstances (poverty, unemployment, housing etc.) and state responsibility for ensuring better conditions. The cause of the problem was in this latter case attributed to the failure of the state to remedy the circumstances, although this frame was clearly not entirely free of the tendency to place some of the responsibility on the Roma. In the "discrimination" frame, blame was usually put on the side of the ethnic majority or the authorities. Official reports sometimes held the state responsible because of its failure to provide good anti-discrimination legislation and to prevent discrimination in public services. At other times, emphasis was placed on the discriminatory attitudes of the non-Romani citizens. The "lack of cultural protection" frame clearly placed responsibility in the lap of policy makers. Documents sometimes associated the current problems with past reluctance to accommodate the rights of the Roma as a minority culture.

Before embarking on an in-depth discussion of these problem frames, three brief points need to be made. First, problem descriptions in official documents are usually rather general, implicit, and vague. Perhaps this is due to the fact that they needed to unite different opinions. Moreover, sometimes within a single government report or resolution one can find *various* contrasting problem frames alongside one another, presumably reflecting some variety of opinion within the government. Overall, however, one sees that in each of the documents one or two main elements were regarded as the "real" problem. This is what we will focus on.

Secondly, emphasis on a particular problem frame reflects a particular moment in time. Government views are susceptible to change, and problem frames did change from one document to another. What was regarded as the principal problem in need of policy attention at a certain point in time was in later periods often construed as a by-product or an effect of a more fundamental problem. Thus, one finds shifting perspectives with regard to cause and effect.

Thirdly, an analysis of government documents should not be confused with a policy assessment. Although I argue that different problem frames give rise to different solution models, it has to be noted that I did not carry out an analysis of what constitutes a "successful" solution. In other words, this section does not seek to analyze either the quality of the policy strategies or their degree of implementation. I am concerned with the discursive construction of a "policy problem" and the formulation of policy strategies to address that problem, rather than with the process of policy implementation itself.

Slovakia

In the period from 1994 to 1998 the resolutions and accompanying explanatory reports introduced by the Slovak government maintained a strong emphasis on Romani social behavior and lifestyle as the core of the problem. For example, Resolution 310, adopted in 1996, disassociated the situation of the Roma from issues of ethnic minority protection (such as discrimination or the protection of minority language and culture) and brought it into a discourse of social needs (Government of the Slovak Republic 1996). The title of the resolution ("Activities and measures in order to solve the problems of citizens in need of special care") did not mention that the resolution was meant to assist the Roma as an ethnic minority and referred only to "citizens in need of special care." However, when reading the text of the resolution, one quickly gets the impression that the resolution was indeed meant to address the situation of the Roma as an ethnically defined group; in each of the seven paragraphs of the document the target group was named "Roma." Through its multiple references to the name Roma, the document as a whole clearly conveyed the idea that the phrase "citizens in need of special care" and the designation "Roma" were to be seen as perfectly interchangeable.

The resolution further identified a number of key areas in which the social behavior of the target group was regarded as problematic. For example, with regard to "pre-schooling and schooling of children" (paragraph A), the document mentioned irregular school attendance, poor language command, and lack of interest from the parents in education as basic problems. In paragraph B the employment situation of the target group was linked to their "low work ethic" and their lack of interest in public service jobs. With regard to housing (paragraph C), the document referred to their lack of interest "in solving their own housing problems," the devastation of apartments, and their arrears with respect to paying rents and bills. To describe health conditions, paragraph E of the resolution referred to teenage pregnancy and the "high rate of mental retardation due to socially retarding environments."

Other elements of problem attribution appeared in the text, but were clearly not the main focus. For example, paragraph A (on education) made mention of the "lack of pre-school education in kindergartens" and the fact that "teachers are not prepared to deal with the specific problems of deprived and poorly motivated children." Although this could be read as a reference to the state's failure to provide these services, in the context of the whole document it mainly served to draw attention to role of the children and their parents in creating the problem. *They* were seen as the reason why new preschool education needed to be established, and teachers needed to receive additional training. In a similar vein, paragraph B seemingly admitted that unemployment was due to lack of opportunities. Yet, the text still placed a large part of the responsibility for the amount of unemployment on the shoulders of the unemployed themselves by adding, "employers are not interested in hiring unqualified citizens." The resolution apparently ruled out the possibility that the problem could in part have been caused by the employers.

The resolution adopted by the Slovak government in 1997 (Government of the Slovak Republic 1997) and the accompanying report by Branislav Baláž (Commissioner of the Government of the Slovak Republic for Solutions of Problems of Citizens with Special Needs 1997), at that time Government Commissioner for Citizens in Need of Special Care, differed from the previous resolution mainly in that it had the name Roma in its title. For the rest, it was quite similar to the 1996 resolution. It claimed to offer concrete measures to remedy problems. In reality, it remained quite vague as to what should be seen as causes of the deplorable situation of the Roma (in areas like education, health, employment, etc.), and on how to address these causes. It did suggest that some of the problems were caused by the "interaction" of Romani and non-Romani populations. The report mentioned "integration," "positive stimulation," and reducing "social tensions" as remedies, without, however, explaining how this was to be translated in concrete policy. In comparison to the 1996 resolution, the 1997 documents were even vaguer on possible solutions for the problems described.

The resolutions adopted by the post-1998 government under premier Dzurinda represented a clear break with the line of policy promulgated by the last Mečiar government. When at the end of 1998 the government announced that it would show more "empathy" with regard to the situation of the Roma, many Romani activists expected a clear initiative in the direction of a policy specifically for Roma.[6] The newly appointed

Deputy Prime Minister for Human Rights, Minorities, and Regional Development, Pál Csáky (SMK), established the position of Government Commissioner for the Solution of the Problems of the Romani Minority, a position filled first by Vincent Danihel and later by Klara Orgovánová, both Romani activists. The Government Commissioner's office, responsible for bringing Romani concerns to the governmental level, completed a policy paper in June 1999 entitled, "Strategy of the Government for the Solution of the Problems of the Roma." In 2000, the government officially adopted a new version of this report as a resolution.

Characteristic of this change in policy was that the situation of the Roma was now seen as a matter of social inequality as well as of protection of cultural diversity. This was illustrated by the fact that besides topics that appeared in the earlier resolutions and reports (housing, employment, and health), the newly approved strategy documents also contained paragraphs on human rights, minority rights, language, and culture (Government of the Slovak Republic 1999a; Government of the Slovak Republic 2000). Also with regard to problem definition, the resolutions of 1999 and 2000 contained new elements. According to the explanatory report of the 1999 resolution, the problems facing the Roma "as a national minority should be understood as a problem concerning the whole society." This suggests that the social behavior frame had diminished in importance, although it had not completely disappeared. It stated, for example, that the Roma were an "ethnic minority whose different way of life traditionally (historically) wakes intolerance among [the] majority population," and by the characterization of the problems addressed as "the problems caused by the specific way of life of a part of the Romany national minority." By subscribing to these two statements the government suggested that the Roma themselves were to some extent the culpable agents.

Characteristic of the 1999 document was, further, that it contained, in contrast to the earlier resolutions, elements of other problem frames. Notable in this respect were the repeated statements that placed responsibility on the shoulders of the state. The Dzurinda government could allow itself to be critical of the Mečiar period since such a critical stance had been the basis of its 1998 electoral success as a democratic opposition, when it had defeated Mečiar's HZDS. Not surprisingly, then, in the 1999 government resolution some elements were included that referred directly to the failure of policy strategies during the last Mečiar government and still earlier. It specifically referred to the past inability or unwillingness of the state to protect Romani citizens from acts of discrimination. And it also held the previous government responsible for the growth of Romani unemployment. The resolution pledged to end discrimination in institutions and to introduce measures to prevent or push back discrimination by the majority population.

At the same time, however, the government tried to strike a delicate balance, and on a number of specific occasions it explicitly denied the existence of discrimination as a basic problem. This was, for example, evidenced by the response of the Slovak government to the criticism from the Council of Europe regarding Slovakia's obligation under the Framework Convention for the Protection of National Minorities (Government of the Slovak Republic 1999b):

> As regards the application of Article 4 (Point 18 of the Opinion) the Advisory Committee notes its concern about the problems related to the implementation of anti-discrimination legislation and "credible reports" concerning discrimination of the Roma minority also in health care facilities. In this respect the Government of the Slovak Republic respectfully states that the Ministry of Health Care has not registered any case of discrimination of the Roma minority in state health care facilities in the Slovak Republic and no complaints by Roma citizens have been received either. (Government of the Slovak Republic 2000a)

Important in this context is that in the resolutions of 1999 and 2000, which were coauthored by the government commissioner, an attempt was made to dissociate the concept of "Romani identity" from that of the "Romani problem." However, this undertaking was not a complete success. The view on Romani identity produced by the 1999 resolution is ambiguous. On the one hand, the accompanying explanatory report was careful not to generalize, and consistently qualified the "Romani problem" as the problem of *a part of* the Romani population. Nevertheless, the document also vaguely suggested that Romani culture and lifestyle were indeed problematic by stating that, "Some aspects of life of a certain part of this minority *cause* social distance in the majority society" or that problems are "*caused* by the specific way of life of a part of the Romany national minority" (Government of the Slovak Republic 1999a, emphasis added).

The suggestion of a natural overlap between "Romani identity" and the "Romani problem" was also reflected in the political debate surrounding the new government resolutions. Consider, for example, Csáky's description of the reason why the government had not been yet able to tackle the problematic situation of the Roma:

> Of course there isn't enough money, but that kind of question reflects a poor understanding of the situation. The Roma problem arises from the absence of a model for mutual coexistence between completely different cultures. If you had an unimaginable amount of money, could you change India into a modern European country in four years? No. Roma mentality, culture, thinking, reactions do not stem from the classic Slovak culture. We have to look for mutual coexistence, and we need time to make changes inside ourselves — both Roma and non-Roma citizens.[7]

A Slovak document distributed at a meeting of the presidents of the Visegrád countries in December 1999 contained the following description of Romani mentality.

The lifestyle of many of them is oriented towards consumption and they live from hand to mouth. Because of their lower educational standard, the philosophy of some of them is to simply survive from one day to the next. If we add their increased propensity to alcohol abuse, absence of an at least minimum degree of planning, and low concern for developing normal habits including the feeling of responsibility, hygienic habits and ethics, this philosophy is changing today to that of living "from one benefit to the next." (Office of the President of Slovakia 1999: 7)

Another characteristic of the resolutions and the surrounding political discourse was that the "Romani problem" was considered to be a "European" affair:

The problems caused by the specific way of life of a part of the Romany national minority and the problems of co-existence with the majority part of society, as well as the right choice of emancipation processes represent an exceptionally difficult multispectral problem, the solution of which is, *also in other European countries*, a topic of an open dialogue. (Government of the Slovak Republic 1999a, emphasis added)

One easily sees the strategic interest that the authorities had in showing that problems were not restricted to Slovakia but also occurred in other countries where Roma live. The "Europeanization" of the issue was a powerful frame since it could rely on the argument promoted by some Romani activists themselves that the Roma are a European nation. The popularity of placing the matter in a European context was further evidenced by Dzurinda. In an unpublished paper entitled, "Problems of the Roma ethnic minority," which was available for a while on the prime minister's website, he communicated his view on what Günter Verheugen, the European Commissioner responsible for enlargement, should learn about the Roma.

I have decided to accompany one day this week the Commissioner of the European Commission Mr. Gunter Verheugen during his journey to Roma villages and settlements. I will use this opportunity to talk in detail about the problem, which all Europe must consider to be its "own" problem. (Dzurinda 2002)

The argument about the European character of the Romani issue surfaced also in the two neighboring countries. Interestingly, it can be linked to the way in which Romani identity was seen in European bodies such as the Council of Europe and the European Commission. For example, in October 1999, Lord Russell-Johnston, the president of the Council of Europe's Parliamentary Assembly, told journalists in Bratislava that the Council of Europe "can and must" play "a significant role" in solving the "Romani problem," because the problem is "not Slovakia's, but Europe's."[8] Furthermore, Dzurinda's point of view was clearly endorsed by the European Commission. After a visit to Prešov in July 1999, European Commission ambassador in Slovakia, Walter Rochel, stated: "the Romany problem is not specific to Slovakia, but also for surrounding countries and therefore it needs to be judged from a broader point of view."[9] The European Parliament correspondent for Slovakia, Jan Marinus Wiersma, was reported to have said in January

2000 that the Romani issue was to be seen in a "pan-European" perspective. "The answer to the Romany issue," he argued, "is a priority not only in Slovakia, but also in all EU countries."[10]

The Czech Republic

Is it possible to find similar ways of problem and subject framing in the Czech case? Between 1993 and 1997 the Czech Republic addressed Romani issues within the context of a general minority policy (the basis of which was established by Resolution 63/1994). The problem framing by Prime Minister Václav Klaus and his government varied over the years. Klaus's initial declarations were that a "Romani problem" did not exist (Fawn 2001: 1208). His view changed sharply when in 1995 the case of a murdered Romani man aroused a great deal of media attention. Klaus convened a special meeting in which he called for a strong response to ethnic-related crimes. At the same time, however, the Romani representatives in the Council of National Minorities had already for some years strongly insisted on the need to pay special attention to the Roma, particularly with regard to manifestations of intolerance and discrimination. The government responded to this with a number of decisions enjoining the appropriate ministries to adopt measures against ethnic violence (Resolutions 67/1993 and 580/1995), and to investigate the situation of children both in education and on the labor market (e.g. Resolution 210/1993). However, Klaus himself remained quite defiant about criticism on such issues as the discriminatory effect of the citizenship law and the increase of Romani marginality.

A clear problem framing of the situation of the Roma only emerged in 1997, when, in response to the persistence of ethnicized violence and the growth of the number of Czech asylum seekers, the then Minister without Portfolio, Pavel Bratinka, submitted a report mapping out "the problems connected with the Romani community" (Council for Nationalities of the Government of the Czech Republic 1997). Unlike the Baláž report in Slovakia, the Bratinka report was quite critical of the ruling government, mostly with respect to its failure to formulate a strong condemnation of intolerance. The Bratinka report also differed significantly from the Baláž report in the area of problem framing. Perusing the report, one quickly finds that the social behavior frame was employed but did not predominate. For example, the assertion that there are "specific acts by members of the Romani community" that cause problems was immediately put into a larger perspective.

> The cause is not only specific acts by members of the Romani community, coming partly from their past experience, but at least equally also the majority's attitudes. (Council for Nationalities of the Government of the Czech Republic 1997: Paragraph ii)

Further down, the report also stated:

> the majority population is not aware of the Roma's recent history and also does not acknowledge the extent to which it has itself caused the Romani community's current situation. (Council for Nationalities of the Government of the Czech Republic 1997: Paragraph 1.3)

When the report alluded to problematic behavior, it added that this had to be seen as a symptom of underlying, more fundamental problems that fall under the responsibility of the ethnic majority or the state administration. Consider, for example, the following statement on unemployment.

> The high level of Romani unemployment is a problem for society as a whole, partly caused by the lifestyle of some members of the Romani community, partly by inadequate measures from state and local government.

The way in which the government under Miloš Zeman (1998–2002) framed the issue from 1998 onwards was clearly based on a similar perception. A frame was constructed in which both the Roma and the state were seen as having contributed to the aggravation of the problem. A certain amount of responsibility for improving the situation was put in the hands of the Roma. In the run-up to the 2002 elections, for example, a party spokesman for the Czech social democrats (ČSSD) said: "the mutual responsibility for the improvement of the social life of the Romany citizens is also in the hands of the Romany organizations, which may exert their natural authority."[11]

Official reports, as well as statements by politicians in power, expressed the view that integration attempts by the authorities had failed in the past and that the government should bear responsibility for providing better opportunities for the Roma. However, official reports and statements remained ambiguous as to whether creating better opportunities and equal chances involved the introduction of any proactive measures (financial or other) and institutions specifically meant to support the Roma. As I noted earlier, while since 1997 there was an increasing tendency to construct special Romani policies and design special institutions for accommodating Romani concerns, major politicians in their communication with Czech citizens sharply emphasized that these were merely "equalizing" measures, meant to be temporary.

The social behavior frame again figured more prominently in the formulations of policy adopted in 1999 and 2000. The sources that I refer to here are in the first place documents that were produced with the participation of the Interdepartmental Commission for Romani Community Affairs (later, the Government Council for Romani Community Affairs). In 1999 the Interdepartmental Commission finished a document presenting the concept of "Romani integration." In April 2000 the government adopted this concept as the principal component of a new strategic Romani policy (Resolutions 279/1999 and 599/2000).

Although the problem framing in these policy strategies was for the most part in line with that of the Bratinka report, one can detect in the former a number of statements that portrayed Romani culture and Romani identity as intrinsic elements of the problem. The problematic character of certain alleged traits of Romani identity was suggested by the dubious position in the texts on whether the development of Romani culture was a desirable strategy. The government document on Romani policy, on the one hand, stated that the emancipation of Romani identity was the ultimate goal. As the translation of a draft resolution distributed by the Czech government stated: "the more Romas [sic] will feel being Roma, the more emancipated and responsible citizens they will be" (Government of the Czech Republic 1999b). But at the same time, the first three pages of that same draft contained a number of statements qualifying this. These statements indicated that assimilation (quite the opposite of what was proposed in the above quote) was not necessarily a bad strategy either, at least for individuals. The draft resolution further argued that assimilation was generally what "the majority of the Czech citizens" expected of the Roma, and that the government would certainly not discourage the phenomenon.

> [The government] is aware that the majority of the Czech citizens is able and willing to accept Romanies only when they adapt to the majority and assimilate into it ... The government will not refuse support to those Romanies who voluntarily wish to assimilate. (Government of the Czech Republic 1999b)

What also became more visible in this period was the tendency of Czech governmental actors to support the idea of the Roma as a European nation. One needs first and foremost to refer to the activities and statements of the Czech Ministry of Foreign Affairs. In December 1998 the Ministry of Foreign Affairs supported a conference organized by the Czech Institute for International Relations under the title, "The Roma community and multi-ethnicity in the countries of Central Europe—A European problem?" It subsequently published the conference papers in English. The foreword by Czech Deputy Minister of Foreign Affairs, Martin Palouš, indicated clearly that the purpose of the conference was to place the Czech "Romani problem" in a European context:

> As the title of the conference reveals, it is an all-European problem ... We must always bear in mind that the successful solution of our domestic difficulties as regards the integration of the Romany ethnic group will to a large extent be inseparable from these broader links. As a result, it is no coincidence that the organizer of the conference was an institution which provides a sort of theoretical groundwork for the Ministry of Foreign Affairs. (Gedlu 1998: 11–12)

A couple of pages further, Palouš briefly mentioned the reason why he believed we should see the matter in a European context. Because of their European identity, the Roma were entitled, Palouš argued, to expect more help from Europe than other European nations, which have their own state. In one passage a boundary was constructed between "the Czechs" as a European nation with a state of their own and "the Roma" as "the most European nation" without a state of their own, for whom the transnational level (European institutions) should bear more responsibility than the Czech Republic.

> If the Roma are the most European nation, then the reason could well be that they hold up a kind of specific mirror to Europe in which Europe can see itself, and where they can expect from European institutions a little bit more than other European nations which have their own European states and enter the process of European integration precisely in the light of their experience. (Gedlu 1998: 16)

The Ministry supported the Europeanization of Romani identity in more than words alone. It supported the fifth World Romani Congress (WRC) and subsequently signed a memorandum with the International Romani Union (IRU) ("Memorandum of Understanding and Cooperation between the Ministry of Foreign Affairs of the Czech Republic and the International Romani Union"). Furthermore, in 2000, the Ministry of Foreign Affairs prepared a document entitled "the Ministry of Foreign Affairs' conception of the Roma issue," meant inter alia to clarify the official Czech response to international criticism about the situation of the Roma. In this document the Europeanization of the Romani problem was literally referred to as the preferential way of framing the issue. Point 65 of the document defined a number of goals toward which Czech foreign policy needed to be oriented. The first was:

> The promotion of the concept of the Europeanization of the Romani problematic on all levels of Czech foreign policy. We understand Europeanization here as to grasp the Romani issue as an affair which concerns every European state where a Romani minority lives today. From this follows also the will to seek a solution for the Romani issue at the international/European level, and this includes a financial safeguard for such a solution.[12]

Furthermore, the document suggested that the Czech Republic needed to reject more consistently the criticism from abroad that anti-Romani racism in the Czech Republic was a ubiquitous phenomenon (Sobotka 2001b: 68).

Hungary

In Hungarian policy documents the social behavior frame received much less attention than in the Slovak case. The Hungarian formulation of policy changed from seeing the Roma as one among the thirteen minorities in Hungary, to seeing them as a *special* minority in need of a *specific* kind of policy treatment and even a long-term strategy extending through several governments. This was also reflected in the problem framing. During the first half of the 1990s, the Romani issue was brought into the larger context of minority integration in general. Thus, there was no explicit problem identification for the situation of the Roma, since this issue was considered to be an element of the "minorities problem" in general. In the philosophy of the Minorities Act, the central issue was that national minority cultures needed to be protected by the state. The introduction of cultural autonomy was seen as the ultimate solution to the disadvantaged position of minorities. In the words of the preamble to the act:

> In preparing this Act, the National Assembly of the Republic of Hungary is guided by the vision of the establishment of a Europe without frontiers, reduction and elimination of the disadvantages which result from living in a minority, and the development of the democratic institutional structures necessary to achieve these goals. (Act LXXVII of 1993 on the Rights of National and Ethnic Minorities, Preamble)

Here one sees a considerable difference between the problem framing of the Hungarian policy makers and that of their Slovak and Czech counterparts. The Slovak case (especially in Resolution 821/1999, section on language and culture) and the Czech case (Government of the Czech Republic 1997 and 1999b, in particular section 5 of the latter resolution) referred to the need to protect the Roma as a minority culture; but in neither of the two cases was a direct link made between the lack of protection of cultural rights and the problem of disadvantage. In Slovakia and the Czech Republic (in the latter case from 1997 onwards), it was argued that language and culture needed to be protected; but the introduction of self-government rights in the field of culture and language were not seen as necessary.

In Hungary, official problem framing changed with two new resolutions in 1995 (resolutions 1125/1995 and 1120/1995) that adjusted the general policy towards the Roma in the direction of designing special measures *only* for the Romani population. In a 1996 discussion paper published by Csaba Tabajdi, at that time State Secretary for Minority Affairs, the shift was formulated in the following way:

> The present Government committed itself in its program to draw up a crisis management package to improve the situation of the Gypsy community, not merely as one of the minorities, but as an ethnic group which merits special and significant attention. (Farkas Szilágyi and Heizer 1996: 12).

The new perspective on the Romani issue that emerged at that time attached importance mainly to the failure of economic and social integration. This means that the Horn government (1994–98), which was dominated by the Socialist party (MSzP), considered the problems facing the Roma mainly as problems of poverty and social exclusion. The central issue for the government, as was illustrated by a speech that Tabajdi gave during a debate in the Hungarian National Assembly in 1996, was not discrimination.

> The Socialists reject as a simplification the assumption which—using a scapegoat philosophy—one-sidedly places the responsibility for creating these problems, and Hungarian–Gypsy conflicts, on the Gypsy community. At the same time, the

> Socialists also view as misguided the opposite to the above approach, which tries to account for all the problems of the Gypsy community with an alleged collective majority anti-Gypsy sentiment and disadvantageous discrimination. (Farkas Szilágyi and Heizer 1996: 29)

The text of Resolution 1125/1995, which introduced an action plan with short- and long-term priorities to improve the position of the Roma in education, employment, and agriculture, contained little information as to what was to be regarded as the chief cause of the failure of social and economic integration. If there was discrimination, it was regarded as an unfortunate *effect* of the lack of social and economic integration. Discrimination was thus more or less discounted as a problem. The policy aimed at tackling it *indirectly* by first targeting aspects of economic and social integration.

It is not completely clear from the Hungarian documents whom or what they blamed for the problems described. The situation of the Roma was certainly not seen as caused by the shortcomings of the general minority policy. The decision to grant cultural autonomy to minorities and develop a system of self-governments was considered to be an element in the facilitation of the emancipation of the Roma, and a means to foster their involvement in the creation of policies aimed at their constituencies. It had not been the task of the system to deal with economic disadvantage. The documents did not, however, specify who or what, then, was responsible for causing the problems of economic disadvantage from which the Roma clearly suffered. The documents and debates from that period seem to suggest that rather general economic difficulties and societal changes were blamed. The Roma were seen as people who were particularly affected by the inevitable hardships of the economic transition after 1989, or they were called the victims of age-old poverty and social exclusion.

What is notable, further, is that, notwithstanding the Horn government's clear focus on the economic aspect of the problem, statements were repeatedly made that emphasized the severe budget limitations to deal with the situation. Although the resolution made no mention of the potential problem of financing a large operation to integrate the Roma, the discussion paper published by Tabajdi did so unambiguously. In a section entitled, "The principles behind current government measures aimed at improving the situation of the Gypsy community," the paper stated the following:

> It should be considered a fact of life that there will be significantly fewer opportunities for direct Government intervention, the scope of the efforts of the Gypsy community will become more limited and there will be a lack of central resources—necessary for an accelerated program enabling Gypsies to 'catch up'. This, however, does not relieve the Government of its duty to develop and implement a medium-term plan of action—taking the economic state of the country into account, on the one hand—and formulating long-term policy on the other. (Farkas Szigály and Heizer 1996: 21)

The documents by the Orban government (1998–2002) did not fundamentally change the dominant perspective. The minority self-government system was still regarded as a successful way of tackling the problem of the Roma's lack of participation in society, while additional programs were meant to remedy such phenomena as massive unemployment and poverty. Nevertheless, in some minor aspects the official framing of the problem did change after 1998. In contrast to the 1995 resolutions, Resolution 1047/1999 strongly emphasized the need to target regular institutions and the majority population in order to prevent anti-Roma discrimination (for example, in the police force and in education). It also pledged to support legal aid organizations and institutions engaged in conflict prevention and management.

Just as Hungarian Romani activists in general were reluctant to support the initiatives of the IRU and the concept of the Roma as a "European nation," so policy makers in Hungary usually referred to the Roma exclusively as a *national* minority. Neither government reports nor program-type documents by politicians in power contained many references to the Roma as a transnational group. One could argue that Hungarian politicians had less incentive to "Europeanize" the Roma than their Slovak and Czech counterparts. For most of the 1990s external actors regarded Hungary's treatment of the Roma as an example of progressive policy rather than as a problem in itself. To be sure, the European Commission and the Council of Europe criticized the Roma's distressing economic and social predicament. But Romani policy never acquired the symbolic value it had in the Czech Republic and Slovakia, where it figured prominently in the debate about EU membership.

At the same time, one cannot go so far as to state that Hungarian policy makers were not at all influenced by the emerging trend to see the situation of the Roma within the European context. One initiative is worth mentioning. In a report for the Parliamentary Assembly of the Council of Europe, Csaba Tabajdi (inspired by the President of Finland, Tarja Halonen) proposed the introduction of a European consultative assembly for Roma. He proposed to establish an elected body of "Romani representatives" to serve as an advisory body for the Committee of Ministers, the Parliamentary Assembly of the Council of Europe, and the European Parliament. This proposal could be interpreted as an attempt to "Europeanize" Romani identity for the purpose of putting the responsibility of designing and financing policy targeted on Romani issues at a level above that of domestic politics.

Assessing the Effectiveness of Romani Movement Frames

One would expect framing attempts by prominent political actors in Central Europe—allies as well as opponents of the Romani movement

—to have had a serious impact on the general public's perceptions of the Romani issue. However, just as movement leaders could not always successfully persuade potential movement participants, neither could other political actors completely regulate and direct the views of the larger public. Their views on the matter had to compete with other ideas present among the public at large, and these were often age-old stereotypes and myths. Moreover, mass media played an important role in distributing powerful images of the Roma, sometimes with a distinct preference for the portrayal of what was regarded as strange and authentic. Both myths and stereotypical images constitute what I earlier called the "cultural setting" of movement framing. To gain a clearer idea of the cultural setting of the Romani movement, one would need to investigate thoroughly the way in which domestic mass media in Central Europe reported about the Roma, what views of the "Romani problem" they propagated, and what they considered to be the markers of Romani identity. The distribution and the role of myths and popular scientific interpretations in the construction of ethnicized divisions between Roma and non-Roma form a fascinating, but largely unexplored, field of study.[13] It would lead me far beyond the scope of this book to engage here in a systematic investigation of this field. However, as the large-scale opinion surveys quoted in Chapter 1 illustrate, there is ample evidence suggesting that views on Romani identity in the last decade were generally not favorable and that there was a sweeping tendency to see the Roma as responsible for their own hardship.

The implication of such negative qualification of Romani identity is that it created a *double bind* situation for many activists desiring to engage in ethnic mobilization. On the one hand, the tendency of governments in Central Europe to recognize the specific character of the Roma's predicament represented a positive response to the demands made by the Romani movement. In the Czech Republic, Slovakia, and Hungary recent policy proposals and resolutions were drafted through a process that involved consultation with selected or elected Romani "representatives." Arguably, with the assistance of external pressure a relatively large group of Romani activists was able to gain some degree of control over the production of documents on "Romani policy." Moreover, one of their crucial demands was realized: the official recognition of the Roma as a single ethnic minority group.

On the other hand, the top-down conception of Romani identity continued to see particular forms of social behavior as essential markers of that identity. This confronted Romani activists with new difficulties. It was especially the close association made between Romani identity and "objectionable behavior" that created an obstacle for Romani mobilization. The identification of social behavior and ethnic identity could easily be maximized in public discourse and lead to a "discourse of otherness." Unsurprisingly, it became difficult for activists to promote alternative understandings of Romani identity and to capture their predicament in an alternative way. In these circumstances, Romani activists found themselves in double jeopardy. The government's ways of framing Romani culture as substantially different neatly fitted the images of Roma prevalent in the public opinion. Thus, when Roma wanted to mobilize protest in the name of their ethnicity, they were confronted with narratives that questioned a positive framing of this very same ethnicity. The more they emphasized their ethnic identity, the more they appeared to be held responsible for what was typically called the "Romani problem."

The double bind that confronted the Roma may have had important implications for the potential resonance among Roma of new frames of Romani identity proffered by the Romani elite. Because of highly salient counterframes, some Roma became ambivalent towards the postulated Romani identities. Some of the people who expressed their Romani ethnic identity in the private sphere became reluctant to be open about that ethnicity in public; they feared that precisely this identification would allow others to discredit them even more. Possibly, it was dominant rhetoric associating Romani identity with social marginality that led many of them to reject Romani political mobilization.

A comparison of Hungary, the Czech Republic, and Slovakia suggests that contextual aspects of Romani identity played an important role in the creation of Romani mobilization. Even if—as was the case in these three countries—international attention stimulates a process of ethnic mobilization, it is not obvious to find large support for a unified movement. In a similar vein, even if—as in the case of Slovakia—ethnic claims play a role in mainstream political competition and activists believe they have a large potential constituency, it is still not easy to mobilize a group on the basis of an ethnic minority identity. The complex discursive struggles surrounding the "Romani problem" mostly rendered a powerful negative valuation of Romani identity. Policy documents that were meant as responses to the demands of Romani activists could be used as a new set of arguments to prove the Roma's reputation as permanent troublemakers. Consequently, at the beginning of the 2000s many Romani activists were stuck with a crucial question: How is one to build a movement on what is regarded by many as a "stigmatized" identity?

Conclusion

This chapter has investigated how government policy documents have interpreted the plight of the Roma and explored the divergent ways in which prominent actors in the Romani movement have understood and framed their cause. The prominent identity and problem framings in the Romani movement have varied according to the degree to which ethnic differentiation or assimilation have been emphasized, and they often represent competing strategic positions. Furthermore, these framings have to some extent been dependent on the dominant ways in which Romani identity has been understood in society at large and the ways in which the "Romani problem" has been constructed in political discourse.

One of the important conclusions is that some of the activists placed the Romani issue in the context of multiculturalism and minority rights protection. By doing so they hoped to increase moral leverage in a geographical area where minority rights protection was increasingly seen as an important precondition for democratic stability and peace. To strengthen their demands for policy change, activists could refer to the existing international norms and standards for recognizing cultural, ethnic, and national minority identities. Governments have used references to other countries and international organizations mainly in order to buttress the argument that improving the situation of the Roma should not be seen as the sole responsibility of the national state.

In sum, the framing attempts constitute an important element in the relationship between activists and policy makers, both in domestic and international contexts. So far I have mainly examined the domestic sphere. The international context is the focus of the next chapter.

Chapter 5

International Responses

In the summer of 2003, a remarkable conference took place in Budapest. Prime ministers and government representatives from eight Central and Eastern European countries gathered in Hungary's capital to meet with Romani activists and international governmental and nongovernmental organizations. The topic of discussion was the "future of the Roma in an expanded Europe." The Hungarian government hosted the conference; the World Bank and the Open Society Institute were the main sponsors. The event followed a call that had been put forward by international financier George Soros, the chairman of the Open Society Institute. The main purpose was to launch the "Decade of Roma Inclusion," a ten-year framework project (from 2005 to 2015) meant to encourage domestic governments to initiate, expand, and implement special policies aimed at the Roma.

In his dinner speech Soros said that since the 1980s it had been one of his priorities to support the Romani movement and stimulate people to be "engaged" in being Roma. He also explained why. "When Roma manage to progress in society," he argued,

> it is a very natural inclination to try not to be Roma ... [W]hat the rest of the population sees, are the disenfranchised, the underclass. And that is the stereotype that prevails in society. ... [T]o break that stereotype you need Roma who are educated and who remain Roma. And they are the ones who can advocate their cause the best.[1]

In February 2005, the "Decade of Roma Inclusion" was officially launched by the organizations and governments involved.[2] Whether the program will be successful remains to be seen, but the fact that the World Bank and the Open Society Institute could mobilize such an impressive amount of political and financial capital for its launching conference demonstrates its potential importance for local Romani activists.[3]

All the processes discussed so far in this book have been mainly domestic in nature. This chapter asks what the impact is of international actors on the development of domestic Romani movements. This question is not only important with regard to the Roma, it concerns an important *general* topic in social movement research, namely how do "transnational spaces for discourse and action" (Guidry et al. 2000: 3) transform the nature of domestic collective action? Anyone who talks to

Romani activists, state representatives, and independent experts in Central Europe soon realizes the significance of the international context. Many of the people I interviewed spontaneously pointed out why international actors were so important to them. They referred to the spread of ideas among movement actors across state borders, the interference of international political institutions, and the importance of international sources of funding.

An increasing number of scholars, too, have acknowledged the importance of the international pressures thrust upon domestic states. There is a large body of literature on the internationalization of minority rights protection and the impact of international relations on other domestic minority issues (e.g. Pentassuglia 2001; Schöpflin 2000). In his *Nationalism Reframed*, Rogers Brubaker has shed new light on this international dimension by conceptualizing national minority issues as a triadic nexus between three dynamic and interdependent political fields: national minorities, nationalizing states, and external national homelands (Brubaker 1996). In Brubaker's view, these three political fields are bound together in a single relational nexus, "linked by continuous mutual monitoring and interaction" (Brubaker 1996: 8). In many cases, one could arguably add to this a fourth political field, one that is characterized by a transnational point of view. This latter field represents universal norms on minority protection. The dominant idea here is that international standards on minority protection should guide the stance that national states take towards their minorities. Here one finds actors who are able to push states to adopt policies that they see as consistent with these standards. In the case of the Roma, the transnational field is more important than the field of external homelands.

This chapter focuses on two related groups of actors. First, I will investigate the impact of specific initiatives by international governmental organizations (IGOs), especially the OSCE, the Council of Europe, and the EU. Secondly, I will examine the role of internationally active nongovernmental organizations (NGOs), which form the core of an emerging cross-border advocacy network focusing on the plight of the Roma. The growing concern of IGOs and international NGOs about the situation of the Roma should be seen in the context of a number of broader developments. One is the process of European integration, or, more generally, the process of growing regional cooperation in Europe. Central European countries have been members of the Conference for Security and Cooperation in Europe (CSCE) since its original founding in 1973, and have from the very beginning been members of the Organization for Security and Cooperation in Europe (OSCE).[4] Early in the 1990s they also joined the Council of Europe.[5] Both the OSCE and the Council of Europe developed specific instruments to monitor the way in which their member states deal with minority demands. Thus, the situation of the Roma in Central Europe has been exposed to widespread international attention from the OSCE and the Council of Europe. More importantly, Central Europe's record on minority protection has also been subject to scrutiny by the EU, which has been involved in a protracted process of enlargement to the East. Since the beginning of the 1990s the Central European governments have realized that domestic policy decisions on minorities could have a profound impact on their bid for EU membership. This has especially been the case since the Copenhagen European Council in 1993 deemed the protection of ethnic and national minorities a precondition for the accession of Central European candidates.

Another element of the larger context pertains to the internationalization of norms on minority treatment. There is an increasing body of literature in political science on the diffusion and internationalization of norms (e.g. Checkel 2000; Finnemore and Sikkink 1998). A part of this literature has focused on the issue area of minority protection in contemporary Central and Eastern Europe (e.g. Amato and Batt 1998; Burgess 1999; Malfliet and Laenen 1998). The purpose of this literature has mainly been to gain insight into the mechanisms that have made states in Central and Eastern Europe adopt new ways of accommodating minority demands. Most of this literature has paid attention to IGOs, but, as for example Margaret Keck and Kathryn Sikkink have pointed out, also nonstate actors should be taken into account (Keck and Sikkink 1998). A large number of NGOs that operate across state borders have explicitly or implicitly promoted norms of minority protection.

Because of the fact that the treatment of the Roma became an important element in the construction of a country's international reputation, one would expect Romani movement actors in Central Europe to have welcomed the interference of both IGOs and international NGOs in domestic affairs. One news magazine hinted precisely at this when it called the EU "the Gypsies' best ally."[6] But have Romani activists indeed experienced IGOs and international NGOs as their best allies? Has the international involvement been conducive to the formation of a Romani movement in Central Europe? In the first part of this chapter I review the initiatives taken by IGOs in this field and argue that IGOs have been actively shaping a view on the Roma that does not always coincide with (and sometimes contradicts) the way in which Romani activists have framed their issues and demands.

In the latter part of this chapter I show that among Romani activists in Central Europe an ambivalent perception of international politics could be detected. On the one hand, because of the interference of IGOs and international NGOs they were able to create a distinct profile of the Roma as a European nation. As a result they became increasingly successful at organizing on a transnational level and lobbying directly towards international organizations. On the other hand, international pressure produced new obstacles hindering the development of the

Roma movement in domestic and local politics. It created new divisions and new controversies among Romani activists. Discussion arose about who had the moral authority to control and represent Romani demands internationally, about whether international financial resources were fairly distributed, and whether Romani activists could and should hold international NGOs accountable for their activities.

International Governmental Organizations: Institutional and Political Responses

The OSCE: Shifting Conceptualizations of the Romani Issue

One of the first major efforts to raise international concern for the Roma in the 1990s took shape within the framework of the OSCE. This fact should perhaps not come as a surprise. In the early 1990s the OSCE had been the first regional organization in Europe to place the issue of minority protection at the center of its activity in Central and Eastern Europe.[7]

The purpose of the original CSCE had been the creation of a dialogue between East and West on the basis of a piecemeal approach to international security. After the end of the Cold War, however, the organization soon found a new mission in the prevention of ethnic conflict and the protection of ethnic and national minorities. The Copenhagen Document (1990) was one of the first international initiatives in post-Cold War Europe to link the preservation of international stability and peace to the question of minority protection. An expert meeting on minority protection in July 1991 in Geneva did not yield a clear strategy for developing legal instruments. In 1992, however, a step was taken in the direction of developing a new *political* instrument. Soon a separate CSCE institution was established that would become responsible for early warning and preventive diplomacy in cases of impending conflict involving national minorities. This was the High Commissioner on National Minorities (HCNM).

The HCNM's mandate was designed for purposes of preventing conflict between states, or dealing with conflicting territorial claims within one state. Although the political implications of the situation of the Roma seemed not to fit in this framework, High Commissioner Max van der Stoel (1993–2001) produced two highly influential reports on the Roma, an initiative that was backed by decision-making bodies in the CSCE/OSCE. In 1993 the Committee of Senior Officials (CSO) requested the HCNM to study the issue of the Roma. After the submission of van der Stoel's report, the CSO decided that the Roma needed to be included as a topic in the Human Dimension Implementation Meeting in Warsaw in the autumn of 1993. A year later an entire Human Dimension Seminar was devoted specifically to the topic of the Roma in

Europe (ODHIR 1994), a fact described by some as "a milestone for Roma advocacy efforts at the international level" (Foundation for Inter-Ethnic Relations 1997: 78–79).

The most tangible result of this growing attention was the establishment in 1994 of a Contact Point for Roma and Sinti Issues (CPRSI)[8] at the Warsaw-based Office for Democratic Institutions and Human Rights (ODIHR).[9] The institutional location of the CPRSI is significant. Since its establishment, the ODIHR has been responsible for the "human dimension" of the OSCE, which means that it has been tasked to encourage member states to respect human rights and strengthen their democratic institutions. Minority groups have never been a *specific* focus of the ODIHR, and no minority issue, beside that of the Roma, has ever led to the establishment of a separate institution within the ODIHR. Arguably this shows the tendency of the OSCE to separate the issue of the Roma from other minority issues, and put it in a human rights-related context, as opposed to a context of ethnic conflict prevention.

The Contact Point was given three main tasks:

1. to act as a clearing house for the exchange of information on Roma and Sinti (Gypsies) issues, including information on the implementation of commitments pertaining to Roma;
2. to facilitate contacts on Roma issues between participating states, international organizations and institutions, and NGOs;
3. to maintain and develop contacts on these issues between OSCE institutions and other international organizations and institutions. (CSCE 1994, Chapter VIII, paragraph 23)

The original task description to some extent still reflected the idea that the problems facing the Roma had to be dealt with in the context of the political commitments of OSCE member states. Documents produced after 1994 show nevertheless that the issue of the Roma was increasingly regarded as an issue in its own right and became separated from the areas of attention of other institutions within the OSCE. Indicative of this development was the proposal discussed at a 1998 roundtable on "Roma and Sinti National Policies" about the establishment of a senior position at the ODIHR to deal specifically with Roma and Sinti issues (a special "advisor on Roma and Sinti issues"). The recommendation had come from the OSCE Parliamentary Assembly and was largely supported by the Romani activists present at the 1998 roundtable. Participants at this roundtable pointed out that the mandate of this advisor could even include some ombudsman-type functions and functions otherwise performed by human rights protection institutions (OSCE 1998). The proposal was accepted, and in 1998 the well-known Romanian Romani activist Nicolae Gheorghe was appointed as the ODIHR's first advisor on Roma and Sinti issues. After 1998 the CPRSI further expanded its range of projects. The most important ones aimed at increasing the participation of Roma in elections (both as candidates and voters), assisting the reintegration of Roma in disrupted communities under the Stability Pact in the Balkans, and stimulating discussions between activists and governments on the topic of Romani asylum seekers.

In summary, the way in which the Romani issue was understood by the OSCE underwent two important developments in the course of the 1990s. The topic of the Roma first became separated from the topic of conflict prevention and national minority protection in order to find a position in the general context of the commitments of states to address the problems of *all* their marginalized minorities (HCNM 1993: 14). Once the CPRSI was created within the ODIHR, the topic of the Roma increasingly became separated from the items related to other marginalized groups. This second shift was prompted by the growing conviction that the Roma needed *special* attention, because their ethnicity was believed to be strongly connected to the problems they encountered. Wherever Roma live, the implicit reasoning went, they are confronted with a consistent pattern of discrimination. A CPRSI newsletter stated in 1996:

> The current developments in Europe show that Roma *regardless of their social status*, are confronted with hostility, which by many is perceived as a result of social prejudices. In order to solve this problem it is not enough to initiate only welfare or development projects. Roma must be granted guarantees for the protection of civil liberties. This means a change in the political status of the Roma toward political, social and ethnic self-determination.[10] (Emphasis added)

The way in which Romani issues were further dealt with by the HCNM confirmed this shift from a general human dimension approach to an identity-based approach. The first report on Roma, written by van der Stoel in 1993, placed the issue of the Roma in the context of the political and economic transition in postcommunist Europe (see also Kovats 2001c: 98). Consider, for example, the following description in the report.

> The significant, simultaneous, and often difficult transitions in the political systems of numerous participating States have sometimes resulted in the lack of institutional capacity to deal with complex problems related to the Roma. Material hardship, associated with economic recession and transformation as well as greater government austerity throughout the CSCE region, have hit the vast majority of the Roma particularly hard. (HCNM 1993: 5–6)

The report even saw a direct connection between the growth of anti-Roma discrimination and the economic and political difficulties of the transition states in Central and Eastern Europe.

> The overall climate of political and economic uncertainty confronting people throughout the region may also encourage the collective "scapegoating" of certain groups, such as the Roma, for the ills of society-at-large. (HCNM 1993: 6)

The report published by the HCNM in 2000 was much larger and included reference to more examples and cases. These examples were taken not only from Central and Eastern Europe, but included virtually all countries with a sizeable Romani minority. Therefore, the report could be read as an attempt to demonstrate that there were common elements in the plight of the Roma, even if circumstances varied. It could also be read as an attempt to determine *what* made the plight of the Roma so unique. The conclusion reached was that, although diversity could not be denied, ultimately the Roma were confronted with the same type of problems in all these countries. It was argued that discrimination had given rise to four typical problem areas: racial violence, unequal access to education, substandard living conditions (housing, health), and lack of political participation. The problem areas listed in this report did not differ fundamentally from the problem areas listed in the first report, but the perspective had clearly shifted. While in the 1993 report by the HCNM the deplorable situation of many Roma was seen as a consequence of a variety of general political and economic circumstances, the 2000 report focused more attention on the role of anti-Roma discrimination as a phenomenon that unified all Roma in Europe as victims.

What were the implications of this development for the position of domestic Romani activists? The OSCE's framing of the problem was not so different from the way in which some of the most influential Romani activists framed their situation. The HCNM's report of 2000 and the growing independence of the CPRSI reflect very much the efforts of the activists who sought to create greater unification among the Roma in Europe on the basis of the conviction that they are all faced with the same type of discrimination. The tendency of including demands made by activists was also apparent in the efforts of the CPRSI to invite consistently a host of Romani organizations and advocacy NGOs to high-level meetings and discussions. To be sure, it is difficult to measure the amount of influence activists really had on the formulation of OSCE priorities and how much they were driven by specific concerns of particular OSCE member states. Nevertheless, one can see the emergence of a mutually reinforcing relationship between international Romani activists and the OSCE. International Romani activists found access to the OSCE; subsequently, they increasingly voiced their concerns on the international level and were increasingly accepted as international "Romani leaders." The concentration of all topics related to Roma within a separate institution of the OSCE clearly supported the emergence of an international Romani movement. Activists were able to attract the attention of the OSCE. In this way they could—borrowing a phrase from Risse and Sikkink (1999: 18)—"amplify" their concerns towards their domestic governments.

Other activists, however, felt less comfortable with the OSCE's position on the issue. In response to the OSCE's promotion of certain Romani activists as "Romani leaders," questions arose about the basis on which these activists were selected. Moreover, activists wondered whether the increasing attention devoted to the Roma at the intergovernmental level would indeed lead to meaningful changes at the domestic and local levels. Some of them feared that the support from national governments for OSCE initiatives merely served to hide the fact that they were not taking appropriate measures at home. Another potential problem was the OSCE's interpretation of the Romani issue as a special area of policy, not related to country-specific circumstances but to universal anti-Roma discrimination. The problem with this approach, some argued, was that it potentially isolated the Romani issue from government responsibility and vaguely linked it to quasi-universal societal attitudes. Some activists considered it a risk pointing to the alleged universality of anti-Roma bias. That Roma are discriminated against everywhere they are, is exactly what some take as evidence for the assertion that the Roma themselves provoke such discrimination. As one activist argued: "The Romani leadership might say, 'The Roma have a problem,' whereas, non-Romani politicians are more inclined to say, or suggest, 'The Roma are the problem'" (PER 2001b: 28).

Related to this was the contention surrounding the special status that certain Romani activists had received within the OSCE. These activists were increasingly approached as the "representatives" of *all* the Roma in the OSCE region. Some of them no doubt were pleased with this status, especially since it gave them the chance to participate in projects supporting the "Romani elite" organized by other organizational forums such as the Princeton-based Project on Ethnic Relations. But others feared their high-level position would associate them increasingly with problems that were not necessarily a close concern to them.

The Council of Europe: Europeanizing the Roma

The second international actor actively involved in promoting the Romani issue is the Council of Europe. The activities of this organization have centered mainly on the promotion of European identity and the protection of human rights in Europe. Concern for the plight of the Roma gradually came to the fore with the expansion of the Council of Europe to postcommunist countries. In the first half of the 1990s, however, the Council's concern for the Roma remained implicit and was subordinate to the general attempts to develop new legal instruments to enforce minority protection. The most important achievements were the 1992 European Charter on the Protection of Minority Languages, which came into force in March 1998, and the adoption of the 1995

Framework Convention on the Protection of National Minorities (FCNM), which entered into force in February 1998.[11]

The first Council of Europe initiative that was specifically concerned with the situation of the Roma dates from January 1993. At that moment the Parliamentary Assembly accepted a report entitled "On Gypsies in Europe," written by Dutch Socialist Josephine Verspaget, which led to the passage of Recommendation 1203 (Parliamentary Assembly of the Council of Europe 1993a) declaring the Roma to be "a true European minority" (Kovats 2001c: 95–96). Much more than the HCNM report that appeared in the same year, Verspaget's report and the ensuing recommendation emphasized the cultural difference between the Roma and the majority. The report argued that exceptional attention from the Council of Europe to the Roma was justified because the Roma were different from any other ethnic group in Europe in that they lacked "a country to call their own" (Parliamentary Assembly of the Council of Europe 1993a, paragraph 2). While the first HCNM report highlighted the various political and economic circumstances determining the fate of many Roma, the Council of Europe, through Verspaget's report, pointed to the need to grant the Roma a "special status" as a special cultural group. It described them as a "cross-border nation" foreshadowing a united Europe. The issue of the Roma was placed squarely into the Council of Europe's project of promoting "the emergence of a genuine European cultural identity" (Parliamentary Assembly of the Council of Europe 1993a, paragraph 1). To lend force to the argument that the Roma had always been, as it were, European *avant la lettre*, Verspaget quoted the following statement by Secretary General of the Council of Europe Cathérine Lalumière:

> You are a truly European people as by definition and tradition Gypsies are nomads, traveling from country to country and without really recognizing frontiers in Europe. You are at home in the Council of Europe because for centuries you have already been Europeans. (Quoted in Parliamentary Assembly of the Council of Europe 1993b, paragraph 20)

With the acceptance of Recommendation 1203 (1993) the Parliamentary Assembly of the Council of Europe quite explicitly defined the Roma as a European group characterized by a common culture (in addition to nomadic lifestyle, the report also referred to music, trades, and crafts). This was no less than a call for the official recognition of the Roma, and it was soon followed by an institutional response. A number of special bodies for Romani issues were established within the Council of Europe. In 1994, the Secretary General appointed a Coordinator of Activities on Roma, Gypsies and Travelers, who became responsible for bringing into line all activities of the Council of Europe that concerned these groups. It was also meant to stimulate dialogue between the Council and domestic Romani organizations, and to foster cooperation with other IGOs on the issue, in particular with the ODIHR and the

European Commission. In 1995, the coordinator was complemented by an advisory body to the Committee of Ministers. This new body was called the Specialist Group on Roma/Gypsies (MG-S-ROM) and consisted of eleven permanent members.

This new institutional framework could not have come into existence without the efforts of the Parliamentary Assembly. Verspaget continued to be one of the main initiatiors. In 1995, she drew up a report on the Roma for the Council of Europe's expert body on migration (the Committee on Migration). Later she became the chair of the Specialist Group on Roma/Gypsies. Other Council of Europe bodies were not necessarily as keen on further institutionalizing Romani identity. In 1997 Verspaget submitted a written question (No. 372) to the Committee of Ministers, asking whether the committee would act on one of the proposals in Recommendation 1203 (1993) to appoint a "mediator for Roma/Gypsies" who, among other things, would have the task of maintaining contact with the "representatives of Gypsies" and advising governments of member states in matters concerning Roma (Parliamentary Assembly of the Council of Europe 1993a, paragraph 11. xxii). In February 1998, the Committee of Ministers replied that it did not see fit to appoint a specific mediator, as it reasoned that there should be no direct interference from a European institution on the domestic relationship between governments and Romani minorities. What should be done, the Committee argued, was to urge governments to find better ways to ensure the full participation of *all* their minorities in the political, social, and economic life of the member state. In the words of the Committee, rather than organizing the inclusion of Roma on a European level, it was considered more appropriate for the Council of Europe to encourage member states individually to take "positive steps to facilitate such participation by Roma/Gypsies" (Committee of Ministers of the Council of Europe 1999).

But even in the presence of this reluctance, the Parliamentary Assembly kept issuing proposals to establish a kind of separate Romani policy on the European level. On January 24, 2001 the President of Finland, Tarja Halonen, addressed the Parliamentary Assembly and proposed to give serious consideration to the need to create for the Roma "some kind of consultative assembly to represent them on the pan-European level."[12] This proposal did not fall on deaf ears, and in October 2001 it was incorporated in a document written by Hungarian Socialist MP Csaba Tabajdi, the rapporteur for the Parliamentary Assembly's Committee on Legal Affairs and Human Rights (Committee on Legal Affairs and Human Rights 2002). I mentioned in earlier chapters that as an MP in Hungary and State Secretary for Minority Affairs under the Horn government, Tabajdi was an important participant in the Hungarian public debate on minority policy. Tabajdi's report for the Council of Europe proposed the promotion of a further institutionalization of Romani identity on both domestic and European levels, very much along the lines of the Hungarian minority self-government system:

> Member states of the Council of Europe should encourage the Roma to set up their own organizations and/or political parties, and participate in the political system as voters, candidates, or members in national parliaments. Romani communities, organizations and political parties should be given the full opportunity to take part in the process of elaborating, implementing and monitoring programs and policies aimed at improving their present situation. (Committee on Legal Affairs and Human Rights 2002, draft recommendation, paragraph 10)

In addition, Tabajdi advocated the establishment of a European body of elected Romani representatives (a European Roma Consultative Forum) to advise European institutions:

> The Roma, having no state of their own, are in need of particular protection. Their specific situation was the reason for the proposal put forward by Mrs Tarja Halonen, President of Finland, for a European Roma Consultative Forum to be set up. Such a democratically established assembly, which would meet regularly, could serve as an advisory body to the Committee of Ministers, the Parliamentary Assembly of the Council of Europe and the European Union. (Committee on Legal Affairs and Human Rights 2002, Explanatory memorandum, paragraph 27)

In 2003, at a meeting of the French and Finnish presidents, a more specific proposal was set forth. The idea was now to set up a Council of Europe partner association under French law, whose representatives would be entitled to sit on the various Council bodies concerned with Roma issues. This led to the official establishment of the European Roma and Travelers Forum (ERTF) in July 2004, which is meant to function as a nonelected independent international body that has close and privileged links with the Council of Europe.[13]

The responses of Romani activists I interviewed in the Czech Republic, Slovakia, and Hungary to the activities and initiatives of the Council of Europe were mixed. On the one hand, they were pleased to see that through Recommendation 1203 (1993) and the establishment of the special institutions, a selection of Romani activists gained more attention than ever. It is important to note that both the coordinator of the activities for Roma and the specialist group were open to dialogue with Romani activists and advocacy organizations. In fact, the uniqueness of the Specialist Group on Roma/Gypsies was not only that it was the only expert body in the Council of Europe dealing with the situation of a separate ethnic group, but also that it included in its meetings the active participation of Romani activists and members of advocacy organizations. This was seen as a positive development not in the least by the activists themselves, especially because they could profit from additional funds made available by the Council of Europe to participate in training sessions and international meetings among Romani activists.

On the other hand, many Romani activists saw the interference of the Council of Europe as a potential source of new problems. First, increasing involvement of Romani activists on the European level did not necessarily integrate them in domestic and local decision making. On the contrary, many of the Romani activists who became progressively more successful on the European level experienced more and more difficulties in gaining support from Romani communities at home. Furthermore, there was some controversy with regard to the selection of activists to attend the meetings of the Council of Europe. Some activists and observers argued that Romani participation on European level remained confined to a small group of always the same activists. There was no complete clarity as to what criteria were applied to select activists or NGOs to the meetings of the specialist group. Other Central European Romani activists were also rather uncomfortable with the strong promotion by the Council of Europe of the European status of the Roma. Some feared this shifted the focus of attention away from the responsibility of national governments. Others pointed to the possibility of increasing stigmatization as a result. They objected to the fact that their problems were lumped together with those of what they regarded as very different groups in Western Europe. This was particularly problematic when it concerned issues of lifestyle. Kovats (2001a: 100) has pointed to one example. The phenomenon of Romani migration has sometimes been viewed by the Council of Europe not as caused by complex societal and political conditions, but as a form of Romani culture. The 1995 report by Verspaget for the Council of Europe's Committee on Migration argued: "The increase of mobility since 1990 must not conjure up pictures of a 'tidal wave' of Gypsies sweeping over the West, it is merely a return to the normal mobility of the Gypsies" (quoted in Kovats 2001c: 100). In other words, the implication was made that Romani migration to the West was motivated by a revival of nomadic lifestyle rather than by political or social circumstances. Many Romani activists in Central Europe did not want to be associated with groups such as the Travelers, *Gitanos, Woonwagenbewoners*, etc. in Western Europe and argued that such remarks undermined their protests against their national governments.[14]

The European Union: Roma in the Enlargement Process

More than any other IGO in Europe, the EU was able to turn policy making on minority issues in postcommunist Central Europe into a matter of international politics. More specifically, the EU had, in theory at least, a rather direct impact on minority policies in its candidate member countries because it explicitly linked normative pressure with membership "conditionality." One wonders to what extent this also had an impact on the Romani movement in Central Europe.

In the course of the 1990s the EU demonstrated a growing concern for the protection of national minorities in Central Europe. In 1997, the European Commission's Agenda 2000 referred to both the Framework

Convention (FCNM) and the Council of Europe's Recommendation 1201 (1993) on minorities. The impact of the EU in this field was far-reaching, at least potentially. The EU had the capacity and the financial resources to influence minority policies of other states and to empower minority citizens to challenge the initiatives of their governments.

The year 1993 was a crucial one. At that time the European Council meeting in Copenhagen decided that the protection of minorities would serve as one of the political prerequisites for future membership.[15] The European Council had hoped that as a consequence of their strong desire to join the EU, the candidate countries would be inclined to acknowledge their accountability with regard to minority treatment and introduce new legal frameworks and policy initiatives. In other words, the introduction of political conditionality was based on the assumption that introducing comprehensive conditions for EU membership would incite prospective members to align their policies with the standards set by the EU. In this way the EU hoped to guarantee the political stability of future Union territory.[16]

In the first half of the 1990s, there was growing concern over the possibility of inter-state minority conflicts arising in Central Europe, but at that time the situation of the Roma as a minority in need of protection was not yet an issue within the enlargement context. The risk that an ethnic conflict involving Roma would develop into a war between two or more states was deemed minimal. In the course of the 1990s, however, the topic of the Roma gradually became an important point of reference for the conditionality policy. This was partly induced by the growing media coverage of the appalling treatment of a great number of Roma, and was partly the result of work by international NGOs like Human Rights Watch, Amnesty International, Project on Ethnic Relations, and the European Roma Rights Center. I will return to the activities of these international NGOs later. In addition, EU attention was stimulated by a small group of independent Roma activists who had been able to voice their concerns in international forums such as the Council of Europe, the OSCE, and the UN. Ian Hancock, a Romani scholar of linguistics and well known for his publications on the history of Romani persecution, did this in the capacity of the United Nations representative of the IRU. As mentioned earlier, during the fifth World Roma Congress in July 2000 in Prague the IRU attempted to garner new credibility as the main representative body of the Roma as a trans-border nation. Attention to the Roma on a European level was also stimulated by the work of Romani activists such as Rudko Kawczynski (the Roma National Congress) and Nicolae Gheorghe.

In 1996, Gheorghe was also one of the key participants at a European Commission-supported roundtable on the situation of the Roma in Europe, which brought together a selection of representatives of Romani interest organizations. The resulting concluding document, "The Roma

— A Truly European people" (European Commission 1996), was a plea to the European Commission to raise awareness about the problems of the Roma in the candidate member states. The document emphasized the responsibilities of European institutions in this field. Although in essence it represented nothing more than a guiding declaration, the document had a relatively high degree of legitimacy; the roundtable had been hosted by the European Parliament, and representatives of the OSCE and the Council of Europe had participated in drafting the declaration. As a result, after 1996 the European Commission referred more systematically to the plight of the Roma when the Copenhagen political criteria were discussed (PER 1999). This led to a significant criticism directed towards the Central European governments in the European Commission's Agenda 2000 (1997). The European Commission pointed out that the treatment of minorities was in general satisfactory, "except for the situation of the Roma minority in a number of applicants, which gives cause for concern" (European Commission 1997). The message was evident—the situation of the Roma was to play a particular role in deciding whether a candidate member would be ready to join the EU.

This became even more apparent when the Commission started publishing its annual "regular reports." In these reports the situation of the Roma in the three countries was repeatedly mentioned as an area of growing international concern and criticism. However, in two of the three cases the apparent inability of the government to radically change the situation was never an obstacle that really blocked the accession procedure. Only in the case of Slovakia did it come to be seen as critical at a certain point. At the Luxembourg European Council in December 1997, Slovakia was for a number of reasons temporarily excluded from the first group of countries to start detailed accession negotiations. Although reference was made in the Agenda 2000 to Slovakia's official treatment of its Magyar and Romani minorities, the plight of the Roma did not emerge from the report as the number one reason for putting the country on the waiting list. Slovakia was judged to have failed to meet the requisite political conditions on the basis of its shortcomings in the functioning of democracy in general and specifically on the country's lack of stable institutions needed to secure democracy. Nevertheless in the year following the European Council's decision, when a significant number of Slovak Roma began seeking asylum in EU member states, protection of Roma suddenly became a much more prominent topic of discussion between Slovakia and the EU. Even after the installment of a new government in Bratislava at the end of 1998, various EU officials considered it to be the most important political problem area.[17] In the Commission's 1999 Accession Partnership on Slovakia the improvement of the situation of the Roma was identified as the single short-term priority under the political criteria (European Commission 2000: 4).

In the literature on conditionality there is considerable debate over the effectiveness of the EU's membership conditionality in general (Checkel 2000: 6–7; Grabbe 1999: 8–9), as well as over the implications of setting specific requirements on minority protection (Amato and Batt 1998; Liebich 1998). A question that is not directly addressed in the literature, however, is whether and to what extent minority activists perceived EU conditionality with regard to minority treatment as beneficial. The Romani activists I interviewed were rather ambivalent towards the EU's pressure on Central Europe. On the one hand, they believed that the international political context of EU enlargement had indeed had a positive impact on their position. On the other hand, in many cases they also pointed to the difficulty of turning the pressure exerted by the EU into an effective tool of Romani mobilization.

To a certain extent, the ambivalence among the Roma had to do with the quality and the content of the EU pressure. By including the requirement of minority protection, the EU had aspired to serve as an anchor of stability for its unstable neighbors to the East. However, until recently the topic of minority protection was neglected in the EU's internal affairs. For example, the EU was long silent on how to deal with discrimination against minorities in EU countries, even when there was rampant growth of extremist rhetoric directed against non-EU immigrants. Despite pressure kept up by the European Parliament since the mid-1980s to adopt protective European legislation in the field of anti-discrimination and anti-racism, it took more than a decade before an important step in this direction was taken with the ratification of the Treaty of Amsterdam (European Parliament 1997).[18] Unsurprisingly, Romani activists were rather confused about whether there were indeed EU standards to be implemented, or whether minority protection was simple a very flexible and minor requirement, subordinate to considerations related to pragmatic interests and international security.

Moreover, some could sympathize with the argument made by some politicians in Central Europe that the minority protection requirement itself was discriminatory. The provenance of the EU's concern over minorities seemed to lie, not with conflicts on EU territory that had led to serious political violence, as seen in Corsica or Northern Ireland, but with ethnic conflict in the Balkans and Central Europe. Arguably, the EU's specific stance towards postcommunist Central and Eastern Europe stemmed from the popular assumption that the "ethnic" East had been historically more inclined to ethnic conflict than the "civic" West. This argument is problematic because it invokes a simplistic stereotype of the "backward East" (Kürti 1997).

Related to these problems was the vagueness of the minority protection criterion. The descriptions of the situation in the Commission's annual "regular reports" were rather brief and general, and, more importantly, they did not indicate exactly to what extent the situation had to be made better in order to result in a positive evaluation. The regular reports did not list any concrete requirements on the introduction of national legislation prohibiting discrimination in crucial areas such as employment, education, or housing. Consequently, there was a broad margin of interpretation on how to satisfy the minority protection requirement. The adoption of the Council of Europe's Framework Convention for the Protection of National Minorities (FCNM) was implicitly referred to as a precondition (it was, for example, mentioned in the Agenda 2000). However, at the beginning of 2001 only nine EU countries had ratified it, and two (France and Belgium) had at that time neither signed nor ratified it.[19] Consequently, the EU's condition on minority protection could easily be put into perspective by the applicants and as such there was a great amount of uncertainty over which commitments Central European states needed to make order to safeguard their accession procedures. According to some Romani activists this eroded the potential power of the conditionality strategy:

> The EU's criticism is not really helpful because it's not clear what we should ask from the government when we refer to it. I don't even know to what extent this is a strict requirement ... . Because there is little communication about this from the European institutions. (Personal interview)

Slovakia is clearly a case in point. Criticism from the European Commission was easily countered by the Slovak government by reference to the international documents that Slovakia had signed. Slovakia had ratified the European FCNM. Thus, in response to criticism from the EU the Slovak government could point out that the EU itself had not even been able to persuade all of its current member states to sign and ratify this convention. For the EU this problem pointed to the essential question of whether it had to aspire to a common core of shared standards in the field of human rights, and if so, whether this would not harm the principle of subsidiarity that permits member states to decide on such matters for itself. Philip Alston and Joseph H.H. Weiler (2000: 26) have argued that a minimum core of shared standards was to be seen as a necessity to enhance the EU's credibility as a human rights proponent, and that the EU at least could play a role in encouraging member states to adhere to such instruments as the FCNM.

Another important problem related to the EU's conditionality policy was the effect of that policy on the image of the Roma. With the growing attention to the Roma in the context of EU accession Romani activists feared that this EU involvement would reinforce widespread negative stereotypes in which the Roma are held responsible for hindering EU accession. That this was not unfounded is again illustrated best by the case of Slovakia—not coincidentally the country in Central Europe that was on the receiving end of some of the most direct EU criticism. The Commission's reports repeatedly mentioned the problem of anti-Roma discrimination in Slovakia. The question, however, is whether by doing so these reports were able to counter the popular negative image of the Roma as a group that "deserves" to be discriminated against. I have shown that a negative framing of Romani identity was one of the most serious obstacles for Romani activists. In such a framing the whole range of problems facing the Roma are lumped together and explained by using a reified idea of Romani mentality or Romani culture. Such a view often excludes an analysis of complex causes and easily leads to blaming the Roma. For example, the discussion on the miserable housing conditions of Romani communities has often been governed by the idea that Roma do not respect housing. As I explained, a similar mechanism has often been at work when Roma migration is discussed. Popular beliefs about nomadism as an allegedly unchanging and innate cultural trait of the Roma has sometimes led people to suggest that the phenomenon of recent Romani migration was inexplicable in terms of political context, but should rather be seen as an illustration of how nomads seek economic advantages as they have always done. This line of thinking matches the argument that the problems Roma are faced with are related to cultural difference and thus to the mere presence of the Roma, and are therefore neither the responsibility nor the problem of the majority communities.

The successful resonance of the latter argument in Central European debates about EU membership created a severe dilemma for Romani activists. They became reluctant to refer to the EU's conditions and the Commission reports because they feared that society would hold them responsible for hindering EU accession. Thus, instead of inadequate minority protection being seen as an obstacle for EU membership, the Roma themselves thought they would be perceived as the obstacle. Activists wondered how they could protest a situation when the situation was framed as being their own responsibility. The EU membership standards did not solve this dilemma. International pressure on Central Europe exerted by individual EU states responding to Romani asylum seekers even exacerbated it.

Third Parties: The Role of Transnational Advocacy Networks

There is a significant body of literature focusing on the role that internationally active NGOs have played in transforming state sovereignty. Thomas Risse and Kathryn Sikkink (1999), for example, have done much to highlight the role of these NGOs in the internationalization of human rights norms. According to these authors, international NGOs have helped establish human rights standards firmly in international law and have managed to link up with domestic social movement organizations in protesting norm-violating states. Through these activities, NGOs have made states realize that their behavior towards their citizens has increasingly become subject to international scrutiny.

Given the growing international concern for ethnic minorities in the last decade, one would expect ethnic movements in Central Europe to feel particularly encouraged by the work of internationally active NGOs. One category of NGOs in particular seems important, namely those that are "distinguishable largely by the centrality of principled ideas or values in motivating their formation" (Keck and Sikkink 1998: 1). These are, in other words, advocacy organizations; they advocate policy changes that cannot be easily linked to a rationalist understanding of their own interests (advocates plead the causes of others) (Keck and Sikkink 1998: 8–9). International advocacy organizations focusing on one ethnic minority should not be confused with representative organizations. Advocacy groups do not aim to *represent* ethnic constituencies. Rather they want to *defend* particular groups which they believe are not treated in accordance with international standards.

Throughout the 1990s, a relatively large group of NGOs in Central Europe became actively involved in criticizing governments for their lack of concern for Roma, demanding new policy and legal changes, inciting Roma to protest, and raising the awareness of IGOs of these issues. Often, these were domestic or international NGOs working in the field of human rights, and their interest in the Roma was temporary. In many cases, however, the latter were complemented by domestic Romani self-help organizations and informal associations of independent experts and activists who specifically focused on the Roma. These actors formed a "transnational advocacy network" (Keck and Sikkink 1998) around the issue of the Roma. This means that they maintained a network of individual people and organizations that were in contact across state borders and concentrated on the situation of the Roma wherever their situation was believed to be problematic. The question now is: What has the presence of such a transnational advocacy network meant for the Roma themselves and, in particular, for those aspiring to represent the Roma?

Transnational Advocacy and Domestic Policy Change

Advocacy actors generally do not engage in supporting particular political movements and parties. On the other hand, the fact that they are nonpartisan does not mean that they are apolitical. They defend norms that are seen as valid across state borders, and that activity often involves criticizing particular politicians and even whole governments when they do not comply with those norms. In theory, such a strategy may lead to important political changes in the targeted country.

During the last decade of the twentieth century a number of international human rights NGOs started to research and document the human rights situation of the Roma in Europe. Particularly in Central and Eastern Europe, they found that the Roma were disproportionately affected by economic and political changes after 1989 and had become the number one victims of discrimination. From the beginning of the 1990s onwards, international human rights NGOs criticized those governments that ignored the plight of the Roma. For example, in the first half of the decade Human Rights Watch published a series of reports on the situation of the Roma in Bulgaria, Romania, Hungary, and Czechoslovakia, concentrating on a wide range of issues from education to unequal access to public and private services (Helsinki Watch 1991a, 1991b; HRW 1992, 1993). In the latter half of the 1990s, the European Roma Rights Center (ERRC) became the first professional international NGO to focus exclusively on the human rights situation of the Roma. Besides documenting and publicizing the systematic lack of human rights protection and sending protest letters to "shame" governments, the ERRC also started to provide targeted legal help, including litigation, to Romani victims of human rights violations. The idea behind this was to fight discriminatory practices through courts of law by engaging in "impact litigation," on both domestic and international levels. The work of these organizations was joined by the activities of a wide range of international NGOs of which the most important were Minority Rights Group International (Liégeois and Gheorghe 1995), Amnesty International (2000), Save the Children (2001), Open Society Institute (Zoon 2001a; Zoon 2001b), and the International Helsinki Federation for Human Rights. These international advocacy NGOs also maintained links with local organizations and local independent activists in the three countries under consideration.

To what extent was the criticism of advocacy organizations taken into account by national governments? A general impression is that their influence on Central European governments was quite substantial, especially when it was combined with criticism from IGOs. Politicians in power as well as civil servants working in specialized government institutions aimed at preparing and implementing Romani policy more than once referred to the growing influence of advocacy NGOs on domestic policy making on Roma. Although it is difficult to measure the exact power of the advocacy network, there are a number of indicators suggesting that it did indeed exert some leverage.

One is the growing number of references to minority rights standards and the role of NGOs in government reports addressing the situation of the Roma. This development correlated with the general increase of government attention to the Roma as a policy theme in their own right. New government programs aimed at Romani communities in many cases included references to issues raised by advocacy organizations. This development was most apparent in the case of Slovakia. As I discussed in an earlier chapter, Resolutions 310 (1996) and 796 (1997), issued by the last Mečiar government, did not frame the issue of the Romani minority in terms of minority rights, but in terms of remedying socially pathological behavior. Moreover, the resolutions did not mention the problem of discrimination—a traditional concern of advocacy organizations—and did not discuss a possible contribution of NGOs and the Romani movement itself to the process of remedying the problematic situation. The contrast with Resolution 821 (1999), issued by the Dzurinda government, is remarkable. Not only did this resolution reflect the typical preoccupations of the advocacy organizations (mainly discrimination and social exclusion), it also placed emphasis on the rights of the Roma, and its explanatory report even included several paragraphs directly addressing the role of advocacy organizations in making society and authorities more aware of those rights.

> NGOs have significantly contributed to the detection of extreme cases of violation of human rights of the Roma, they have helped the victims and they have demanded a fair sentencing of the perpetrators. They have significantly contributed to the lifting of state power concealment of human rights violations—thus, they have become significant actors in the enhancement of civic awareness ... It is therefore desirable that the enhancement of legal awareness in human rights and rights of persons belonging to [a] national minority be continued so that it achieves not only a comparable level with the majority population but also a higher standard of legal awareness in the field of human rights protection and the protection of persons belonging to national minorities. (Government of the Slovak Republic 1999a)

The fact that advocacy organizations, both domestic and international, were able to influence the Dzurinda government should come as no surprise. Independent criticism by NGOs and campaigns for democratization had been a critical factor in the victory of Dzurinda's coalition party SDK in the 1998 elections (see e.g. Bútora and Demeš 1999).

In the Czech Republic the influence of advocacy networks on policy formation was most visible after 1996. Publications from advocacy organizations about the disparate impact on Roma of the 1993 citizenship law, combined with criticism from abroad as a consequence of the rising number of Czech asylum seekers, made the government adopt a rather self-critical report in 1997 (Resolution 686). Following this the Government Council of Human Rights paid increasing attention to the situation of the Roma and the policy concept adopted by the government in 1999 (Resolution 279) devoted considerable attention to concerns of activists (see, for example, Paragraph 1 of the resolution, which addresses the issue of discrimination).

From the early 1990s onwards Hungarian government reports and resolutions on the situation of the Roma framed the situation of the Roma in terms of their minority rights, more specifically in terms of the need to protect their cultural autonomy. The influence of independent organizations on government proposals is less clear in Hungary than in the other two cases. Nevertheless, the Hungarian government acknowledged that independent international actors such as the Soros Foundations were important sources of funding (Farkas Szilágyi and Heizer 1996: 19). The government also became more open to discussions with advocacy organizations. For example, in 2001 a discussion paper on a "long-term Roma social and minority policy strategy" was adopted by the government (Resolution 1078) which was distributed to advocacy organizations such as the ERRC, among others, in order to create what was called a "social debate."

Another development is reflected in the personal career paths of those civil servants who later were employed in the newly established special institutions for the design or implementation of Romani programs. In the latter half of the 1990s the Czech Republic, Slovakia, and Hungary experimented with commissions aimed at bringing the "Romani voice" into the policy-making process. Especially in the Czech and Slovak cases, a number of the people selected to take part in these bodies came from a background in advocacy organizations, most of them well entrenched in an international network. The Secretariat of the Czech Inter-ministerial Commission for Romani Community Affairs, for instance, employed people with a background in organizations such as the Helsinki Citizens Assembly and the Open Society Foundation. The Secretariat of the Slovak Government Commissioner for the Solution of the Problems of the Roma employed people who had been working for the Slovak Helsinki Committee and the Foundation InfoRoma (sponsored by the Open Society Fund in Bratislava).

The influence of advocacy organizations is to a large degree dependent on reputation. Organizations with a serious image are more likely to be taken seriously by governments. Governments are sometimes more willing to view these advocates as credible critics of the situation of the oppressed than they are prepared to accept the criticisms that are formulated by ethnic representatives. Advocacy actors represent internationally valid principles, and not the private interests of only one group. However, international advocacy organizations are not always successful in constructing a solid image of themselves as neutral defenders of universal principles. In some cases advocacy NGOs remain unsupported by potentially supportive politicians and potential local allies (media and local advocacy organizations). This happens when the strategies of "information politics" employed by the advocates are met with negative responses from both governments and potential partners in the domestic arena. Information politics refers here to the "ability to quickly and credibly generate politically usable information and move it to where it will have the most impact" (Keck and Sikkink 1998: 16). Activists "gain influence by serving as alternate sources of information." They "interpret facts and testimony, usually framing issues simply, in terms of right and wrong, because their purpose is to persuade people and stimulate them to act" (Keck and Sikkink 1998: 19). However, information politics can fail when the credibility of the information is questioned by potential supporters.

That is exactly what happened to some of the initiatives in Central Europe. In 2001, for example, the Open Society Institute (OSI) published a report on the situation of the Roma in Slovakia that would soon lose some of its potential impact. The report was published in October of that year, noncoincidently a month before the publication of the European Commission's yearly regular report on Slovakia's progress towards EU membership. On the basis of testimonies from Roma who had requested political asylum in Finland and direct observations of medical personnel working with NGOs, the report raised concerns over possible cases of recent forced sterilization of Romani women in eastern Slovakia (Zoon 2001b: 67–68). This information was, however, not detailed enough to persuade domestic Romani activists to mobilize around the issue. Moreover, it provoked a negative response from some activists, and most importantly, from the Government Commissioner for Romani Issues, Klára Orgovánová. She dismissed the OSI's publication as being "on a level between inaccurate information and opinion."[20] In a press statement issued on November 14, 2001, Minister for Minorities, Human Rights and Regional Development Pál Csáky found it "regrettable that the OSI distributed material that was prepared on a low professional level and contained false information."[21]

Another example was the controversy surrounding an advertisement for Amnesty International which had appeared in the December 9 issue of *NRC Handelsblad* in the Netherlands. The advertisement depicted an image of a toothless child, accompanied by text which, Hungary's National Image Center claimed in a letter of complaint to Amnesty International, unfairly suggested systematic abuse of Roma by the Hungarian Police. Although Hungarian National Chief of Police Péter Orbán did not deny that police abuses had occurred in Hungary, Amnesty felt itself forced to apologize to the Hungarian government because the advertisement had "given the mistaken impression that Amnesty International has reports of children in Hungary being given electric shocks or having their teeth punched or kicked out in Hungarian police stations."[22] The response of Amnesty International's European Director, Anne Burley, illustrates very well the importance of reputation and credibility in this matter. During a press conference in Budapest following the controversy she stated:

> We depend very much on our credibility ... and if anything we report turns out to be incorrect the public and governments take a less trusting view of our information. This matter is especially unfortunate as we are convinced that reports on which it was based are thoroughly researched and accurate.[23]

Transnational Advocacy and Romani Activists: A Complex Relationship

Not only is the relationship between these NGOs and the governments they criticize complex, but also the relationship between the NGOs in question and those they seek to defend.

One of the arguments proposed in literature on the diffusion of human rights norms contends that through emphasizing the norms of universal human rights, international NGOs are able to support domestic opposition movements demanding political change in norm-violating states. Thomas Risse and Kathryn Sikkink, for example, have argued that international NGOs advocating human rights might have played a crucial role in mobilizing domestic opposition and legitimating the claims of local social movements in such diverse regions as Latin America, Africa and Eastern Europe (Risse and Sikkink 1999). In Central Europe, many Romani activists did indeed welcome the growth of a transnational advocacy network on Romani issues. International NGOs provided domestic Romani activists with a powerful tool in the language of international human and minority rights with which to make their claims to the government and attract support from ordinary Romani citizens.

Moreover, advocacy organizations could support the efforts of local activists through their special relationship with international press. International NGOs had better access to international mass media than local activists and were able to draw attention to the issue of the Roma and the international Romani movement. Arguably, the information politics of advocacy organizations directed the attention of the international press to such organizations as the Roma National Congress (RNC) and the International Romani Union (IRU).

Furthermore, the increased attention to Roma by advocacy organizations went hand in hand with a flow of financial and technical resources to the new democracies through private foundations and international organizations in the context of what has been called "civil society development." This term is most often understood as the development of civic awareness of citizens through their voluntary participation in NGOs of all kinds. At the end of the 1990s and the beginning of the 2000s, the EU was one of the main financial supporters of projects on involving Roma in Central Europe (see Table 5.1).

Organizations that explicitly aimed at defending the rights of Romani minorities and supported the establishment of new Romani organizations could also profit from new funds made available by private donors. The Soros Foundations network, for instance, was a most prominent defender of such a strategy and made financial support available to a large number of projects and initiatives. In 1999, the Soros Foundations network spent a total of approximately €7 million on Romani programs;

Table 5.1 EU funding through the Phare programs. Grants made available for projects that explicitly support Romani communities (in euros).

	1998	1999	2000	2001
Czech Republic	900,000	500,000	2,850,000	3,000,000
Hungary	141,850	6,900,000	2,500,000	5,000,000
Slovakia	591,850	3,800,000	3,800,000	10,000,000

Source: European Commission (2002).

in 2000 the figure rose to about €7.4 million.[24] This is considerable if one compares these figures with the annual budgets of the Central European governments reserved for programs directly targeting Roma. In Hungary, the Horn government used to spend around 3 billion Forints (approximately €11.7 million) annually (Kadét 2001). According to one government report, the special budgetary resources made available in 2000 for the medium-term package of measures amounted to 4.86 billion Forints (approximately €19 million) (Inter-Ministerial Committee on Roma Issues of the Hungarian Government 2001). In 2002, the Slovak government earmarked 50 million Crowns (about €1.1 million) to fund its Romani policy (Government Commissioner for the Romani Community 2002). In 2000, the annual report of the national Soros Foundation in Hungary indicated that 13 percent of its total expenditures was spent on projects specifically aimed at the Roma, while no other minorities were mentioned as a special category for targeted projects.

The advocacy network, furthermore, aspired to stand for values of democracy. Several international NGOs tried to bring education on democracy and political organization to a Romani audience, or they tried to provide a wider audience with a new perspective on the social situation of the Roma by emphasizing the importance of human rights norms. Advocates also criticized discriminatory language and thus helped to produce a more positive image of Romani activists and Romani politicians. Moreover, as the lack of political representation of Roma was increasingly seen as a democratic deficit, certain NGOs started to take the lead in fostering the involvement of Roma in politics. Some recent OSI programs, for example, were explicitly meant to stimulate the engagement of Roma in elections and parties. One international NGO — Project on Ethnic Relations (PER)—contributed directly to the formation of a credible Romani leadership by organizing roundtable discussions at which both politicians in power and a selection of Roma were brought together.

It was not the intention of these and other human rights NGOs to act as "representatives" of the Roma. Although in most cases they received backing from well-known Romani personalities in advisory boards, they did not aim to speak *for* the people. One could say that they did not seek to defend all particular claims made by Romani activists. They contributed to defending a common "negative interest," meaning an interest in being rid of a certain condition, namely the condition of inequality and discrimination.[25] However, parallel to the activities of these international NGOs ran the aspiration of some Romani activists to speak for the Roma and form some sort of political representation. This means that the latter organized efforts to represent "positive interests," which are particular claims and particular views on specific strategic ways of remedying discrimination and increasing the well-being of the entire Roma community. It goes without saying that the second type of interest representation is likely to lead to much more differentiation among Romani activists. Activists may disagree with regard to which opinion to support or which strategic decision to take. And it entails all kinds of challenging problems, such as defining for whom to speak (the boundaries of the Romani community) and defining representative claims. Hence, for example, the sometimes fierce debates among Romani activists about whether to ally with non-Roma political forces or whether to support or contest certain government initiatives.

However positive the influence of advocacy networks on the position of the Roma may at first sight appear, it nonetheless confronted Romani activists with new questions, and it raised new controversies among them. In particular, the problem surrounding the creation of a legitimate Romani representation loomed large. The indirect or direct support from the international advocacy network for ethnic activism created the impression that some of the problems could be solved by identifying the appropriate Romani representatives. But the question then was: Who was to have the democratic or moral mandate to speak on behalf of the Roma?

Romani activism in Central Europe was severely plagued by discussions on this matter. Non-Romani advocacy organizations, like the ERRC, were sometimes bitterly criticized by both Romani organizations and independent observers for reducing complex cases to simple stories of discrimination, seeing a solution for the problems facing the Roma only in the narrow area of increased protection of rights, *and*, most significantly, for not appropriately representing the Roma. Some of the critics argued that advocacy organizations have tended to neglect the real needs of Romani communities since they have acted only from the perspective of their own normative agenda (see, for example, Barany 2002: 276; Trehan 2001). In the strict sense, advocacy organizations, even if they are based on Romani membership, are of course not representative of the entire Romani population of a country. They have no mandate to speak for the people; rather they aim to speak and act in the name of an idea (for example, in this case, the idea that Roma have specific rights and that they should not be discriminated against). In this way, advocacy organizations (Romani as well as non-Romani) are not accountable to a Romani constituency in the same way democratically elected representatives would be.

These organizations have nevertheless had a strong impact on the position of Romani activists and can therefore not claim that they should be judged only taking into account their record on defending principles. In the three countries covered in this book, the activities of advocacy organizations led to the emergence of an identifiable group of influential Roma—a Romani political elite—who came to be regarded as representative of the Roma. These people were often quoted in the media, were able to voice their opinions, and were often invited to international conferences. A number of them were even approached by their government to participate in dialogues or act as experts.

The discussion about what constitutes legitimate representation became especially apparent when the newly designed special bodies for advising, coordinating, and implementing Romani policy were under scrutiny. As discussed earlier, in response to a lack of democratically elected Roma in the deliberation process, some governments established advisory and expert bodies in which Roma, mostly from NGOs, were included. The status of the Roma in these advisory and expert bodies was often not entirely clear. Governments sometimes emphasized that Romani representation was one of the major concerns in policy deliberation, and subsequently they argued that the consultation of experts and Romani spokespersons was in fact a form of ethnic representation. In Hungary, such a process of consultation had taken place in the period prior to the elaboration of the Minorities Act in 1993. More recently, the Office for Ethnic and National Minorities in Hungary claimed to maintain a dialogue with a variety of well-known leaders of Romani organizations. In Slovakia, the person who was appointed to the position of Government Commissioner for the Solution of the Problems of the Romani Minority in 2001 was a well-known Romani personality who had previously worked in a Romani organization. The best example is perhaps the Czech Republic where the Government Council for Romani Community Affairs brought together people from a broad range of organizations and literally called them the Czech "Romani elite."

Such initiatives were often supported by Romani activists, because they found it important to have a say in policy preparation. A number of Romani activists probably saw this kind of expert function as a way to influence government without having to go through the process of mobilizing mass support. Moreover, for many Romani activists it was important that governments discussed new policy proposals with at least some members of the communities in question, even if these were not officially elected representatives.

But as a by-product of this development a new division arose between officially acknowledged Romani advisors and Romani activists who were not officially recognized. Discussions about who should be recognized as legitimate advisors surfaced in the three countries. The context of these discussions differed to a large extent between the Czech Republic and Slovakia on the one hand, and Hungary on the other. In the Czech and Slovak Republics, the Romani participants in these bodies increasingly functioned as a substitute for Romani representation through elected representatives (and were probably regarded as such by many ordinary Roma). Therefore, discussion in the Czech Republic and Slovakia mostly concerned the very weak connection that some of the selected Romani activists were claimed to have with local Romani communities. As said, the governments of the two countries to some extent created the illusion that the Romani elite could form an alternative political representation, while the problem of the lack of inclusion of Roma in regular political bodies moved into the background.

In Hungary, the problem was different. As a result of the minority law, Hungary has a fifty-three-member elected National Gypsy Self-Government that is the official ethnic partner of the government for discussing matters related to the rights of the Roma. One can therefore say that in Hungary there has indeed been a form of democratically elected Romani representation. However, a debate about the legitimacy of this representation arose among Romani activists. One part of the discussion related to the way in which the National Gypsy Self-Government was elected, another aspect concerned the way the government treated this body. The National Gypsy Self-Government was seen by the government as the exclusive partner for dialogue, and thereby it largely illegitimatized alternative Romani advocacy organizations that sought to influence policy but were not engaged in the self-government system. Some Roma also felt that through the establishment of this minority self-government system the state neglected to care about the overall inclusion of Roma in regular political institutions.

The idea that ethnic representation was needed gained further ground through the actions of IGOs. On the European level, international organizations repeatedly emphasized the demand that initiatives targeted at the situation of the Roma be codesigned by Romani representatives. But since there were too few elected representatives, the Council of Europe and the OSCE set up special offices in which a selection of Romani members from advocacy organizations and Romani leaders could have an advisory seat. Romani organizations that are active across borders responded by trying to establish a firm basis for further dialogue with IGOs and the people in these advisory bodies. It is, however, debatable if Roma are better represented simply by letting a selected number of members of advocacy organizations (or those promoted by advocacy organizations) have a say in the process of policy preparation. It is undoubtedly important that ideas on how to improve the situation of the Roma can be discussed publicly and that Roma themselves are included in such debates. However, there is a problem when the inclusion of a selected group of Roma in the discussion is portrayed as the establishment of a "representative" Romani body that will ensure the effectiveness of the initiatives taken by these international organizations.

Another problem was that the involvement of interest advocates, who bring substantial financial resources with them, created new controversies among Roma about whether that money was fairly distributed. Romani activists to whom I talked in the three countries frequently brought up this issue, not only in the context of the criteria for resource distribution, but also in the context of the power that these organizations have. Many of the activists interviewed believed that dependence on private money also meant dependence on the programmatic priorities of the funding organizations. They also believed that these funding organizations favored certain types of activists (for example, those who know English and favor the development of an international Romani movement) and neglected others.

Advocacy organizations were also criticized for reinforcing the gap between intellectual activists and "ordinary" Romani citizens. Advocacy organizations generally stood for the empowerment of the Roma in an ethnic movement. Yet, the support from below for such a movement has not visibly grown in recent years. One could speculate about the various reasons for this failing mass mobilization, but in the context of the above, one should certainly refer to the role of advocates in constructing and reinforcing an ethnic boundary between the Roma and non-Roma (for purposes of advocacy), without at the same time having been able to foster more positive images of the people whose interests they have sought to defend. Apparently, they have so far not been able to effectuate the acceptance of the Roma as an integral part of the national "imagined communities." Under such circumstances it is difficult to mobilize mass support (from Roma and from non-Roma) for the ideas and norms of minority rights protection.

Conclusion

This chapter began with an exploration of the institutional and political responses from IGOs to the plight of the Roma in Central Europe. It has shown that in the last decade European institutions have increasingly highlighted the Romani issue within their general policies towards Central Europe. I asked whether this development was perceived as beneficial by domestic Romani activists. The answer was mixed. It was certainly perceived as favorable by one part of the Romani movement, namely by those activists who from the very beginning had attempted to give the Roma the status of a European nation. Other Romani activists, however, were clearly more doubtful and feared that such status would reinforce stereotypes and subsequently undermine their efforts to pressure domestic governments.

The growing international concern for the Roma in Central Europe should not be seen as brought about only by IGOs; international attention was to a large extent also excited by transnational advocacy NGOs. The actions of IGOs and NGOs in this field were mutually reinforcing. On the one hand, the pressure strategies applied by IGOs were crucial in creating new opportunities for advocacy. And on the other hand, transnational advocacy groups stimulated IGOs to step up their monitoring activities. From this perspective, one can easily understand why advocacy organizations actively sought to maintain contacts in international forums and consistently aimed their information campaigns at IGOs. It is difficult to establish whether advocacy organizations indeed became more powerful when IGOs joined them in criticizing domestic governments. It is clear, however, that Central European governments in their communication towards EU institutions increasingly highlighted the Romani issue, especially when these governments had received criticism from both IGOs and advocacy organizations—Slovakia before 1998 being the most striking example. The EU's handling of the issue of minority protection had for a large part its own dynamics. Nevertheless, organizations and activists advocating Romani rights were able to utilize EU concerns in order to scrutinize governments of candidate EU member states, and they were also able to highlight the lack of minority protection standards within the EU.

To what extent, then, were advocacy organizations able to influence the position of the Romani movement in Central Europe? Developments in the Czech Republic, Hungary, and Slovakia show that the typical concerns of advocacy networks were increasingly incorporated in domestic policy documents, a fact that undoubtedly gave a number of local Romani activists a stronger negotiating position. Advocacy organizations also gave local Romani activists an international profile. But these organizations were not able to create mass Romani mobilization, and the involvement of interest advocates created a number of new controversies among Roma about the distribution of private money, the content of Romani demands, and the legitimate representation of those demands.

Chapter 6

The Romani Movement in Theoretical Perspective

In the first chapter of this book I outlined the dominant theoretical approaches to ethnic mobilization in the current literature and described how the examination of different aspects of ethnic protest animated authors to develop different models of explanation. I also argued that the complex "political process" model represented a viable and preferable alternative to models that assigned weight to only one factor, in particular those that singled out either culture, relative deprivation, or elite competition as an isolated causal factor. The general tenet of the political process approach to ethnic movements is that the prospects of ethnic mobilization are dependent on the changes in the institutionalized political system, the availability of organizational structures around ethnic identity, and the presence of powerful schemes of interpretation conducive to ethnic mobilization. Doug McAdam in his book *Political Process and the Development of Black Insurgency, 1930–1970*—still one of the most sophisticated theoretically based studies of the civil rights movement in the United States—described the political process model as one that suggests that "neither environmental factors nor factors internal to the movement are sufficient to account for the generation and development of social insurgency." The political process model, he went on to say:

> rests on the assumption that social movements are an ongoing product of the favorable interplay of *both* sets of factors. The specific mix of factors may change from one phase of the movement to another, but the basic dynamic remains the same. Movements develop in response to an ongoing process of interaction between movement groups and the larger sociopolitical environment they seek to change. (McAdam 1982: 39–40)

The question I will ask in this concluding chapter goes back to the theoretical point of departure of this book. Is the political process model an apt and sufficiently comprehensive theoretical framework for understanding and explaining the developments of the Romani movement? And if so, what can we learn about the Romani movement in Central Europe by examining it from this perspective? And what are the remaining problem areas?

Revisiting the findings so far and applying the theoretical models developed at the beginning of this book, this chapter seeks to redress some of the weaknesses of the culturalist and reactive ethnicity explanations of ethnic minority mobilization. Following this, and further applying theoretical perspectives to the story of the Romani movement in Central Europe, the chapter will gradually move into the direction of the political process model. I will examine the role of competition as a causal factor and gauge the usefulness of the political opportunities approach. Finally, I will briefly address the question of the limits of these latter two perspectives and propound additional explanations needed to make sense of the empirical observations made in earlier chapters. In particular, I will focus on the importance of social psychological dynamics (what has been called "framing processes") and assess the extent to which an emerging international opportunity structure should be taken into account.

Culture, Inequality, and Ethnic Mobilization

One of my aims at the outset of this book was to find out how post-communist governments in Central Europe responded to questions of inequality and cultural differentiation. This response was particularly visible in the way the countries under study responded to the issue of the Roma. As has been seen, a common characteristic has been the substantial difference between the policies towards Roma in this period and those employed in communist times. Communist regimes operated on the premise that Romani identity was not to be seen as an ethnic identity and would consequently disappear, although in practice the position of the authorities was often ambiguous. After 1989, the dominant view was that Romani identity needed to be viewed as an ethnic minority identity and was therefore a legitimate basis for political participation and the representation of group-specific interests.

The most important consequence of this shift was that after 1989 ethnic divisions in society were considered the preferred basis for policy making. Ethnic-blind approaches aimed at economic equalization and cultural assimilation lost their dominant status. A specific implication of the ethnicization of policy towards the Roma was the promotion of a single ethnic categorization to deal with this group. The distinction between Roma and non-Roma became politically meaningful, while lesser-known ethnic categorizations such as Vlach, Romungre, Lovari, Kalderashi, or Beash were seen as less important and were made subordinate to the official designation "Roma." Instead of being considered as potential members of other target groups in social policy, such as the poor or the unemployed, the Roma were increasingly seen as a special target group of their own.

This clearly generated an enormous change in the opportunity structure for the Romani movement. Activists increasingly promoted the view that Romani ethnic identity needed to be seen as an overarching ethnic identification, encompassing a wide variety of other identifications, and in need of special policy measures. This points to the existence of an intriguing correlation between the growing success of the discourse of Romani activism and the increase in the number of policy measures aimed specifically at the Roma. One also sees a spectacular increase in the attention devoted to the Roma by international actors (IGOs and international NGOs). It is impossible to determine which of these developments have been causes and which have been effects. It can, however, be hypothesized that the growing attention paid to Romani ethnicity in the development of policies was stimulated from below (activists influenced the policy-making process), while at the same time the development of Romani activism was fostered by attention coming from above (policies influenced Romani mobilization). Moreover, the increasing use of an ethnic discourse by activists may have been stimulated by the tendency of the mass media, domestic mainstream politicians and IGOs to consider ethnic divisions in Central European societies as crucial political dividing lines.

But along with this central characteristic common to the postcommunist era one sees considerable variation among the three countries with regard to the development of policies towards the Roma. During the course of the 1990s, states went about institutionalizing Romani ethnicity in different ways. Hungary between 1989 and 1995 created special institutions for all ethnic minorities and placed the Roma on an equal footing with the other officially recognized minorities. In the latter half of the decade, the Roma were differentiated from the other minorities and we saw the introduction of additional measures and institutions specifically for the Roma. Czechoslovakia at the beginning of the decade placed Roma on an equal footing with other minorities, but in contrast to Hungary at that time attached much importance to the "civic principle" and was very reluctant to institutionalize ethnic differentiation. Later on, in independent Slovakia, the Roma were deemed a special group of "citizens in need of special care," while in legal terms they had a status similar to that of the other minorities. After 1998 the Roma in Slovakia became an important topic of international concern and new specific measures and strategies were designed. A similar development was visible in the Czech Republic.

Within these changing contexts Romani activism changed. Romani activists attempted to form a movement in different ways, and with varying degrees of success. Movement strategies varied in accordance with their decisions on three central choices:

1. The choice between cooperation with the established political institutions for minority or Romani policies (institutional access,

becoming partners instead of challengers), or contention (civil disobedience, public protest against state institutions and government behavior, shaming).
2. The choice between building a movement on the basis of a separate ethnic Romani identity (as a national or a European minority), or making Romani identity subordinate to other solidarities (on the basis of socioeconomic position).
3. The choice between cooperation with non-Romani actors (such as mainstream political parties and advocacy and solidarity NGOs), or isolation in organizations exclusively for the Roma (Romani political parties and Romani NGOs).

In Hungary at the beginning of the 1990s, Romani activists organized mainly in independent organizations. Some of them allied with the democratic opposition; others attempted to organize a movement within the structures that had been set up during the latter half of the 1980s. Unification of both wings into one Romani movement was realized for only a very brief period. In the latter half of the 1990s Hungarian Romani activists primarily organized themselves through minority self-governments. Through this channel they found access to institutionalized dialogue with the government. Independent Romani activists formed alliances with advocacy organizations. In Czechoslovakia before 1993 Romani mobilization occurred mainly in coalition with the anticommunist forces. Romani activists were elected to the parliament and formed ethnic political parties. This changed after the country split up in 1993. In Slovakia, Romani activists engaged in independent Romani political parties or forged alliances with mainstream political parties. Other activists organized themselves into self-help NGOs—often supported by foreign donors. In the Czech Republic Romani activism before 1998 mainly occurred within the Council of Nationalities. Later a number of activists maintained their focus on particular, symbolic events, while others increasingly cooperated with the Government Council for Romani Community Affairs. At the beginning of the new century, a number of Czech activists were particularly interested in participating in a Europe-wide Romani movement.

In the most recent periods, one sees an increasing preference among Romani activists for cooperation with the established political institutions, which could indicate the growing institutionalization of the Romani movement and the marginalization of confrontational action. Hungary between 1995 and 2001 is perhaps the most obvious case, but it is possible to observe this trend in the other two countries as well. Moreover, one discerns a growing conviction among Romani activists that Romani identity is an appropriate, and even the most suitable, basis for the representation of their interests. Independent of whether ethnic mobilization was successful or not, activists increasingly came to regard the "ethnic way" as the most adequate form of mobilization. With regard to the question of whether Romani activists found it appropriate to cooperate with non-Romani actors, the picture is more mixed. Some Romani activists sought to forge alliances with national and international advocacy NGOs, while others increasingly attempted to create a Romani movement exclusively on the basis of ethnic membership. But antagonistic as well as cooperative forms of Romani mobilization were able to find support from non-Romani actors.

What theoretical conclusion should be drawn from this? One of the premises of the political process perspective is that the political opportunity structure (POS) leads to particular mobilization patterns. This brings us to the following question: How plausible is a theory that proposes a causal relationship between the variation in the POS and the changing patterns of Romani mobilization? I will argue that ways of organizing a Romani movement changed in response to political opportunities, but that the process was influenced by other factors as well. These factors were linked to the way the Romani movement was framed on domestic levels, and the additional opportunities and obstacles provided by the international environment (including both international organizations and independent advocacy and shaming networks).

The Deficiency of Culturalist and Reactive Ethnicity Approaches

Before dealing with the merits and demerits of the competition and political process explanations of ethnic minority mobilization, it might be useful to briefly reconsider the older approaches. What I meant by a culturalist theory of ethnic mobilization in Chapter 1 was a model based on the idea that ethnic minorities are fixed cultural entities. Because of the existence of a cultural core, culturalists argue, these entities are likely to show typical patterns of mobilization. According to this perspective, the Romani movement should show little variation and develop in similar patterns wherever Roma live. As was mentioned, one of the fundamental theoretical criticisms of this approach has argued that the existence of ethnic minorities is to a large extent dependent on processes of perception, interpretation, and evocation. That ethnic minority identities are politically and socially constructed is a matter that is often neglected in culturalist approaches.

In earlier chapters, I documented attempts by activists to construct Romani ethnicity for strategic reasons. I showed how Romani culture and Romani ethnicity were frames created and promoted primarily by those activists who were able to position themselves as ethnic leaders. Identity construction was, at one and the same time, influenced by non-Romani political leaders who supported the Romani movement and by those who opposed it, the latter having usually constructed a negative image of Romani identity. Thus, Romani ethnicity cannot be separated from the process in which such an ethnicity is constructed by social and political actors. This does not mean that the cultural setting plays no role in this process. However, culture should not be seen as an objectively identifiable set of group characteristics. It should rather be regarded as a reservoir of interpretations, such as traditional beliefs and myths, which actors can utilize for purposes of ethnic group formation, and which make certain political and social constructs more accepted and more effective than others.

In light of these observations, it should come as no surprise that Romani mobilization varied substantially not only between countries, but also between various political levels. As was seen earlier, for example, the idea of the Roma as a European nation became the predominant notion within IGOs and the international Romani movement, but this frame did not enable mass ethnic mobilization in the domestic arena. Moreover, within various domestic contexts, it was possible to identify divergent organizational trends within the Romani movement. While in the Czech Republic a number of important activists attempted to mobilize in a Europe-wide Romani movement and targeted IGOs, the European level was of marginal importance to many Romani activists in Hungary. A culturalist perspective comes up empty-handed when it comes to explaining such variations. The mere fact that collective action on the basis of Romani identity did indeed vary during recent years, and in the different countries studied, is an empirical observation that contradicts the assumptions of a rigid culturalist perspective. According to such a culturalist paradigm, Romani mobilization should have been constant over different periods and in different countries simply because the theory holds that mobilization patterns are closely related to what is regarded as the objectively identifiable characteristics of the ethnic group.

Popular descriptions sometimes argued that patterns of Romani mobilization were consistently lackluster exactly because of Romani culture. Many observers argued that factionalism within the Romani movement was related to the exceptional nature of the Roma as an extremely heterogeneous conglomerate of ethnic subgroups. As one journalist argued: "They belong to many different, and often antagonistic, clans and tribes, with no common language or religion."[1] However, on the basis of a closer analysis of the events in the three countries, I contend that mobilization and unification processes were not uniformly unsuccessful.

Moreover, the ethnic heterogeneity among the Roma need not only be understood as cause of failing mobilization, but also as a consequence of it. The process of Romani mobilization itself gave rise to competing understandings of Romani identity. Thus, Romani mobilization was hindered, not by the alleged universally low levels of Romani ethnic awareness, but by crucial factors of political organization such as strategic disputes between movement elites about how to conceptualize Romani identity, how to promote their conceptualizations, and how to organize around them.

The reactive ethnicity approach is also difficult to maintain in the case of the Roma. The essential argument of this approach was that the level of mobilization is directly linked to the level of deprivation and inequality. Compelling as this view may seem, the idea that ethnic mobilization naturally arises in response to disturbances experienced by members of an ethnic group was strongly criticized in the literature. Neither is it entirely supported by the case of the Roma. The model has two fundamental problems. First, much like the culturalist approach, this theory separates ethnicity from the role of social and political actors. The ethnic group is treated as though it had material existence prior to processes of interpretation and construction. Secondly, the events of Romani mobilization show that those who did attempt to mobilize an ethnic movement did not spontaneously react to marginality or deprivation, but rather made rational calculations about ways to communicate with the state. There are many poor communities in the three countries under study that were not interested in participation in the Romani movement, and did not believe that ethnic mobilization would ameliorate their situation (hence the complaints made by Romani activists who failed to attract voters during elections). Conversely, instances of relatively successful mobilization (some Romani activists were indeed elected and a number of successful protest actions did occur) did not always involve those communities that experienced the most troublesome circumstances.

In short, deprivation as such does not determine patterns of ethnic mobilization. Social movement scholars have pointed out that problems have to be *perceived* as grievances before they can lead to mobilization (della Porta and Diani 1999: 70). That this holds true for the Romani movement was illustrated in Chapter 3. The descriptions in that chapter suggest that the situation of economic inequality, although it did play a certain role in bringing about Romani mobilization, did not provide a sufficient explanation for the upsurge and decline of ethnic mobilization. Moreover, the chapter provided examples where it was not the inequalities in themselves, but the *attention* coming from media and advocacy groups, the input of financial resources, and the symbolic value of the events that led to some of the most successful moments of ethnic mobilization (for example, the Matični Street affair in the Czech Republic, or the responses in the three countries to the issue of the asylum seekers). In these cases, some actors were able to draw the people's attention to the situation and to promulgate the interpretation that the root cause of the problem was the injustice done at the expense of the Roma.

Solving the Puzzle? Strengths and Problems of the Competition and Political Process Approach

Some aspects of the Romani movement that remain puzzling when merely seen from the perspective of the reactive ethnicity model become more easily explainable when viewed within the perspective of a theory of ethnic competition. Competition for particular rewards was a powerful force causing contenders to organize themselves along ethnic lines. Inequality in itself did not lead to mobilization, but competition among elites for particular rewards did. Incentives may have been financial (governmental funding or funding from international private donors, distributed on the basis of ethnic categorization) or political (offices specifically for ethnic minority members, filled through election or appointment). What is important is that such incentives were able to boost ethnic group formation when individual material or political payoffs were experienced as conditional upon ethnic group membership.

The competition perspective clearly provides a better understanding of many of the observations I made in earlier chapters. Its main virtue is that it draws our attention to the role of ethnic leaders in constructing an ethnic group and in promoting ethnicity as an instrument for achieving a better political and material position. However, it is not able to offer a complete explanation for all of the findings. For example, it is not able to clarify why activists sometimes persistently organized in forms that clearly offered only marginal financial or political rewards. Consider the attempts of Romani activists in Hungary to organize outside the self-government system, or the sustained attempts by Czech and Slovak Romani activists to participate in parliamentary elections in ethnically based Romani parties even after a succession of failures.

One way to make sense of these developments is to assume that it was the institutional environment that impelled ethnic actors to organize in particular kinds of organization and has discouraged other kinds. This is the POS approach. It does not preclude the role of competition, but contends that competition is not the only factor at play. The form that competition takes, it argues, is shaped by the available institutional context. In contrast to what the competition model suggests, the dynamics of ethnic mobilization are dependent not merely on the tactical choices of ethnic leaders, but also on the opportunities and constraints offered by the political and institutional environment. In this way, the POS approach offers a more complete view of the dynamics of ethnic competition.

Let me mention just a few examples. In Hungary the greater part of the internal organization of the Romani movement developed in response to the financial and political rewards offered by the minority self-government system. Before the introduction of the self-government system, Romani activists engaged in attempts to unify under a broad nongovernmental umbrella organization. In the latter half of the 1990s, a tangible dividing line emerged between those activists who focused their activities on the state-funded self-government system and those who tried to mobilize independently, often seeking funds from international private donors.

In Slovakia, Romani mobilization did not seem to have been particularly rewarding, either financially or politically. However, the consistent pattern of attempts to organize in ethnically based political parties is explicable if seen as a response to existing patterns of ethnic competition in the political system of the country. In the 1990s, the Magyar minority in Slovakia reached high levels of ethnic mobilization, mainly in opposition to the nationalist Slovak parties, which for their part increasingly sought to attract voters on the basis of their ethnic Slovak identity. To achieve some influence on politics, Slovak Romani activists tried to compete with Slovaks and Magyars, and sought to establish a third ethnic political force in the country. Although Romani activists could not attract a popular base, they were able to position themselves as Romani representatives, mainly because the state authorities for their own purposes recognized them as the group's representatives.

At least at first sight, there appear to have been few incentives in the Czech Republic to organize in ethnic groups. The Czech state did not offer many financial or political incentives to foster ethnic politics. This may be part of the reason why many Czech Romani activists were more hesitant than their Slovak and Hungarian counterparts about the merits of ethnic mobilization. Nevertheless, mainly from 1997 onwards, Czech Romani activists were able to find support from the state budget and from international private donors to engage in projects that specifically targeted Romani communities. Moreover, they increasingly responded to what they considered to be the tendency of mainstream politicians to represent exclusively the interests of ethnic Czechs. Maneuvered into the position of *not* belonging to the Czech ethnic group, some of them may have felt more compelled than before to engage in Romani mobilization.

What these examples demonstrate is that it is at least not unreasonable to assume that ethnic mobilization can be pushed in a particular direction (and restricted from developing in other directions) by the surrounding political and institutional context. One might say that ethnic leaders use "particular dimensions of ethnicity according to some measure of utility" (Nagel 1996: 23), but with regard to what concrete strategies will be used, the catalogue of choices is limited by the surrounding political opportunities and constraints.

Dimensions of the POS

Let me consider the POS of the Romani movement in a more sustained manner. In Chapter 1, I quoted Kriesi et al. (1995: xiii–xvi) as offering the following practical categorization of the various elements of the POS:

- national cleavage structures;
- formal institutional structures;
- prevailing informal strategies;
- alliance structure.

The first aspect relates to the "political space which is available for challengers to introduce new conflicts into a polity" (Koopmans and Statham 2000: 33). The term "national cleavage" must be understood as a division which (a) is experienced as historical, (b) is currently politicized, (c) functions as a relatively stable basis for group formation, and (d) potentially leads to conflict. In Central Europe, countries had different national cleavage structures with regard to ethnic identity, and the position of the Roma differed accordingly. The clearest example of a country characterized by a politicized ethnic cleavage is Slovakia. Although I argued earlier that one cannot characterize the Slovak party system as one that is completely dominated by ethnic divisions, the specific position of the Roma in relation to the political competition between Magyars and ethnic Slovaks became increasingly apparent over the course of the 1990s. Influential populist and nationalist parties in Slovakia increasingly appealed to an ethnic Slovak audience, while Magyar leaders usually distanced themselves from the position of the Roma. Within this cleavage structure Romani activists found it logical to emphasize their separate Romani ethnicity and engage in ethnic political parties (or quasi political parties). A minority of Romani activists mobilized in cooperation with the Magyars, or sought to cooperate with Slovak nationalist parties. Most Romani activists, however, thought it was more logical to compete with both the Magyars *and* the Slovaks.

In contrast to Slovakia, Hungary has been perceived as a country that is not characterized by an important ethnic cleavage. Nevertheless, through the minority self-government system, the Roma, since 1993, have been considered as one of the non-Magyar minorities. Arguably, this is a development that stimulated their mobilization as an ethnic minority, and discouraged Romani activists from invoking nonethnic ways of mobilization. The Czech Republic, for its part, has since 1993 not known any significant ethnic cleavages. Rather, the country adhered to the homogenizing "civic principle," which was meant to suppress the politicization of ethnic cleavages and stimulate inclusive conceptions of Czech identity. However, the controversy surrounding the 1993 citizenship law and its strong impact on Roma has persuaded many Romani activists that ethnic Czechs consider Czech ethnic identity incompatible with Romani identity. This has no doubt stimulated the willingness of Roma to establish ethnic protest organizations.

The most tangible element of the POS pertains to the formal domestic institutional context, the second point in Kriesi's list. I have discussed this dimension at length in earlier chapters. One of the conclusions reached was that Romani mobilization was geared to the institutions introduced by the authorities. The existence of the minority self-government system in Hungary strongly shaped patterns of Romani mobilization. Not only did it provide access to the policy-making process on the basis of minority membership, it also made hundreds of Romani activists familiar with playing an ethnic-based role in public life. In Slovakia and the Czech Republic, formal ethnic political representation was not introduced, but the participation of Romani activists in governmental bodies whose task it was to deliberate Romani policy clearly changed the status of Romani activism. The selected activists were sometimes perceived as representatives, even though they were not elected. In Slovakia, the Government Commissioner for the Solution of the Problems of the Romani Minority was crucial in shaping Romani mobilization patterns. Independent Romani activists directed their political and financial demands to the Government Commissioner.

With regard to the prevailing informal strategies of the authorities to deal with ethnic minority movements, one must consider the difference between the Czech Republic on the one hand, and Hungary and Slovakia on the other. Informal strategies have to do with traditions and historically embedded practices. The individual histories of the ways in which the three countries dealt with ethnic movements actually have a great deal in common. These countries all dealt with the legacy of a half-century of communist-inspired policy, and they all shifted from assimilationist-oriented policies to strategies that, whether weakly or strongly, support ethnic-based politics. In recent times the policies for dealing with minorities increasingly converged in these three states. Nevertheless, the legacies are considerably different when viewed against the background of the development of Magyar, Slovak, and Czech nationalism since the nineteenth century.

The differences are especially apparent in the case of Hungary and Slovakia, which both were involved in long struggles to express in more satisfactory ways their respective ethnic identities in political institutions. The Magyar (ethnic Hungarian) struggle for national unity first resulted in a form of greater autonomy under Habsburg rule (the *Ausgleich*, or Compromise, of 1867). After the fall of the multinational Habsburg Monarchy, Magyar nationalists centered on regaining the territories that were lost as a result of the Trianon Treaty and which were inhabited by large Magyar populations. With the establishment of Czechoslovakia (the "First Republic") in the aftermath of the First World War, Slovak leaders tried to make Slovakia secure from Hungary's irredentist claims. Historical strategies for dealing with nationalism and ethnic identity provide part of the explanation for current attitudes towards ethnicity. One argument, for example, is that the Magyar and Slovak nationalist movements have had a strong influence on the currently prevailing strategies for dealing with ethnic diversity in Hungary and Slovakia. In this view, it is understandable that Slovakia and Hungary were much more oriented towards a policy of ethnic differentiation than the Czech Republic. This perspective offers a clue as to why people tended to see Magyar and Slovak identities as incompatible with Romani identity. Conversely, in such a context it is not unreasonable to expect Romani leaders to feel compelled to organize on an ethnic basis. Czech political leaders traditionally promoted a strategy of inclusion towards the Slovaks, celebrating the emergence of Czechoslovakia after the First World War as the climax of the Czech national liberation effort (Rychlík 1995: 102). The historical roots of Czech nationalism differ from those of Slovak and Magyar nationalism, but nevertheless, in this case also ethnic exclusion did occur.

It was not only the formal institutional context, but also domestic alliance structures that played a role in establishing the dynamics of Romani mobilization. I discussed various elements of this aspect of the problem in earlier chapters. Literature on the situation of the Roma in Central Europe has often focused on the role of political opponents. As I explained, these were not only found among far-right and nationalist parties, but repeatedly included politicians from the political mainstream. Yet, in the three countries under study there were instances during the 1990s and early 2000s when Romani activists were supported by political allies.

Problems

On the basis of the above considerations, it is possible to conclude that the POS approach can be profitably used to explain the development of Romani ethnic mobilization. Nevertheless, there are still a number of problems that need to be addressed.

First, POS explanations take as their point of departure a simple causal relationship between political environment and movement patterns. I contend, however, that that various movement patterns can exist *at the same time* within a single domestic POS. In other words, different movement actors may come to different conclusions about how to deal with the POS. Dominant patterns of mobilization do not rely only on the available opportunities, but also on the willingness of movement activists to seize these opportunities. For a variety of reasons, activists may not always want to use political opportunities.

Some authors have warned against drawing overly simplistic conclusions about a causal link between structure and movement action on the basis of the political opportunities approach (Koopmans and Kriesi 1995: 37). A POS approach sees the relationship between environmental structure and movement pattern as unilateral. However, there are indications that in the case of the Roma the relationship between activists and the surrounding political structure should rather be seen as interactive. This is also a criticism that has been made regarding social movements in general. Hanspeter Kriesi and Marco Guigni argue that "once the mobilizing process has been set in motion, the strategies adopted by the social movements will have feedback on the strategies adopted by the authorities" (Kriesi and Guigni 1995: xv). With regard to the Romani movement, it is clear that once the ethnicization of Romani policy was set in motion, Romani activists themselves usually lobbied in favor of establishing *more* ethnic-specific institutions. Indeed, the social and political construction of Romani identity was both a top-down and a bottom-up process.

Secondly, in the case of the Roma it was not always clear what should be considered a political opportunity and what should not. What might well be considered political factors facilitating ethnic mobilization were not in fact always perceived as such by activists and potential movement adherents. Consider, for example, the institutionalization of cultural autonomy in Hungary. Some Romani activists regarded this institutional environment as a political opportunity, while others saw it as a system that divided the Romani movement. As argued in current social movement literature, opportunities refer not only to the reality of institutions and practices, but also to the world of symbols and discourse. Institutional design created the possibility for numerous Romani actors to engage in ethnic mobilization. However, such mobilization attempts were sometimes hindered by framing disputes within the movement. It is obvious from my investigations that particular political opportunities sometimes resulted in complex, changing, and sometimes contradictory developments.

The Interpretative Turn

Political process theorists have argued that the POS approach should be complemented with a framing perspective. Attention to framing processes is indispensable for anyone seeking to explain the dynamics of Romani mobilization. This conclusion accords with the recent interpretative turn in theorizing on social movements (Koopmans and Duyvendak 1995: 244). The interpretative turn refers to the growing interest among social movement scholars in the way mobilization constructs identities, problems, and grievances. Analyses of Romani mobilization from the viewpoint of the framing model as developed by Benford and Snow have shown that by focusing on processes of interpretation and persuasion it is possible to gain insight into precisely those developments in Romani mobilization that have puzzled many observers.

Competition and political opportunities theorists draw our attention to such matters as leadership, networks, allies, and political and institutional opportunities as central elements in the emergence and the success of an ethnic movement. The material I explored in this book, however, showed that the growing number of institutions and opportunities, and the existence of powerful allies were not sufficient to further a successful Romani mass movement. Romani parties failed to attract voters, Romani activists were not able to organize mass protests, and even the number of people publicly identifying themselves as Roma in censuses fell short of expectations. Although Romani activists increasingly found national and supranational authorities responsive, they usually failed to find a mass constituency willing to support their demands. Even in times of a serious crisis—like when in early 2004 Romani communities rioted and looted shops in the eastern part of Slovakia in response to a social measure—it remains difficult for Romani activists to transform local worries into a general concern for the Romani movement at large.

One of the important obstacles to such mass mobilization was not related to the POS, but to the way reality was interpreted within and outside the movement. A crucial factor was the *inability* of activists to use Romani identity, with all of its stigmas, and turn it into a mobilizing identity. I explained how this relates to processes of counterframing in politics, traditional perceptions among the population at large (colored by romantic myths and stereotypes), and the increasingly dominant media portrayal of Roma as violators of "normal" social behavior.

In addition, one should perhaps also point to the inability of Romani movement actors to realize a "cognitive liberation" among their potential constituencies. "Cognitive liberation" is a term coined by Doug McAdam, who used it to refer to "a transformation of consciousness within a significant segment of the aggrieved population" (McAdam 1982: 51). The term describes a necessary condition of mobilization. "Before collective protest can get under way, people must collectively define their situations as unjust and subject to change through group action" (McAdam 1982: 51). As the example of the riots in Slovakia in 2004 illustrates, people who felt discriminated against by the government's measure did not seek to organize protest through existing movement activists, leaders, or civic organizations. Even though international Romani activists immediately traveled to the region in order to speak to the international media, negotiate with the police, and "streamline" the protests, local populations remained more focused on short-term survival than on the overall interests of the Romani movement.

The authors of a book on new social movements in Western Europe explain why the process of cognitive liberation is difficult to set in motion within certain populations: "poor and powerless people often seem to deny the few opportunities they do get because they have accustomed themselves to the idea that those 'up there' will never listen to their kind anyway" (Kriesi et al. 1995: 246). It is not unreasonable to assume that this was an important reason why Romani mass mobilization remained lackluster, especially in Slovakia and the Czech Republic. During my interviews, Romani activists frequently complained about the difficulty of winning the hearts and minds of their targeted audiences.

The International Dimension

Another important area of influence that has usually not attracted much attention in the study of ethnic movements is the international environment. Much of the literature focusing on ethnic mobilization takes domestic states as the principal referents. However, it should be clear from my accounts in earlier chapters that the patterns of domestic ethnic minority mobilization in contemporary Central Europe cannot be understood without taking the international context into account.

Social movement literature has recently seen a surge of writing on the position of social movements in a globalizing world. Indeed, there is a school of social movements scholars who argue that the growth of a "transnational public sphere" (Guidry et al. 2000: 5) has modified, and in many cases amplified, "the ability of national movement organizations to frame their claims in terms that resonate beyond territorial borders, thereby allowing national organizations to obtain resources from abroad" (Guidry et al. 2000: 2). Particularly important for the understanding of the influence of globalization on social movement formation has been the work by Keck and Sikkink (1998) on transnational advocacy networks.

The findings set out in this book suggest the importance of political opportunities on the transnational level. To go back to one notorious example—when in the Czech town of Ústi nad Labem a fence was built that isolated an apartment building inhabited by Roma—Romani activists and transnational human rights organizations turned what was seen in the Czech Republic primarily as a national or even a local issue into a European one. The European integration process and the emergence of transnational organizations working on issues such as human rights provided Romani activists with ideological and material resources that helped sustain their ethnic mobilization attempts. In other words, domestic Romani mobilization was influenced not only by domestic policies and institutions, but also by an international POS. Domestic ethnic minority mobilization in Central Europe was at particular times determined by the attention devoted to it in the realm of European politics and in the international media.

That ethnic minority mobilization is to some extent influenced by international developments does not necessarily mean that we should take the supranational European level as the *predominant* realm of influence. Although the process of European integration was a point of support for the ethnic mobilization of the Roma, the findings indicate that this support only reached a small group of Romani activists, and only "worked" during particular events. Although the process of EU enlargement, for example, offered unprecedented opportunities for a particular group of Romani activists, many others experienced it as a marginally important and confusing development, or even as an obstacle. Moreover, additional funding offered by European institutions and the increasing political concern of EU leaders did not lead to increased levels of mass mobilization. In this regard, one should perhaps keep in mind the point that Favell and Geddes have made about ethnic mobilization within the EU:

> the organizational behaviour of different ethnic groups is still strongly structured by national political structures and/or the nature of local opportunities, and, despite a great deal of talk about new European opportunities, there is a clear underinvestment in the European level, or worse, the EU remains remote and uninteresting, indeed irrelevant, to these ethnic groups' self-perceived interests. (Favell and Geddes 2000: 412)

The EU remains less remote for particular sections of the Romani movement than it perhaps has been for immigrant ethnic activists within the EU. Nevertheless, its facilitating role should not be overestimated since it did certainly not make the Romani movement as a mass movement more successful.

Concluding Note

Studying the dynamics of Romani mobilization in Central Europe one finds a host of indicators that confirm the main contentions of what has become known as the political process perspective on ethnic mobilization. This perspective combines the competition and POS models with systematic attention to framing processes. In light of this theoretical conclusion, one may ask now what the *prospects* of Romani mobilization in Central Europe are.

While there is still inadequate information to make a conclusive argument, it seems unlikely that the Romani movement in Central Europe will soon reach higher levels of mass mobilization. One can expect continuing difficulties, especially with regard to turning Romani identity into an identity that will have positive connotations. Since Romani identity has popularly become associated with negative characteristics, it is likely that precisely this identity will continue to be a crucial obstacle to successful mass mobilization.

Romani activists are faced with an extraordinary task. On the one hand, they demand equality and thus protest against those who see them as different. On the other hand, they must define their own group for political purposes, so that policies can be directed towards them; and, to do this, they must reaffirm the difference between Roma and non-Roma. This is the paradox of identity politics; or, as one author accurately described it, "the terms of protest against discrimination both refuse and accept the group identities upon which discrimination has been based" (Scott 1999: 6). Turning the group that one is perceived to belong to into "the group of one's affirmative identification" (Scott 1999: 7) is certainly not an easy task for Romani activists. Indeed, even a number of Romani activists themselves have doubted whether it will be possible to achieve this.

At the same time, Romani identity has increasingly been accepted as a reality by important political forces, and ethnic mobilization has continued to be an important channel for political expression in Central Europe. It is therefore unlikely that Romani ethnic identity and attempts at forming a Romani movement in this region will disappear soon. Both national and international political actors have supported the development of Romani ethnic group formation. Today, there seem to be few nonethnic movements in Central Europe that are able to mobilize a similar degree of attention and similar amounts of money for addressing problems of marginalization, poverty, unemployment, discrimination, and spatial segregation. Moreover, both on the national and international level, Romani identity has increasingly found an institutional niche. A growing institutionalization of Romani identity is thus likely to continue on both the domestic and international levels—domestic governments, international organizations, and independent nongovernmental networks have in recent times already stepped up their efforts to establish Romani programs.

But seeing and portraying the problems that face the Roma exclusively through the prism of ethnicity is clearly not without its dangers. It might at best attract attention to these problems, and it might encourage Roma to engage in political and civic action and provide a channel through which they can help to change their situation. But if relations between communities do not improve, if problems of poverty, inequality, discrimination, segregation, and social distance persist, then ethnic politics may merely galvanize ethnic group feeling, sharpen boundaries between ethnic groups, reinforce stereotypes on both sides of the boundaries, and strengthen discourses of mutual recriminations. If important changes do not come into effect, one might perhaps see noninstitutionalized activists engaging in less cooperative and more radical forms of ethnic-based protest, without, however, necessarily having strong support from a large mass of people. And more importantly, if ethnically framed programs for whatever reason do not lead to any palpable changes, they run the risk of reinforcing the idea that there is something in the ethnicity of the target group that prevents these programs from being successful (Vermeersch 2005).

So far, Romani identity has served to generate attention for problems that were too often dismissed as not being the responsibility of society as a whole. But movement actors will have to make sure that the emancipatory potential of the act of group construction will not open the way to a discourse of oppressive essentialism and a "blame the victim" rhetoric. At times it may be necessary to apply a discourse that constructs a stable notion of Romani identity; at other times it may be more useful to *deconstruct* such a notion and emphasize the existence of strong ties with other groups in the population. In other words, it might be useful for activists and supportive organizations to pursue a complex movement strategy that pays attention to the existing patterns of social differentiation and identification, but at the same time demonstrates that such patterns can be changed, that boundaries between groups may shift, and that new solidarity ties between Roma and other (nonethnic) groups may arise in response to certain common interests.

In order to be able to strike this delicate balance, actors in and around the Romani movement will need creativity and skill for public framing. Only then, will Romani identity continue to be, as Nicolae Gheorghe (1997: 157) once called it, "a political crutch."

Notes

Introduction

1. There are a number of scholars who have addressed issues related to the Romani movement. See, for example, books by Thomas Acton (2000), Zoltan Barany (2002), Will Guy (2001a), Ilona Klímová-Alexander (2005), and Diane Tong (1998). In 2001, Graham Holliday edited a special issue of the online *Journal on Ethnopolitics and Minority Issues in Europe* that featured a discussion on Romani political participation (Barany 2001; Fox 2001; Kovats 2001a; Sobotka 2001a; Vermeersch 2001).

1. Identities, Interests, and Ethnic Mobilization

1. There is no complete consensus on the spelling of these names in English, so one finds different versions of the same appellations in the available literature.
2. The link between the language of the Roma, their alleged Indian descent, and the need to regard them as a discrete people (*Volk*) was first formulated at a time when German philosophers—most notably Johan Gottfried von Herder—laid the intellectual foundations for a romantic understanding of the "nation" as a natural political unit characterized by a common language, culture, and *Volksgeist*.
3. Petr Bakalář is an example of an author seriously defending the use of biological categories to explain variations in IQ results and patterns of socioeconomic differentiation between Romani and non-Romani populations (Bakalář 2004). Bakalář's work is morally suspect and scientifically questionable. For a response, see Laubeová (2003). As has been pointed out by William H. Tucker (1996), research into racial differences in intelligence has provided no results of any scientific value; it has been used primarily, if not exclusively, to legitimate racist ideology.
4. It is clear from other data that one's ability to speak the Romani language does not always determine how someone is registered in censuses. The 1990 and 2001 Hungarian censuses give different figures for the number of Romani language speakers (48,072 and 48,685 respectively) and the number of people who identify themselves as having a Romani ethnic identity ("nationality") (142,683 and 190,046 respectively). In the 1991 Slovak census, the percentage of Romani speakers was 1.5 percent, and thus more or less as high as the percentage of people declaring Romani nationality. In the 2001 Slovak census, there were 37,803 people (0.7 percent of the total population) who indicated "Slovak" as their nationality and Romani language as their mother tongue. No comparative data are available for the Czech Republic.
5. Liégeois and Gheorghe (1995), for example, do not include any critical note on the figures they present, and neither do they offer any information on how the figures were compiled. An example of a political use of a crude estimation was offered by Slovak MP Róbert Fico, formerly deputy of the Party of the Democratic Left (SDL') and since 2000 leader of the populist party Smer (Direction), who during a press conference in June 2000 estimated that there would be 1.2 million Roma in Slovakia by 2010. He referred to this figure as a legitimization for his proposal to change the

current Slovak system of child allowance and limit benefits for families with more than three children.
6. There are no uniform standards applied for identifying and registering Romani settlements. Different authors have cited different statistics. According to the explanatory report appended to the government strategy of the Slovak Republic that was published in 1999, there were 591 Romani settlements at the end of 1998. According to the government report at the time, a total of 124,031 registered inhabitants were living in these settlements, or 22,732 families occupying 13,882 dwellings. The government report characterizes the dwellings as "simple shelters built mostly in wood, clay and plate. In the better cases they would have plaster on the outside walls" (Government of the Slovak Republic 1999a). The Slovak Government Commissioner for the Romani Community presented a figure of 620 Romani settlements for the second half of 2000. According to this report, 250 settlements are located in the Prešov region, 168 in the region of Košice (Government Commissioner for the Romani Community 2001).
7. Personal observation at the "Conference 2000: Romani Studies in the New Millennium: Where Do We Go From Here," University of Greenwich and University of Birmingham, June 28 to July 1, 2000.
8. This concept of culture as "interpretation" is close to the influential semiotic concepts of culture that have been developed in anthropology by, for example, Geertz (1993).
9. Not all versions of the reactive ethnicity approach preclude the role of a manipulating elite; one example is an article by Nielsen (1980) with reference to the Flemish case.
10. Hechter's recent work is clearly a departure from his earlier writings on "reactive ethnicity" in the 1970s.
11. Davis (1991), for example, shows that the meaning of "blackness" in the United States has varied considerably over the course of history. It changed under the influence of ongoing negotiations within the group and under the influence of varying patterns of top-down classification. Authors such as Hall (1990) and Gilroy (2000), writing within British Cultural Studies, have emphasized that "black identity" is constructed in relation and in contrast to "white identity." To demonstrate this, they have paid attention to both political and cultural elites. For example, they have examined the cultural representation regimes in cinema and music that maintain or break the categorization scheme dominant in society.

2. The Development of Minority Policies in Central Europe

1. Horváth's victory was short-lived. In June 2003 the members of the National Gypsy Self-Government dismissed him from his position as president of the body and elected Orbán Kolompár as his successor. Horváth did not accept this decision (Roma Press Center, *Newsletter*, July 1, 2003).
2. It is well beyond the scope of this book to engage in a discussion of this topic. I just want to point out that the Marxist-Leninist argument that nationalism is a bourgeois ideology and a by-product of capitalist state-building was the primary inspiration for communist leaders to commit themselves to dismissing national distinctions as temporary phenomena.
3. The fate of the Hungarian Roma during that period is poorly documented, and there are widely differing estimations of the number of people deported to concentration camps and murdered. Crowe (1995: 91) cites a figure of 32,000 Hungarian Romani

victims, while Helsinki Watch (1993:5) refers to two different figures: 60,000–70,000, as supplied by the Hungarian Romani umbrella organization Roma Parliament, and 5,000, as estimated by Karsai (1992).

4. The fact alone that in 1971 a pioneer study could be carried out that examined poverty in relation to ethnicity exemplifies the changing attitude of official policy toward problems of poverty and ethnic differentiation in society. Before 1956 it had been impossible to examine ethnicity as a factor or a phenomenon; research on poverty, too, was banned, since authorities argued that it would bring unjust discredit upon the socialist system (Fábián 1994).

5. The MCKSz established in 1986 was a new institution and not a revival of the association with a similar name in the 1950s.

6. After the Second World War Germans fled or were deported *en masse* from the Czech lands, leaving, according to the 1950 census, only 165,000 Germans from a previous population of 3,391,000 (Bugajski 1994: 296). Between 1945 and 1948, about 90,000 Magyars—according to census figures about one-fifth of the total Magyar population in Slovakia—were transferred to Hungary in exchange for over 70,000 Slovaks (Bugajski 1994: 323).

7. Guy (1998: 32) notes that in 1966 the transfer plan was officially 85 percent fulfilled, in 1967, 51 percent, and in 1968 only 20 percent. Between 1966 and 1968, 494 Romani families were transferred, while in that same period 1,096 unplanned family migrations took place.

8. The most notorious policies of complete assimilation or attempts to let the group "disappear" have been exposed by human rights groups. Charta 77 accused the state of pursuing a policy of targeted sterilization of Romani women in the 1970s, following a 1972 decree on sterilization. A 1992 report by Human Rights Watch claimed that many Romani women in the 1980s were urged to undergo sterilization in return for grants.

9. These "historical minorities" do not include refugees, newly arrived groups, or people residing in Hungary without Hungarian citizenship.

10. The organization that became known as the Democratic Opposition came into existence in the latter half of the 1970s and can be compared to the Czechoslovak-based movement formed around Charta 77. These people were left-wing intellectuals who had given up the socialist project but engaged in underground mass mobilization around issues of human rights and democracy. In 1988 the Democratic Opposition formed a political party called Alliance of Free Democrats (SzDSz). During 1988 and 1989 the SzDSz, together with the liberal and free market-oriented Federation of Young Democrats (Fidesz), favored a radical change in regime (see Körösényi 1999: 39–44).

11. The use of the word "Gypsies" is deliberate here. In my interview with him, MCDSz President Gyula Náday emphasized that the Gypsy people ("*cigányság*") were not to be ashamed of their "real" name, because, he argued, it is this that connects them to the majority population. It is possible that his tenacity in using the name "Gypsy" was to a certain extent related to his dispute with organizations such as Phralipe and Roma Parliament, which have tended to espouse the name "Roma."

12. To give just one example: According to the 1990 census on the basis of mother tongue, the Greek minority numbered only 1,640 Hungarian citizens.

13. The issue was included in the Tošovský Government program. The program stated that the government would take up the pledge of the previous cabinet "to erect a dignified monument on the site of the former internment camp at Lety u Pisku" (Program Statement of the Government of the Czech Republic, January 27, 1998). In early 1999 a proposal to buy the farm and turn it into a commemorative site was rejected as being too costly. In May of that same year, the government decided to

make new funding available to improve the monument that had been unveiled by Havel in 1995.
14. There are other elements in the law that point to political compromise. Paragraph 2 of the law ("Definition of basic concepts") defines a national minority as "a community of citizens who live on the territory of the present Czech Republic and as a rule differ from other citizens by their common ethnic origin, language, culture and traditions." However, as has been noted by Hofmann (2003), for the provisions of the act that relate to privileges, such as the right to multilingual topographic names for localities (section 8) or the right to use the language of the national minority before public organs and courts (section 9), the law introduces the extra criterion of "living traditionally and for a long period of time" on the territory of the Czech Republic.
15. In the 1990 elections for the Slovak National Council, SNS won 13.9 percent of the vote, in 1992 7.9 percent, and in 1994 only 5.4 percent. After each of these elections, however, the party was invited by the HZDS to form a government coalition. In the 1998 parliamentary elections the number of votes for SNS rose again to 9.07 percent, but it lost its position in the government.

3. Ethnic Politics from Below

1. Statements conveying this message were made in written interviews with party spokespersons conducted by the editorial office of the Romani magazine *Amaro gendalos* in the period just before the elections in June 2002. The interviews were published on the web pages of the organization Dženo, at <http://www.dzeno.cz/czech/volby/index.htm>.
2. See the interview with Lívia Járóka by Stephen Moss in *The Guardian*, December 15, 2004, pp. 6–7.
3. These are parties that have a reference to Romani identity (*Cigány* or *Roma*) in their party name. See, <http://www.valasztas.hu>.
4. See, <http://www.volby.cz> and <http://www.mvrc.cz>.
5. A full version of the agreement can be found in the October–December 2000 issue of the Slovak Romani newspaper *Romano nevo l'il* (*Romano nevo l'il* 10, no. 455–67, 2000).
6. Results are available on <http://www.statistics.sk/volby01/webdata/angl/home.htm>.
7. Observers have noted that the life expectancy in poor Romani communities is often low, while birth rates tend to be high (see, e.g., Liégeois and Gheorghe 1995: 12).
8. See, for example, the discussions about the controversial work of the American sociologist Charles Murray (Murray 1984), who argues that welfare support in the USA has undermined the ability of the poor to help themselves and has created a culture of welfare dependency. For arguments against this theory, see for example the work by Gregory (1998) on the black urban experience in New York.
9. Quoted in *The Budapest Sun* 9, no. 13, 2001.
10. This was especially the case when a news item was published which suggested that the migration of the Roma from Zámoly was seen by some as a plot by Russian agents to undermine Hungary's bid for EU membership. The conspiratorial theory that the Russian secret service had masterminded the Romani migration to darken Hungary's human rights record first appeared in 2001 in a series of articles in *Jane's Intelligence Digest*, a UK journal devoted to the study of secret service operations ("The New Russian Offensive," *Jane's Intelligence Digest*, February 26, 2001; "Questions in Budapest," *Jane's Intelligence Digest*, March 9, 2001). Although these allegations were strongly denied by Romani activists, political commentators, *and*

Russian officials, they caused a stir in Hungary, both in the media and in public opinion.
11. Quoted in *The Budapest Sun* 8, no. 31, 2000.
12. Quoted in *The Budapest Sun* 8, no. 34, 2000.
13. This was even acknowledged by a report by Czech experts that was adopted by the Czech government in 1997. With regard to the condition of having a clean criminal record for the past five years, the report stated, "This condition was interpreted as imposing a new penalty ex post facto, and as a violation of Art. 15 of the International Covenant on Civic and Political Rights and Art. 40, par. 6 of the Charter of Fundamental Rights and Freedoms in the sense that it imposed a higher penalty than the one prescribed by the law at the time the crime was committed. In addition, the five-year clean criminal record requirement did not take into account the seriousness of the crime, and this violated the generally recognized principle of proportionality" (Council for Nationalities of the Government of the Czech Republic 1997).
14. In 1994 the CSCE quoted a report by the human rights organization, Tolerance Foundation, suggesting that as many as 100,000 Roma residing in the Czech Republic were excluded from Czech citizenship under the 1993 law. The same source quoted an official of the Czech government's Council of National Minorities as speculating that 15,000 to 20,000 Roma may been without citizenship at that time. The authorities officially, and strongly, contested both figures. The Interior Ministry did not maintain any public statistics on the ethnicity of applicants, while the Czech embassy in Washington claimed at that time that only 100 applications for citizenship had been denied (CSCE 1994: 18). Šiklová and Miklušáková (1998) noted that the Advisory Center for Citizenship of the Czech Helsinki Committee had roughly 4,000 clients registered with it. Among them were many Romani children who had been put, wilfully or not, into Czech foster homes by their Slovak parents.
15. Radio Prague, *Newsview*, August 2, 2001.
16. Radio Prague, *Newsview*, August 15, 2001.
17. Opinions of the Lords of Appeal for Judgment in the Cause "Regina v. Immigration Officer at Prague Airport and another (Respondents) ex parte European Roma Rights Center and others (Appellants)," December 9, 2004.
18. Michele Legge, "Canadian Asylum for Czech Romanies," *The Prague Post*, April 22, 1998.
19. Quoted in Siegfried Mortkowitz, "Tear Down the Walls," *The Prague Post*, October 20, 1999.
20. On October 23, 1999, *The New York Times* published an editorial entitled, "Europe's Walls for Gypsies." The editorial was reprinted in *The International Herald Tribune* on October 25, 1999. It described the events as follows: "Ten days ago, the Czech town of Usti nad Labem managed to symbolize both of Europe's 20th-century pathologies —communism and Nazism—when it erected a six-foot-high concrete wall to separate a Gypsy neighborhood from one of ethnic Czechs. The wall, called a 'law and order' measure by the town's mayor, has been condemned by the Czech Republic's government and Parliament, and by President Vaclav Havel. But it still stands, and is very popular in Usti nad Labem." The article went on to describe the plight of the Roma in several postcommunist countries, focusing on the situation in Kosovo, Hungary, and Slovakia.
21. Quoted in Luke Allnutt, "Confronting Racism's Roots," *The Prague Post*, November 18, 1998.
22. *Romano nevo l'il*, no. 455–67, 2000.
23. The figures for 2000 and 2001 only take into account asylum applicants in twenty-six industrialized countries. This excludes Greece, New Zealand, and the UK, for which comparative data are not available.
24. SITA News Agency, July 8, 1999.

25. Czech News Agency (ČTK), February 9, 2000.
26. The decisions of the Helsinki European Council were positive for Slovakia. Recalling an earlier decision in 1997 to exclude Slovakia from the first group of candidate countries to start negotiations, the Presidency Conclusions of the Helsinki European Council contained the decision to begin negotiations with Slovakia in February 2000.
27. In the spring of 2000, a number of police investigations were initiated into the possible involvement by Romani organizations in the organization of the migration, but no formal charges were laid.
28. RFE/RL Newsline vol. 8, no. 34, part II, February 23, 2004.
29. Roma Press Agency, "FÍZIK: Parliament Rómov pripravuje protesty proti sociálnym reformám," press release, February 12, 2004.
30. RFE/RL Newsline vol. 8, no. 34, part II, February 23, 2004.
31. RFE/RL Newsline vol. 8, no. 34, part II, February 23, 2004.
32. ERRC, "Urgent measures needed to address deep-seated racism issues in Slovakia," press release, February 26, 2004.

4. The Power of Framing

1. One has to see the writing of the European Charter on Romani Rights against the backdrop of the organizational structure of the Romani movement in Germany. The RNC was founded at the beginning of the 1990s to represent the interests of Romani refugees and asylum seekers from Central and Eastern Europe who had arrived in Germany. Its basic conception of Romani interests conflicted with that of the Central Council for German Roma and Sinti (*Zentralrat Deutscher Roma und Sinti*), the organization that since 1982 had successfully lobbied for German Roma and Sinti (i.e. those with German citizenship) and had been able to get them recognized as a German national minority in 1995 (Abdikeeva 2002).
2. Romani activists from thirty-five countries were elected to sixty-one positions within four IRU institutions (the Cabinet, the Parliament, the Court of Justice, and the Presidium). Most of the countries were represented by one or two elected officers; three countries (Sweden, Romania, and Belarus) had three representatives. The Czech Republic was the only country that was represented by as many as six elected officers. Hungary was not represented (based on the official list of elected officers as printed in Acton and Klímová 2001: 199–200).
3. International Romani Union, *Newsletter*, No. 1, July 2002.
4. Alena Borovičková, "Prezident Medzinárodnej rómskej únie Emil Ščuka pre Pravdu: My sme národ, nie minorita," *Pravda*, August 2, 2000.
5. Mann quotes point 13 of the action program of the party: "In our work, we do not want to isolate ourselves and create a legal Romany nationality from part of the population of the Slovak Republic, but we want to assist the more rapid assimilation of the Romany ethnic group by our political and educational work" (Mann 1992: 263).
6. Ivan Remiaš, "Slovak Romanies get glimpse of better future," *The Slovak Spectator* 5, no. 4, 1999.
7. Matthew Reynolds and Zuzana Habšudová, "Pál Csáky: SMK not 'Byzantine swindlers,'" *The Slovak Spectator* 7, no. 4, 2001.
8. RFERL/Newsline, October 11, 1999.
9. Reported by SLOVAKIA press agency, July 8, 1999.
10. Reported by SITA press agency, January 11, 2000.
11. Quoted on the website of the magazine *Amaro Gendalos* (http://www.dzeno.cz/english/election/parties/cssd_en.htm).

12. The document (No. C.j. 140892/2000-LP) was published by the Ministry of Foreign Affairs in December 2000. A copy of page 15 of the original Czech document containing the Section V entitled, "Goals and tasks for the organs of the Ministry of Foreign Affairs connected with the Romani problematic" (*Cíle a úkoly související romskou problematikou pro útvary MZV*), was published in Sobotka (2001b: 68).
13. Willems and Lucassen have studied the formation of popular understandings of "Gypsies" in Western European countries by focusing on prevailing views in popular scientific texts and encyclopedias (Willems and Lucassen 1998).

5. International Responses

1. See http://www.soros.org/initiatives/roma/news/decade_20030708.
2. See the official website of the program, http://www.romadecade.org.
3. For a critical assessment of the program, see http://www.eumap.org.
4. Czechoslovakia and Hungary were both admitted to the CSCE in 1973 and signed the Helsinki Final Act in 1975. In 1990, the governments of both countries also signed the Charter of Paris—the document which started converting the CSCE from a process into an organization. This also led to a new name (OSCE), adopted at the s immediately became members of the CSCE/OSCE.
5. Hungary joined the Council of Europe in November 1990, the Czech Republic and Slovakia in June 1993.
6. "Europe's spectral nation," *The Economist* 359, no. 8221, 2001, 29–31.
7. The status of the OSCE is quite unique. It is not a classic international organization: it has no legal status under international law, and its decisions are politically but not legally binding. The OSCE does, however, have some attributes of a normal international organization, such as permanent institutions and standing decision-making bodies. Its authority is based on the fact that its commitments have been signed on the highest political level. Moreover, the OSCE is considered the only European "regional arrangement" in the sense of Chapter VIII of the United Nations Charter, and is therefore the primary instrument for early warning, conflict prevention, crisis management and post-conflict rehabilitation in the region (see, http://www.osce.org).
8. The name "Sinti" was included here in response to a demand from German Sinti activists, who perceived the exclusive use of the name "Roma" as a claim for superior authenticity from those groups who called themselves "Roma" (Gheorghe and Acton 2001: 58).
9. The decision was taken at the Budapest Summit in December 1994, (*CPRSI Newsletter* 1, no. 1, 1995).
10. *CPRSI Newsletter* 2, no. 4, 1996.
11. The FCNM is the first legally binding multilateral instrument on the protection of national minorities in general. In March 2001 there were thirty-three State Parties (Albania, Armenia, Austria, Azerbaijan, Bosnia and Herzegovina, Bulgaria, Croatia, Cyprus, Czech Republic, Denmark, Estonia, Finland, Germany, Hungary, Ireland, Italy, Liechtenstein, Lithuania, Malta, Moldova, Norway, Poland, Romania, Russian Federation, San Marino, Slovakia, Slovenia, Spain, Sweden, Switzerland, the former Yugoslav Republic of Macedonia, Ukraine and the United Kingdom).
12. Council of Europe, *Newsletter, Activities on Roma/Gypsies*, no. 21, 2001, 3.
13. See, http://www.ertf.org.
14. These and other reports by Verspaget have been very influential, but do not represent the *only* point of view within the institutions of the Council of Europe. An alternative view on Romani migration was submitted by external expert Yaron Matras to the same Committee on Migration a year later. According to Matras, "the

extraordinary feature of Romani migration is that so many Roma are prepared to take the risk of migrating *despite their lack of nomadic tradition.*" (Matras 2000: 32, emphasis in original).

15. Apart from a number of political preconditions, the Copenhagen European Council also formulated a number of economic requirements. Together they formed what became known as the "Copenhagen criteria"—conditions that had to be met before a country could start accession negotiations and that were under constant scrutiny during the process of negotiations. Typical of the political Copenhagen criteria is that they fell outside the more technical body of laws and regulations applicant states had to adopt before becoming a member (the chapters of the *acquis communautaire*). The Copenhagen political criteria were more general and were never the subject of legislation within the EU (Vachudova 2000 : 65). The negotiations revolved around the thirty-one chapters of the *acquis communautaire*. The Copenhagen criteria were not a part of this *acquis*, so, in theory, even if the complete *acquis communautaire* was incorporated by a candidate member state, accession could still be refused on the basis of the Copenhagen criteria.

16. Conditionality strategies were traditionally associated with World Bank and IMF lending programs, but have since 1989 extensively been used by organizations such as NATO, the Council of Europe, and the EU to instigate both the economic and political transformation of the former communist states. Conditions imposed on candidate states by these latter organizations go far beyond those of the World Bank and IMF because they aim to change the fundamental sociopolitical attributes of the applicant states (Checkel 2000: 1–2).

17. European Commissioner Günter Verheugen emphasized this during his visit to Slovakia in February 2001. He called "respect of minorities, and in particular of the Roma population" one of the three important issues that needed further monitoring under the Copenhagen political criteria. The other two were the independence of the judiciary and the fight against crime and corruption (Verheugen 2001).

18. In the Treaty of Amsterdam, the principle of non-discrimination on the basis of "racial or ethnic origin" was added as article 13. This may be regarded as an attempt to turn the minority protection requirement into an enforceable condition within the Union. Also the Council Directive 2000/43/EC of June 29, 2000, implementing the principle of equal treatment between persons irrespective of racial or ethnic origin, and the Council Directive 2000/78/EC of November 27, 2000, determining the general framework for equal treatment at work, demonstrate the fact that the EU did take some steps in this direction.

19. Belgium signed the FCNM in the summer of 2001, but at the time of writing had not ratified it.

20. Ed Holt and Chris Togneri, "Report slams Slovakia on Minorities," *The Slovak Spectator* 7, no. 40, 2001.

21. Urád vlády SR, *Tlačová správa*, November 14, 2001.

22. Fraser Allan. "Gypsy-abuse ad irks Government." *The Budapest Sun* 9, No. 1, 2001.

23. Fraser Allan. "Amnesty visit after advert controversy." *The Budapest Sun* 9, No. 5, 2001.

24. See, http://www.soros.org/netprog.html.

25. I borrow the distinction between negative and positive interest from Stone (1998: 214–15).

6. The Romani Movement in Theoretical Perspective

1. "Are they a nation?" *The Economist*, Vol. 357, No. 8198, 2000, 61–62.

References*

Abdikeeva, Alphia A. 2002. "Germany's Policies toward Sinti and Roma: Living Apartheid?" Unpublished paper, Center for Policy Studies, Budapest.
Acton, Thomas. 2000. *Scholarship and the Gypsy Struggle. Commitment in Romani Studies.* Hertfordshire: University of Hertfordshire Press.
Acton, Thomas, and Ilona Klímová. 2001. "The International Romani Union: An East European Answer to West European Questions?" In: *Between Past and Future: The Roma of Central and Eastern Europe,* ed. W. Guy. Hertfordshire: University of Hertfordshire Press, pp. 157–219.
Allahar, Anton. 1996. "Primordialism and Ethnic Political Mobilisation in Modern Society." *New Community* 22:1, pp. 5–21.
Allen, Garland. 1990. "Genetic Indexing of Race Groups is Irresponsible and Unscientific." *The Scientist* 4: 10.
Alston, Philip, and Joseph H.H. Weiler. 2000. "An 'Ever Closer Union' in Need of Human Rights Policy: The European Union and Human Rights." Harvard Jean Monnet Working Paper 1/99, Harvard Law School.
Amato, Guiliano, and Judy Batt. 1998. "Minority Rights and EU Enlargement to the East." RSC Policy Paper 98/5, European University Institute, Florence.
Amnesty International. 2000. "Amnesty International Report 2000."
Anderson, Ingrid D. 2000. "The Role of Framing in Public Policy Debate: An Experimental Research Design." Unpublished paper presented at the Midwest Political Science Association Annual Meeting, April 27–30, 2000. Chicago, Illinois.
Ash, Timothy G. 1999. "The Puzzle of Central Europe." *The New York Review of Books* 46: 5 (March), pp. 18–23.
Bačová, Viera, and L. Bača. 1994. "Analýza bývania rómskeho spoločenstva na sídlisku Lunćk IX v Košicach." *Sociológia* 26: 5–6, pp. 447–53.
Bakalář, Petr. 2004. "The IQ of Gypsies in Central Europe." *Mankind Quarterly* 44: 3–4, pp. 291–300.
Bakker, Peter, Milena Hübschmannová, Valdemar Kalinin, Donald Kenrick, Hristo Kyuchukov, Yaron Matras, and Giulio Soravia. 2000. *What is the Romani Language?* Paris: Gypsy Research Center. Hatfield: University of Hertfordshire Press.
Barany, Zoltan. 2001. "Romani Electoral Politics and Behaviour." *Journal of Ethnopolitics and Minority Issues in Europe* 1, pp. 1–13.
———. 2002. *The East European Gypsies. Regime Change, Marginality, and Ethnopolitics.* Cambridge: Cambridge University Press.
Barnes, Samuel H., Max Kaase, and Klaus R. Allerbeck. 1979. *Political Action: Mass Participation in Five Western Democracies.* Beverly Hills: Sage.
Barry, Brian. 2001. *Culture and Equality.* Cambridge: Polity Press.
Barth, Fredrik. 1969. *Ethnic Groups and Boundaries: The Social Organization of Cultural Difference.* Boston: Little Brown Co.

---

* This is a reference list of journal articles (including those published in electronic journals), books, book chapters, reports, unpublished papers, and official documents. References to websites, press releases, public letters, and newspaper articles are provided in the endnotes.

———. 1994. "Enduring and Emerging Issues in the Analysis of Ethnicity." In: *The Anthropology of Ethnicity. Beyond 'Ethnic Groups and Boundaries'*, ed. H. Vermeulen and C. Govers. Amsterdam: Het Spinhuis, pp. 11–32.

Baumgartner, Frank R. and Beth L. Leech. 1998. *Basic Interests. The Importance of Groups in Politics and Political Science*. Princeton: Princeton University Press.

Bell, Daniel. 1975. "Ethnicity and Social Change." In: *Ethnicity. Theory and Experience*, ed. N. Glazer, and D. Moynihan. Cambridge MA, London: Harvard University Press, pp. 141–74.

Benford, Robert D., and David A. Snow. 2000. "Framing Processes and Social Movements: An Overview and Assessment." *Annual Review of Sociology* 26, pp. 611–39.

Benkovič, B., and L. Vakulová. 2000. *Image of the Roma in Selected Slovak Media (June 1998–May 1999)*. Bratislava: Slovak Helsinki Committee.

Benz, Wolfgang. 2002. "The Other Genocide: The Persecution of the Sinti and Roma." *Journal of Holocaust and Genocide Studies* 1, (http://zfa.kgw.tu-berlin.de/journal/wbenz001.htm).

Bernáth, Gábor and Vera Messing. 1999. "Seen From Afar: Roma in the Hungarian Media." *Roma Rights* 4, pp. 35–42.

Blauner, Robert. 1969. "Internal Colonialism and Ghetto Revolt." *Social Problems* 16, pp. 393–408.

Bonacich, Edna. 1972. "A Theory of Ethnic Antagonism: The Split Labor Market." *American Sociological Review* 37: 5, pp. 547–59.

Bousetta, Hassan. 2001. "Immigration, Post-Immigration Politics and the Political Mobilisation of Ethnic Minorities. A Comparative Case-Study of Moroccans in Four European Cities." Unpublished doctoral dissertation, KU Brussel.

Braham, Mark and Matthew Braham. 2003. "Romani Migrations and EU Enlargement: Reply to Critics and Some Epistemological Considerations for Policy-Making." *Nationalities Papers* 31: 1, pp. 47–32.

Brass, Paul R. 1991. *Ethnicity and Nationalism: Theory and Comparison*. Newbury Park: Sage.

Brubaker, Rogers. 1996. *Nationalism Reframed: Nationhood and the National Question in the New Europe*. Cambridge: Cambridge University Press.

———. 2002. "Ethnicity without Groups." *Archives Européennes de Sociologie* 43: 2, pp. 163–89.

Buček, Jan. 1999. "Land, Ownership and Living Environment of Roma Minority in Slovakia." Unpublished paper. Department of Human Geography, Comenius University, Bratislava.

Bugajski, Janusz. 1994. *Ethnic Politics in Eastern Europe: A Guide to Nationality Policies, Organizations, and Parties*. New York: M.E. Sharpe.

Bulmer, Martin, and John Solomos. 1998. "Re-thinking Ethnic and Racial Studies." *Ethnic and Racial Studies* 21: 5, pp. 819–37.

Burgess, Adam. 1999. "Critical Reflections on the Return of National Minority Rights Regulation to East/West European Affairs." In: *Ethnicity and Democratisation in the New Europe*, ed. K. Cordell. London, New York: Routledge, pp. 49–60.

Burleigh, Michael. 2000. *The Third Reich: A New History*. New York: Hill and Wang.

Burns, Tom. 1992. *Erving Goffman*. London, New York: Routledge.

Bútora, Martin, and Pavol Demeš. 1999. "Civil Society Organizations in the 1998 Elections." In: *The 1998 Parliamentary Elections and Democratic Rebirth in Slovakia*, ed. M. Bútora, G. Mesežnikov, Z. Bútorová, and S. Fisher. Bratislava: Institute for Public Affairs, pp. 155–67.

Bútora, Martin, Grigorij Mesežnikov, and Zora Bútorová. 1999. "Introduction: Overcoming Illiberalism—Slovakia's 1998 Elections." In: *The 1998 Parliamentary*

Elections and Democratic Rebirth in Slovakia, ed. M. Bútora, G. Mesežnikov, Z. Bútorová, and S. Fisher. Bratislava: Institute for Public Affairs, pp. 9–23.

Cahn, Claude, and Peter Vermeersch. 2000. "The Group Expulsion of Slovak Roma by the Belgian Government: A Case Study of the Treatment of Romani Refugees in Western Countries." *Cambridge Review of International Affairs* 13: 2, pp. 71–82.

Castles, Stephen. 1995. "How Nation-States Respond to Immigration and Ethnic Diversity." *New Community* 21: 3, pp. 293–308.

Castle-Kaněrová, Mit'a. 2003. "Round and Round the Roundabout: Czech Roma and the Vicious Circle of Asylum Seeking." *Nationalities Papers* 31: 1, pp. 13–26.

Central Committee of the Hungarian Socialist Workers' Party (MSzMP). 1961. "Decision on Certain Tasks for Improving the Situation of Gypsy Inhabitants." (A cigánylakosság helyzetének megjavításával kapcsolatos egyes feladatokról. Az MSzMP KB Politikai Bizottságának határozata).

Checkel, Jeffrey T. 2000. "Compliance and Conditionality." Arena Working Papers WP 00/18, University of Oslo.

Chirico, David. 1997. "The Long, Hot Czech Summer." *Roma Rights* 3, (http://errc.org/rr_aut1997/noteb2.shtml).

Cibulka, Frank. 1999. "The Radical Right in Slovakia." In: *The Radical Right in Central and Eastern Europe Since 1989*, ed. S.P. Ramet. Pennsylvania: Pennsylvania State University Press, pp. 109–31.

Clark, Colin. 1998. "Counting Backwards: The Roma 'Numbers Game' in Central and Eastern Europe." *Radical Statistics* 69, pp. 35–46.

———. 1999. "Britain and Human Rights: Should Travellers Be Allowed to Retain Their Way of Life?" *Patrin Web Journal*, (http://www.geocities.com/Paris/5121/britain-rights.htm)

Clébert, Jean-Paul. 1972. *Les Tsiganes*. Paris: Arthaud.

Cohen, Abner. 1996. "Ethnicity and Politics." In: *Ethnicity*, ed. J. Hutchinson and A.D. Smith. Oxford: Oxford University Press, pp. 83–84.

Cohen, Jean L., and Andrew Arato. 1995. *Civil Society and Political Theory*. Cambridge, MA: MIT Press.

Commissioner of the Government of the Slovak Republic for Solutions of Problems of Citizens with Special Needs. 1997. "Conceptual Intends of the Government of the Slovak Republic for Solution of the Problems of Romany Population Under Current Social and Economic Conditions. Annex: the Analysis of Problems of Romany Population and the Bases for Their Solution."

Committee on Legal Affairs and Human Rights (Parliamentary Assembly of the Council of Europe). 2002. "Legal Situation of the Roma in Europe. Doc. 9397. Rapporteur: Csaba Tabajdi."

Committee of Ministers of the Council of Europe. 1999. "Appointment of a Mediator for Roma/Gypsies. Doc. 8314. Reply to Written Question No. 372 by Mrs. Verspaget."

Connor, Walker. 1984. *The National Question in Marxist-Leninist Theory and Strategy*. Princeton: Princeton University Press.

———. 1994. *Ethnonationalism. The Quest for Understanding*. Princeton: Princeton University Press.

Coughlan, Reed, and S.W.R.d.A. Samarasinghe. 1991. *Economic Dimensions of Ethnic Conflict: International Perspectives*. New York: St. Martin's.

Council for Nationalities of the Government of the Czech Republic. 1997. "Report on the Situation of the Romani Community in the Czech Republic and Government Measures Assisting Its Integration in Society." (Zpráva o situaci romské komunity v České republice a opatření vlády napomáhající její integraci ve společnosti).

Crampton, Richard J. 1994. *Eastern Europe in the Twentieth Century—and After*. London, New York: Routledge.

Crowe, David M. 1995. *A History of the Gypsies of Eastern Europe and Russia*. London, New York: I.B. Tauris Publishers.

———. 2003. "The International and Historical Dimensions of Romani Migration in Central and Eastern Europe." *Nationalities Papers* 31: 1, pp. 81–94.

Crowley, John. 2001. "The Political Participation of Ethnic Minorities." *International Political Science Review* 22: 1, pp. 99–121.

CSCE (Commission on Security and Cooperation in Europe). 1994. "Human Rights and Democratization in the Czech Republic."

———. 1996. "Ex Post Facto Problems of the Czech Citizenship Law."

Csepeli, György. 1998. "Claimed Consensus as a Means of Justification of Hostile Stereotypes Against the Roma Minority Among Hungarian Policemen." *Intermarium* 2: 3, pp. 1–3.

Csepeli, György, Zoltán Fábián, and Endre Sik. 1999. "Xenophobia and Opinions about the Roma." In *Social Report 1998*, ed. T. Kolosi, G.I. Tóth, and G. Vukovich. Budapest: TÁRKI, Social Research Informatics Center, pp. 452–82.

Davis, James F. 1991. *Who is Black? One Nation's Definition*. University Park: Pennsylvania State University Press.

Dedinszky, Erika. 1997. *Vers vuur. Over zigeunerliteratuur in Hongarije*. Haarlem: In de Knipscheer.

Demeš, Pavol. 1999. "The Third Sector and Volunteerism." In: *Slovakia 1998–1999. A Global Report on the State of Society*, ed. G. Mesežnikov, M. Ivantyšyn, and T. Nicholson. Bratislava: Institute for Public Affairs, pp. 347–64.

Department of Science, Education, and Culture of the Central Committee of the Hungarian Socialist Workers' Party (MSzMP). 1984. "Report on the Situation of the Gypsy Inhabitants in Hungary and the Current Tasks." (A MSzMP KB Tudományos, Közoktatási és Kulturális Osztályának jelentése).

Doncsev, Toso. 1999. "Minorities: Recent Changes in the Condition of National and Ethnic Minorities." Lecture at the conference of the Hungarian Academy of Sciences and the Office for National and Ethnic Minorities, April 8–9, 1999, Budapest.

Druker, Jeremy. 1997. "Present but Unaccounted for." *Transitions* 4: 4, pp. 22–23.

Drury, Beatrice. 1994. "Ethnic Mobilisation: Some Theoretical Considerations." In: *Ethnic Mobilisation in a Multi-Cultural Europe*, ed. J. Rex and B. Drury. Aldershot: Avebury, pp. 13–22.

Dzurinda, Mikuláš. 2002. "Problems of the Roma Ethnic Minority." Unpublished paper (http://www.vlada.gov.sk/dzurinda_en/tema/tema03.php3).

Edwards, Mike. 1996. "The Fractured Caucasus." *National Geographic* 189: 2, pp. 126–32.

Eisinger, Peter K. 1973. "The Conditions of Protest Behavior in American Cities." *American Political Science Review* 67, pp. 11–28.

Entzinger, Han. 2000. "The Dynamics of Integration Policies: A Multidimensional Model." In: *Challenging Immigration and Ethnic Relations Politics: Comparative European Perspectives*, ed. R. Koopmans and P. Statham. Oxford: Oxford University Press, pp. 97–118.

Eriksen, Thomas H. 2002. *Ethnicity and Nationalism*, second edition. London, Boulder, CO: Pluto Press.

European Commission. 1996. "Brussels Declaration: The Roma—A Truly European People. Roma Rountable."

———. 1997. "For a Stronger and Wider Union. Agenda 2000." DOC 97/6.

———. 2000. "1999 Accession Partnership—13 October 2000 (Revised February 2000)."

———. 2002. "EU Support for Roma Communities in Central and Eastern Europe. Enlargement Briefing."

European Parliament. 1997. "European Union Anti-Discrimination Policy from Equal Opportunities between Women and Men to Combating Racism." Working Document LIBE 102.
Fábián, Zoltán. 1994. "Review of the Main Research on Poverty." Working paper, TÁRKI, Budapest.
Fábián, Zoltán, and Endre Sik. 1996. "Előítéletesség és tekintélyelvűség." In: *Társadalmi riport 1996*, ed. R. Andorka, T. Kolosi and G. Vukovich. Budapest: TÁRKI, pp. 381–413.
Farkas Szilágyi, Zsuzsa, and Antal Heizer. 1996. "Report on the Situation of the Gypsy Community in Hungary." Budapest: State Secretary for Minority Affairs at the Office of the Prime Minister.
Favell, Adrian. 1998. *Philosophies of Integration: Immigration and the Idea of Citizenship in France and Britain*. Basingstoke: Macmillan.
Favell, Adrian, and Andrew Geddes. 2000. "Immigration and European Integration: New Opportunities for Transnational Mobilization?" In: *Challenging Immigration and Ethnic Relations Politics: Comparative European Perspectives*, ed. R. Koopmans and P. Statham. Oxford: Oxford University Press, pp. 407–28.
Fawn, Rick. 2001. "Czech Attitudes towards the Roma: 'Expecting More of Havel's Country'." *Europe-Asia Studies* 53: 8, pp. 1193–219.
Ficowski, Jerzy. 1989. *Cyganie w Polsce: Dzieje i obyczaje*. Warszawa: Wydawnictwo Interpress.
Finnemore, Martha, and Kathryn Sikkink. 1998. "International Norm Dynamics and Political Change." *International Organization* 52: 4, pp. 887–917.
Forray, Katalin R., and Erzsébet Mohácsi. 2002. "Opportunities and Limits: The Roma Community in Hungary at the Millennium." Budapest: Ministry of Foreign Affairs.
Foundation on Inter-Ethnic Relations. 1997. *The Role of the High Commissioner on National Minorities in OSCE Conflict Prevention: An Introduction*. The Hague: Foundation on Inter-Ethnic Relations.
Fox, Jonathan. 2001. "Patterns of Discrimination, Grievances and Political Activity among Europe's Roma: A Cross-Sectional Analysis." *Journal on Ethnopolitics and Minority Issues in Europe* 1, pp. 1–25.
Fox Piven, Frances, and Richard A. Cloward. 1995. "Collective Protest: A Critique of Resource-Mobilization Theory." In: *Social Movements: Critiques, Concepts, Case-Studies*, ed. S.M. Lyman. London: Macmillan, 137–67.
Fraser, Angus. 1995. *The Gypsies*. Oxford: Blackwell Publishers.
———. 2000. "The Present and Future of the Gypsy Past." *Cambridge Review of International Affairs* 13: 2, pp. 15–31.
Friedman, Eben. 2002. "Explaining the Political Integration of Minorities: Roms as a Hard Case." Unpublished doctoral dissertation, University of California.
Gedlu, Mesfin. 1998. *The Roma and Europe. Romové a Evropa*. Štiřín Castle: Institute of International Relations.
Geertz, Clifford. 1993. *The Interpretation of Cultures: Selected Essays*. London: Fontana.
Gheorghe, Nicolae 1991. "Roma-Gypsy Ethnicity in Eastern Europe." *Social Research* 58: 4, pp. 829–45.
———. 1997. "The Social Construction of Romani Identity." In: *Gyspsy Politics and Traveller Identity*, ed. T. Acton. Hertfordshire: University of Hertfordshire Press, pp. 153–63.
Gheorghe, Nicolae, and Thomas Acton. 2001. "Citizens of the World and Nowhere: Minority, Ethnic and Human Rights for Roma during the Last Hurrah of the Nation-State." In: *Between Past and Future: The Roma of Central and Eastern Europe*, ed. Will Guy. Hertfordshire: University of Hertfordshire Press, pp. 54–70.

Gilroy, Paul. 1998. "Race Ends Here." *Ethnic and Racial Studies* 21: 5, pp. 838–47.
———. 2000. *Between Camps. Nations, Culture and the Allure of Race*. London: Penguin Books.
Glazer, Nathan. 2000. "Disaggregating Culture." In: *Culture Matters*, ed. L. Harrison and S. Huntington. New York: Basic Books, pp. 219–30.
Glazer, Nathan, and Daniel P. Moynihan. 1974. "Why Ethnicity?" *Commentary* 58: 4, pp. 33–39.
Goffman, Erving. 1975. *Frame Analysis: An Essay on the Organization of Experience*. Harmondsworth: Penguin Books.
Government Commissioner for the Romani Community (Slovak Republic). 2001. "List of Communities on which Territory Romani Settlements are Located." (Zoznam obcí SR na území ktorých sa nachádzajú rómske osady).
———. 2002. "Priorities of the Government of the Slovak Republic with Regard to Roma Communities for 2002." (Priority vlády SR vo vzťahu k rómskym komunitám na rok 2002).
Government of the Czech and Slovak Federative Republic. 1991. "Resolution No. 619/1999 on the Principles of Government Policy of the Czech and Slovak Federative Republic towards the Romani Minority." (Zásady politiky vlády České a Slovenské Federativní Republiky k romské menšině, Usnesení vlády ČSFR č. 619/1991).
Government of the Czech Republic. 1997. "Resolution on the Report About the Situation of the Romani Community in the Czech Republic and on the Present Situation within the Romani Community, Resolution No. 686/1997." (Usnesení č. 686/1997 ke zprávě o situaci romské komunity v České republice a k současné situaci v romské komunitě).
———. 1998. "Policy Statement."
———. 1999a. "Report Submitted by the Czech Republic Pursuant to Article 25, Paragraph 1 of the Framework Convention for the Protection of National Minorities."
———. 1999b. "Conception of Government Policy Towards Members of the Romani Community, Facilitating Their Integration in Society, Resolution No. 279/1999." (Koncepce politiky vlády vůči příslušníkům romské komunity, napomáhající jejich integraci do společnosti, Usnesení č. 279/1999).
Government of the Republic of Hungary. 1997. "Report No. J/3670 of the Government of the Republic of Hungary to the National Assembly on the Situation of the National and Ethnic Minorites Living in the Republic of Hungary." (J/3670. számú Beszámoló a Magyar Köztársaságban élő nemzeti és etnikai kisebbségek helyzetéről).
———. 1998. "Government Programme for a Civic Hungary."
———. 1999. "Government Resolution No. 1047/1999 (V.5.) About Medium-Term Measures to Improve the Living Standards and Social Position of the Gypsy Population." (1047/1999. (V.5.) kormhatározat a cigányság életkörülményeinek és társadalmi helyzetének javítására irányuló középtávú intézkedéscsomagról).
Government of the Slovak Republic. 1991. "Principles of Government Policy Towards the Roma, Resolution No. 153/1991." (Zásady vládnej politiky k Rómom, Uznesenie č. 153/1991).
———. 1996. "Resolution to the Proposal of the Activities and Measures in Order to Solve the Problems of Citizens in Need of Special Care, Resolution No. 310/1996." (Uznesenie k návrh úloh a opatrení na riešenie problémov občanov, ktorí potrebujú osobitnú pomoc, Uznesenie č. 310/1996).
———. 1997. "Resolution on the Conceptual Aims of Government of the Slovak Republic Regarding the Solution of the Problems of the Roma Under the Current Social-Economic Circumstances, No. 796/1997." (Uznesenie vlády slovenskej repub-

liky k návrhu koncepčných zámerov vlády SR na riešenie problémov Rómov v súčasných spoločensko-ekonomických podmienkach, Uznesenie č.796/1997).
———. 1999a. "Resolution About the Strategy of the Government of the Slovak Republic for the Solution of the Problems of the Romani National Minority and the Set of Measures for Its Implementation—Stage I, Resolution No. 821/1999." (Uznesenie k stratégii na riešenie problémov rómskej národnostnej menšiny a súboru opatrení na jej realizáciu—I. etapa, Uznesenie č. 821/1999).
———. 1999b. "Report Submitted by the Slovak Republic Pursuant to Article 25, Paragraph 1 of the Framework Convention for the Protection of National Minorities."
———. 2000. "Comments of the Government of the Slovak Republic to the Opinion of the Advisory Committee on the Report on the Implementation of the Framework Convention for the Protection of National Minorities in the Slovak Republic."
Grabbe, Heather. 1999. "A Partnership for Accession? The Implications of EU Conditionality for the Central and Eastern European Applicants." RSC Policy Paper 99/12, European University Institute Florence.
Gregory, Steven. 1998. *Black Corona: Race and the Politics of Place in an Urban Community*. Princeton: Princeton University Press.
Grosby, Steven. 1994. "The Verdict of History: The Inexpungeable Tie of Primordiality—A Reply to Eller and Coughlan." *Ethnic and Racial Studies* 17: 1, pp. 164–71.
Guidry, John A., Michael Kennedy, and Mayer N. Zald, eds. 2000. *Globalizations and Social Movements: Culture, Power, and the Transnational Public Sphere*. Ann Arbor: University of Michigan Press.
Gurr, Ted Robert, and Barbara Harff. 1994. *Ethnic Conflict in World Politics*. Boulder, San Francisco, Oxford: Westview Press.
Guy, Will. 1998. "Ways of Looking at Roma: The Case of Czechoslovakia." In: *Gypsies: An Interdisciplinary Reader*, ed. D. Tong. New York, London: Garland, pp. 13–68.
———, ed. 2001a. *Between Past and Future: The Roma of Central and Eastern Europe*. Hertfordshire: University of Hertfordshire Press.
———. 2001b. "Romani Identity and Post-Communist Policy." In: *Between Past and Future: The Roma of Central and Eastern Europe*, ed. W. Guy. Hertfordshire: University of Hertfordshire Press, pp. 3–32.
———. 2001c. "The Czech Lands and Slovakia: Another False Dawn." In: *Between Past and Future: The Roma of Central and Eastern Europe*, ed. Will Guy. Hertfordshire: University of Hertfordshire Press, pp. 287–323.
———. 2001d. "Introduction", In: *Between Past and Future: The Roma of Central and Eastern Europe*, ed. Will Guy. Hertfordshire: University of Hertfordshire Press, pp. xiii–xvii.
———. 2002. "Late Arrivals at the Nationalist Games: Romani Mobilisation in the Czech Lands and Slovakia." In: *The Shaping of Ethnonational Identities*, ed. S. Fenton and S. May. London: Macmillan, pp. 48–83.
———. 2003. "'No Soft Touch': Romani Migration to the U.K. at the Turn of the Twenty-First Century." *Nationalities Papers* 31: 1, pp. 63–80.
Győri Szabó, Róbert. 1998. *Kisebbségpolitikai rendszerváltás Magyarországon*. Budapest: Osiris Kiadó.
Hall, Stuart. 1990. "Cultural Identity and Diaspora." In: *Identity: Community, Culture, Difference*, ed. J. Rutherford. London: Laurence and Wishart.
Hancock, Ian. 1992. "The East European Roots of Romani Nationalism." In: *The Gypsies of Eastern Europe*, ed. David Crowe and John Kolsti. Armonk, New York: M.E. Sharpe, pp. 133–50.
———. 1997. "The Struggle for the Control of Identity." *Transitions* 4: 4, pp. 36–44.

———. 2000. "The Emergence of Romani as a Koïné outside of India." In: *Scholarship and the Gypsy Struggle: Commitment in Romani Studies*, ed. Thomas Acton. Hertfordshire: University of Hertfordshire Press, pp. 1–13.

Hann, Chris, and Elizabeth Dunn, eds. 1996. *Civil Society. Challenging Western Models.* London: Routledge.

Harrison, Lawrence E., and Samuel P. Huntington, eds. 2000. *Culture Matters.* New York: Basic Books.

Haughton, Tim. 2001. "HZDS: The Ideology, Organisation and Support Base of Slovakia's Most Successful Party." *Europe-Asia Studies* 53: 5, pp. 745–69.

Havas, Gábor, Gábor Kertesi, and István Kemény. 1995. "The Statistics of Deprivation: The Roma in Hungary." *Hungarian Quarterly* 36: 3, pp. 67–80.

Havas, Gábor, and István Kemény. 1999. "The Statistics of Deprivation." In: *Encounters: A Hungarian Quarterly Reader*, ed. Z. Zachár. Budapest: The Hungarian Quarterly Society, Balassi kiadó, pp. 361–70.

HCNM (High Commissioner on National Minorities). 1993. "Roma (Gypsies) in the CSCE Region." The Hague: HCNM.

———. 2000. "Report on the Situation of the Roma and Sinti in the OSCE Area." The Hague: HCNM.

Hechter, Michael. 1975. *Internal Colonialism: The Celtic Fringe in British National Development, 1536–1966.* London: Routledge and Kegan Paul.

———. 1996. "Ethnicity and Rational Choice Theory." In: *Ethnicity*, ed. J. Hutchinson and A.D. Smith. Oxford: Oxford University Press, pp. 90–98.

Heizer, Antal. 1999. "State Policies toward the Romani Communities in Candidate Countries to the EU: Government and Romani Participation in Policy-Making in Hungary." Speech delivered at the European Commission, July 26, 1999, Brussels.

Helsinki Watch. 1991a. *Destroying Ethnic Identity: The Gypsies of Bulgaria*, New York: Helsinki Watch.

———. 1991b. *Destroying Ethnic Identity: The Persecution of Gypsies in Romania*, New York: Helsinki Watch.

———. 1993. *Struggling for Ethnic Identity. The Gypsies of Hungary.* New York, Washington, Los Angeles, London: Helsinki Watch.

Henderson, Karen. 1999. "Minorities and Politics in the Slovak Republic." In: *Minorities in Europe — Croatia, Estonia and Slovakia*, ed. S. Trifunovska. The Hague: T.M.C. Asser Press, pp. 143–73.

de Heusch, Luc. 1997. "L'ethnie: vicissitudes d'un concept." *Archives européennes de sociologie* 38: 2, pp. 185–206.

Hirschfeld, Lawrence A. 1996. *Race in the Making: Cognition, Culture, and the Child's Construction of Human Kinds.* Cambridge, MA: MIT Press.

Hofmann, Mahulena. 2003. "The 2001 Law on National Minorities in the Czech Republic." *European Yearbook of Minority Issues* 1, pp. 623–28.

Holomek, Karel. 1998. "Romany Civic Initiative (ROI)." *Helsinki Citizens Assembly—Roma Section Newsletter* 3.

———. 1999. "Vývoj romských reprezentací po roce 1989 a minoritní mocenská politika ve vztahu k Romům." In: *Romové v České republice (1945–1998)*, ed. Helena Lisá. Prague: Socioklub, pp. 290–310.

Hornung-Rauh, Edit, and István Fretyán. 2000. "Summary of Measures Taken by the Government Affecting the Roma Minority over the Past Two Years." Unpublished paper, Office for Ethnic and National Minorities.

Horowitz, Donald L. 1985. *Ethnic Groups in Conflict.* Berkeley: University of California Press.

Horváthová, Emilia. 1964. *Cigáni na Slovensku.* Bartislava: Vydavateľstvo Slovenskej adadémie vied.

HRW (Human Rights Watch). 1992. *Struggling for Ethnic Identity: Czechoslovakia's Endangered Gypsies.* New York: Human Rights Watch.
———. 1993. *Struggling for Ethnic Identity: The Gypsies of Hungary.* New York: Human Rights Watch.
———. 1996. *Roma in the Czech Republic. Foreigners in Their Own Land.* New York: Human Rights Watch.
Hungarian Government. 1999. "Report of the Republic of Hungary. Implementation of the Council of Europe Framework Convention for the Protection of National Minorities." Budapest.
Information Center of the Hungarian Coalition in Slovakia. 1997. "The Hungarians in Slovakia." Bratislava: Information Centre of the Hungarian Coalition in Slovakia.
Inter-Ministerial Committee on Roma Issues of the Hungarian Government. 2001. "Guiding Principles of the Long-Term Roma Social and Minority Policy Strategy. Discussion Paper. Adopted by the Government in Resolution 1078/2001 (VIII. 13)." (A kormány 1078/2001. (vii.13.) korm. határozata a hosszú távú roma társadalom- és kisebbségpolitikai stratégia irányelveit tartalmazó vitaanyag elfogadásáról és társadalmi vitájáról).
IOM (International Organization for Migration). 2000. "Social and Economic Situation of Potential Asylum Seekers From the Slovak Republic." Bratislava: IOM.
Ireland, Patrick. 1994. *The Policy Challenge of Ethnic Diversity: Immigrant Politics in France and Switzerland.* Cambridge, MA: Harvard University Press.
———. 2000. "Reaping What They Sow: Institutions and Immigrant Political Participation in Western Europe." In: *Challenging Immigration and Ethnic Relations Politics: Comparative European Perspectives,* ed. R. Koopmans and P. Statham. Oxford: Oxford University Press, pp. 233–82.
Jacobs, Dirk. 2005. "Arab European League (AEL): The Rapid Rise of a Radical Immigrant Movement." *Journal of Muslim Minority Affairs* 25: 1, pp. 97–115.
Jenkins, Richard. 1997. *Rethinking Ethnicity: Arguments and Explorations.* London, Thousand Oaks, New Dehli: Sage.
Jenkins, Robert M. 1998. "Stablizing the Democratic Transition: The 1990 Hungarian Parliamentary Elections." *Szelényi 60,* (http://hi.rutgers.edu/szelenyi60).
Jenson, Jane. 1998. "Social Movement Naming Practices and the Political Opportunity Structure." Working paper, Instituto Juan March de Estudios e Investigaciones, Madrid.
Johnston, Hank. 1995. "A Methodology for Frame Analysis: From Discourse to Cognitive Schemata." In: *Social Movements and Cultures,* ed. H. Johnston and B. Klandermans. London: UCL Press, pp. 217–46.
Kadét, Ernő. 2001. "Creative Accounting: State Spending on Programmes for Roma in Hungary." *Roma Rights* 2–3, (http://errc.org/rr_nr2-3_2001/noteb3.shtml).
Kállai, Ernő, and Erika Törzsök. 2001. *A Roma's Life in Hungary: Report 2000.* Budapest: Bureau for European Comparative Minority Research.
Kaltenbach, Jenő. 1995. *National and Ethnic Minority Rights Parliamentary Commissioner's Report 1995.* Budapest: Parliamentary Commissioner for National and Ethnic Minority Rights.
———. 2003. *Report 2002.* Budapest: Parliamentary Commissioner for National and Ethnic Minority Rights.
Kaplan, Petr. 1999. "Romové a zaměstnanost neboli zaměstnatelnost Romů v České republice." In: *Romové v České republice (1945–1998),* ed. Helena Lisá. Prague: Socioklub, pp. 352–77.
Karsai, László. 1992. *A cigánykérdés Magyarországon.* Budapest: Scientiae Hungariae.

———. 1999. "The Radical Right in Hungary." In: *The Radical Right in Central and Eastern Europe Since 1989*, ed. S.P. Ramet. Pennsylvania: Pennsylvania State University Press, pp. 133–46.

Keck, Margaret, and Kathryn Sikkink. 1998. *Activists beyond Borders: Transnational Advocacy Networks in International Politics*. Ithaca, London: Cornell University Press.

Kellas, James. 1991. *The Politics of Nationalism and Ethnicity*. Basingstoke and London: Macmillan.

Kemény, István. 2000. "Employment, Jobs and Joblessness." In: *A Roma's Life in Hungary*, ed. E. Kállai and E. Törzsök. Budapest: Bureau for European Comparative Minority Research, pp. 29–36.

Kende, Pierre. 1988. "Communist Hungary and the Hungarian Minorities." In: *The Hungarians: A Divided Nation*, ed. S. Borsody. New Haven: Yale Center for International and Area Studies, pp. 274–88.

Kenrick, Donald. 1978. "Romanies without a Road." *Contemporary Review* 232, pp. 153–56.

Kertesi, G. and G. Kézdi. 1998. *A cigány népesség magyarországon. Dokumentáció és adattár*. Budapest: Socio-typo.

Kertzer, David I., and Dominique Arel. 2002. *Census and Identity. The Politics of Race, Ethnicity, and Language in National Censuses*. Cambridge: Cambridge University Press.

Klímová, Ilona. 2002. "Romani Struggle for Legitimacy in Central Europe: Institutionalisation of Formal External Romani Political Representation and Administration (15th Century up to Present)." Unpublished paper presented at the conference on Contours of Legitimacy in Central Europe: New Approaches in Graduate Studies. Oxford, St. Anthony's College.

Klímová-Alexander, Ilona. 2005. *The Romani Voice in World Politics. The United Nations and Non-State Actors*. Hampshire: Ashgate.

Koopmans, Ruud, and Jan Willem Duyvendak. 1995. "Conclusion." In: *New Social Movements in Western Europe: A Comparative Analysis*, ed. H. Kriesi et al. London: UCL Press, pp. 238–51.

Koopmans, Ruud, and Hanspeter Kriesi. 1995. "Institutional Structures and Prevailing Strategies." In: *New Social Movements in Western Europe: A Comparative Analysis*, ed. H. Kriesi et al. London: UCL Press, pp. 26–52.

Koopmans, Ruud, and Paul Statham, ed. 2000. *Challenging Immigration and Ethnic Relations Politics: Comparative European Perspectives*. Oxford: Oxford University Press.

Kornblum, William, and Paul Lichter. 1972. "Urban Gypsies and the Culture of Poverty." *Urban Life and Culture* 1: 3, pp. 239–53.

Körösényi, András. 1999. *Government and Politics in Hungary*. Budapest: Central European University Press, Osiris.

Kosztolányi, Gustav. 2001. *Out of the Ghetto*. Central Europe Review.

Kovats, Martin. 1998. "The Development of Roma Politics in Hungary 1989–95." Unpublished doctoral dissertation, University of Portsmouth.

———. 2001a. "The Political Significance of the First National Gypsy Self-Government (Országos Kisebbségi Önkormányzat)," *Journal of Ethnopolitics and Minority Issues in Europe* 1, pp. 1–24.

———. 2001b. "Hungary: Politics, Difference and Equality." In: *Between Past and Future: The Roma of Central and Eastern Europe*, ed. W. Guy. Hertfordshire: University of Hertfordshire Press, pp. 333–50.

———. 2001c. "The Emergence of European Roma Policy." In: *Between Past and Future: The Roma of Central and Eastern Europe*, ed. W. Guy. Hertfordshire: University of Hertfordshire Press, pp. 93–116.

Kriesi, Hanspeter. 1993. *Political Mobilization and Social Change: The Dutch Case in Comparative Perspective*. Aldershot: Avebury.

Kriesi, Hanspeter, and Marco G. Guigni. 1995. "Introduction." In: *New Social Movements in Western Europe: A Comparative Analysis*, ed. H. Kriesi, R. Koopmans, J.W. Duyvendak, and M.G. Guigni. London: UCL Press, pp. ix–xxvi.
Kriesi, Hanspeter, Ruud Koopmans, Jan Willem Duyvendak, and Marco G. Giugni. 1995. *New Social Movements in Western Europe: A Comparative Analysis*. London: UCL Press.
Krizsán, Andrea. 2000. "The Hungarian Minority Protection System: A Flexible Approach to the Adjudication of Ethnic Claims." *Journal of Ethnic and Migration Studies* 26: 2, pp. 247–62.
Küpper, Herbert. 1998. *Das neue Minderheitenrecht in Ungarn*. München: R. Oldenbourg Verlag.
Kürti, László. 1997. "Globalisation and the Discourse of Otherness in the 'New' Eastern and Central Europe." In: *The Politics of Multiculturalism in the New Europe*, ed. Tariq Modood and Pnina Werbner. London, New York: Zed Books, pp. 29–53.
Kymlicka, Will. 1995. *Multicultural Citizenship: A Liberal Theory of Minority Rights*. Oxford: Clarendon Press.
———. 2000. "Nation-Building and Minority Rights: Comparing West and East." *Journal of Ethnic and Migration Studies* 26: 2, pp. 183–212.
———. 2001a. "Western Political Theory and Ethnic Relations in Eastern Europe." In: *Can Liberal Pluralism Be Exported? Western Political Theory and Ethnic Relations in Eastern Europe*, ed. W. Kymlicka and M. Opalski. Oxford: Oxford University Press, pp. 13–105.
———. 2001b. *Politics in the Vernacular: Nationalism, Multiculturalism, and Citizenship*. Oxford: Oxford University Press.
Ladányi, János. 2002. "A romák választási tényezővé válásáról." *Beszélő* (March), (http://www.beszelo.hu).
Laitin, David D. 1998. *Identity in Formation. The Russian-Speaking Populations in the Near Abroad*. Ithaca, London: Cornell University Press.
Laubeová, Laura. 2003. "Some Social Science and Public Policy Responses to Racism in the Czech Republic." Unpublished paper presented at the international congress of the Austrian Sociological Association, November 23–26. Vienna.
Leudar, Ivan, and Jiří Nekvapil. 2000. "Presentations of Romanies in the Czech Media: On Category Work in Television Debates." *Discourse and Society* 11: 4, pp. 487–513.
Liebich, André. 1998. "Ethnic Minorities and Long-Term Implications of EU Enlargement." RSC Working Paper 98/49, European University Institute, Florence.
Liégeois, Jean-Pierre. 1994. *Tsiganes et voyageurs: données socio-culturelles et socio-politiques*. Strasbourg: Conseil de l'Europe.
———. 1996. "Roma Policy: Gypsy National Self-Government and Local Self-Governments (Hungary)." Strasbourg: Council of Europe, Report DECS/SE/DHRM (96) 23.
Liégeois, Jean-Pierre, and Nicolae Gheorghe. 1995. *Roma/Gypsies: A European Minority*. London: Minority Rights Group International.
Linz, Juan J., and Alfred Stepan. 1996. *Problems of Democratic Transition and Consolidation*. Baltimore: Johns Hopkins University Press.
Lucassen, Leo, Wim Willems, and Annemarie Cottaar. 1998. *Gypsies and Other Itinerant Groups: A Socio-Historical Approach*. London: Macmillan.
Lutz, Brenda Davis, and James M. Lutz. 1995. "Gypsies as Victims of the Holocaust." *Holocaust and Genocide Studies* 9: 3: pp. 346–59.
Malfliet, Katlijn, and Ria Laenen. eds. 1998. *Minorities in Central and Eastern Europe: The Link between Domestic Policy, Foreign Policy and European Integration*. Leuven: Garant.

Mann, Arne B. 1992. "The Formation of the Ethnic Identity of the Romany in Slovakia." In: *Minorities in Politics—Cultural and Language Rights*, ed. J. Plichtová. Bratislava: The European Cultural Foundation, pp. 260–65.

———. 2000. "The Problem of the Identity of Romany People." In: *Identity of Ethnic Groups and Communities: The Results of Slovak Ethnological Research*, ed. G. Kiliánová and E. Riečanská. Bratislava: Institute of Ethnology of Slovak Academy of Sciences, pp. 51–78.

Mansfeldová, Zdenka. 1998. "The Czech and Slovak Republics." In: *The Handbook of Political Change in Eastern Europe*, ed. S. Berglund, T. Hellén, and F.H. Aarebrot. Cheltenham, Northampton: Edward Elgar, pp. 191–229.

March, James G., and Johan P. Olsen. 1989. *Rediscovering Institutions: The Organizational Basis of Politics*. New York: The Free Press.

Martiniello, Marco, and Paul Statham. 1999. "Introduction." *Journal of Ethnic and Migration Studies* 25: 4, pp. 565–73.

Marushiakova, Elena, and Vesselin Popov. 2001a. "Historical and Ethnographic Background: Gypsies, Roma, Sinti." In: *Between Past and Future: The Roma of Central and Eastern Europe*, ed. Will Guy. Hertfordshire: University of Hertfordshire Press, pp. 33–53.

———. 2001b. "The Roma — a Nation without a State? Historical Background and Contemporary Tendencies." Unpublished paper.

Matras, Yaron. 2000. "Romani Migrations in the Post-Communist Era: Their Historical and Political Significance." *Cambridge Review of International Affairs* 13: 2, pp. 32–50.

McAdam, Doug. 1982. *Political Process and the Development of Black Insurgency, 1930–1970*. Chicago: University of Chicago Press.

———. 1996. "Conceptual Origins, Current Problems, Future Directions." In *Comparative Perspectives on Social Movements: Political Opportunities, Mobilizing Structures and Cultural Framings*, ed. D. McAdam, J.D. McCarthy, and M.N. Zald. Cambridge: Cambridge University Press, pp. 23–40.

McAdam, Doug, John D. McCarthy, and Mayer N. Zald, eds. 1996. *Comparative Perspectives on Social Movements: Political Opportunities, Mobilizing Structures and Cultural Framings*. Cambridge: Cambridge University Press.

Mesežnikov, Grigorij. 1999. "The 1998 Elections and the Development of the Party System in Slovakia." In: *The 1998 Parliamentary Elections and Democratic Rebirth in Slovakia*, ed. M. Bútora, G. Mesežnikov, Z. Bútorová, and S. Fisher. Bratislava: Institute for Public Affairs, pp. 49–61.

Miles, Robert. 1989. *Racism*. London: Routledge.

Ministry of Labor and Social Affairs of the Czech Republic. 2002. "Operational Programme for Human Resource Development in the Czech Republic."

Mirga, Andrzej, and Lech Mróz. 1994. *Cyganie: odmiennosc i nietolerancja*. Warszawa: Wydawnictwo Naukowe PWN.

Moynihan, Daniel P. 1993. *Pandaemonium: Ethnicity in International Politics*. Oxford: Oxford University Press.

Murray, Charles. 1984. *Losing Ground: American Social Policy, 1950–1980*. New York: Basic Books.

Nagel, Joane. 1996. *American Indian Ethnic Renewal: Red Power and the Resurgence of Identity and Culture*. New York, Oxford: Oxford University Press.

Nečas, Ctibor. 1995. *Romové v České republice včera a dnes*. Olomouc: Univerzita Palackého.

———. 1999. *Holocaust českých Romů*. Praha: Prostor.

Népegészségügyi Iskola. 2001. "Telepek és telepszerű lakóhelyeken élő kisebbségek környezetegészségügyi problémái." Debreceni Egyetem.

———. 2004. "Telepek és telepszerű lakóhelyek felmérése." Debreceni Egyetem.

Nielsen, François. 1980. "The Flemish Movement in Belgium after World War II: A Dynamic Analysis." *American Sociological Review* 45, pp. 76–94.
Oberschall, Anthony. 1973. *Social Conflict and Social Movements*. Englewood Cliffs: Prentice-Hall.
———. 2000. "The Manipulation of Ethnicity: From Ethnic Cooperation to Violence and War in Yugoslavia." *Ethnic and Racial Studies* 23: 6, pp. 982–1001.
ODHIR (Office for Democratic Institutions and Human Rights). 1994. "ODIHR Human Dimension Seminar on Roma and Sinti in the CSCE Region." Warsaw.
Office of the President of Slovakia. 1999. "Meeting of the Presidents of the Visegrad Four Countries: Working Dokument [sic] on the Roma Issue in the V4 Countries." Unpublished paper presented at the meeting of presidents of the Visegrád Four Countries, December 3. High Tatras.
Okely, Judith. 1983. *The Traveller-Gypsies*. Cambridge: Cambridge University Press.
Olzak, Susan. 1998. "Ethnic Protest in Core and Periphery States." *Ethnic and Racial Studies* 21: 2, pp. 187–217.
OSCE (Organization for Security and Cooperation in Europe). 1998. "ODIHR Human Dimension Implementation Meeting. Roundtable on Roma and Sinti National Policies."
Parliamentary Assembly of the Council of Europe. 1993a. "Recommendation 1203 (1993) on Gypsies in Europe."
———. 1993b. "Gypsies in Europe. Report Doc. 6733."
Parliament of the Czech Republic. 2001. "Act 273/2001 on the Rights of Members of National Minorities and on the Amendment of Some Acts." (Zákon 273/2001 o právech příslušníků národnostních menšin a o změně některých zákonů).
Patterson, Orlando. 2000. "Taking Culture Seriously: A Framework and an Afro-American Illustration." In: *Culture Matters: How Values Shape Human Progress*, ed. L.E. Harrison and S.P. Huntington. New York: Basic Books, pp. 202–18.
Pentassuglia, Gaetano. 2001. "The EU and the Protection of Minorities: The Case of Eastern Europe." *European Journal of International Law* 12: 1, pp. 3–38.
PER (Project on Ethnic Relations). 1999. "Political Participation and the Roma in Hungary and Slovakia." Princeton.
———. 2001a. "Parliamentary Representation of Minorities in Hungary: Legal and Political Issues." Princeton.
———. 2001b. "Romani Representation and Leadership at National and International Levels." Princeton.
Petrova, Dimitrina. "The Roma: Between a Myth and the Future." *Social Research* 70: 1, pp. 111–61.
Phralipe. 1989. "From the Documents of Phralipe Independent Gypsy Organization." Unpublished manuscript, Budapest.
Pithart, Petr. 1995. "Towards a Shared Freedom, 1969–89." In: *The End of Czechoslovakia*, ed. J. Musil. Budapest, London, New York: Central European University Press, pp. 201–22.
della Porta, Donatella, and Mario Diani. 1999. *Social Movements: An Introduction*. Oxford: Blackwell Publishers.
Puxon, Grattan. 2000. "The Romani Movement: Rebirth and the First World Romani Congress in Retrospect." In: *Scholarship and the Gypsy Struggle: Commitment in Romani Studies*, ed. T. Acton. Hertfordshire: University of Hertfordshire Press, pp. 94–113.
Ragin, Charles. 1987. *The Comparative Method: Moving beyond Qualitative and Quantitative Strategies*. Berkeley: University of California Press.
Rath, Jan. 1991. *Minorisering: de sociale constructie van 'etnische minderheden'*. Amsterdam: SUA.

Riba, István. 1999. "Minority Self-Governments in Hungary." *The Hungarian Quarterly* 40: 155, pp. 80–99.
Risse, Thomas, and Kathryn Sikkink. 1999. "The Socialization of International Human Rights Norms into Domestic Practices: Introduction." In: *The Power of Human Rights: International Norms and Domestic Change*, ed. T. Risse, S.C. Ropp, and K. Sikkink. Cambridge: Cambridge University Press, pp. 1–38.
Roosens, Eugène. 1998. *Eigen grond eerst? Primordiale autochtonie: dilemma van de multiculturele samenleving*. Leuven: ACCO.
Rothstein, Bo. 2000. "Political Institutions: An Overview." In: *A New Handbook of Political Science*, ed. R. Goodin and H.-D. Klingemann. Oxford: Oxford University Press, pp. 133–66.
Rueschemeyer, Dietrich, Marylin Rueschemeyer, and Björn Wittrock. 1998. *Participation and Democracy: East and West. Comparisons and Interpretations*. Armonk, London: M.E. Sharpe.
Rychlík, Jan. 1995. "National Consciousness and the Common State (A Historical-Ethnological Analysis)." In: *The End of Czechoslovakia*, ed. J. Musil. Budapest, London, New York: Central European University Press.
Sághy, E. 1999. "Cigánypolitika Magyarországon 1945–1964." *Regio* 10: 1, pp. 16–35.
Save the Children. 2001. *Denied a Future? The Right to Education of Roma/Gypsy and Traveller Children in Europe*. London: Save the Children.
Schöpflin, George. 2000. *Nations, Identity, Power: The New Politics of Europe*. London: Hurst & Company.
Scott, Joan W. 1999. "The Conundrum of Equality." Occasional Paper of the School of Social Science, Institute for Advanced Study Princeton.
Šebesta, Michal. 2003. "The Roma Political Scene." In: *Čačipen pal o Roma*, ed. M. Vašečka, M. Jurásková, and T. Nicholson. Bratislava: Institute for Public Affairs, pp. 199–210.
Šiklová, Jiřina. 1999. "Romové a nevládní, neziskové romské a proromské občanské organizace přispívající k integraci tohoto etnika." In: *Romové v České republice (1945–1998)*, ed. Helena Lisá. Prague: Socioklub, pp. 271–89.
Šiklová, Jiřina, and Marta Miklušáková. 1998. "Denying Citizenship to the Czech Roma." *East European Constitutional Review* 7: 2, pp. 58–64.
Smith, Anthony D. 1981. *The Ethnic Revival*. Cambridge: Cambridge University Press.
———. 1997. "Structure and Persistence of Ethnie." In *The Ethnicity Reader. Nationalism, Multiculturalism and Migration*, ed. M. Guibernau and J. Rex. Cambridge: Polity Press, pp. 27–33.
———. 1998. *Nationalism and Modernism: A Critical Survey of Recent Theories of Nations and Nationalism*. London, New York: Routledge.
Snow, David A., and Robert D. Benford. 1998. "Ideology, Frame Resonance, and Participant Mobilization." *International Sociological Movement Research* 1, pp. 197–218.
Sobotka, Eva. 2001a. "The Limits of the State: Political Participation and Representation of Roma in the Czech Republic, Hungary, Poland and Slovakia." *Journal on Ethnopolitcs and Minority Issues in Europe* 1, pp. 1–23.
———. 2001b. "Crusts from the Table: Policy Formation towards Roma in the Czech Republic and Slovakia." *Roma Rights* 2–3, pp. 66–70.
Solomos, John, and Les Back. 1995. "Marxism, Racism, and Ethnicity." *American Behavioural Scientist* 38: 3, pp. 407–21.
Sontag, Susan. 2003. *Regarding the Pain of Others*. New York: Farrar, Straus & Giroux.
Soysal, Yasemin N. 1996. "Changing Citizenship in Europe." In: *Citizenship, Nationality and Migration in Europe*, ed. D. Cesarani and M. Fulbrook. London, New York: Routledge, pp. 17–29.

Stalin, J.V. 1954. "Marxism and the National Question." In: *Works*, J.V. Stalin. Moscow: Foreign Languages Publishing House, pp. 300–81.
Stewart, Michael. 1997. *The Time of the Gypsies*. Colorado: Westview Press.
———. 2001. "Communist Roma Policy 1945–1989 as Seen Through the Hungarian Case." In: *Between Past and Future: The Roma of Central and Eastern Europe*, ed. W. Guy. Hertfordshire: University of Hertfordshire Press, pp. 71–92.
Stone, Deborah. 1998. *Policy Paradox: The Art of Political Decision Making*. New York, London: W.W. Norton & Co.
Sulitka, Andrej. 1999. "Vývoj a súčasný stav praktických riešení kompetencií vrcholných orgánov štátu po roku 1989." In: *Romové v České republice (1945–1998)*, ed. Helena Lisá. Prague: Socioklub, pp. 219–43.
Sus, Jaroslav. 1961. *Cikánska otázka v ČSSR*. Prague: Státni nakladatelství politické literatury.
Tancerova, Barbara. 2004. "Slovakia: Looting Subsides, Tensions Remain." *Transitions Online*, February 24–March 1.
Tarrow, Sidney. 1983. *Struggling to Reform: Social Movements and Policy Change During Cycles of Protest*. Ithaca, New York: Cornell University.
———. 1994. *Power in Movement: Social Movements, Collective Action and Politics*. Cambridge: Cambridge University Press.
———. 1996. "States and Opportunities: The Political Structuring of Social Movements." In: *Comparative Perspectives on Social Movements: Political Opportunities, Mobilizing Structures and Cultural Framings*, ed. D. McAdam, J.D. McCarthy, and M.N. Zald. Cambridge: Cambridge University Press, pp. 41–61.
Taylor, Rupert. 1996. "Political Science Encounters 'Race' and 'Ethnicity.'" *Ethnic and Racial Studies* 19: 4, pp. 884–95.
Tilly, Charles. 1978. *From Mobilization to Revolution*. Reading, MA: Random House.
———. 2003. "Political Identities in Changing Polities." *Social Research* 70: 2, pp. 605–20.
Tóka, Gábor. 1998. "Hungary." In: *The Handbook of Political Change in Eastern Europe*, ed. S. Berglund, T. Hellén, and F.H. Aarebrot. Cheltenham, Northampton: Edward Elgar, pp. 231–74.
Tomka, M. 1991. "Gazdasági változás és a cigánysággal kapcsolatos közvélemény." In: *Cigánylét*, ed. Á. Utasi and Á. Mészáros. Budapest: MTA PTI.
Tong, Diane, ed. 1998. *Gypsies: An Interdisciplinary Reader*. New York, London: Garland.
Tőkés, Rudolf L. 1996. *Hungary's Negotiated Revolution*. Cambridge: Cambridge University Press.
Trehan, Nidhi. 2001. "In the Name of the Roma? The Role of Private Foundations and NGOs." In: *Between Past and Future: The Roma of Central and Eastern Europe*, ed. W. Guy. Hertfordshire: University of Hertfordshire Press, pp. 134–49.
Tucker, Aviezer. 1999. "The Politics of Conviction: The Rise and Fall of Czech Intellectual-Politicians." In: *Intellectuals and Politics in Central Europe*, ed. A. Bozóki. Budapest: Central European University Press, pp. 185–205.
Tucker, William H. 1996. *The Science and Politics of Racial Research*. Urbana, Chicago: University of Illinois Press.
Uhl, Petr. 1998. "The Interdepartmental Commission for Affairs of the Roma Community of the Government of the Czech Republic." In: *The Roma and Europe. Romové a Evropa. Conference Proceedings*, ed. M. Gedlu. Štiřín Castle: Institute of International Relations, pp. 46–49.
Ulč, Otto. 1995. "Czech Republic and the Gypsies." *Freedom Review* 3, pp. 1–7.
UNDP (United Nations Development Programme). 2001. *Human Development Indicators*. Bratislava: UNDP.

―――. 2002. *The Roma in Central Europe: Avoiding the Dependency Trap. A Regional Human Development Report*. Bratislava: UNDP.

UNHCR (United Nations High Commissioner for Refugees). 1999. "Refugees and Others of Concern to UNHCR—1998 Statistical Overview." Geneva: UNHCR.

―――. 2000. "Refugees and Others of Concern to UNHCR, 1999 Statistical Overview." Geneva: UNHCR Population Data Unit, Population and Geographical Data Section.

―――. 2001. "Asylum Applications in industrialized countries: 1980–1999." Geneva: UNHCR Population Data Unit, Population and Geographical Data Section.

―――. 2002. "Trends in Asylum Applications Lodged in Europe, North America, Australia and New Zealand: Analysis of the Provisional 2001 Asylum Application Data in 29 Countries." Geneva: UNHCR Population Data Unit, Population and Geographical Data Section.

Vachudova, Milada A. 2000. "EU Enlargement: An Overview." *East European Constitutional Review* 9: 4, pp. 64–69.

Vašečka, Michal. 1999a. "Roma and the 1998 Parliamentary Elections." In: *The 1998 Parliamentary Elections and Democratic Rebirth in Slovakia*, ed. M. Bútora, G. Mesežnikov, Z. Bútorová, and S. Fisher. Bratislava: Institute for Public Affairs, pp. 255–63.

―――. 1999b. "The Roma." In: *Slovakia 1998–1999. A Global Report on the State of Society*, ed. G. Mesežnikov, M. Ivantyšyn, and T. Nicholson. Bratislava: Institute for Public Affairs, pp. 395–415.

―――. 2001. "Rómovia." In: *Slovensko 2000. Súhrnná správa o stave spoločnosti*, ed. M. Kollár and G. Mesežnikov. Bratislava: Inštitút pre verejné otázky, pp. 191–238.

Vašečka, Imrich and Michal Vašečka. 2003. "Recent Romani Migration from Slovakia to EU Member States: Romani Reactions to Discrimination or Romani Ethno-Tourism?" *Nationalities Papers* 31: 1, pp. 27–47.

Verheugen, Günter. 2001. "Slovakia on its Path towards the European Union." Speech held at the Technical University of Košice, February 21, 2001.

Vermeersch, Peter. 2001. "Advocacy Networks and Romani Politics in Central and Eastern Europe." *Journal on Ethnopolitics and Minority Issues in Europe* 1, pp. 1–22.

―――. 2002. "Ethnic Mobilisation and the Political Conditionality of European Union Accession: The Case of the Roma in Slovakia." *Journal of Ethnic and Migration Studies* 28: 1, pp. 83–101.

―――. 2003. "Ethnic Minority Identity and Movement Politics: The Case of the Roma in the Czech Republic and Slovakia." *Ethnic and Racial Studies* 26: 5, pp. 879–901.

―――. 2004. "Minority Policy in Central Europe: Exploring the Impact of the EU's Enlargement Strategy." *Global Review of Ethnopolitics* 3: 2, pp. 3–19.

―――. 2005. "Marginality, Advocacy, and the Ambiguities of Multiculturalism: Notes on Romani Activism in Central Europe." *Identities: Global Studies in Culture and Power* 12: 4, pp. 451–78.

Vermeulen, Hans, and Cora Govers. 1994. *The Anthropology of Ethnicity: Beyond "Ethnic Groups and Boundaries."* Amsterdam: Het Spinhuis.

Willems, Wim. 1995. *Op zoek naar de ware zigeuner. Zigeuners als studieobject tijdens de Verlichting, de Romantiek en het Nazisme*. Utrecht: Jan van Erkel.

Willems, Wim, and Leo Lucassen. 1998. "The Church of Knowledge: Representation of Gypsies in Encyclopedias." In: *Gypsies and Other Itinerant Groups: A Socio-Historical Approach*, ed. L. Lucassen, W. Willems, and A. Cottaar. London: Macmillan, pp. 35–52.

Wolchik, Sharon. 1991. *Czechoslovakia in Transition: Politics, Economics and Society*. London: Pinter.

———. 1994. "The Politics of Ethnicity in Post-Communist Czechoslovakia." *East European Politics and Societies* 8: 1, pp. 153–88.

World Bank. 2001. *Slovak Republic: Living Standards, Employment and Labor Market Study* (Report No. 22351-SK). Bratislava: World Bank.

Young, John. 1996. "Mission to Eastern Slovak Roma Settlements, 21–24 April 1996." Unpublished report of the Slovak Helsinki Committee with the participation of UNHCR.

———. 1999. "Present Situation and Development of Roma Nationality in Slovakia." Unpublished report of the Working Seminar of Romani Political Parties, Movements and Citizens' Associations in Slovakia, January 12, 1999, Lucenec.

Zald, N. Mayer, and Roberta Ash. 1966. "Social Movement Organizations: Growth, Decay, and Change." *Social Forces* 44, pp. 327–41.

Zeigler, D.J. 2002. "Post-communist Eastern Europe and the Cartography of Independence." *Political Geography* 21: 5, pp. 671–86.

Zoon, Ina. 2001a. *On the Margins: Roma and Public Services in Romania, Bulgaria, and Macedonia*. New York: Open Society Institute.

———. 2001b. *On the Margins: Roma and Public Services in Slovakia*. New York: Open Society Institute.

Index

A
Acton, Thomas, 13, 105, 160, 162, 164, 231n 1, 236n 2, 237n 8, 239, 243, 245, 251
Adam, Gejza, 107
advocacy networks, 8, 18, 135, 137, 138, 140, 157, 185, 188, 190, 194, 200–12, 227, 247, 254
Alliance of Free Democrats (SzDSz), 45, 70, 71, 75, 78, 79, 101, 112–14, 125–28, 132, 233n 10
Amnesty International, 196, 202, 205, 239
ANO
  See New Citizen's Alliance
Arel, Dominique, 19, 248
Assembly for the Republic-Czechoslovak Republican Party (SPR-RSČ), 139
assimilation, 15, 16, 30, 47, 49, 52, 54–60, 66, 81, 160, 167, 176, 183, 214, 223, 233, 236
Association of Gypsies-Roma, 59, 60, 63
Association of Roma in Hungary for Safeguarding of Interests (MCESz), 156
asylum seekers, 82, 83, 92, 130–33, 138–40, 144–47, 155, 174, 189, 197, 200, 203, 205, 219, 235n 18, 235n 23, 236n 1, 237n 14, 241, 247, 254
  and border controls, 140
  in Canada, 83, 99, 130, 139
  from Czech Republic, 138–40
  from Hungary, 130–33
  and Romani culture, 145
  from Slovakia, 144–47
  and visa requirements, 139, 140, 145, 146

B
Baláž, Branislav, 89, 170, 174
Balkans, 2, 7, 104, 189, 198
Barany, Zoltan, 15, 48, 103, 208, 231n 1, 239
Barth, Fredrik, 3, 33, 36–38, 239
Báthory, János, 62, 70, 124,
Belgium, 30, 199, 238n 19, 250
  asylum seekers in, 144, 145
Beneš, Edvard, 56, 97
Benford, Robert D., 42, 43, 150, 151, 168, 226, 240, 252
Bernáth, Gábor, 22, 240
Body, Ladislav, 107, 108, 138
Bonacich, Edna, 34, 35, 240
Borrow, George, 14
Bousetta, Hassan, 41, 240

Bratinka, Pavel, 82, 83, 174, 176
Brubaker, Rogers, 3, 4, 5, 49, 240

C
Cahn, Claude, 145, 241
Canada, 83, 99, 130, 139
categorization, 3, 4, 13, 14, 19, 34
census, 18–20, 73, 80, 88, 117, 118, 226, 231nn 4, 5, 233n 6, 12
  See also population figures
Christian Democratic Union – Czech People's Party (KDU-ČSL), 82, 109
CIT
  See International Gypsy Committee
citizenship law of 1993 (Czech Republic), 82, 135–38, 153, 174, 203, 235n 14
Civic Democratic Alliance (ODA), 82
Civic Democratic Party (ODS), 82, 84, 86, 99, 107, 109
Civic Democratic Union (ODÚ), 107
Civic Forum (OF), 82, 101, 106, 107, 134
Civic Movement (OH), 106
civic principle, 80, 86, 81, 87, 94, 215, 222
civil unrest, 1, 147–49, 226
Clark, Colin, 15, 19, 241
Clébert, Jean-Paul, 15, 241
CMSP
  See Hungarian Gypsy Solidarity Party
cognitive liberation, 226, 227
collective action
  See social movements
communism
  collapse of, 1, 101, 125, 134
  in Czechoslovakia, 56–60
  in Hungary, 49–56
  and minority policy, 48–60, 214, 223
  and mobilization, 62, 63, 105, 106, 125, 126, 133, 167, 216
  in the Soviet Union, 48–50, 52
Communist Party of the Soviet Union (KPSS), 49
Conference for Security and Cooperation in Europe (CSCE), 185, 188, 189
Connor, Walker, 32, 49, 59, 241
Contact Point for Roma and Sinti Issues (CPRSI), 8, 166, 188
Copenhagen criteria
  See European Union

Council for National Minorities (*Rada pro národnosti vlády České republiky*), 25, 81, 82, 84, 97, 138, 174, 175, 216
Council of Europe, 6, 8, 25, 72, 87, 131, 135, 141, 166, 172, 173, 180, 185, 186, 191–97, 199, 210, 237nn 5, 12, 14, 238n 16, 241, 247, 249, 251
  See also Framework Convention for the Protection of National Minorities
Council of Nationalities
  See Council for National Minorities
CPRSI
  See Contact Point for Roma and Sinti Issues
criminality, 3, 21, 22, 51, 137, 164, 174, 234n 13, 238n 17
Crowe, David, 13, 47, 50, 52, 53, 59, 103, 130, 134, 232n 3, 241, 245
Csáky, Pál, 91, 92, 145, 171, 172, 205, 236n 7
CSCE
  See Conference for Security and Cooperation in Europe
Csepeli, György, 22, 242
cultural autonomy, 45, 49, 59, 158, 178, 203, 225
Czechoslovak Communist Party (KSČ), 57, 79, 107, 138
Czech Social Democrat Party (ČSSD), 86, 109, 175

D
Danihel, Vincent, 92, 107, 135, 171
Daróczi, Ágnes, 62, 112, 124, 127
Dávid, Ibolya, 79
Decade of Roma Inclusion, 163, 184
  See also World Bank, Open Society Institute
della Porta, Donatella, 35, 36, 40, 219, 251
Democratic Alliance of Hungarian Gypsies (MCDSz), 70, 124, 125–27, 135, 156, 233n 11
Democratic Party of the Hungarian Gypsies (MCDP), 115
Democratic Union (DÚ), 110
Democratic Union of Roma (DÚRS), 116
Diani, Mario, 35, 36, 40, 219, 251
discrimination, 1, 2, 20–23, 26, 28, 35, 37, 44, 45, 82–84, 89, 92, 96, 120, 132, 138, 141, 146, 147, 152, 164–69, 171–74, 178–80, 189–91, 198–200, 202, 203, 208,

229, 238n 18, 242, 243, 254
and problem definition, 151–59, 168
Dobal, Viktor, 82, 83, 140
Doncsev, Toso, 72, 73, 76, 78, 242
double bind, 181, 182
Dzurinda, Mikuláš, 91, 98, 111, 148, 149, 170, 171, 173, 203, 242

E
education, 21, 23, 25, 26, 27, 44, 45, 50, 53–55, 64, 66, 67, 72, 75, 77, 87, 89, 114, 120, 136, 154, 158, 169, 170, 173, 174, 179, 180, 190, 199, 202, 207, 252
elections
  in Czech Republic, 86, 98, 106–12, 115, 116, 136, 175
  and electoral competition, 119, 120
  and electoral thresholds, 119
  and European Parliament, 114
  in Hungary, 79, 98–100, 112–15, 125, 128
  for minority self-governments (Hungary), 45, 46, 65, 72 74, 115, 121–23, 129
  and Romani candidates, 90, 95, 105, 106–15, 119, 128, 207
  and Romani parties, 105, 115–21, 119, 163, 189, 207, 220
  and Romani voters, 114, 117–20, 128, 142, 219
  in Slovakia, 77, 90, 98, 100, 106–12, 115–17, 142, 163, 203, 234n 1, 234n 15
ERRC
  See European Roma Rights Center
essentialism
  See primordialism
ethnicity
  concept of, 3, 4, 32, 34
ethnic mobilization theories, 12, 28–43
  culturalist perspective, 30, 31–34, 38, 214, 217–19
  ethnic competition theory, 31, 36–38, 44, 213, 214, 217, 220–22, 226, 228
  liberal expectancy, 30
  political process theory, 31, 38–43, 44, 213, 217, 220, 222–28
  reactive ethnicity, 30, 34–36, 214, 219
  See also framing, political opportunity structure
European Court of Human Rights, 131
European Roma Rights Center (ERRC), 140, 148, 155, 157, 158, 202, 204, 208
European Roma and Travelers Forum, 194

European Union (EU)
  and conditionality policy, 195, 196, 198, 199
  Copenhagen criteria, 91, 186, 196, 197, 237n 15, 238n 17
  enlargement of, 8, 155, 173, 195–200, 242, 249, 254
  European Commission, 8, 88, 141, 173, 180, 195–97, 199, 205, 207, 242, 246
  European Parliament, 114, 131, 162, 173, 180, 197, 198, 242
  Phare program, 207
  Treaty of Amsterdam, 198, 238n 8
extreme right parties, 97–98, 139

F
Fábián, Zoltan, 22, 242, 243
Farkas, Flórián, 62, 112, 113, 126, 127, 133
Favell, Adrian, 41, 228, 243
Fawn, Rick, 21, 99, 100, 139, 174, 243
Fico, Róbert, 145, 148, 231n 5
Ficowski, Jerzy, 105, 243
Fidesz, 77, 99, 100, 112–14, 233n 10
Finnemore, Martha, 186, 243
Fízik, Ladislav, 148
Forray, Katalin R., 122, 243
Fox, Jonathan, 231n 1, 243
Framework Convention for the Protection of National Minorities (FCNM), 25, 87, 94, 172, 192, 196, 199, 237n 11, 238n 19, 244, 245, 247
  See also Council of Europe
framing, 42, 43, 139, 150–51, 225–27
  diagnostic framing, 43, 151
  and ethnic discrimination, 151–54
  and identity, 150, 159–67, 168
  and policies, 168–80
  and problem definition, 150–59, 168
  prognostic framing, 43, 151, 156
France, 105, 130–32
Fraser, Angus, 13, 14, 15, 243
Free Democrats/National Socialist Liberal Party (SD-LSNS), 109
Freedom Union (US), 108, 109
Freedom Union/Democratic Union (US-DEU), 110
Friedman, Eben, 120, 243

G
Geertz, Clifford, 232n 7, 243
Gheorghe, Nicolae, 10, 17, 18, 196, 202, 231n 5, 234n 7, 237n 8, 243, 249
  and Contact Point for Roma and Sinti Issues (CPRSI), 166, 188, 189
  and Romani identity, 13, 166, 230

Giňa, Ondřej, 82, 107, 133, 134, 141
Glazer, Nathan, 30, 33, 240, 244
Goffman, Erving, 42, 240, 244
Government Commissioner for the Solution of the Problems of the Romani Minority (*Splnomocnec vlády SR na riešenie problémov rómskej menšiny*), 8, 89, 91, 92, 153, 171, 172, 204, 205, 207, 209
Government Council for Romani Community Affairs (*Rady vlády pro záležitosti romské komunity*), 8, 86, 175
Government Council on National Minorities and Ethnic Groups (*Rada vlády pre národnostné menšiny a etnické skupiny*), 91
Grellman, Heinrich, 14
Guigni, Marco G., 39, 225, 248
Gurr, Ted Robert, 166, 245
Guy, Will, 13, 25, 28, 58–60, 105, 130, 231n 1, 233n 7
"Gypsy", 10, 13, 15, 51, 52, 54, 58, 98, 159, 233n 11
  See also terminology
Gypsy Council (*Cigányszövetség*), 54

H
Hága, Antónia, 62, 112, 113, 125
Halonen, Tarja, 193, 194
Hancock, Ian, 13–16, 196, 245
Harff, Barbara, 166, 245
Haughton, Tim, 98, 246
Havas, Gábor, 20, 25, 53, 54, 100, 125, 246
Havel, Václav, 100, 140, 163, 233n 13, 235n 20, 243
Hechter, Michael, 34, 38, 232n 9, 246
Heizer, Antal, 76, 121, 178, 179, 204, 243, 246
Helsinki Watch
  See Human Rights Watch
Henderson, Karen, 88, 246
High Commissioner on National Minorities (HCNM), 21, 23, 135, 187, 189, 190, 192, 246
  See also van der Stoel, Max
Holomek, Karel, 63, 107, 109, 134, 165, 166, 246
Horáková, Monika, 85, 108, 109
Horn, Gyula, 67, 75–78, 178, 179, 193, 207
Horváth, Aladár, 45, 61, 62, 71, 100, 112, 113, 124, 125, 127–29, 158, 159, 232n 1
housing, 23, 24, 44, 53, 60, 74, 89, 100, 125, 131, 136, 155, 156, 166, 168–71, 190, 199, 200
  See also settlements
HSD/SMS
  See Self-governing Democracy Movement/Association for Moravia and Silesia

Index

human rights, 1, 21, 26, 54, 82, 83, 86, 89, 91, 92, 95, 102, 106, 112, 120, 125, 128, 131, 135, 137, 139, 140, 142, 157, 159, 162, 166, 171, 188, 191, 193, 194, 196, 199, 200–7, 227, 233n 1, 234n 10, 235n 14
Human Rights Watch (HRW)/Helsinki Watch, 71, 83, 135, 138, 196, 202, 246, 247
Hungarian Democratic Forum (MDF), 77, 79, 98, 99
Hungarian Gypsy Cultural Alliance (MCKSz), 52, 56
Hungarian Gypsy Social Democratic Party (MCSzDP), 115
Hungarian Gypsy Solidarity Party (CMSP), 115
Hungarian Party of Justice and Life (MIÉP), 98, 100
Hungarian Socialist Party (MSzP), 67, 75, 76, 78, 79, 100, 112, 113, 123, 127, 128, 178
Hungarian Socialist Workers' Party (MSzMP), 51, 52, 55, 123, 124
Hungarian Workers' Party (MDP), 50
Huntington, Samuel P., 32, 33, 244, 246, 251
HZDS
See Movement for a Democratic Slovakia

I

ILO
See International Labor Organization
immigrant minorities, 3, 33–35, 37, 41, 198, 228
Independent Smallholders' Party, Hungary (FKGP), 77, 99
instrumentalism, 37, 38
integration policy, 49, 54–56, 59, 76, 79, 87, 175, 177, 179
Interdepartmental Commission (*Meziresortní komise*), 8, 84–87, 175
International Gypsy Committee (CIT), 105
International Labor Organization (ILO), 25, 26
International Organization for Migration (IOM), 144, 247
International Romani Union (IRU), 154, 160–64, 177, 180, 196, 206, 236n 2
interpretative turn, 225, 226
IRU
See International Romani Union

J

Jenson, Jane, 42, 43, 150, 247
Johnston, Hank, 42, 247

K

Kádár, János, 51, 123,
Kaltenbach, Jenő, 70, 73–75, 77, 247
See also Parliamentary Commissioner for Ethnic and National Minority Rights
KDU-ČSL
See Christian Democratic Union – Czech People's Party
Keck, Margaret, 186, 201, 204, 205, 227, 247
Kemény, István, 20, 25, 26, 246, 248
Kenrick, Donald, 13, 248
Kertesi, Gábor, 20, 248
Kertzer, David I. 19, 248
Kézdi, Gábor, 20, 248
Klaus, Václav, 82, 140, 174
Klímová, Ilona, 103, 105, 160, 162, 164, 239, 248
Kompuš, Jan, 110
Koopmans, Ruud, 3, 41, 150, 222, 225, 242, 243, 247, 248
Koptová, Anna, 108
Kovats, Martin, 53–55, 62, 72–74, 77, 198, 192, 195, 231n 1, 248
Kozma, Blanka, 62, 113
KPSS
See Communist Party of the Soviet Union
Krasznai, József, 130–32
Kriesi, Hanspeter, 29, 39, 222, 223, 225, 227, 248
Krizsán, Andrea, 69–71, 249
KSČ
See Czechoslovak Communist Party
KSS
See Slovak Communist Party
Kymlicka, Will, 30, 64, 65, 159, 249

L

Ladányi, János, 27, 100, 249
Laitin, David D., 5, 249
Lakatos, Menyhért, 54, 55, 62, 156
Lety u Pisku, 48, 82, 86
Liégeois, Jean-Pierre, 15, 17, 18, 72, 202, 231n 5, 234n 7, 249
lifestyle, 15, 27, 54, 55, 57, 58, 60, 142, 154, 156, 157, 159, 172, 173, 175, 192, 195
Lucassen, Leo, 15, 236n 13, 249, 254
Lungo Drom, 46, 73, 99, 112, 113, 122, 126, 128, 129
Luník IX, 155, 156, 239

M

Magyar Coalition Party (SMK), 91, 95, 111, 171, 236n7
Magyar minority (in Slovakia), 88, 91, 94–96, 103, 104, 110, 111, 164, 165, 197, 221–24, 233n6
Mann, Arne, 60, 236n 5, 249
Mansfeldová, Zdenka, 106, 119, 120, 250

Marushiakova, Elena, 18, 104, 105, 160, 250
Matras, Yaron, 237n 14, 250
McAdam, Doug, 39, 40, 42, 213, 226, 250, 253
MCDP
See Democratic Party of the Hungarian Gypsies
MCDSz
See Democratic Alliance of Hungarian Gypsies
MCESz
See Association of Roma in Hungary for Safeguarding of Interests
MCKSz
See Hungarian Gypsy Cultural Alliance
MCSzDP
See Hungarian Gypsy Social Democratic Party
MDF
See Hungarian Democratic Forum
MDP
See Hungarian Workers' Party
Mečiar, Vladimír, 90, 110, 117, 120, 124, 153, 157, 170, 171, 203,
Medgyessy, Péter, 79
media, 2, 22, 27, 67, 79, 82, 97, 151, 156, 161, 174, 181, 215, 219, 226, 228, 234n 10
and criminality, 22
Messing, Vera, 22, 240
MG-S-ROM
See Specialist Group on Roma/Gypsies/Travelers
MIÉP
See Hungarian Party of Justice and Life
migration
See asylum seekers
Mikloško, Jan, 80
Miklušáková, Marta, 136, 137, 235n 14, 252
minority ombudsman
See Parliamentary Commissioner for Ethnic and National Minority Rights
minority rights, 64–65, 112, 132, 142, 148, 158, 159, 164–66, 171, 183, 185, 202, 203, 206, 211
Minority Rights Group, 17, 20, 202, 249
Minority Roundtable in Hungary, 45, 69, 71, 127
minority self-government system in Hungary, 45, 65–67, 71, 72–75, 121–23, 129
Mirga, Andrzej, 15, 250
Miskolc, 125, 152
Mlynář, Vladimír, 85, 86
Mohács, Attila, 127
Mohácsi, Viktória, 114

260   Index

Movement for a Democratic Slovakia (HZDS), 88, 90, 91, 97–100, 107, 110, 111, 107, 117, 120, 142, 145, 153, 156, 171, 234n 15, 246
Moynihan, Daniel P., 30, 33, 240, 244
Mróz, Lech, 15, 250
MSzMP
   See Hungarian Socialist Workers' Party
MSzP
   See Hungarian Socialist Party

N
Náday, Gyula, 62, 124
Nagel, Joane, 37, 250
National Gypsy Self-Government (OCÖ), 46, 62, 129
National Gypsy Council (*Országos Cigánytanács*), 56, 69
nationalism, 32, 57, 104, 185, 223, 224, 232n 2
   communist view on, 49, 50, 57
New Citizen's Alliance (ANO), 111

O
ODA
   See Civic Democratic Alliance
ODIHR
   See Office for Democratic Institutions and Human Rights
ODS
   See Civic Democratic Party
ODÚ
   See Civic Democratic Union
OF
   See Civic Forum
Office for Democratic Institutions and Human Rights (ODIHR), 8, 166, 188, 198, 192, 251
Office of Ethnic and National Minorities (*Nemzeti és Etnikai Kissebségi Hivatal*), 8, 62, 68–69, 72, 76
OH
   See Civic Movement
Okely, Judith, 13, 14, 251
Oláh, Vladimír, 82
Open Society Institute (OSI), 143, 163, 184, 202, 204, 205, 207, 255
   and Decade for Roma inclusion, 163
Orbán, Viktor, 77, 133, 180, 205
Organization for Security and Cooperation in Europe (OSCE), 6, 8, 21, 160, 162, 185–91, 196, 197, 210, 237n 4, 237n 7, 251
Orgovánová, Klára, 92, 106, 143, 153, 171, 205
Orsós, Éva, 96, 113
OSCE
   See Organization for Security and Cooperation in Europe
OSI

   See Open Society Institute
Osztojkán, Béla, 62, 124, 125, 127, 129

P
Parliamentary Commissioner for Ethnic and National Minority Rights (Minority Ombudsman), 68–70, 74, 96
   See also Kaltenbach, Jenő
Party for Labor and Security (SPI), 116
Party for Social Security (SŽJ), 109
Party for the Protection of Roma in Slovakia (SOPR), 110, 111
Party of the Democratic Left (SDL'), 91
Péli, Tamás, 112
PER
   See Project on Ethnic Relations
Petrova, Dimitrina, 2, 251
Phralipe, 45, 70, 71, 101, 123–29, 152, 156–58, 233n 11
police, 22, 52, 87, 152, 180, 205, 226, 235n 27
Political Movement of the Roma in Slovakia (ROMA), 117
political opportunity structure (POS), 12, 38–42, 94, 101, 217, 225
Popov, Vesselin, 18, 104, 105, 160, 250
population figures, 17–20
   See also census
Pořajmos, 48
   See also Romani Holocaust, Lety u Pisku
POS
   See political opportunity structure
poverty, 1, 3, 20–28, 35, 44, 60, 82, 96, 152–57, 168, 178–80, 229
Prague Spring, 135, 136
primordialism, 3, 5, 33, 34, 36, 37
Project on Ethnic Relations (PER), 71, 160, 163, 164, 167, 191, 196, 197, 207, 251
Public Against Violence (VPN), 106–8
Puxon, Grattan, 105, 251

R
Raduly, József, 62, 127
Rákosi, Mátyás, 50, 52
Ravasz, József, 110, 111
refugees
   See asylum seekers
RIS
   See Slovak Romani Initiative
Risse, Thomas, 190, 200, 206,
Ritter, Robert, 14, 16
RIZS
   See Romani Intelligentsia for Coexistence

RNC
   See Roma National Congress
ROI
   See Romani Civic Initiative
ROI-SR
   See Romani Civic Initiative
ROMA
   See Political Movement of the Roma in Slovakia
Roma Civic Initiative (ROI and ROI-SR), 89, 91, 107, 110, 111, 116, 117, 134, 140, 148, 152–54, 162–66
Roma Civil Rights Foundation, 45
Roma National Congress (RNC), 160, 162, 206
Romani Holocaust, 16, 19, 47, 48, 82
   See also Pořajmos, Lety u Pisku
Romani identity
   and categorization, 3, 4, 13, 14, 19, 214, 220
   and class, 30, 32, 35, 37, 58, 166
   and diaspora, 13, 14, 16
   and ethnoclass, 166, 167
   and kinship, 16, 17
   and lifestyle, 15
   and national minority, 163, 164–66
   and nonterritorial nation, 160–64
Romani Intelligentsia for Coexistence (RIZS), 111, 153
Romani language, 10, 14, 18, 27, 47, 52, 99, 120, 122, 156–59, 167, 231n 4
Romani political parties, 102, 103, 115–21
Romani political representation
   and electoral competition, 119
   in national parliaments, 107–15
   and Romani political parties, 115–17
   and voter turnout, 118, 119
Roma Parliament, 45, 69, 71, 123, 126–28, 130, 232n 3, 233n 11
Rüdiger, Johann, 14

S
Samková, Klara, 106, 107
Save the Children, 26, 202, 252
Schöpflin, George, 31, 32, 49, 68, 252
Ščuka, Emil, 85, 133, 140, 154, 161–64, 236n 4
SDK
   See Slovak Democratic Coalition
SDKÚ
   See Slovak Democratic and Christian Union
SDL'
   See Party of the Democratic Left
SD-LSNS
   See Free Democrats/National Socialist Liberal Party

Index 261

Second World War, 16, 19, 47, 48, 50, 51, 56, 82, 233n 6
See also Holocaust, Poṛajmos
Self-governing Democracy Movement/Association for Moravia and Silesia (HSD/SMS), 107
settlements, 23, 24, 26, 27, 53, 55, 58, 77, 173, 231n 6
Sikkink, Kathryn, 186, 201, 204, 205, 227, 247
Šiklová, Jiřina, 136, 137, 235n 14, 252
skinheads, 21, 82, 135, 138
Slovak Communist Party (KSS), 111
Slovak Democratic and Christian Union (SDKÚ), 91, 111
Slovak Democratic Coalition (SDK), 91, 110, 111
Slovak National Party (SNS), 90, 91, 97–99
Slovak Romani Initiative (RIS), 111, 116, 117, 146, 153
Smer (Direction), 111, 145, 231n 5
Smith, Anthony D., 5, 32, 35, 241, 246, 252
SMK
See Magyar Coalition Party
Snow, David A., 42, 43, 150, 151, 168, 226, 240, 252
SNS
See Slovak National Party
Sobotka, Eva, 177, 231n 1, 236n 12, 252
social behavior, 15, 154, 155, 168, 169, 171, 174, 175, 177, 181, 226
social benefits 1, 23, 24, 136, 147
social movements, 29, 35, 36, 38–43, 150, 184, 200, 206, 213, 219, 225, 227
and resource mobilization theory, 36, 40
structural-functionalist theories on, 35, 40
See also ethnic mobilization theories, framing, political opportunity structures
SOPR
See Party for the Protection of Roma in Slovakia
Soros, George, 143, 163, 184
Soviet Union, 48, 49, 59
Soysal, Yasemin, 162, 252

Specialist Group on Roma/Gypsies/Travelers (MG-S-ROM), 8, 193
SPI
See Party for Labor and Security
Split labor market theory, 35
See also ethnic mobilization theories
SPR-RSČ
See Assembly for the Republic-Czechoslovak Republican Party
Stalin, J.V., 50, 57
Statham, Paul, 3, 41, 150, 222, 242, 243, 247, 248, 250
stereotypes, 16, 21, 181, 184, 198, 199, 212, 226, 229
Stewart, Michael, 13, 51, 25, 118, 159, 252
Sudeten Germans, 56
Sus, Jaroslav, 58
SzDSz
See Alliance of Free Democrats
SŽJ
See Party for Social Security

T
Tabajdi, Csaba, 67, 158, 178–80, 193, 194, 241
Tarrow, Sidney, 39, 40, 253
Teleki, László, 79, 113, 122
terminology, 10, 13
Tilly, Charles, 28, 35, 40, 253
Tošovský, Josef, 84, 86
transfer and dispersal program, 58
Trebišov, 1, 147, 148
Trehan, Nidhi, 208, 253

U
Uhl, Petr, 86–88, 253
UN
See United Nations
undifferentiated citizenship, 64, 65, 80
UNDP
See United Nations Development Program
unemployment, 1, 20, 23–27, 44, 82, 83, 96, 146, 148, 152, 157, 167, 168, 170, 171, 175, 180, 229
and informal economy, 26
UNHCR
See United Nations High Commissioner for Refugees
United Kingdom, 15, 35, 83, 105, 140, 144, 145, 237n 11

United Nations (UN), 2, 8, 196, 237n 7
United Nations Development Program (UNDP), 2, 23, 25, 26, 118, 122, 253
United Nations High Commissioner for Refugees (UNHCR), 130, 139, 144, 253, 254
US
See Freedom Union
US-DEU
See Freedom Union/Democratic Union
Ústí nad Labem, 99, 140–42, 219, 227, 235n 20

V
van der Stoel, Max, 187, 198
See also High Commissioner on National Minorities
Vašečka, Michal, 24, 90, 103, 110, 111, 130, 134, 144, 252, 254
Verheugen, Günter, 155, 173, 238n 17, 254
Verspaget, Josephine, 192, 193, 195, 237n 14, 241
Vote for the Future (VPB), 109
VPB
See Vote for the Future
VPN
See Public Against Violence

W
Willems, Wim, 13, 14, 16, 236n 13, 249, 254
Workers' Association of Slovakia (ZRS), 90
World Bank, 2, 17, 18, 23, 24, 163, 184, 238n 16, 254
World Romani Congress (WRC), 60, 105, 160, 177, 251
WRC
See World Romani Congress

Z
Zámoly, 130–33, 234n 10
See also asylum seekers
Zeman, Miloš, 86, 175
Zoon, Ina, 202, 205, 255
ZRS
See Workers' Association of Slovakia
Zsigó, Jenő, 124, 128

Recent Volumes in the Series

Volume 5

MODERNITY AND SECESSION
The Social Sciences and the Political Discourse of the lega nord in Italy
Michel Huysseune

The northern Italian, 'Padanian' identity, fostered by the Lega Nord, is rooted in the long-standing tradition, in political and scholarly discourse, of casting regional differences within Italy in terms of a North-South geographic divide. Trying to come to terms, in the late 1980s and 1990s, with Italy's (real or presumed) inadequacies – such as inefficient government, corruption, and organized crime – this imagined geography acquired political centrality in that the North became associated with the virtues of modernity and the South with the vices of un-modernity. The author provides a new, systematic, and interdisciplinary approach that re-interprets the premises behind Italy's imagined geography of modernity. He moves beyond an understanding of the South as a "backward" and implicitly inferior society and problematizes normative notions of modernity, thus offering a new perspective on the North-South divide, which has a significance well beyond the case of Italy.

Michel Huysseune teaches Political Science at the Vrije Universiteit, Brussels).

2006. 288 pages, bibliog., index
ISBN 1-84545-061-2 Hb $80.00/£45.00

Volume 3

RADICAL ETHNIC MOVEMENTS IN CONTEMPORARY EUROPE
Edited by Stefan Troebst and Farimah Daftary

Nation states and minorities resort more and more to violence when safeguarding their political interests. Although the violence in the Middle East has been dominating world politics for some time now, European governments have had their share of ethnic violence to contend with as this volume demonstrates. And as the case studies show, ranging as they do from the Basque Country to Chechnya, from Northern Ireland to Bosnia-Herzegovina, this applies to western Europe as much as to eastern Europe. However, in contrast to other parts of the world, instances where political struggles for power and social inclusion between minorities and majorities lead to full-fledged inter-ethnic warfare are still the exception; in the majority of cases conflicts are successfully de-escalated and even resolved. In a comprehensive conclusion, the volume offers a theoretical framework for the development of strategies to deal with violent ethnic conflict.

Stefan Troebst is Professor of East European Cultural Studies at the University of Leipzig.
Farimah Daftary is a former Senior Research Associate of the European Centre for Minority Issues (ECMI), Flensburg, Germany.

2004. 224 pages, index
ISBN 1-57181-695-X Pb $25.00/£15.00
ISBN 1-57181-622-4 Hb $70.00/£42.00 [2003]

Berghahn Books, Inc. 150 Broadway, Suite 812, New York, NY 10038, USA

Berghahn Books, Ltd. 3 Newtec Place, Magdalen Rd. Oxford OX4 1RE, UK

orders@berghahnbooks.com   www.berghahnbooks.com